The Psychology of Terrorism

Recent Titles in Psychological Dimensions to War and Peace

Perpetration-Induced Traumatic Stress: The Psychological Consequences of Killing
Rachel M. MacNair

Memory Perceived: Recalling the Holocaust
Robert N. Kraft

The Psychological Impact of War Trauma on Civilians: An International Perspective
Stanley Krippner and Teresa M. McIntyre, editors

The Psychology of Terrorism

◆

Volume II
Clinical Aspects and Responses

Edited by Chris E. Stout
Foreword by Klaus Schwab

Psychological Dimensions to War and Peace
Harvey Langholtz, Series Editor

PRAEGER

Westport, Connecticut
London

Library of Congress Cataloging-in-Publication Data

The psychology of terrorism / edited by Chris E. Stout ; foreword by Klaus Schwab.
    p. cm.—(Psychological dimensions to war and peace, ISSN 1540–5265)
    Includes bibliographical references and index.
    ISBN 0–275–97771–4 (set)—ISBN 0–275–97865–6 (vol. I)—ISBN 0–275–97866–4
(vol. II)—ISBN 0–275–97867–2 (vol. III)—ISBN 0–275–97868–0 (vol. IV)
    1. Terrorism—Psychological aspects. 2. Terrorists—Psychology. 3.
Terrorism—Prevention. I. Stout, Chris E. II. Series.
HV6431 .P798 2002
303.6'25—dc21   2002072845

British Library Cataloguing in Publication Data is available.

Library of Congress Catalog Card Number: 2002072845
ISBN: set: 0-275-97771-4
       v.I: 0-275-97865-6
       v.II: 0-275-97866-4
       v.III: 0-275-97867-2
       v.IV: 0-275-97868-0
ISSN: 1540-5265

First published in 2002

Praeger Publishers, 88 Post Road West, Westport, CT 06881
An imprint of Greenwood Publishing Group, Inc.
www.praeger.com

Printed in the United States of America

To my parents, Carlos L. and Helen E. (Simmons) Stout,
to my wife and soulmate, Dr. Karen Beckstrand, and
to my children and heroes, Grayson Beckstrand Stout and
Annika Beckstrand Stout.

You all have taught and continue to teach me so very much.

Contents

Foreword

First of all, I want to note the impressive collection of academics, thinkers, activists, and clinicians congregated in this set of volumes. Through their active engagement, the result is a series of works that crosscut an immense range of related factors—historical contexts; group dynamics; social psychological aspects; behavioral, forensic, psychopathological, evolutionary theory, peace-building, and conflict resolution perspectives; as well as the political, clinical, and social aspects of prevention, intervention, and security issues. Global perspectives vis-à-vis understanding, empathy, bias, prejudice, racism, and hate are also represented.

This group of authors offers a unique combination of talents and viewpoints rarely seen in the worlds of academia or activism. Their work and voices move knowledge and understanding forward in a way that will serve as a framework and catalyst for readers to consider ways in which to respond to terrorism in its various displays. Dr. Stout has fostered a self-organizing environment that has enabled this work to be a collaboration of ideas that goes beyond the traditional and almost complacent; instead it is realistically erudite and even provocative in some instances.

I suspect that the readership will likewise be broad and crosscutting—including academics and departments of psychology, political science, religious studies, military sciences, law enforcement, public health, sociology, anthropology, social work, and law, as well as the lay public and the media, policy makers, elected government officials, leaders of nongovernmental organizations, ambassadors and diplomats, military leaders, law enforcement professionals, the intelligence community, and members of think tanks and private and public policy institutes and centers.

Such integration of diversity in thought and perspective parallels our "Forum Plus" strategy at the World Economic Forum. This strategy aims to advance critical issues on the global agenda through the creation of task forces and initiatives that integrate business, governments, international organizations, civil society, academics, and technical experts.

Similarly, Dr. Stout has been successful in gathering some of the greatest thinkers on this topic from around the world, including Fulbright scholars, a Kellogg International fellow, a Pulitzer Prize winner, a Beale fellow (Harvard), a *boursier de la Confédération Suisse*, a Medical Research Council fellow, American Psychological Association fellows, a Royal College of Physicians fellow, an American College of Psychiatrists fellow, American Psychiatric Association fellows, and a Regents scholar. Authors represent a wide array of academic institutions: the University of Pennsylvania; Harvard Medical School; Rutgers University; Princeton University; Northwestern University Medical School; Mount Sinai School of Medicine; Nelson Mandela School of Medicine, University of Natal, South Africa; George Mason University; University of Massachusetts; University of Michigan; Civitan International Research Center at the University of Alabama; Institute for Mental Health Initiatives at George Washington University; Marylhurst University; Portland State University; Southwest Texas State University; Al Aksa University in Gaza; University of Lagos, Akoka-Yaba, Lagos, Nigeria; University of Wisconsin; Northern Arizona University; Bryn Mawr College; Randolph-Macon College; Illinois State University; University of South Florida; Elmhurst College; Howard University; University of Texas Health Science Center; Texas A&M College of Medicine; University of California; Saybrook Graduate School and Research Center; New School University; and New York University. Authors also represent the United Nations (a Humanitarian Affairs Officer, an Assistant to the Under-Secretary-General for Peacekeeping, and an Assistant to the Special Representative of the Secretary-General to the former Yugoslavia and to NATO), the Disaster Mental Health Institute; the Comprehensive Medical Center in Dubai, United Arab Emirates; GGZ Den Bosch/Outpatient and Daytreatment Centre for Refugees in the Netherlands; the Human Sciences Research Council in South Africa; Delta Psychiatric Teaching Hospital in Poortugaal, the Netherlands; Maagalim–Institute of Psychotherapy and Counseling in Tel Aviv; the United Nations Development Program for Women; the USAID Rwanda Rule of Law Project; and the Christian Children's Fund.

Many of the authors are also current or past officers of a wide variety of professional associations and other organizations: the World Psychiatric Association on Urban Mental Health; the Commission on Global Psychiatry of the American Psychiatric Association; the South African Institute for Traumatic Stress; Solomon Asch's Center for Ethno-Political Conflict at the University of Pennsylvania; the American Psychological Association Committee on Global Violence and Security within Division 48; the Society for the Study of Peace, Conflict, and Violence; the Association for Humanistic Psychology; the Non Governmental Organizations Executive Committee on Mental Health—UN; Psychologists for Social Responsibility; the Conflict Resolution Action Committee; the Conflict Resolution Working Group (of Division 48 of the American Psychological Association); the Philadelphia Project for Global Security; the American Academy of Psychiatry and the Law; the National Council of State Medical Directors; the Board of Presidents of the Socialist Countries' Psychiatric Associations in Sofia, Bulgaria; the Society for the Study of Peace, Conflict and Violence: Peace Psychology Division of the American Psychological Association (APA); the International Society for Political Psychology; the Committee for International Liaisons for the Division of International Psychology (APA); and the Common Bond Institute.

Dr. Stout has also assembled some of the best and the brightest to serve as his Editorial Advisory Board: Terrance Koller, Dana Royce Baerger, Malini Patel, Ron Levant, and Stephen Kouris.

The rapid growth of global communications, information technology, and international business in the second half of the twentieth century increased the need for a common platform where the stakeholders of society could be brought together to consider and advance the key issues on the global agenda. The World Economic Forum's goal is to provide that platform, asking a mix of individuals to articulate the major problems facing the world and to find solutions. Works like this are catalytic to our thinking and dialogue.

It is our hope at the Forum to support the global public interest and to improve the state of the world. I believe this series adds to such a mission by its integration of thinking and facilitation of dialogue among different stakeholders and across different regions and intellectual disciplines. This series promotes progress by expanding common ground and developing new approaches.

Klaus Schwab
Founder and President
World Economic Forum

Acknowledgments

A project such as this one—with authors from all over the world covering a breadth and depth of examination of such a complex topic—can only happen as the result of a team effort. As such, I would like first of all to thank my family. Annika, Grayson, and I have sacrificed many a weekend of playing together; and I have also missed time with my very supportive partner and wife, Dr. Karen Beckstrand. Debora Carvalko, our editor at Greenwood, has been the crucial link in this project. She has worked with herculean effort to keep things organized and working. In fact, it is thanks to her that this project was even undertaken. The Editorial Advisory Board worked diligently, reading and commenting on many more manuscripts than those seen herein. The work of Terrence Koller, Malini Patel, Dana Royce Baerger, Steven P. Kouris, and Ronald F. Levant was impeccable and key to ensuring the quality of the chapters. I am also indebted to the council of Hedwin Naimark for invaluable help and thinking.

Professor Klaus Schwab has been a valued resource to me over the years and he was kind enough to provide the foreword. Harvey Langholtz has been an ongoing source of inspiration and mentorship to me. He is without a doubt the most diplomatic of all psychologists I know (it must have been all those years at the United Nations). And, this project would have been no more than an idea without the intellectual productivity of the contributing authors. We were fortunate to have more submissions than we could use in the end, but even those whose works were not used surely had an impact on my thinking and perspective, and I am very grateful. Finally, behind-the-scenes thanks to Ralph Musicant, Lawrence W. Osborn, Phillip Zimbardo, Patrick DeLeon, and Michael Horowitz.

I am markedly indebted to you all at a level that I shall never be able to repay. My sincere thanks to each of you.

Introduction

In thinking about the words to write here, I am struck with the vast array of ironies.

I had been writing and presenting talks on issues of terrorism for a while before September 11, 2001. In June 2001, I had submitted a proposal dealing with issues of terrorism for a clinical practice conference in November 2001, and I cannot help but suspect that the proposal could easily have been rejected because of a busy agenda and other competing topics that would have been considered more important to attendees. Instead, the proposal was accepted and it was the largest crowd I have ever addressed. Standing room only, and the only presentation over the course of a three-day conference that was videotaped. Sad, indeed, how some things change. I now often find myself reminding audiences that terrorism existed before September 11, 2001. In fact, that was what my talk was about. Terrorism in Japan, in Lebanon, in Ireland. In the world. In our world. For many of us who are U.S. citizens, the term "our world" now has a new and different meaning.

I have presented and written a fair amount on terrorism, and war, and trauma, and civilian casualties. I've worked with children who have been tortured, talked with traumatized refugees, broken bread with former political prisoners, and worked with a center offering pro bono clinical services to refugees who are victims of torture. I've seen the aftermath of atrocities—exhumed corpses, mass graves, and murdered infants. I have gone on medical missions to far-off places around the world. I have slides and statistics, bar graphs and citations; I can quote numerous facts and figures. But prior to September 11, 2001, all of that was done with a certain degree of clinical detachment. I would go somewhere else, and then come home. I have not ever been in an active war zone, nor have I been a victim of a terrorist attack. After September 11, I feel a bit different.

More people now know what is meant by a "dirty bomb," or what anthrax and Cipro are, than knew before September 11. I'm not sure if that is a good thing or not. I work in Chicago, the city that again has title to the tallest building in the United States. Who could have ever imagined such an odd occurrence? The reclaiming of such a title as the result of a kiloton of destructive force toppling the towers of the World Trade Center, all for the price of a plane ticket and a box cutter. Unbelievable.

I cannot help but wonder what might have been different if the West/North had dealt before September 11 with brewing, yet largely ignored, issues—from an intelligence perspective, a psychological perspective (in all its varieties, forms, and flavors), a diplomacy and foreign policy perspective. I wonder what might have been achieved in tackling the larger dynamics of both the good and the bad that accompany globalization. All of this juxtaposed with issues of religious fundamentalism and politics. I'd like to believe things would have been better, but perhaps they would not.

Terrorism is a complex issue that does not respond well to reductionism. I apologize in advance if somehow this project looks as if it tries to simplify the complexities. My objective is not to teach the reader everything he or she ever wanted to know about terrorism in four easy lessons, but rather to offer a sampling of diverse and rich thought. Perhaps this can be the spark that starts a dialogue or a debate. That is OK by me. I have been amazed at the diversity, if not downright division, of some of the opinions and resultant debates following September 11. There are arguments regarding violent and aggressive responses versus forgiveness and passivism, evil versus good, behavioral reinforcement versus social psychology theories, isolationism versus globalism, "we are victims" versus "we brought this on ourselves," and my favorite dichotomy—"this is a start of the end" versus "this is the start of a new beginning." I think back to the horrible nature of the Oklahoma City bombing. That event was not at the same level as the New York and D.C. attacks in terms of the loss of life, damage, destruction and, frankly, vast media coverage. But the horror may also be mitigated by the fact that it was done by a McVeigh, not a bin Laden.

Everything is a political act, it simply cannot be escaped. A lack of political participation (such as not voting) or a lack of political activism (such as not supporting a cause) is still a political act (as in support of a status quo). As you will see, some of our authors are academics, some are clinicians, and some are activists. Try as we all do to check our political biases at the door, they surely squeak in, and most likely in ways that are difficult to see. I hope that an Editorial Advisory Board makes it more difficult to miss these biases, but I still suggest that readers, like all good academics, seek to understand by questioning assumptions and looking for empirical evidence wherever possible. Certainly this topic may often not comply with such methods, but we have all tried our best to present good scholarship herein.

This project started out as one book. It quickly grew to four volumes. Many more chapters went unused due to space limitations, duplication, or other technical reasons. There simply is no singular psychology of terrorism, no unified field theory if you will. None of the chapters is a stand-alone work; they are best understood in the greater context of the book, and then likewise in the wider context of the series. In some instances, the reader may see differences of perspectives or tensions between viewpoints. None of the books is a homogenized or sterile rendition of information. Personally, I find it difficult to talk about terrorism without also talking about war. And it's hard to discuss war without getting into issues of torture. Similarly, it's difficult to discuss torture without also discussing violence, and so forth. Thus, in this project on terrorism, readers will see discussions concerning such various related issues, because none of these issues can easily or correctly be dis-integrated from terrorism. Thus these four books emanated from an organic, self-organizing developmental process, resulting in:

I.   The Psychology of Terrorism: A Public Understanding

II. The Psychology of Terrorism: Clinical Aspects and Responses

III. The Psychology of Terrorism: Theoretical Understandings and Perspectives (with a special section on the Roles and Impacts of Religions)

IV. The Psychology of Terrorism: Programs and Practices in Response and Prevention

While there is no unifying perspective per se, I hope that these books may act as a unified source of perspectives. Also, they are incomplete. Individuals representing even more perspectives had hoped to contribute, but the realities prevented them from doing so. Certainly there will be continued interest, and I hope to see much more on these issues as we all become more aware and wise.

Volume I—A Public Understanding—provides an overview of issues in a way to help the public, in general, better understand the various issues involved. Volume II—Clinical Aspects and Responses—is an adequately telling title and offers much in the way of dealing with the emotional impacts of such traumas. Volume III—Theoretical Understandings and Perspectives—offers various perspectives of psychological understanding and theory intertwined with culture, context, politics, globalization, and social injustice as well as diplomatic processes. This volume also has a special section on the roles and impacts of religions that covers apocalyptic dreams, cults, religious archetypes, Islamic fundamentalism, and religious fanaticism.

Volume IV—Programs and Practices in Response and Prevention—provides a mix of preventative ideas and methods for youth and communities, as well as therapeutic aspects for those in trouble. For example, it includes articles on ethnopolitical warfare, family traumatic stress and refugee children; children's responses to traumatic events; aggression in adolescents; peace building; cooperative learning communities; antiviolence programming in school settings; and raising inclusively caring children. Granted, not all of these programs can be applied to a global set of venues, but they may offer much to those interested in developing their own variations on the theme.

What is my goal with this project? As noted earlier, I hope it provides readers with a mix of opinion and perspectives from which further thought and dialogue may occur. As you read these volumes, I would like you to keep in mind that through the work you do, no matter who you are, you can have an impact upon others that affects not only the individuals you encounter today, but potentially generations thereafter.

1

Refugees and Terrorism: Cultural Innovations in Clinical Practice

Fred Bemak and Rita Chi-Ying Chung

As a result of political conflict, refugee migration continues to be a major global problem. In the 1950s following World War II, there were 1.5 million refugees and displaced persons (Berman, 2001). Current estimates are significantly higher, with projections that there are 26 million refugees worldwide today (Balian, 1997). This dramatic increase in the numbers of refugees is reflective of the changing circumstances around the world. An outcome of armed conflict is terrorism, which is a strategy to terrorize and target civilian populations, frequently resulting in displacement and migration (Widgren, 1988) so that vast numbers of people worldwide are seeking political asylum as refugees.

The plight of refugees and their migration has been characterized by exposure to serious life-threatening traumatic events (Bemak & Chung, 2002; Bemak & Chung, 2003) and is further exacerbated by acts of terrorism. Migration and relocation is a tumultuous process for refugees. Rather than a self-determined choice, refugee migration is forced and involuntary, without preparation or planning. This sudden flight in an attempt to escape dangerous conditions dramatically disrupts one's life and has the potential to cause significant short- and long-term mental health problems.

Research has identified premigration as a major predictor of psychological problems (e.g., Bemak & Greenberg, 1994; Chung & Bemak, 2002; Chung & Kagawa-Singer, 1993; Hinton, Tiet, Tran, & Chesney, 1997; Mollica et al., 1998; Nicolson, 1997). These experiences have been characterized as culture shock

(Berry, 1990), cultural fatigue (Guthrie, 1975), acculturative stress (Padilla, 1980), and the effects of political victimization and repression (Sluzki, 1990, 1993). Common features in each of these characterizations are the multiple losses of family, friends, and one's own culture (Bemak & Chung, 2002; Berman, 2001), which further contribute to the devastating psychological effects of terrorism. The mourning for one's past life and adaptation to a new way of living and new culture present formidable obstacles that need to be addressed (Aroian, 1990; Bemak & Chung, 2002), and compound the already traumatic experiences of terrorism.

As a result of forced migration, some refugees idealize the past and live with both an intense desire to return to their homeland and guilt about having left (Roizblatt & Pilowsky, 1996). Refugees must also deal with numerous psychosocial adjustment challenges, such as loss of employment, a downgrading of socioeconomic status, difficulty in learning a new language, and acculturation and adjustment to a new country, as well as marked changes in family and social relationships and in defined gender roles. Furthermore, research has found a relationship between refugees' success in postmigration adjustment and subsequent mental health problems and their war experiences (e.g., Bathien & Malapert, 1987; Eberly & Engdahl, 1991; Hauff & Vaglum, 1995; Herber, Robins, & McEvoy, 1987; Somasundaram & Sinayokan, 1994; Weine et al., 1995). It has been established that witnessing traumatic war events or terrorism, such as people being tortured, murdered, raped, and beaten, is a predictor of serious mental health problems, identified by Bemak and Chung (1998) as the "psychological recoil effect."

Given the numerous issues and challenges encountered by refugees as a result of terrorism and war, this chapter will begin with a review of the psychosocial challenges encountered by refugee populations in resettlement countries, followed by a discussion of the impact of terrorism on refugee mental health during dislocation and relocation. Due to the complexity of refugee premigration experiences of terrorism and trauma, to assist clinicians in resettlement countries, a discussion of cultural belief systems and their impact on mental health will be presented, along with a discussion of barriers perceived by refugees in the utilization of Western mental health services. The chapter will conclude with the presentation of the Multi-Level Model of Psychotherapy for Refugees (MLM), an innovative clinical intervention model that incorporates a culturally sensitive macro approach to refugee mental health treatment.

PSYCHOSOCIAL ADJUSTMENT CHALLENGES FOR REFUGEES IN RESETTLEMENT COUNTRIES

The impact of terrorism on refugees in resettlement countries is complicated by challenges in postmigration adjustment. These challenges range from acculturation, or the degree of adjustment and integration within the resettlement country's culture—including issues related to speaking and understanding the resettlement country's language—to employment and education issues and changing family dynamics. This section will discuss the various psychosocial challenges encountered by refugees during their postmigration resettlement.

Acculturation

There have been numerous studies on migration and mental illness (e.g., Eitinger, 1960; Hitch & Rack, 1980; Mezey, 1960; Odegaard, 1932) that illustrate the unique challenges that refugees encounter during postmigration. The concept of acculturative stress has been associated with refugees. Acculturative stress is a unique type of distress that involves adjusting to a foreign culture and requires changes in identity, values, behaviors, cognitions, attitudes, and affect (Berry, 1990; Berry & Anis, 1974; Liebkind, 1996; Miranda & Matheny, 2000). Research suggests that acculturative stress combines the ameliorating effects of environmental, familial, demographic, and other factors (Miranda & Matheny, 2000). Liebkind (1996) suggested that for refugees, acculturative stress is influenced by multiple factors that include sociodemographics, premigration experiences, the social and political context of the resettlement society, and postmigration acculturation experiences. One criticism of acculturative stress models points toward the inclusion of external factors while neglecting internal psychological resources, such as coping strategies and resiliency. Acculturation models, in general, include the following dimensions: assimilation, integration or biculturalism, rejection, and deculturation, with research pointing toward biculturalism or integration as the healthier acculturation outcome (Berry, 1986; Szapocznik & Kurtines, 1980). Clearly, acculturative stress will be complicated by experiences of terrorism.

In addition, acculturative stress is further exacerbated by premigration trauma that includes terrorism. Mollica, Wyshak, and Lavelle (1987) categorized four major categories of trauma experienced by refugees, all of which may have origins in terrorist activities. These categories are: deprivation (e.g., of food and shelter), physical injury and torture, incarceration and re-education camps, and witnessing torture and killing. Premigration trauma correlates with the mental health problems of refugees and hinders positive postmigration adjustment and adaptation.

Further complicating this process, postmigration frequently includes culture shock that precipitates feelings of helplessness and disorientation when refugees are separated by migration or war from members of their nuclear and/or extended families and community networks. Arrival in resettlement countries introduces new cultures and reference groups that are more frequently individualistic rather than collective in nature (Bemak & Greenberg, 1994), contributing to feelings of alienation and loneliness. Thus refugees who have faced terrorism during premigration must contend with a new society that often values self rather than family or group, while simultaneously dealing with the loss of their family, community, and social network reference group (Bemak & Chung, 2002; Bemak & Greenberg, 1994).

Psychosocial Adjustment and Adaptation

Implicit in the discussion of acculturation is the issue of psychosocial adjustment. The antecedents of flight, the period of flight, and the process of resettlement have been described as important elements in psychosocial adjustment (Ben-Porath, 1991). Terrorist acts are most likely to occur for refugees during the first two phases of adjustment, the antecedents of flight and period of flight. In providing treatment for refugee trauma, the psychotherapist must carefully evaluate dynamics in each phase of the therapeutic relationship to understand the past experiences within a present context.

Bemak (1989) outlined a three-phase development model of acculturation that influences psychosocial adjustment. The first phase is a period of security and safety, in which the refugee attempts to use existing skills to master the new environment and feel psychologically safe. During this phase, traumatic issues from the past are worked through and there is greater internal consistency between affect and cognitions and subsequently behavior. Successful integration and resolution of past trauma and completion of phase one will lead to the second phase, in which former skills from the culture of origin and newly acquired skills are integrated as acculturation takes place. This is also accompanied by further resolution of past trauma and a deeper consistency between affect and cognitions. Phase three follows successful adaptation and is highlighted by a growing sense of future. In this developmental model it is only after a basic mastery of culture and language, a "coming to terms" with past traumatic experiences, and an ensuing sense of psychological safety that the refugee begins to contemplate and plan for future realistic and attainable goals and to implement strategies to achieve those objectives.

The premigration trauma experienced by refugees may continue to interfere with psychosocial adjustment and present barriers to successful adaptation. Adaptation for refugees in the resettlement country includes learning new coping skills as well as new behavioral and communication patterns. Many refugees learn survival skills that may appear aversive, antisocial, or even psychopathological in the host country (Stein, 1986). For example, Cambodian refugees who experienced or witnessed torture, rape, and other incidents of abuse or death, remained alive by acting "dumb," a reaction that is common to survivors of atrocities (Chung & Okazaki, 1991). Mollica and Jalbert (1989) described the Khmer term *Tiing Mooung* ("dummy" personality, puppet, or scarecrow) as a common Cambodian way to describe refugee behavior under the Khmer Rouge regime—being deaf, stupid, foolish, obedient, and confused. When this behavior is continued after the terrorist events in resettlement countries, it appears strange and inappropriate and contributes to adjustment difficulties.

Another contributing factor in refugees' adaptation to a new country is ambivalence about leaving their country of origin. The refugee experience is characterized by involuntary flight and the lack of control over decisions regarding where one lives and works. Furthermore, there may even be resentment on the part of the refugee toward the host country. For example, some Southeast Asian refugees felt exploited by the United States during the Vietnam War and hence resentment in being resettled in the United States. These feelings may contribute to a difficult adaptation process.

Survivor's guilt is also a common problem for refugees (Brown, 1982; Lin, Tazuma, & Masuda, 1979). Many refugees remain guilty about escaping from dangerous conditions in their home country and leaving behind family, friends, and loved ones. A lack of knowledge about the condition of those left behind adds to existing trauma and mental health problems. The cycle of guilt may continue so that the more the refugee works through past trauma and finds enjoyment and success, the greater the sense of hurt and associated guilt.

Language Barriers

Language plays an important part in refugee adjustment. Learning the language of the resettlement country symbolizes leaving one's homeland and may be a catalyst for feelings of cultural identity loss (Bemak & Chung, 2003). Losing one's identity may create high levels of emotional distress, particularly for those individuals who have not adequately dealt with past trauma. The El Salvadorian refugee who struggled to learn English after migrating to the United States provides a good example. During a particularly difficult time, she finally exclaimed in Spanish, "To learn English is to forget my country. I don't want to lose myself and speak English!" Similarly, a resettled Cambodian adolescent whose mother was executed during the period of mass genocide under the Khmer Rouge regime reported that in a dream her mother angrily entreated her to "Stop speaking English. You must speak Khmer! Remember you are Cambodian!"

Experiencing the frustration of trying to learn a new language may also bring back memories of "better times and easier communication" with neighbors, friends, and family. The struggle with language may exacerbate emotional problems and frustrations in understanding the new environment and re-ignite deeply rooted trauma. Language classes may also create helpless feelings, causing regression. This may evoke questions about self-worth and cause a loss in social status marked by feelings of inadequacy and low self-esteem, all of which add to existing difficulty of resolving past experiences with terrorism.

Finally, learning the language of the new culture may stimulate a redefinition of family relationships and roles. Thus, attempting to deal with trauma in a country of relocation may be complicated as the family loses tradition and social restructuring, causing role confusion. This can be seen with the child from a patriarchal society who rapidly acquired language skills in school, resulting in her parents becoming dependent on her for cultural and language translation.

Education and Employment

Many refugees face not only social readjustment problems, but also difficulties in transferring past training, education, and skills to equivalent employment. Educational qualifications from countries of origin may not be transferable in resettlement countries, and jobs in more developed societies that require technological skills may not be applicable. Subsequently, the status and recognition for previous skills and education is often neglected in the new culture, creating a situation whereby the refugee must "begin again," resulting in a decrease in status, poor self esteem, and feelings of hopelessness (Bemak & Chung, 2002). Downward mobility and employment devaluation are serious concerns, adding to traumatized individuals' existing problems.

Unemployment or underemployment of refugee men commonly forces wives to work outside the home, creating another new dynamic in families. This produces a dramatic shift in gender roles for many cultures, causing a conflict between the values of the culture of origin and those of the host country (Chung & Okazaki, 1991). Ironically, whereas refugee men may experience a downward socioeconomic status, refugee women from developing countries may experience upward socioeconomic mobility (Chung & Okazaki, 1991). These changes in familial and gender roles add to the already strained family situation and cause additional psychological problems in individuals who have experienced trauma.

Changes in Family Dynamics

Refugees may be forced to change traditional child-rearing practices to comply with the resettlement country's laws regarding children and discipline. Practices such as marriage during the early teen years that may have been commonplace in their home country may be infractions of the law in the new environment. New rules may create confusion and adjustment difficulties within the refugee family.

Parents' appreciation for the host culture may diminish as children rapidly acculturate to the society in their new home, resulting in the loss of adult authority by and creating intergenerational conflicts. Furthermore, to compound the situation, refugee children and adolescents may witness a transformation in their parents. In the home country, parents may be seen as autonomous and culturally competent caretakers, whereas in the resettlement country they may be viewed as depressed, overwhelmed, helpless, scared, and dependent individuals. Confidence in parents is inevitably undermined when their roles transform from independent to dependent caretakers who are slow to acquire a new language and understand new customs (Bemak & Chung, 2002).

Conflicts between parents and children may also emerge regarding acceptable practices and customs. Dating, marriage, curfews, and other supervisory guidelines may become negotiated issues rather than prescribed parental norms. The fact that these issues become open for discussion rather than remain nonnegotiable may create intense anxiety for the parents as they experience a loss of authority and control. These postmigration adjustment issues may have serious implications for individuals who are attempting to recover from past trauma.

School

School presents a number of problems for refugee students who may be prone to extreme risk for truancy and dropout (Goldberg, 1999). The overall structure of schools, including the norms regulating classroom and social behavior, may be different from that of the home country. Refugee students who experienced war and forced migration, causing situational and psychological chaos, may benefit from the structured environment that schools can offer (Bruce, 2001). Expectations for academic and personal growth may not fit with life perspectives and worldviews. For example, in Western resettlement countries, the expectations for academic success are traditionally defined by an emphasis on scores, grades, early course and vocation choices, and rankings, which may be contradictory to cultural norms for refugee students (Hertzberg, 1998).

Being a foreigner in a school may create added problems. Different language, dress, ways of socially interacting, habits, and foods may elicit prejudicial responses from peers, teachers, and staff. Behaviors of children may be misconstrued. For example, school personnel and other mental health professionals may be confused and misdiagnose aggressive behavior that has been clearly documented as likely in regarding children who have been exposed to sustained trauma (Freud & Dann, 1951; Pinsky, 1949; United Nations Educational, Scientific, and Cultural Organization, 1952). Van der Kolk (1987) found that children who had been traumatized were both self-destructive and destructive toward other children, because of the difficulties they had controlling their aggression. Research is congruent with these findings; for example, Dadfar (1994) (regarding Afghan refugees), Ajdukovic and Ajdukovic (1993) (regarding Croatians), and Boothby (1994) generalized these concerns to all refugee children. Bemak and Chung (2003) present a detailed description of issues encountered by refugee children in U.S. schools.

Discrimination and Racism as Barriers in Psychosocial Adjustment

In addition to the above psychosocial adjustment issues encountered by refugees, this group may also face discrimination and racism in resettlement countries. Resettlement countries' refugee immigration policies may create tension with members of that country, especially during economically difficult times. As seen after the September 11 attacks on the United States, if the host country was affected either directly or indirectly by terrorism, some members of the host country may respond negatively to refugees from the same countries or ethnic/racial background as the terrorists. Racism and discrimination contribute to the already-existing difficulties of dealing with trauma and may manifest overtly or covertly (Beiser et al., 1988; Bemak, Chung, & Pedersen, 2003; Noh, Beiser, Kaspar, Hou, & Rummens, 1999).

PSYCHOLOGICAL PROBLEMS ENCOUNTERED BY REFUGEES

Premigration Trauma

To understand the refugee experience, it is critical that mental health professionals be aware of and understand the premigration experiences of refugees. Studies on premigration traumatic experiences of refugees are extensive (e.g., Ajdukovic & Ajdukovic, 1993; Bottinelli, 1990; Dadfar, 1994; El-Sarraj, Tawahina, & Heine,

1994; Farias, 1991; Karadaghi, 1994; Kinzie, 1993; Kozaric-Korvacic, Folnegovic-Smalc, Skringjaric, Szajnberg, & Marusic, 1995; Mollica et al., 1987). Studies have found that many refugees are subjected to the atrocities of war and terrorism, such as experiencing and witnessing starvation, rape and sexual abuse, physical beatings and injury, and torture and killing; being forced to commit atrocities; and being incarcerated. Due to the premigration traumatic experiences, refugees are at risk for developing serious mental health problems that include depression, anxiety, post-traumatic stress disorder (PTSD) and generalized psychological difficulties. It has been found that this population experienced a higher incidence of psychopathology than the general population of the resettlement country (e.g., Kinzie, 1993; Marsella, Friedman, & Spain 1993; Mollica & Lavelle, 1988; Weisaeth & Eitinger, 1993). For example, it was estimated that in a clinical refugee population, PTSD occurs 50 percent of the time or higher and depressive disorders range from 42 percent to 89 percent (e.g., Hauff & Vaglum, 1995; Mollica et al., 1987; Ramsay, Gorst-Unsworth, & Turner, 1993). In the refugee community it was found that depression ranged from 15 percent to 80 percent (e.g., Carlson & Rosser-Hogan, 1991; Pernice & Brook, 1994). Premigration experience with war and terrorism has a dramatic impact on the lives of refugees and contributes to the psychosocial postmigration resettlement adjustment and adaptation.

Six groups of refugees have been identified as at-risk for developing serious mental health disorders during postmigration adjustment as a result of their exposure to premigration war and terrorism. One group is older refugees. Due to their age and therefore deeply ingrained cultural behavior patterns, this group may have more difficulties in adjusting to a new and foreign environment that requires learning a new language, skills, and patterns of behavior (Chung, Bemak, & Okazaki, 1997). A second group is single men (under 21 years in age) because of the lack of familial and social support (Lin et al., 1979). A third group is unaccompanied minors, that is, children and adolescents who are not accompanied by adult family members during the resettlement process. Fourth, refugee women and girls are at risk due to the high prevalence of rape and sexual abuse (frequently multiple times) during premigration (Refugee Women in Development, 1990). The fifth group is the high percentage of refugee women whose husbands and/or children were killed or lost during war, leaving them widowed (Mollica et al., 1987). Chung (2000) found in a community study of three hundred Cambodian refugee women that 22 percent reported death or loss of a spouse and 53 percent reported loss of a close family member (e.g., children, sibling, parents, etc). A sixth group is also composed of women, but of refugee women who experienced problems during postmigration due to minimal or no amounts of one or more of the following: prior education, literacy in their own language, English proficiency or proficiency in the resettlement country's language, family and emotional support, and community resources (Chung, 2000).

The process of acculturation takes place within the context of these mental health concerns, contributing to the difficulty of adjustment following the refugee's exposure to war and terrorism. In its broadest sense, acculturation is defined as a changing process that facilitates adaptation from one culture to another. Many refugees are in the unique position of having to undertake this major life-changing event while also dealing with the painful issues of premigration trauma, which causes highly intense and complex clinical challenges for mental health professionals.

CULTURAL BELIEF SYSTEMS

The World Health Organization defines *health* as a "state of complete physical, mental and social well-being" (World Health Organization Division of Mental Health, 1987, p. 1). Psychotherapy has generally tended to focus on promoting mental health that is based on individualized treatment as a means to enhance optimal independent functioning, coping strategies, and adaptation. This contradicts the cultural context for most refugees, who generally come from countries where family and community networks are the foundation for the culture. As a result, the standard clinical interventions in Western resettlement countries are frequently in conflict with fundamental societal beliefs and value systems that foster family and community interdependence. These social and cultural constructs must be considered when providing culturally relevant mental health treatment for refugees.

The Western clinicians and the refugee client will typically have different perceptions of both the mental health problem and effective intervention strategies. An example of this would be the Somalian who believes her ancestor's spirit can help deal with a particular problem. She calls on this person, talks to her, and takes very seriously her guidance and advice. Traditional Western clinicians may view these symptoms as psychotic, calling for medication to alleviate the symptomatology (the "hallucination") and treat the underlying psychosis. Indigenous healing methods would approach the same symptoms from a different cultural belief system, incorporating the concept of the deceased relative and spirit as important and relevant personal and spiritual communication contributing to the treatment of the individual, which may include the entire family (Bemak, Chung, & Pedersen, 2003).

Kleinman and colleagues (Kleinman, Eisenberg, & Good, 1978; Kleinman & Good, 1985) have discussed disparities in cultural beliefs, values, philosophical constructs, and spiritual and religious customs, citing the need to validate the client's cultural conceptualization of the problem. The cultural conceptualization of mental illness affects the manifestation of symptoms (Chung & Kagawa-Singer, 1993), the help-seeking behavior (Chung & Lin, 1994), and expectations of treatment and outcome. For example, insomnia or loss of appetite may be viewed in some cultures as having upset ancestral spirits and thus would require assistance from individuals who respect and honor that cultural belief system, such as a spiritualist who could communicate with the ancestors to establish the cause of the problem and the subsequent solution. Clinicians must be knowledgeable and aware and able to develop culturally sensitive therapeutic interventions and skills (Kagawa-Singer & Chung, 1994; Pedersen, 1988) that have applicability to deeply rooted trauma.

UTILIZATION OF WESTERN MAINSTREAM MENTAL HEALTH SERVICES

Studies have reported that a disproportionate number of refugees have serious mental health problems; however, there is a historical reluctance on the part of this population to seek help from Western mainstream mental health services (Higginbotham, Trevino, & Ray, 1990). This may be related to several factors. First, a resettlement country's mainstream mental health services may be the last treatment choice of refugees. Before seeking mental health treatment, there is typically an exploration of indigenous healers, elders, family and social support networks, and religious leaders. Only after failing to receive help from these sources do refugees seek out, by default, mainstream mental health professionals. This also presents an added complication in treatment since, by the time a connection is made with a mental health professional, the problem has grown more unmanageable and acute (Higginbotham et al., 1990).

A second reason is cultural insensitivity on the part of mainstream services. The lack of cultural responsiveness by mainstream services has been shown to account for low utilization, high dropout, and premature termination of these services (Sue, Fujino, Hu, Takeuchi, & Zane, 1991). A third reason is language within the treatment context. The lack of native language speakers or trained bilingual workers who can translate creates an obstacle for mental health treatment. Equally important is the inability of many bilingual translators to work effectively within the mental health spectrum, to go beyond the literal translation and provide additional information, such as the meaning of personality within the culture, the innuendoes of tone, interpretation of nonverbal behavior, and the social relationships and definition of self that are culturally bound (Bemak, Chung, & Pedersen, 2003).

A fourth reason for low utilization of mainstream mental health services is inaccessibility (Higginbotham et al., 1990). Clinics and private offices are frequently located in areas that may be difficult to reach. Public transportation systems may be confusing, especially for someone who is traumatized. Public transportation may also be time consuming, causing refugees to assess the value of negotiating a myriad of trains or buses. Furthermore, mental health facilities are sometimes located in poorer communities that may be perceived as dangerous and trigger traumatic memories.

A fifth reason is "welcomeless service systems" (Bemak & Chung, 2002). Refugees may encounter insensitive receptionists, staff, or professionals. For example, a refugee who arrives late at a mental health clinic for an appointment, yet is within appropriate time parameters for his or her culture, may be greeted by a hostile receptionist who scolds the person for missing the appointment. A loud or forceful voice or rudeness on the part of the receptionist may trigger the refugee's own past trauma and raise questions for the refugee about treatment.

Finally, in many refugee communities, the problem of one person is the problem of the family or community. Individual experiences are reflections on the family or clan rather than solely the responsibility of one person. Thus, individual treatment may create a stigma for the entire family and/or community. This shared responsibility for mental health problems, coupled with negative stereotypes of mainstream mental health practices, may result in an avoidance of mental health services. Furthermore, clinicians need to be aware that although refugees may seek mainstream mental health services, they may also concurrently utilize their own traditional methods of healing (Chung & Lin, 1994).

CULTURAL INNOVATIONS IN CLINICAL PRACTICE

Providing effective clinical interventions with refugees who are experiencing mental health problems due to terrorism requires a high degree of awareness and understanding of the relationship of the refugee experience to acts of terrorism. The combination of premigration trauma, postmigration adjustment difficulties, and terrorist acts of intentional violence creates multiple levels of deeply rooted issues that require significant time, attention, and skill. Added to this already highly complex situation is the need for significant skills in cross-cultural psychotherapy, since refugees migrate from one culture to another. This requires that the psychotherapist be able to conceptually understand and apply effective treatment to cultural differences in help-seeking behaviors, conceptualization of mental illness, manifestation of symptoms, and treatment expectations and outcomes, as well as an integration of Western and Eastern healing methodologies and familiarity with the limitations of Western-based diagnoses in assessment.

Unfortunately, the overwhelming majority of graduate and in-service training programs for the various mental health disciplines do not provide training for working with terrorism and refugees. Thus professionals' training leaves them limited in their understanding of clinical interventions in these areas. In this section we will discuss treatment for refugees who have experienced significant trauma and terrorism, treatment that is rooted in culturally appropriate interventions. The interventions discussed will be derived from the Multi-Level Model (MLM) of Psychotherapy for Refugees (Bemak & Chung, 2002; Bemak, Chung, & Bornemann, 1996; Bemak, Chung, & Pedersen, 2003) and expanded to incorporate elements that are conducive to working with refugees who are also traumatized by terrorism.

To work with traumatized refugees who have experienced terrorism, it is essential to understand the following: the psychological realities of forced migration; premigration trauma; postmigration adjustment challenges; historical and sociopolitical context of the refugee situation; transition; deeply rooted losses; and understanding of political and social concerns for the refugee and the resettlement country's refugee policies. All of these are critical in undertaking clinical work. The Multi-Level Model (MLM) of psychotherapy for refugees reconceptualizes working with this population and offers a framework for clinical interventions that incorporates these key issues in a culturally responsive manner, as well as a macro holistic approach.

Embedded in the four levels of the MLM are several important therapeutic constructs. The first concept is "clinical dignity," which emphasizes the sociocultural and historical background of the client that is at the root of a refugee's identity and must be respected at all times. A second construct is cross-cultural empathy, which is different from a generalized concept of empathy (Chung & Bemak, 2002) and results in the demonstration of culturally appropriate verbal and nonverbal displays of support and understanding.

A third construct is the consideration of how racism and discrimination, which have been identified as a natural outcome of Western individualism (Pedersen, 2000), contribute to the mental health problems of already-traumatized refugee individuals. Fourth is a clear understanding of postmigration acculturation and adjustment issues and their intersection with mental health and trauma. A fifth construct is the importance of racial and ethnic identity development and its impact on overcoming experiences of terrorism and trauma.

Finally, it is essential that there is a fundamental cross-cultural understanding that each culture is unique. This requires taking into account cross-cultural issues relevant to different refugee groups, such as the cultural belief systems and world-views, unique cross-cultural perspectives on help-seeking behaviors, and conceptualizations about health and illness that are culturally bound. Each of these constructs is important in undertaking the difficult and complex work of providing treatment to refugees who have experienced terrorism.

The Multi-Level Model of Psychotherapy for Refugees incorporates four phases: Level I: mental health education; Level II: individual, group and/or family psychotherapy; Level III: cultural empowerment; and Level IV: indigenous healing. It is important to note that these phases are not sequential and may be implemented simultaneously or independently. They may be utilized at any stage of treatment and be reintroduced as needed at different stages of the therapeutic process.

The MLM is a psycho-educational model that incorporates affective, behavioral, and cognitive intervention and prevention strategies. The following is a description of the MLM model for refugees that is expanded to include interventions dealing with terrorism.

Level I—Mental Health Education

Refugee clients who have been traumatized may be distrustful of mainstream mental health services and hesitant about participating in mental health practices and interventions that are unfamiliar. In fact, many refugees from war-torn countries come from cultures where personal problems are not usually shared with people outside the family network. Thus it is important to educate refugee clients about what happens in psychotherapy and during the treatment process.

A critical element in Level I is establishing a trusting therapeutic relationship, which has been recognized as an essential ingredient of effective psychotherapy (Wohl, 2000) and is heightened as an issue following exposure to terrorism. It is highly important in establishing trust and rapport to sensitively take into account the cultural background of the refugee client and his or her subsequent perception of help seeking and support within that framework. It has been pointed out that refugees need more time to explore and discuss these issues (Root, 1998), which can naturally take place within the framework of Level I discussions.

Early sessions using the MLM model would emphasize "mental health basics." The following issues would all be discussed at the beginning of treatment: how long sessions last, information gathered during intake assessments, the recounting and sharing of personal feelings and experiences, confidentiality with particular relevance to government or military authorities, the role of an interpreter, different possible psychotherapeutic techniques that may be employed, interpersonal space, relationship boundaries, and usage or nonuse of medications. Refugee clients may feel less awkward or uncomfortable participating in the therapeutic relationship after discussing these important and relevant fundamentals of mental health. Thus Level I provides information, education, and clarification for the individual, group, or family about the process of psychotherapy and the mental health treatment encounter.

It is important to note that Level I is a two-way process. While educating and providing and clarifying the parameters of psychotherapy, the psychotherapist is gathering information about the client's (or clients') mental health belief system and cultural views about help-seeking behaviors for use and application at other MLM levels. Bridging the divide between the client's and the psychotherapist's conceptualization of mental illness is central to effective interventions (Kleinman, 1980) and includes an exploration of etiology, course, help-seeking behavior, and treatment outcome as well as culturally unique symptom manifestation and the preferred treatment expectations and outcomes.

Distrust stemming from the experience of terrorism must also be considered during Level I when working with refugee clients. Disregard for this may result in further resistance and difficulty in treatment. It is essential that the psychotherapist provide a psychologically safe environment and consider distrust as one of many strategies to survive rather than as a pathological symptom.

Level II—Psychotherapy

Level II is the application of individual, group, and family psychotherapy in culturally responsive ways to effectively work with clients who have experienced trauma. After evaluating the client's needs, the clinician would make a determination of what treatment would be most suitable and culturally appropriate for that particular client. Although traditional Western techniques are foreign to most refugee clients, Zane and Sue (1991) demonstrated applicability of individual and family therapy to several culturally distinct groups. An example of this is Kinzie's (1985) recommendation that psychotherapists be more directive and active with Southeast Asian refugees.

A number of treatment interventions can be employed in Level II and have been found effective in cross-cultural refugee work and applicable to clients who have experienced terrorism. Cognitive-behavioral interventions have been successful with refugees (Arce & Torres-Matrullo, 1982; Bemak & Greenberg, 1994; Comas Diaz, 1985; Egli, Shiota, Ben-Porath, & Butcher, 1991; Stumphauser & Davis,

1983), facilitating a reorientation to the present, moving beyond traumatic premigration memories and anxiety about the future (Beiser, 1987). Storytelling and projective drawing have helped traumatized children to regain control over their lives (Pynoos & Eth, 1984). Another method of reducing the psychological effects of terrorism on children is the involvement of caring adults in their lives (Melville & Lykes, 1992). This is consistent with family therapy being viewed as a culturally sensitive intervention (Bemak, 1989; Szapocznik & Cohen, 1986). Bemak and Timm (1994) presented a case study in which dreamwork played a central role in therapy for a previously tortured Cambodian refugee. A focus on the moral development of strongly valued cultural traits such as honesty was found to be an effective intervention with Haitian refugees (Charles, 1986). In their work with traumatized individuals, Waitzkin and Magana (1997) found that narrative reconstruction, or storytelling that is integrated with culture and specific traumatic life events, was helpful in treatment with this population. Other interventions that may be employed in Level II include gestalt, relaxation, role playing, and psychodrama.

To provide effective treatment for trauma, clinicians must employ culturally relevant techniques and processes. Given the history of terrorism, persecution, trauma, torture, and forced migration that many refugees encounter, it is vital to understand and consider the refugee's background as it impacts present psychological functioning and the ability to work with symptoms exhibited in post-traumatic stress disorder (PTSD), despite controversy regarding the applicability of PTSD across cultures (see Diagnoses section below).

When working with traumatized refugee populations, it is necessary to take into consideration that many political governments or groups have invaded their lives, creating a distrust and fear of authority. This has resulted in their developing survival skills and a healthy paranoia regarding personal inquiries by authorities. In resettlement countries, clinicians may well be considered threatening and inappropriate, especially when they ask questions that are highly personal. Since psychotherapy requires self-disclosure and a level of intimacy with the psychotherapist, trust must be fostered cautiously, keeping in mind the client's previous trauma based on premigration history.

An example of this is the Bosnian woman who was raped by soldiers who terrorized her village. She subsequently became distrustful of people in authority and withdrew when strange men were around. Unknowingly, the clinic where she sought treatment in the resettlement country assigned her to a male therapist. She was wary, could not make eye contact, and was reluctant to express any feelings or opinions, not wanting to garner further attention from the therapist. Understanding her behavior was critical to effective mental health interventions with her and with other traumatized individuals.

Given that most refugees come from collectivist cultures, we would strongly recommend group and family work to foster interdependence in social and family networks (Bemak, Chung, & Pedersen, 2003; Morris & Silove, 1992). These therapeutic modalities are viewed as key elements in the MLM and have been used in refugee group therapy to resolve painful psychological issues. Examples of effective group therapy with this population include: refugee children in group counseling discussing their shared experience of a traumatic event (Galante & Foa, 1986), personal exploration and sharing in group therapy with traumatized refugee clients (Friedman & Jaranson, 1994), and longer-term group therapy for Southeast Asians that incorporated discussions about somatizations, cultural conflicts, and loss while maintaining loosely constructed time boundaries (Kinzie et al., 1988). Thus with the MLM it is recommended that group therapy be utilized, particularly when it is consistent with the refugee's cultural background.

Strong family bonds for most refugees, the loss of family, and the necessity of family adaptation in countries of migration lead us also to recommend family therapy as a natural means of addressing problems from a family systems perspective. Since World War II, studies have illustrated the negative impact of family separation on the mental health of children affected by war (Berman, 1999; Fox, Muennich, & Montgomery, 1994; Freud & Burlingham, 1943; Henshaw & Howarth, 1941; Laor, Wolmer, Mayes, & Gershon, 1997). Direct work with refugees during postmigration has identified separation from family members as threatening to mental health (Porte & Torney-Purta, 1987; Rumbaut, 1991; Servan-Schreiber, Lin, & Birmaher, 1998). Roizblatt and Pilowsky (1996) identify the need to help families who have forcibly migrated to grieve their losses together and address acculturation as a family unit.

Placement in a new and strange country helps make MLM-embracing family treatment a major therapeutic intervention. This may include work with both nuclear and extended families. It is essential that professionals who provide family therapy for refugee populations have a clear understanding and knowledge about the context of family within the culture of origin of the refugee. For example, in the MLM, we recommend an assessment of extended family—that is, whether or not to include grandparents, aunts, uncles, cousins, friends, and/or spiritual leaders who are identified as part of the family. Other times, even more distant relatives would be important to include in the treatment process, given the importance of their roles within the family constellation. This is unlike Western family therapy, which most often includes immediate family members. Of equal importance is the determination of family hierarchy, which, in turn, should guide protocol and appropriate interactions within the family system. Family therapy with this population has been demonstrated by Bemak (1989), Charles (1986), Lee (1989), and Szapocznik and Cohen (1986).

Diagnoses

There are fundamental questions regarding the cultural sensitivity of applying Western-based frameworks of diagnoses (e.g., DSM-IV, ICD-10) to refugee populations. As mentioned previously, given the cultural influence on conceptualizing mental health problems and symptom manifestation, it is often the case that patterns of symptoms do not correspond exactly with discrete classifications of Western disorders. However, psychotherapists may try to make sense of culturally expressed symptomatology and force refugee clients into discrete categorizations, resulting in erroneous diagnoses and subsequently ineffective treatment (Chung & Kagawa-

Singer, 1995). Research has shown that the misclassification of psychiatric disorders of ethnic clients in the United States (Asians, African Americans, and the Latin population) has been due to the psychotherapist's lack of understanding of cultural and/or linguistic differences (e.g., Baskin, Bluestone, & Nelson, 1981; Sue, Chun, & Gee, 1995). Therefore, clinicians must become knowledgeable about how refugee clients conceptualize mental illness and express their distress before effective diagnosis and treatment can take place. This includes the awareness of ethnocentric biases inherent in diagnostic categories (Chung & Kagawa-Singer, 1995).

For example, there has been controversy regarding PTSD and diagnoses for individuals who have experienced terrorism, arguing that PTSD itself is a cultural construct that may not be accurate in depicting psychological problems (Waitzkin & Magana, 1997). Others have criticized PTSD, indicating that violence is an everyday occurrence for many people and thus is not in accordance with the American Psychiatric Association definition (1987) of trauma being outside the normal range of typical experience. This is consistent with Garbarino, Kostelny, and Dubrow's (1991) contention that trauma becomes a core condition in one's life rather than an extension of a later mental health problem. We would suggest that, in working with clients who have been exposed to terrorism, these issues be considered very carefully prior to determining diagnostic categories.

Level III—Cultural Empowerment

Given the nature of past terrorism, forced migration, and resettlement into a new country, it is our firm conviction that treatment must go beyond traditional Western therapeutic interventions. Level III of the MLM, cultural empowerment, provides this additional important dimension in the healing of refugee clients. Cultural empowerment is a critical element in postmigration, assisting refugees who have experienced a loss of control and helplessness through terrorism and war to gain cultural and environmental mastery over their world. Refugees who are traumatized and seek mental health treatment are also faced with pressing resettlement survival needs such as housing, employment, language, and accessing social services and assistance programs. These concerns may have greater immediate urgency than the trauma itself, which requires a stable environment to facilitate treatment. Mental health professionals, especially if they become trusted partners in the healing process, may be essential as providers of resource information.

Given the varied needs, many refugees find themselves involved with multiple agencies. For example, due to premigration and refugee transitional camp conditions, many refugees have health problems. Many are afraid and confused by the symptoms, which most often contributes further to their poor mental health status. In such instances it would be important for clinicians to work across disciplines, acquire an understanding of the nature and projected outcome for the health problem, and explore this with refugee clients.

Cultural empowerment also suggests that clinicians assume a proactive role in ensuring social justice. We believe that an advocacy role is essential, since issues of human rights and resettlement policies and practices may be unfair and need to be proactively addressed with clients. Since these issues are an important part of resolving past exposure to terrorism and interfere with successful psychosocial adjustment for refugee clients, attention to issues such as family reunification, food, clothing and housing benefits, financial support for heating or electricity costs, employment discrimination, and so on may be essential in the therapeutic process. Thus it is recommended that clinicians redefine their role when working with traumatized refugees and incorporate advocacy and support that aim toward social justice, equity, and fair treatment.

It should be noted that this is a redefinition of the professional's role in treatment rather than an extension of time. An example would be with the refugee parents who are severely traumatized from having observed the mass killing of people and relatives in their village. They migrated six months before and recently decided to move to another geographic region within the resettlement country. The task of moving, changing schools for their two children, affiliating with another resettlement agency, finding health care, and so forth, is overwhelming and adds to their already-existing mental health problems. Using the MLM, the psychotherapist could be helpful in working with them to determine whom to call to transfer school records, what forms to fill out, how to contact the resettlement agency in another city, where to find bilingual interpreters to assist them, and so on. Therefore, at this particular time, effective treatment would be to attend to these pressing issues that are causing significant stress and escalating the symptoms exhibited by the already-existing trauma.

Finally, cultural empowerment provides client assistance in gaining skills to deal with racism, discrimination, and oppression that may be encountered in the resettlement country and significantly contribute to already-existing trauma. Hostility and rejection by host countries is increased when the host society rejects the refugees' differences, including different customs, behaviors, dress, religion, and/or language. This was evident after the September 11 attacks on the United States when there was an outcry of dislike of people from Arab and Muslim backgrounds and numerous hate crimes were targeted at these groups throughout the United States. This type of negativity may result in individual, group, and/or institutional racism, making acculturation more difficult and adding to the aftermath of resolving premigration trauma. The literature has clearly documented the negative effects of racism on psychological well-being (e.g., Aponte & Johnson, 2000; Asamen & Berry, 1987; Hughes & Demo, 1989) and would certainly have serious impact on individuals dealing with the psychological effects of terrorism.

Thus, we strongly believe that clinicians working with refugees who have experienced terrorism must be attuned and highly sensitive to the difficulties inherent in adapting to a new culture and must expand beyond traditional roles to provide case management–type assistance, guidance, and resource information that will empower the refugee. In the MLM, the clinician is not expected to become a case manager for the client, but rather to assume responsibilities as a "cultural systems information guide and advocate," assisting the refugee with relevant information about how systems work, how to solve problems within those systems, what new coping strategies are needed to master the new culture, and how to deal with unfair, unequal, and discriminatory treatment. The resultant mastery of the world around them is instrumental in helping the refugee client acculturate successfully and address the deeper traumatic issues that pose serious psychological problems.

Level IV—Integration of Western and Indigenous Healing Methodologies

Level IV of the MLM—indigenous healing—integrates Western traditional and nontraditional or indigenous healing methodologies. The World Health Organization (1992) has acknowledged that an integration of Western traditional mental health practice and indigenous healing results in more effective outcomes. This is highly important in treating refugees who have experienced terrorism and war and is consistent with findings that more than three quarters of people worldwide regularly utilize some form of alternative or indigenous (non-Western) methods of healing (Micozzi, 1996).

Pedersen (2000) has reported that Western and non-Western approaches to healing are becoming more complementary as psychology gives increasing attention to this area. Despite this knowledge in some spheres of Western treatment, indigenous practices are generally disregarded in the West due to a lack of knowledge and experience working across cultures. Thus we would recommend that psychotherapists working with traumatized individuals establish relationships with community leaders, priests, monks, and other spiritual and religious healers. These individuals may provide important information about the client's culture as well as assist in treatment.

Traditional cultural practices that ensure the refugee the rich combination of healing sources from the culture of origin and culture of resettlement are important in dealing with trauma. "Treatment partnerships" with indigenous and spiritual healers and community leaders provide insight and co-treatment interventions ensuring a cultural context. Hiegel (1994) identified four approaches to indigenous healing that include: (a) physical treatments, (b) magic healing methods, (c) counseling, and (d) medications. We would add another dimension—that of religion and spirituality.

The need for receptivity to culture-bound practices is essential. Making referrals and maintaining open communication with indigenous healers, spiritual leaders, and community leaders in "treatment partnerships" provides a linkage between the culture where the terrorism and trauma originated and the relocation country and adjustment issues. Receptivity to the client's preference for treatment and frequent usage of both treatment interventions (Chung & Lin, 1994) are also important.

Although the MLM recommends that psychotherapists work collaboratively and in partnership with indigenous healers, it is also necessary to mention a few words of caution. It would be false to assume that all refugee clients prefer traditional healing as the treatment of choice. The MLM recommends an exploration of treatment preference, initiated by either the client or the professional. A second caution would be to ascertain the credibility of the traditional healer within the culture of the refugee, to ensure trustworthiness.

CONCLUSION

With the events of September 11, 2001, it became evident that terrorism is no longer restricted to certain parts of the world, but has become a global issue. An ongoing outcome of terrorism is that vast numbers of people are forced to migrate and to seek refuge in other countries, so that the issues of terrorism and refugees go hand in hand. The forced migration of refugees frequently results in relocation to countries that are culturally different from home countries, causing serious acculturation challenges during the postmigration period. These adjustment issues are complicated by premigration histories of terrorism, trauma, and war. Mental health professionals in resettlement countries are therefore confronted with an enormous challenge—how to provide effective treatment to deal with the psychological aftermath of terrorism, premigration trauma, and postmigration adjustment. Interwoven with these issues are the cultural, historical, and sociopolitical backgrounds of refugees.

The Multi-Level Model of Psychotherapy for Refugees is presented in this chapter to assist psychotherapists in being effective with this population. This model provides a culturally sensitive holistic approach to working with refugees and takes the psychotherapist beyond the traditional Western role of a clinician, providing a conceptual model for addressing terrorism and its associated problems with the refugee population.

REFERENCES

Ajdukovic, M., & Ajdukovic, D. (1993). Psychological well-being of refugee children. *Child Abuse and Neglect, 17*, 843–854.

American Psychiatric Association (1987). *Diagnostic and statistical manual of mental disorders* (3rd ed., rev). Washington, DC: Author.

Aponte, J., & Johnson, L. R. (2000). The impact of culture on intervention and treatment of ethnic populations. In J. Aponte & J. Wohl (Eds.), *Psychological intervention and cultural diversity* (pp. 18–39). Needham Heights, MA: Allyn and Bacon.

Arce, A., & Torres-Matrullo, C. (1982). Application of cognitive behavioral techniques in the treatment of Hispanic patients. *Psychiatric Quarterly, 54*, 230–236.

Aroian, K. J. (1990). A model of psychological adaptation to migration and resettlement. *Nursing Research, 39*, 5–10.

Asamen, J. K., & Berry, G. L. (1987). Self-concept, alienation, and perceived prejudice: Implications for counseling Asian Americans. *Journal of Multicultural Counseling and Development, 15*, 146–160.

Balian, K. (1997). *Overview of issues and the United Nations roles.* Paper presented at the meeting on Survivors of Torture: Improving our Understanding Conference. Washington, DC.

Baskin, D., Bluestone, H., & Nelson, M. (1981). Mental illness in minority women. *Journal of Clinical Psychology, 37*, 491–498.

Bathien, K. N., & Malapert, B. (1987). Psychological problems following war and migration traumas. *Neuropsychiatrie de l'enfance et de l'adolescence, 35,* 505–523.

Beiser, M. (1987). Changing time perspective and mental health among Southeast Asian refugees. *Culture, Medicine, and Psychiatry, 11,* 437–464.

Beiser, M., Barwick, C., Berry, J., da Costa, G., Fantino, A., Ganesan, S., Lee, C., Milne, W., Naidoo, J., Prince, R., Tousignant, M., & Vela, E. (1988). *After the door has been opened: Mental health issues affecting immigrants and refugees.* Ottawa, ON: Ministries of Multiculturalism and Citizenship, and Health and Welfare.

Bemak, F. (1989). Cross-cultural family therapy with Southeast Asian refugees. *Journal of Strategic and Systemic Therapies, 8,* 22–27.

Bemak, F., & Chung, R. C.-Y. (1998). Vietnamese Amerasians: Predictors of distress and self-destructive behavior. *Journal of Counseling and Development, 76,* 452–458.

Bemak, F., & Chung, R. C.-Y. (2002). Counseling and psychotherapy with refugees. In P. B. Pedersen, J. G. Draguns, W. J. Lonner, & J. E. Trimble (Eds.), *Counseling across cultures* (5th ed., pp. 209–232). Thousand Oaks, CA: Sage Publications.

Bemak, F., & Chung, R. C.-Y. (2003). Multicultural counseling with immigrant students in schools. In P. B. Pedersen & J. Carey (Eds.), *Multicultural counseling in schools.* Needham Heights, MA: Allyn and Bacon.

Bemak, F., Chung, R. C.-Y., & Bornemann, T. (1996). Counseling and psychotherapy with refugees. In P. B. Pedersen, J. Draguns, W., Lonner, & J. Trimble (Eds.), *Counseling across cultures* (4th ed., pp. 243–266). Thousand Oaks, CA: Sage Publications.

Bemak, F., Chung, R. C.-Y., & Pedersen, P. B. (2003). *Counseling refugees: A psychosocial cultural approach to innovative multicultural interventions.* Westport, CT: Greenwood Publishing Group.

Bemak, F., & Greenberg, B. (1994). Southeast Asian refugee adolescents: Implications for counseling. *Journal of Multicultural Counseling and Development, 22,* 115–124.

Bemak, F., & Timm, J. (1994). Case study of an adolescent Cambodian refugee: A clinical, developmental and cultural perspective. *International Journal of the Advancement of Counseling, 17,* 47–58.

Ben-Porath Y. (1991). The psychosocial adjustment of refugees. In J. Westermeyer, C. Williams, & A. Nguyen (Eds.), *Mental health services for refugees* (pp. 1–23). (DHHS Publication No. ADM 91-1824). Washington, DC: U.S. Government Printing Office.

Berman, H. (1999). Stories of growing up amid violence by children of war and children of battered women living in Canada. *Image: Journal of Nursing Scholarship, 31,* 57–63.

Berman, H. (2001). Children and war: Current understandings and future directions. *Public Health Nursing, 18,* 243–252.

Berry, J. W. (1986). The acculturation process and refugee behavior. In C. L. Williams & J. Westermeyer (Eds.), *Refugee mental health in resettlement countries* (pp. 25–37). Washington, DC: Hemisphere.

Berry, J. W. (1990). Psychology of acculturation. In R. W. Brislin (Ed.), *Applied cross-cultural psychology* (pp. 232–253). Newbury Park, CA: Sage Publications.

Berry, J. W., & Anis, R. C. (1974). Acculturative stress: The role of ecology, culture, and differentiation. *Journal of Cross-Cultural Psychology, 5,* 382–406.

Boothby, N. (1994). Trauma and violence among refugee children. In A. J. Marsella, T. Bornemann, S. Ekblad, & J. Orley (Eds.), *Amidst peril and pain: The mental health and well-being of the world's refugees* (pp. 239–259). Washington, DC: American Psychological Association.

Bottinelli, M. (1990). *Psychological impact of exile: Salvadoran and Guatemalan families in Mexico.* Washington, DC: Center for Immigration Policy and Refugee Assistance.

Brown, G. (1982). Issues in the resettlement of Indochinese refugees. *Social Casework, 63,* 155–159.

Bruce, B. (2001). Toward mediating the impact of forced migration and displacement among children affected by armed conflict. *Journal of International Affairs, 55,* 24–35.

Carlson, E. B., & Rosser-Hogan, R. (1991). Trauma experiences, posttraumatic stress, dissociation and depression in Cambodian refugees. *American Journal of Psychiatry, 148,* 1548–1551.

Charles, C. (1986). Mental health services for Haitians. In H. P. Lefley & P. B. Pedersen (Eds.), *Cross-cultural training for mental health professionals* (pp. 183–198). Springfield, IL: Charles C. Thomas.

Chung, R. C.-Y. (2000). Psychosocial adjustment of Cambodian refugee women: Implications for mental health counseling. *Journal of Mental Health Counseling, 23,* 115–126.

Chung, R. C.-Y., & Bemak, F. (2002). Revisiting the California Southeast Asian mental health needs assessment data: An examination of refugee ethnic and gender differences. *Journal of Counseling and Development, 80,* 111–119.

Chung, R. C.-Y., & Bemak, F. (2002). The relationship of culture and empathy in cross-cultural counseling. *Journal of Counseling and Development, 80,* 154–159.

Chung, R. C.-Y., Bemak, F., & Okazaki, S. (1997). Counseling Americans of Southeast Asian descent: The impact of the refugee experience. In C. C. Lee & B. L. Richardson (Eds.), *Multicultural issues in counseling: New approaches to diversity* (pp. 207–232). Alexandria, VA: American Counseling Association.

Chung, R. C.-Y., & Kagawa-Singer, M. (1993). Predictors of psychological distress among Southeast Asian refugees. *Social Science and Medicine, 36,* 631–639.

Chung, R. C.-Y., & Kagawa-Singer, M. (1995). Interpretation of symptom presentation and distress: A Southeast Asian refugee example. *Journal of Nervous and Mental Disease, 193,* 639–648.

Chung, R. C.-Y., & Lin, K. M. (1994). Helpseeking behavior among Southeast Asian refugees. *Journal of Community Psychology, 22,* 109–120.

Chung, R. C.-Y., & Okazaki, S. (1991). Counseling Americans of Southeast Asian descent: The impact of the refugee experience. In C. C. Lee & B. L. Richardson (Eds.), *Multicultural issues in counseling: New approaches to diversity* (pp. 107–126). Alexandria, VA: American Association for Counseling and Development.

Comas-Diaz, L. (1985). Cognitive and behavioral group therapy with Puerto Rican women: A comparison of group themes. *Hispanic Journal of Behavioral Sciences, 7,* 273–283.

Dadfar, A. (1994). The Afghans: Bearing the scars of a forgotten war. In A. J. Marsella, T. Bornemann, S. Ekblad, & J. Orley (Eds.), *Amidst peril and pain: The mental health and well-being of the world's refugees* (pp. 125–139). Washington, DC: American Psychological Association.

Eberly, R. E., & Engdahl, B. E. (1991). Prevalence of somatic and psychiatric disorders among former prisoners of war. *Hospital and Community Psychiatry, 42,* 807–813.

Egli, A., Shiota, N., Ben-Porath, Y., & Butcher, J. (1991). Psychological interventions. In J. Westermeyer, C. Williams, & A. Nguyen (Eds.), *Mental health services for refugees* (pp. 157–188). Washington, DC: U.S. Government Printing Office.

Eitinger, L. (1960). The symptomatology of mental disease among refugees in Norway. *Journal of Mental Science, 106,* 315–326.

El-Sarraj, E. R., Tawahina, A. A., & Heine, F. A. (1994). The Palestinians: An uprooted people. In A. J. Marsella, T. Bornemann, S. Ekblad, & J. Orley (Eds.), *Amidst peril and pain: The mental health and well-being of the world's refugees* (pp. 141–152). Washington, DC: American Psychological Association.

Farias, P. (1991). Emotional distress and its sociopolitical correlates in Salvadoran refugees. *Culture, Medicine and Psychiatry, 15,* 167–192.

Fox, P., Muennich, C. J., & Montgomery, A. (1994). The effects of violence on health and adjustment of Southeast Asian refugee children: An integrative review. *Public Health Nursing, 11,* 195–201.

Freud, A., & Burlingham, D. (1943). *War and Children.* New York: Medical War Books, Ernst Willard.

Freud, A., & Dann, S. (1951). An experiment in group upbringing. *Psychoanalytic Study of the Child, 6,* 127.

Friedman, M., & Jaranson, J. (1994). The applicability of the posttraumatic stress disorder concepts to refugees. In A. J. Marsella, T. Bornemann, S. Ekblad, & J. Orley (Eds.), *Amidst peril and pain: The mental health and well-being of the world's refugees* (pp. 207–228). Washington, DC: American Psychological Association.

Galante, R., & Foa, D. (1986). An epidemiological study of psychic trauma and treatment effectiveness for children after a natural disaster. *Journal of the American Academy of Child Psychiatry, 25,* 33–57.

Garbarino, J., Kostelny, K., & Dubrow, N. (1991). *No place to be a child: Growing up in a war zone.* Lexington, MA: D. C. Heath.

Goldberg, M. E. (1999). Truancy and dropout rates among Cambodian students: Results from a comprehensive high school. *Social Work in Education, 21,* 49–63.

Guthrie, G. M. (1975). A behavioral analysis of culture learning. In R. W. Brislin, S. Bocher, & W. J. Lonner (Eds.), *Cross-cultural perspectives on learning* (pp. 95–115). New York: Wiley/Halsted.

Hauff, E., & Vaglum, P. (1995). Organized violence and the stress of exile: Predictors of mental health in a community cohort of Vietnamese refugees three years after resettlement. *British Journal of Psychiatry, 166,* 360–367.

Henshaw, E. M., & Howarth, H. E. (1941). Observed effects of wartime conditions on children: Children living under various types of war conditions: Impressions of children in a heavily bombed area. *Mental Health. London, 2,* 93–101.

Herber J. E., Robins L. N., & McEvoy, L. (1987). Post-traumatic stress disorder in the general population: Findings of the epidemiological catchment area survey. *New England Journal of Medicine, 317,* 1630–1634.

Hertzberg, M. (1998). Having arrived: Dimensions of educational success in a transitional newcomer school. *Anthropology & Educational Quarterly, 29,* 391–418.

Hiegel, J. P. (1994). Use of indigenous concepts and healers in the care of refugees: Some experiences from the Thai border camps. In A. J. Marsella, T. Bornemann, S. Ekblad, & J. Orley (Eds.), *Amidst peril and pain: The mental health and well-being of the world's refugees* (pp. 293–310). Washington, DC: American Psychological Association.

Higginbotham, J. C., Trevino, F. M., & Ray, L. A. (1990). Utilization of curanderos by Mexican Americans: Prevalence and predictors findings from HHANES 1982–1984. *American Journal of Public Health, 80* (Suppl.), 32–35.

Hinton, W. L., Tiet, Q., Tran, C. G., & Chesney, M. (1997). Predictors of depression among refugees from Vietnam: A longitudinal study of new arrivals. *Journal of Nervous and Mental Disease, 185,* 39–45.

Hitch, P. J., & Rack, P. H. (1980). Mental illness among Polish and Russian refugees in Bradford. *British Journal of Psychiatry, 137,* 206–211.

Hughes, M., & Demo, D. H. (1989). Self-perceptions of Black Americans: Self-esteem and personal efficacy. *American Journal of Sociology, 95,* 135–159.

Kagawa-Singer, M., & Chung, R. C.-Y. (1994). A paradigm for culturally based care in ethnic minority populations. *Journal of Community Psychology, 22,* 192–208.

Karadaghi, P. (1994). The Kurds: Refugees in their own land. In A. J. Marsella, T. Bornemann, S. Ekblad, & J. Orley (Eds.), *Amidst peril and pain: The mental health and well-being of the world's refugees* (pp. 115–124). Washington, DC: American Psychological Association.

Kinzie, J. D. (1985). Overview of clinical issues in the treatment of Southeast Asian refugees. In T. C. Owan (Ed.), *Southeast Asian mental health: Treatment, prevention, services, training, and research* (pp. 113–135). Washington, DC: National Institute of Mental Health.

Kinzie, J. D. (1993). Posttraumatic effects and their treatment among Southeast Asian refugees. In J. Wilson & B. Raphael (Eds.), *International handbook of traumatic stress syndromes* (pp. 311–320). New York: Plenum Press.

Kinzie, J. D., Leung, P., Bui, A., Ben, R., Keopraseuth, K. O., Riley, C., Fleck, J., & Ades, M. (1988). Group therapy with Southeast Asian refugees. *Community Mental Health Journal, 23,* 157–166.

Kleinman, A. (1980). *Patient and healers in the context of culture: An exploration of the borderland between anthropology, medicine, and psychiatry.* Berkeley, CA: University of California Press.

Kleinman, A., Eisenberg, L., & Good, B. (1978). Culture, illness and care. *Annals of Internal Medicine, 88,* 251–258.

Kleinman, A., & Good, B. (1985). *Culture and depression: Studies in the anthropology and cross-cultural psychiatry of affect and disorder.* Berkeley: University of California Press.

Kozaric-Korvacic, D., Folnegovic-Smalc, V., Skringjaric, J., Szajnberg, N., & Marusic, A. (1995). Rape, torture and traumatization of Bosnian and Croatian women: Psychological sequelae. *American Journal of Orthopsychiatry, 65,* 428–433.

Laor, N., Wolmer, L., Mayes, L., & Gershon, A. (1997). Israeli preschool children under Scuds: A 30-month follow-up. *Journal of the American Academy of Child & Adolescent Psychiatry, 36,* 349–356.

Lee, E. (1989). Assessment and treatment of Chinese-American immigrant families. *Journal of Psychotherapy, 6,* 99–122.

Liebkind, K. (1996). Acculturation and stress: Vietnamese refugees in Finland. *Journal of Cross-Cultural Psychology, 27,* 161–183.

Lin, K. M., Tazuma, L., & Masuda, M. (1979). Adaptational problems in Vietnamese refugees. *Archives of General Psychiatry, 36,* 955–961.

Marsella, A. J., Friedman, M., & Spain, H. (1993). Ethnocultural aspects of PTSD. In J. Oldham, M. Riba, & A. Tasman (Eds.), *Review of psychiatry* (pp. 157–181). Washington, DC: American Psychiatric Press.

Melville, M. B., & Lykes, M. B. (1992). Guatemalan Indian children and the sociocultural effects of government-sponsored terrorism. *Social Science and Medicine, 34,* 533–548.

Mezey, A. (1960). Personal background, emigration and mental health in Hungarian refugees. *Journal of Mental Science, 106,* 618–627.

Micozzi, M. S. (1996). *Fundamentals of complementary and alternative medicine.* New York: Churchill Livingstone.

Miranda, A. O., & Matheny, K. B. (2000). Socio-psychological predictors of acculturative stress among Latino adults. *Journal of Mental Health Counseling, 22*, 306–317.

Mollica, R. F., & Jalbert, R. R. (1989). *Community of confinement: The mental health crisis on Site Two: Displaced persons' camps on the Thai-Kampuchean border.* Boston, MA: Committee on World Federation for Mental Health.

Mollica, R. F., & Lavelle, J. (1988). Southeast Asian refugees. In L. Comas-Diaz & E. H. Griffith (Eds.), *Clinical guidelines in cross-cultural mental health* (pp. 262-303). New York: John Wiley.

Mollica, R. F., McInnes, K., Pham, T., Fawzi, M. C. S., Murphy, E., & Lin, L. (1998). The dose-effect relationships between torture and psychiatric symptoms in Vietnamese ex-political detainees and a comparison group. *Journal of Nervous and Mental Disease, 186*, 543–553.

Mollica, R. F., Wyshak, G., & Lavelle, J. (1987). The psychosocial impact of war trauma and torture on Southeast Asian refugees. *American Journal of Psychiatry, 144*, 1567–1572.

Morris, P., & Silove, D. (1992). Cultural influences in psychotherapy with refugee survivors of torture and trauma. *Hospital & Community Psychiatry, 43*, 820–824.

Nicolson, B. F. (1997). The influence of premigration and postmigration stressors on mental health: A study of Southeast Asian refugees. *Social Work Research, 21*, 19–31.

Noh, S., Beiser, M., Kaspar, V., Hou, F., & Rummens, J. (1999). Perceived racial discrimination, depression, and coping: A study of Southeast Asian Refugees in Canada. *Journal of Health & Social Behavior, 40*, 193–207.

Odegaard, O. (1932). Emigration and insanity: A study of mental disease among the Norwegian born population of Minnesota. *Acta Psychiatrica et Neurologica Supplement, 4*, 1–206.

Padilla, A. M. (1980). The role of cultural awareness and ethnic loyalty in acculturation. In A. M. Padilla (Ed.), *Acculturation: Theory, model, and some new findings* (pp. 47–84), Boulder, CO: Westview Press.

Pedersen, P. B. (1988). *A handbook for developing multicultural awareness.* Alexandria, VA: American Association for Counseling and Development.

Pedersen, P. B. (2000). *A handbook for multicultural awareness* (3rd ed.). Alexandria, VA: American Association for Counseling and Development.

Pernice, R., & Brook, J. (1994). Relationship of migrant status (refugee or immigrant) to mental health. *International Journal of Social Psychiatry, 40*, 177–188.

Pinsky, L. (1949). *The effects of war on displaced children.* Unpublished materials. World Federation for Mental Health, National Committee for Mental Hygiene, Second World Mental Health Assembly, New York. (Available from Centre for Documentation of Refugees, United Nations High Commissioner for Refugees [UNHCR], Geneva, Switzerland.)

Porte, Z., & Torney-Purta, J. (1987). Depression and academic achievement among Indochinese refugee unaccompanied minors in ethnic and nonethnic placements. *American Journal of Orthopsychiatry, 57*, 536–547.

Pynoos, R., & Eth, S. (1984). Children traumatized by witnessing acts of personal violence: Homicide, rape or suicide behavior. In S. Eth & R. Pynoos (Eds.), *Post-traumatic stress disorder in children* (pp. 17–44). Washington, DC: American Psychiatric Press.

Ramsay, R., Gorst-Unsworth, C., & Turner, S. (1993). Psychiatric morbidity in survivors of organised state violence including torture: A retrospective series. *British Journal of Psychiatry, 162*, 55–59.

Refugee Women in Development (1990). What is refugee? (Available from RedWID, 5225 Wisconsin Avenue, N.W., #502, Washington, DC 20015.)

Roizblatt, A., & Pilowsky, D. (1996). Forced migration and resettlement: Its impact on families and individuals. *Contemporary Family Therapy, 18,* 513–521.

Root, M. P. P. (1998). Women. In L. C. Lee & N. W. S. Zane (Eds.), *Handbook of Asian American psychology* (pp. 211–232). Thousand Oaks, CA: Sage Publications.

Rumbaut, R. G. (1991). The agony of exile: A study of the migration and adaptation of Indochinese refugee adults and children. In F. L. Ahearn & J. L. Athey (Eds.), *Refugee children: Theory, research and services* (pp. 53–91). Baltimore, MD: The Johns Hopkins University Press.

Servan-Schreiber, D., Lin, B. L., & Birmaher, B. (1998). Prevalence of posttraumatic stress disorder and major depressive disorder in Tibetan refugee children. *Journal of the American Academy of Child & Adolescent Psychiatry, 37,* 874–879.

Sluzki, C. E. (1990). Disappeared: Semantic and somatic effects of political repression in a family seeking therapy. *Family Process, 29,* 131–143.

Sluzki, C. E. (1993). Toward a model of family and political victimization: Implications for treatment and recovery. *Psychiatry: Interpersonal and Biological Processes, 56,* 178–187.

Somasundaram, D. J., & Sinayokan, S. (1994). War trauma in civilian population. *British Journal of Psychiatry, 165,* 524–527.

Stein, B. N. (1986). The experience of being a refugee: Insights from the research literature. In C. L. Williams & J. Westermeyer (Eds.), *Refugee mental health in resettlement countries,* (pp. 5–23). Washington, DC: Hemisphere.

Stumphauser, J., & Davis, J. (1983). Training Mexican-American mental health personnel in behavior therapy. *Journal of Behavior Therapy and Experimental Psychiatry, 14,* 215–217.

Sue, S., Chun, C., & Gee, K. (1995). Ethnic minority intervention and treatment research. In J. F. Aponte, R. Young Rivers, & J. Wohl (Eds.), *Psychological interventions and cultural diversity* (pp. 266–282). Boston: Allyn and Bacon.

Sue, S., Fujino, D., Hu, L., Takeuchi, D., & Zane, N. (1991). Community mental health services for ethnic minority groups: A test of cultural responsive hypothesis. *Journal of Consulting and Clinical Psychology, 59,* 533–540.

Szapocznik, J., & Cohen, R. E. (1986). Mental health care for rapidly changing environments: Emergency relief to unaccompanied youths of the 1980 Cuba refugee wave. In C. L. Williams & J. Westermeyer (Eds.), *Refugee mental health in resettlement countries* (pp. 141–156). New York: Hemisphere Publishing Corporation.

Szapocznik, J., & Kurtines, W. (1980). Acculturation, biculturalism, and adjustment among Cuban-Americans. In A. M. Padilla (Ed.), *Recent advances in acculturation research: Theory, models, and some new findings* (pp. 914–931). Boulder, CO: Westview Press.

United Nations Educational, Scientific, and Cultural Organization (1952). *The psychological and social adjustment of refugee and displaced children in Europe.* Geneva, Switzerland: Author.

Van der Kolk, B. A. (1987). *Psychological trauma.* Washington, DC: American Psychiatric Press.

Waitzkin, H., & Magana, H. (1997). The black box in somatization: Unexplained physical symptoms, culture, and narratives of trauma. *Social Science and Medicine, 45,* 811–825.

Weine, S. M., Becker, D. F., McGlashan, T. H., Laub, D., Lazrove, S., Vojvoda, D., & Hyman, L. (1995). Psychiatric consequences of "ethnic cleansing": Clinical assessments and trauma testimonies of newly resettled Bosnian refugees. *American Journal of Psychiatry, 152,* 536–542.

Weisaeth, L., & Eitinger, L. (1993). Posttraumatic stress phenomena: Common themes across wars, disasters, and traumatic events. In J. Wilson & B. Raphael (Eds.), *International handbook of traumatic stress syndromes* (pp. 69–78). New York: Plenum Press.

Widgren, J. (1988). The uprooted within a global context. In D. Miserez (Ed.), *Refugees: The trauma of exile* (pp. 1–9). Dordrecht, Netherlands: Martinus Nijhoff.

Wohl, J. (2000). Psychotherapy and cultural diversity. In J. F. Aponte & J. Wohl (Eds.), *Psychological intervention and cultural diversity* (2nd ed., pp. 75–91), Boston, MA: Allyn and Bacon.

World Health Organization. (1992). *Refugee mental health: Draft manual for field testing.* Geneva, Switzerland: Author.

World Health Organization, Division of Mental Health. (1987). *Care for the mentally ill: Components of mental health policies governing the provision of psychiatric services.* Geneva, Switzerland: Author.

Zane, N., & Sue, S. (1991). Culturally responsive mental health services for Asian Americans: Treatment and training issues. In H. Myers, P. Wohlford, P. Guzman, & R. Echemendia (Eds.), *Ethnic minority perspectives on clinical training and services in psychology* (pp. 49–58). Washington, DC: American Psychological Association.

2

Ethnopolitical Warfare, Traumatic Family Stress, and the Mental Health of Refugee Children

Solvig Ekblad

"I was in Kosova and was surprised to see that a human life was worth nothing. Compared to everything else it was the cheapest thing."

> Interview with a mass-evacuated person from Kosovo
> staying temporarily in Sweden (Ekblad, 2000, p. 42)

"Opposing terrorism by understanding the human capacity for evil."

> The American Psychological Association's president-elect on why
> efforts to prevent future terrorist acts must begin with understanding
> the root causes of the hatred against America (Zimbardo, 2001, p. 48)

INTRODUCTION

The Impact: Several New Destructive Areas

In recent decades, more than one hundred regions around the world have been disrupted by war and social conflicts (for example, Afghanistan, Burma, Central America, the former Yugoslavia, Sri Lanka, and Rwanda). The new element is the sporadic acts of terror, such as shootings, bombings, and hijackings, to which groups of civilians are exposed, even in Western countries. Destructive international conflict following the Cold War has entered a new destructive era. Rather than wars between countries, there are now wars between ethnic, racial, religious, and cultural groups within countries, which are destroying the very fabric of families, communities, institutions, and governments.

The most recent sign is terror attacks with biological and chemical weapons anywhere on earth, with the aim of inducing fear, confusion, and uncertainty in everyday life among innocent children and adults. We are exposed daily in the media (in newspapers, on the radio and TV, by email and on the Internet, and so forth) to the fact that violence worldwide exacts an awful toll on children, families, communities, ethnic minorities, and society as a whole.

A second new destructive phenomenon is violence in many of the metropolises, particularly in zones in which violence, gang activity, and homicide are common. Such horrible violence causes deep physical, social, and psychological wounds and plants the seeds of violence in the next generation. Those afflicted become uprooted, communities are devastated, and on both the individual and large-scale level people are showing immediate or delayed post-traumatic stress reactions.

A third destructive area is seen in victims and/or family members who have suffered state-organized violence, including torture and other forms of inhuman or degrading treatment. Torture by its very nature is one of the most extreme forms of trauma perpetrated by one human on another (Silove, 1996), with medical staff quite often being involved. One consequence is a growing distrust of medical experts and government officials, thus robbing state institutions of the trust they need to facilitate recovery (as in the Gulf War and in the Balkans). According to Silove, Steel, McGorry, Miles, and Drobny (2002), "despite international attempts to prevent torture and related human rights violations, such abuses remain endemic, being prevalent in over a third of countries worldwide" (p. 49).

Silove et al. (2002) suggest several elements of torture that may act to accentuate its impact on post-traumatic symptoms:

> . . . the abuse is deliberate, and the perpetrators use methods that maximise fear, dread, and the debility in the victim; the trauma is inescapable, uncontrollable, often repetitive, and conditions between torture sessions (such as solitary confinement) undermine the recovery capacity of the victim; feelings of guilt, shame, anger, betrayal and humiliation—deliberately induced by tortures—tend to erode the victim's sense of security, integrity and self worth; and head injury or other bodily damage may add to risk of psychosocial disability. (p. 49)

Thus, extreme traumatic life events such as torture interfere with intimacy, empathy, emotional expressiveness, control, sexuality, and regulation of anger and hostility toward family members as well as the individual's coping strategies.

Torture survivors are at high risk of developing the various kinds of post-traumatic psychological reactions identified in the literature. According to a recent review by Silove and Kinzie (2001, p. 165), longitudinal studies of civilian violence generally show that the highest rates of post-traumatic stress disorder (PTSD) occur soon after exposure, with decreasing rates in morbidity over time, although a minority of cases do become chronic and severe. Such long-term morbidity seems to have a greater association with exposure to intentional human violence compared with that associated with natural disasters. Professional and public awareness of these burdens and costs in human, social, and economic terms is weak.

A fourth destructive area is characterized by domestic violence. Societies differ in the types of dominant familial structures, in expectations and valuations of marital and family roles, and in prescriptions of normative or accepted aggression and non-normative aggression between spouses and between parents and children. Domestic violence is strongly related to the general level of acceptance of interpersonal violence in a society. In supporting the war against terrorism, we should not forget that two of the most certain outcomes of violence are violence within the family (Janson, 2002) and a large flow of refugees seeking asylum. We should all remember the lessons of history, and the purpose of the Refugee Convention, a landmark international instrument that commits ratifying countries to provide humane protection to persons fleeing persecution worldwide (Ekblad, in press). The United Nations Convention on the Rights of the Child, adopted in 1989, was a watershed in the recognition of children's rights. But "instead of providing special care for the most traumatised individuals fleeing persecution, Western countries may be subjecting them to the very conditions that are likely to hinder psychosocial recovery" (Silove, Steel, & Mollica, 2001, p. 1437). Contemporary refugee policies in Western countries have been thrown into stark relief by the effects of the terror attacks in the United States.

The absence of severe, generalized psychiatric outcomes in war-affected societies is usually attributed to the cushioning effects of social solidarity and to a sense of common purpose provoked by an identifiable external threat (Curran, 1988). However, multiple methodological limitations increase the number of questions about the validity and generalizability of such results (Silove & Kinzie, 2001). In reviewing more recent studies, Silove and Kinzie (2001) found somewhat different results: the use of more systematic and sophisticated sampling and diagnostic methods yielded much higher rates of manifest psychiatric disturbance in the general population.

What do we know about the impact of severe trauma on children and their families?

THE RISK OF A LOST GENERATION

Poor Socioeconomic Conditions—A Risk Factor

A recent study of children's health in Europe stresses the important impact of relative poverty on children's health. It also indicates that the primary factor concerning inequalities in health among children and youth is the unequal distribution of risk and protective factors among the total population (Janson, 2001).

Biological Changes

The literature shows that exposure to trauma in childhood may differentially influence maturation of various brain regions by overstimulating areas involved in fear and alarm reactions (limbic, midbrain, and brain stem) and by retarding cortical development through neglect and sensory deprivation. Development and responsiveness of various stress-related neuroendocrine systems may influence a child's ability to regulate impulses, aggression, and emotions and to accurately process information. It also is possible that early trauma-related neurobiological alterations might predispose an individual to develop PTSD in the future. Combat veterans, for instance, with histories of childhood abuse are more likely to develop combat-related PTSD than are soldiers without histories of abuse (Southwick & Friedman, 2001). Disturbances in arousal are of special concern because they may lead to alterations in the normal maturation of biological systems (for a review, see Pynoos, Kinzie, & Gordon, 2001).

The Range, Prevalence, and Developmental Effects of Trauma Exposure

Recent research findings show that there is a risk among adolescents who are "exposed to chronic political violence and oppression or prolonged inadequate postdisaster community recovery" and that the evidence "indicates that without proper therapeutic attention and commitment of societal resources, this age group can become a so-called lost generation" (Pynoos et al., 2001, pp. 211–212). Of major importance is the impact of chronic traumatic stress and danger on the child's worldview, social map, and moral development (Garbarino, Kostelny, & Dubrow, 1991). This is in line with the view of Cairns (1996), who argued that, in addition to areas of stress and coping, adequate attention needs to be given to levels of aggression, moral development, and political socialization, as well as to the complex interaction of these factors.

There is a huge number of studies from many parts of our globe regarding the alarming prevalence of children and young people who are being exposed to trauma—in war zones and as a result of state-sponsored violent propaganda and repressive environments, terrorism, community violence, interpersonal and domestic violence, and accidents of different kinds. Besides these trauma from war or political violence, many also endure other types of trauma or victimization when these chronic societal conditions give rise to high rates of interpersonal and domestic violence (Bawa, 1995).

Anyone May Be Affected

Among the factors identified in the literature that influence the incidence of post-traumatic reactions after trauma are

- The nature and intensity of the traumatic event
- The duration of the event

- Whether the incident was manmade
- The degree of resistance to trauma
- The degree of mental readiness with regard to the specific event
- The degree of sense of coherence and interpersonal cohesiveness and support that the child and family had before the event
- The effects of trauma on children's symptoms are age-related in connection with developmental delay effects

The literature suggests the importance of extended family networks to buffer the loss of parents in civil war. In a review by Pynoos et al., (2001) it was concluded that "continuing posttraumatic stress symptoms and adversities may lead to disturbances in conscience functioning that are strongly influenced by negative self-attributions and negative expectations about others, the world and the social contract" (p. 216).

There is increased marital and family conflict in families of survivors of torture and related trauma, which, according to Gordon (2001)

> may be a result of (a) the direct effects of trauma-coping behavior and symptoms on interpersonal relationships, (b) the inability of trauma survivors to function in expected family and social roles because of physical or psychological disability resulting from traumatic experiences, and (c) conflicts associated with changes in gender and family roles during the following prolonged detention or refugee migration. (p. 232)

A finding from studies of the psychiatric effects of genocidal wars (e.g., Bosnia and Africa), and in particular from a report on twenty-five Bosnian women who had been raped and impregnated (in addition to experiencing family deaths, dislocations, and beatings), indicated strong feelings of alienation from their unborn fetuses and, among those who carried a pregnancy to term, a desire to allow their babies to be adopted (Kozaric-Kovacic, Folnegovic-Smalc, Skrinjaric, Szajnberg, & Marusic, 1995). The effects of traumatic sexual life events on the intimate relationships of trauma survivors, and changed views of sexual status, may lead to marital conflict and dissatisfaction in intimate relationships. In cultures in which chastity or monogamy are a prerequisite for marriage, the wife will be abandoned by the husband. For this reason, sexual trauma is seriously underreported in torture and refugee populations (for a review, see Gordon, 2001, p. 239).

Younger Children and Girls At Risk

Younger children are extremely vulnerable to such traumatic experiences as violently imposed separation from parents, siblings, and other significant people; abduction; and the traumatic disappearance or death of primary caregivers. In a study of historical-political and individualistic determinants of coping modes and fears among Palestinian children (age 4–14 years), Punamäki (1988) found that older children employed more active, purposeful, and courageous coping modes, that the level of fear was determined by gender rather than by the political-historical situation, and that girls expressed more fears than boys. Imposed poor nutrition and lack of adequate hygiene and medical treatment constitute physical traumatization that may compromise brain development and future health status and could result in physical disabilities or mortality.

However, many preschool and school-aged children witness brutality toward parents and significant adults, which may degrade the parent and purposely traumatize the child. There is a strong association between PTSD in mothers following political violence and symptoms of psychological distress in their children (Dawes, 1989). Maternal trauma-related avoidance (Laor et al., 1997; Stuber, Nader, Yasuda, Pynoos, & Cohen, 1991) and overt anxious responses by parents to traumatic reminders and fears of recurrence (Green et al., 1991) increase young children's post-traumatic distress. The death of family members and significant persons in their surroundings under traumatic circumstances can seriously complicate childhood bereavement by keeping the child and family focused on the circumstances of the death and surrounding issues of human accountability. Various post-traumatic reactions as well as secondary stresses and adversities strongly affect the recovery of children from violence and disaster (for a review, see Pynoos et al., 2001, p. 214).

In a study of psychosocial adaptation of children who were housed in a Swedish refugee camp, my conclusion was that perception of the mother's health and well-being is very important in understanding the child's health. The risk factors for mental ill-health among the children included experience of direct violence, apathetic or unstable mother, a long time living in Sweden waiting for asylum, and lack of proper information about the flight. The buffers were an optimistic mother and the perception of social support. Family members should therefore not be separated during the processing of their asylum application, and follow-up is needed before they have obtained permission to stay (Ekblad, 1993).

It has been shown that the reestablishment of relationships with other significant surviving family members after prolonged massive trauma is associated with improved PTSD outcome for children and adolescents (Kinzie, Sack, Angell, Manson, & Rath, 1986). Montgomery (1998) observed that keeping refugee families intact throughout the process of seeking political asylum and eventual resettlement significantly modifies children's anxieties. She also reported that 50 percent of the children of Middle Eastern refugee families seeking political asylum in Denmark live with a parent who survived various forms of torture. She commented that the more frequent use of corporal punishment by these parents during the resettlement period had an adverse effect on their children's anxiety.

Children May Also Be Tortured

Population-based studies from Kuwait (Eisa & Nofel, 1993, mentioned in Pynoos et al. 2001) and the former Yugoslavia region (United Nations Children's Fund [UNICEF], 1995) documented that school-age children and adolescents were tortured. The UNICEF study of children who were exposed to a wide spectrum of war-related traumatic experiences in the former Yugoslavia region has provided clear evidence that children and adolescents who had been tortured reported the most severe and persistent levels of comorbid post-traumatic stress disorder and depression (UNICEF, 1995). Cambodian refugee studies have shown how PTSD symptoms, especially those that are intrusive, tend to wax and wane over time and therefore require serial evaluations for proper assessment (Kinzie, Sack, Angell, Clarke, & Binn, 1989).

PTSD Surmounts Barriers of Language and Culture Context: Cross-Cultural Findings

In their review of studies of children and adolescents exposed to extreme forms of violence, Pynoos et al. (2001) report high levels of persistent hypervigilance, sleep disturbance (including parasomnias), and exaggerated startle. These findings are consistent across cultures and languages. Longitudinal studies of Cambodian child survivors of the Pol Pot regime and child survivors of the 1988 catastrophic earthquake in Armenia have shown that post-traumatic distress persists for many years (for a review, see Pynoos et al., 2001). Glod, Teicher, Martin, Hartman, and Harakal (1997) reported that physical abuse is associated with enduring sleep disturbance, which poses a need for clinical attention among children who have been tortured or physically beaten while interned. Among children exposed to a sniper attack at school, those with chronic sleep disturbances reported serious difficulties with daytime learning (Pynoos et al., 1987). The facts will be illustrated by the two vignettes below, which concern violence encountered by the author during her work.

Two Vignettes of Violence

The first vignette is a general observation by the author and her colleague, Professor Derrick Silove (Ekblad & Silove, 1998), co-chairs of the International Committee on Refugees and Other Migrants, World Federation for Mental Health, that conditions in the refugee camps in East Africa (Kenya and Tanzania) had certain features in common. Women and children were over-represented in the camps. The population had been exposed to substantial levels of human rights violations, interethnic war, enslavement, and dispossession. In many instances (in Somalia, Sudan, and Burundi), the neighboring countries from which refugees had fled remained in a state of civil war and social disruption.

Most refugees had arrived with few possessions or material resources. Separations and losses were extensive, with families often experiencing multiple deaths or "disappearances" of close relatives. The potential for productive agriculture in most camps was limited. The camps' population was therefore almost entirely dependent on food supplies provided fortnightly by the United Nations High Commissioner for Refugees (UNHCR).

The conditions of camp life and the collective stress associated with an uncertain future may contribute to problems such as criminality, violence, use of drugs (alcohol and other substances), and stress-related mental health problems. The potential for resettlement in third countries was relatively limited for the majority of the camp population. Repatriation therefore appeared to be the only durable long-term solution.

Infants in the perinatal phase and children under five years of age appeared to be high-risk groups vulnerable to the consequences of birth injury, severe infections (such as malaria, dysentery, and respiratory illnesses), and malnutrition. The integrity of maternal-child bonds was often undermined by the refugee experience, yet the proximity and capacity of the primary caregiver was critical to the psychosocial development and health of the child.

Inactivity was a major issue in camps for all inhabitants, but particularly for men. Vocational, educational, and recreational activities were not sufficient in the camps visited to meet the needs of all population groups. The impact of idleness on the status and roles of men, who by tradition were breadwinners for the family and clan, may shape maladaptive reactions such as sexual violence, interethnic friction, and alcohol and drug use.

Vulnerable groups were identified across most camps and fell into the following categories:

- Unaccompanied minors
- Accompanied minors (i.e., young people without parents, living with relatives or other members of their clan)
- Single parents who had lost their spouses as a consequence of war
- Women who had suffered or continued to suffer sexual violence and associated risk of stigma and rejection, and the impact (physical and psychological) on infants born as a consequence of rape. It seemed that many women maintained secrecy about such experiences, thus suffering in silence and isolation. They also often shouldered a disproportionate burden of care for the whole family
- The elderly
- Those who were disabled by physical injury, perceptual impairments and head trauma
- Those with chronic physical illnesses, especially communicable diseases
- Those with severe mental illness

A second vignette concerns asylum-seeking children and their parents in detention centers. Increasingly, industrialized countries are building or extending facilities to detain asylum seekers. In 2000, the United States had about five thousand asylum seekers in detention at any one time (Silove, Steel, & Mollica, 2001). Before September 11, 2001, Australia stood alone in mandating the detention of all individuals entering the country without valid visas, irrespective of whether or not they were seeking asylum. According to a UNHCR report in 2000, Australia ranked seventeenth out of twenty-one industrialized countries in terms of the absolute number of asylum applications received during 1999 (UNHCR, 2000).

In a review of research studies in Australia and elsewhere, Steel and Silove (2001) suggested that detained asylum seekers may have suffered greater levels of past trauma than other refugees, and this may contribute to their mental health problems, with detention providing a re-traumatizing environment. After the terror attacks, there was bipartisan political support in Australia for an international war against terrorism. At the same time, those fleeing from terrorist states are treated as criminals when they reach Australia. Recent asylum seekers are mainly confined in detention centers in remote areas and in economically poor island communities to the north of Australia, a policy that has been criticized by the United Nations and other international agencies.

One afternoon in August 2001, the author, together with Dr. Zachary Steel, visited Villawood detention center in the Sydney area of Australia. We met Aamer Sultan, a medical practitioner who had fled persecution in Iraq after providing casualty medical care to Shiite Muslim rebels. He has been detained since May 1999, because his claim for protection under the United Nations Convention has not been endorsed by the Australian authorities. He cannot be returned to Iraq because Australia currently has no diplomatic ties with that country and no international flights go to Iraq. He is bilingual (Arab/English) and as a health professional he is a confidant for many detainees. In a recent issue of the *Medical Journal of Australia*, Sultan (a detained medical practitioner) and O'Sullivan (a mental health professional who has worked in the same facility) provide a unique picture of the daily difficulties that detained asylum seekers in Australia experience with flagging hopes and mental reactions (Sultan & O'Sullivan, 2001). Steel and Silove (2001) comment on this picture in the same issue and it is suggested that the policy of mandatory detention of asylum seekers is leading to serious psychological harm.

During a few minutes of conversation with Aamer Sultan, the author was deeply impressed by his courage and positive worldview despite being detained for an indeterminate period of time. Children living in Villawood are at special risk of being influenced by a secondary affect that is mediated via their parents, whose ability to provide a normal caring and nurturing environment is more or less nonexistent. There is also the risk that these parents will neglect and physically abuse their children.

How can we understand the effects of refugee trauma? A theoretical framework is presented below.

A FRAMEWORK FOR CONCEPTUALIZING UNDERSTANDING

A Holistic Model

It is useful to consider the major psychosocial systems, both within the individual and across the family, organizational, community, and policy levels, that are disrupted or threatened by the refugee experience (Silove, 1999, revised by Lindencrona, Johansson Blight, & Ekblad, 2001). The theoretical framework on which this chapter is based is presented in the figure below.

FIGURE 1. LEVELS OF "MENTAL HEALTH PROMOTING INTRODUCTION" FOR NEWLY ARRIVED REFUGEES— A THEORETICAL FRAMEWORK

(Silove, 1999, revised by Lindencrona, Johansson Blight, & Ekblad, 2001)

Health system level of action	Attachment	Security	Identity/ roles	Human rights	Existential/ meaning
Individual level					
Interpersonal level					
Organizational level					
Community level					
Policy level					

Ekblad and Silove (1998) identified five fundamental psychosocial systems, presented in the model above, in order to conceptualize the sources of stress experienced by refugees in camps. This has been further developed in the model to also include experiences in the host country (Lindencrona, Johansson Blight, & Ekblad, 2001). The idea is to embrace mental health aspects in an ecological context, in order to allow the inclusion of the refugee's premigration, migration, and postmigration experiences as well as the interaction between the refugee and the host country. The model can then be used to identify individual or group protective and risk factors, in relation to, for example, reception routines in the host country. The *levels of action* refer to the different levels in society (McLeroy, Bibeau, Steckler, & Glanz, 1998), in this case the host country, where (for example) identification of risk and protective factors in the "health systems" can be made. The *individual level* is concerned with the way the person confronts and deals with his or her emotional, cognitive, behavioral, and interpersonal reactions stemming from his or her trauma and its consequences. On the *interpersonal level* we see the influence of the trauma on the immediate family, the family of origin, and the family patterns of behavior and interaction in relation to the trauma. The *organizational level* deals with the person's place among his or her peers, his or her colleagues at the workplace, and in the social group to which he or she belongs. The *community level* concerns the recognition (formal or informal) of the trauma by the community, how the community relates to it on the community level, and the subject of collective responsibility. Lastly, the *policy level* is the recognition (formal or informal) of the trauma by society, how society relates to it on a policy level, and as a matter of collective responsibility.

The author (Ekblad, 2001) is currently in charge of a four-year research project entitled "Health Promoting Introduction" that focuses on all the different levels of action noted above. The project addresses various questions, such as: What type of interventions are needed in the organization of the municipality to enable the refugee (children and adults) to access health care? What policies are in place to prevent further loss of identity or role?

There are five fundamental "systems" that can be identified in the framework.

- The *attachment system* concerns the traumatic losses and separation from close attachment figures that many refugees experience. Significant factors here include sustained disruptions of the family, deterioration of family functioning, and demoralization of parents—factors that can undermine early positive parent-child attachment and parental capacity to buffer the effect of trauma and stress on their children, all of which impair the family's recovery. Disruptions to bonds in this category are often of the most threatening nature, for example, being witness to the murder or kidnapping of close relatives. Such losses and bereavements are often unresolved, with family members living in a state of uncertainty for prolonged periods of time, not knowing the fate of important relatives. The disruption to attachments poses major threats to particular groups, such as single women with children and unaccompanied minors, since they do not have the capacity to "repair," or "substitute" for, their losses. It can also include less severe attachment difficulties, such as loss in relation to the country of origin versus the new relation to the host country. Emotional difficulties (such as unresolved grief, difficulties in forming and maintaining relationships, and separation anxiety) are some of the psychological reactions that may supervene if individual and collective coping mechanisms break down. Preschool children who have been exposed to trauma may show disturbances in attachment and separation anxiety. School-children may show extremes of externalizing and/or internalizing behaviors, including withdrawal and inhibitions, disruptive behaviors, and attentional disturbances. Adolescents may exhibit symptoms very similar to those shown by adults (PTSD, depression, anxiety, somatic symptoms, substance abuse, or antisocial behavior) but also guilt and revenge fantasies that mediate distress and severe acting-out behavior or inhibitions that affect taking initiative in daily life. They may also show reduced impulse control. On the other hand, these symptoms may depend on cultural and socio-environmental factors.

- The *security system* involves physical safety and security that have been violated through, for example, exposure to war, combat, bombardment, land mines, and torture. Once in the host country, security issues such as financial security, the ability to be self-sufficient and not have to depend on others for money, is included in the security concept. Core psychic reactions are post-traumatic stress symptoms, but other reactions may also occur, including severe panic anxiety, depression, anger, phobias, and reactive psychosis.

- The *identity/role system* embraces such issues as loss of land, possessions, and profession. In the host country, this can also include loss of professional status (work identity)—for example, when being forced to take on unqualified jobs—as well as loss of identity/role in relation to a more or less forced change of culture. The loss of community leaders, elderly people, traditional healers, and group knowledge about customs, traditions, and rituals may further undermine the sense of group identity and the sense of control over the situation. Those who have not defined their role in the camp environment can be severely adversely affected by the idleness and inactivity that prevail in refugee camps. We also know from case studies that refugee children who are given responsibilities by their parents during the family's flight (such as caring for siblings, seeking food, and so forth) feel confirmed and that this experience seems to provide a buffer against illness. Hysteria and dissociation may play a role in severe identity and role conflicts. For instance, a newly arrived asylum seeker must understand how his or her status, identity, and role are perceived in the host culture and how cultural modes of behavior are directed toward him or her. There is a danger of imposing Western identities, values, and approaches rather than respecting and collaborating with the asylum seeker, who will be the concern of primary service providers.

- The *human rights system* deals with violations against human rights, which are a very common experience for refugees. These include violence, persecution, and in some cases torture. Violations of human rights in the host country can be, for example, discrimination because of ethnicity, language, religion, etc., or may concern the right to health care. Such experiences may provoke long-lasting feelings of dehumanization, anger, and resentment, especially if there are no mechanisms available to redress feelings of grievance.

- The *existential-meaning system* refers to the sense of coherence and meaning. Loss of the stability that the community used to provide contributes to the refugee's being left in a state of bewilderment and uncertainty, and questioning the meaning of life. Historical continuities linking past, present, and future have been radically disrupted by the upheavals associated with the refugee experience, often leaving those affected in a state of bewilderment and uncertainty. A search for ways to reestablish a sense of coherence in life may result, for example, in becoming more religious and believing than before, or, if the person was religious before may result in abandoning religion. The host country may contribute to the loss of sense of coherence by, for example, failing to provide places for religious activities or keeping people in long-term unemployment. Commitment to the social ideology of the threatened or repressed group can serve as a protective factor. How can we reeducate a child who has been a child-soldier?

A Sense of Coherence Between Person, Event, and Environmental Factors: "Ecological Fit"

The clinician should always be aware of whose purposes are served by an intervention or service and bear in mind the conflicts that can occur when interventions challenge equity, social justice, or participation. Further, he or she must be concerned and transparent about his or her role and work in this process in order to build up local facilities and to encourage the sense of coherence that develops sustainability. Silove, Ekblad, and Mollica (2000), in a comment in the *Lancet,* suggested that a consequence of excessive dissent among mental health experts in the field is that the casualties of mass conflict may become the unintended victims of our neglect. Thus, this process requires mentors, partners, and success.

Mistrust and hostility between individuals and groups, as well as a strong feeling of a low sense of coherence and mutual victimization, feed future negative cycles of violence, thus affecting the next generation. Similarly, armed conflicts—including torture, murder, mass rape, and ethnic cleansing—also encourage violence, with concomitant hate and fear, and create deep-seated individual and communal memories of such traumatic life events. Civilians are the targets, and child soldiers are forced to violate human rights and kill, often on a massive scale. The ultimate expressions of ethnopolitical warfare are genocide and ethnic cleansing.

Factors affecting health are included in Antonovsky's (1987) term "sense of coherence": *comprehensibility,* the extent to which sense can be made of the perception of the internal or external stimuli experienced; *manageability,* the extent to which the perception holds that there are resources available, in oneself or in one's environment, to cope with the stimuli; and *meaningfulness,* the extent to which a person perceives that life is meaningful, despite its hardships, and worth living. However, Somerfield and McCrae (2000), in their review and discussion about research on stress and coping, point out that many people cannot develop further in their coping behaviors than they already have through the years of learning to cope with environmental and intrapsychic problems. Coping behaviors vary from individual to individual and some of life's problems, where coping options are limited, cannot be solved by the efforts of individuals alone but require the input of a group, organization, or agency. With regard to refugees, the trauma they experience may induce a feeling of hopelessness and lack of control that is partly due to the fact that coping mechanisms are no longer working (Ekblad, 1996).

This can be further described by using Harvey's ecological model of psychosocial trauma. The theory of this model is that post-traumatic response and recovery, as well as pre-post-traumatic stress, depend on the interaction between the person, the event, and environmental factors. The impact of this is, for example, that every individual's reaction to violence and traumatic events depends on 1) person-specific factors such as age and personality, and 2) event factors such as the extent and frequency of violence or trauma. All this is affected by 3) the individual's environment with which he or she identifies. The interaction is the same when it comes to recovery, and finally, "the efficiency of trauma-focused interventions depends on the degree to which they enhance the person–community relationship and achieve 'ecological fit' within individually varied recovery contexts." (Harvey, 1996, p. 3).

Family Risk Factors for Post-traumatic Reactions After Extreme Traumatic Life Events

Among the *family risk factors* identified for post-traumatic reactions after extreme traumatic life events are physical fatigue (lack of sleep, food, heating, or shelter from the heat, and so forth); enforced passivity (lack of a normal life because of being deprived of work, including that entailed in taking care of the household); decreased morale (the degree of support the family members receive in the family); and the degree of identification with the sense of coherence (how much each family member feels the trauma in which he or she is involved).

When are professional guidelines needed?

- When disturbing behaviors or emotions last more than about two months
- When a person's behavior or emotions make it difficult to function normally (including at work, in the family, or at school)
- Any time a person feels mentally unstable or concerned about his or her behavior or emotions

MENTAL HEALTH INTERVENTIONS AND RESEARCH RECOMMENDATIONS

Resistance to Trauma—Prevention Number One

One of the major factors is the person's resistance to trauma prior to the traumatic event. The specific resistance is composed of the individual's state of readiness before the stressful traumatic event. Such preparedness usually neutralizes to a certain extent the effect of suddenness and unexpectedness. Nonspecific resistance consists of the social and interpersonal relationships the person had before the exposure to the traumatic event (see the figure above). Feelings of social and inter-personal support, cohesiveness, and manageability (Ekblad, 2000) increase resistance to an extreme traumatic event, whereas feelings of loneliness, marginalization, and isolation decrease it.

The length of time it takes for parents and children to heal and recover from the emotional effects of the traumatic event or events varies. It is, however, important to return to normal life and family routines and the feeling of having some sense of order and control in life. Being afforded the opportunity to tell the psychological trauma story is essential (Ekblad, in press). However, being emotionally upset may lead to the abuse of alcohol and/or other substances, causing other problems.

At a time when the infrastructure has been more or less destroyed due to violence, there is a great need for all kinds of services that promote public health and integration in the society. An important conclusion drawn from findings on the effect of parental trauma on children is that mental health interventions for traumatized parents should include strategies to repair disturbances in the family milieu (Pynoos et al., 2001). According to Shaw, Dorling, and Davey Smith (1999), social exclusion is a concept with several dimensions (such as unemployment, housing, education, health, discrimination, and integration). The concept concerns multi-dimensional disadvantages and refers to the relationship between the ones who are included and the ones who are excluded, and can also refer to people who are stigmatized and marginalized. It does, however, entail a ranking process, which means that the people who are included in society—as opposed to excluded from it—have better access to societal resources, not only economic but also education, social networks, and support. Refugees, especially those experiencing mental ill health, are at high risk of becoming socially excluded both as a group and as individuals, due to factors such as those mentioned above.

Psychologists for Social Responsibility (http://www.psysr.com/IPN.htm) concern themselves with the requirements of psychosocial intervention for building peace. This includes changing people's minds and hearts and improving intergroup relations as prerequisites for political and economic reforms for peace. Fears need to be addressed, and nonviolent options for handling conflict should be encouraged at all levels, from the family to the national and international policy levels.

These psychologists have identified the following important psychosocial tasks that must be tackled:

- Healing the wounds of war
- Nonviolent conflict resolution/reconciliation
- Education for peace, tolerance, and human rights
- Support of work on social justice, human rights, and sustainable development

According to the Psychologists for Social Responsibility, the above list requires a formal and informal education in order to nourish tolerance and to respect human rights and peaceful values and behavior. However, in order to be possible and effective, these tasks should be looked upon with reference to all levels in the figure above regarding individual biological, psychological, social, and spiritual needs. They should also be coordinated with community and policy reconstruction of economic and political tasks.

Evidence-based research suggests that the most important intervention to reduce the high rates of mental distress—including fear, instability, and anger—among asylum seekers is the implementation of strategies to prevent unnecessary stress. According to Pynoos et al. (2001), "Public mental health and social programs to assist the recovery of young people and their families exposed to traumatic situations, particularly those involving youth in armed conflict, are likely to be more successful if they include community outreach efforts to provide remedial education opportunities, job training, and organised pro-social activities" (p. 221). Here lies the importance of adult-led "processing" of the young child's experience regarding his or her psychological coping and moral development (Garbarino, Kostelny, & Dubrow, 1991). When there are relatively stable school systems in the society, the literature shows that schools may be a relevant setting in which to provide mental health promotion support to children and their families in the aftermath of disaster, war, or political violence. However, sometimes there is a limitation in communication between the researchers and the field because of a lack of equivalence.

Equivalence

Lonner and Ibrahim (1996) state that "culture-comparative researchers in psychology often deal with four types of equivalence" (p. 301). These are *functional equivalence*, that is, the assessment of the common ground of functional prerequisites in different cultures; *conceptual equivalence*, the meaning that individuals attach to a specific item or question; *linguistic equivalence* (also called translation equivalence), which is described as a variant of conceptual equivalence but which focuses on what words and sentences in the questionnaires convey the same meaning to everyone and the adequate translation of the words; and, finally, *metric or scalar equivalence*. This last is considered the most challenging type of equivalence and means that "data themselves that result from tests and scales should be functionally equivalent; i.e., they should measure the same behavioural property or properties in different groups of people. Sets of data from different cultures or ethnic groups should show the same coherence of psychometric structure if they are to form the basis for legitimate comparisons" (Lonner & Ibrahim, 1996, p. 303).

Health Is a Human Right

At the present time, when there is an eagerness to combat terrorism and war in many places on our earth, the result may be a climate of discrimination, hostility, and racism. In the light of this, we recommend the following interventions.

- Access to the same social and health services that are available to permanent residents should be provided for asylum seekers until the final determination of their refugee applications, in order to minimize the hardships they face.
- The Convention on the Rights of the Child should be implemented by screening the psychological effect of refugee trauma on asylum seekers. Refugee and mass displaced children should be followed up by social and health services as required.
- Flexible and adaptable methods of social inquiry and service should be developed that are appropriate and sensitive to local customs and needs. The socioeconomic status of resettled refugees appears to be a robust predictor of integration in the host country.
- A policy to assess longitudinally the psychological needs of asylum seekers is highly recommended. The literature shows that providing preventive psychosocial interventions for asylum seekers in a safe, supportive, and predictable environment is instrumental to recovery for those suffering from high levels of exposure to premigration trauma. A comprehensive assessment should include a structured screening for context-specific and culturally informed traumatic (violent) experiences, and documentation of objective features and subjective appraisals and responses. Discrepancies are likely to occur in repeated interviews with asylum seekers, but recall of details rated by the interviewee as peripheral to the account is more likely to be inconsistent than recall of details that are central to the account (Herlihy, Scragg, & Turner, 2002). This has implications for national and international policy in the assessment of asylum seekers. Thus, if discrepancies continue to be used as a credibility criterion, then asylum seekers who have post-traumatic stress at the time of their interviews are systematically more likely to be rejected the longer their applications take.
- Sequential or serial traumatization can be approached by having the child or adolescent rank his or her worst experiences and worst moments. Age-appropriate instruments should be used to assess post-traumatic stress, grief, and depressive reactions, separation anxiety in younger children, and attentional or behavioral disturbances in older children and adolescents.
- In cases of child torture, beating, injury, or rape, a comprehensive medical examination with appropriate specialized consultation is required, similar in scope to that recommended for adult survivors (Vesti & Kastrup, 1995).
- Much more emphasis must be given to studying factors that may protect populations that have experienced domestic, manmade, and natural violence.

- However, there is a paucity of data on the psychological effects of mass trauma on entire communities (such as terrorist attacks, mass shootings of innocent civilian targets, etc.). It seems that at times individuals may be victims as well as perpetrators of extreme traumatic life events such as torture, other traumatic life events, and displacement. Awareness of this fact is important to both rehabilitation work and research design, as these roles are conflicting and influence recovery.

- More research is needed on the transcultural validity of diagnostic constructs and community mechanisms that either exacerbate or mitigate the experience of trauma. Therefore, emic and etic constructs are recommended to be included in future studies of ethnically diverse communities that have been exposed to domestic, manmade, and natural violence. (The emic perspective includes "the evaluation of studied phenomena from within the culture and its context in an attempt to explicate the phenomena's significance and interrelationship with other intra-cultural elements 'from the inside'" [Canino, Lewis-Fernandes, & Bravo, 1997, p. 166]. The etic perspective "is fundamentally comparative, and is directed at eliciting overarching categories of phenomena out of local specificities. Its goal is to identify and compare equivalent phenomena across different cultural contexts" [Canino et al., 1997, p. 166].) Multiple factors determine the onset and course of the disorder, thus necessitating a longitudinal design.

- The challenge in screening is the equivalence concept of the communication, especially when the person and the researcher and clinician do not share the same language. For instance, according to Swedish law, an interpreter should be made available "if needed" in contacts with public authorities. The right to an interpreter within the health service is not explicitly stated, but is generally presupposed to exist.

- More flexible sampling techniques may be necessary in investigating "hidden" or dispersed groups. The outcome would have a wide array of psychiatric, psychological, and social indices both as direct causes of disability and as contributors to psychiatric disorder; this would also contribute to normalization, resilience, coping, and endurance. In the realm of ethical issues, besides confidentiality, researchers need to be mindful of the risk of re-traumatization and to handle this potential challenge with care. A useful line of inquiry would be to conduct "research into research, i.e. inquiries into the effect (positive or negative) of the research process on individual trauma survivors and their communities" (Silove & Kinzie, 2001, p. 171).

- A three-tier approach to intervention is suggested. The first tier provides general support to a wide population of parents and children through their schools, community agencies, and religious institutions. The second-tier interventions are specifically directed toward children, adolescents, and adults with severe levels of personal traumatic exposure and continuing post-traumatic distress, grief, and depression. The third tier provides appropriate referral to adult mental health services and child mental health services for those identified as requiring evaluation and treatment for a broader range of adult, child, and adolescent psychiatric disorders, respectively.

- A national forum for dialogue between politicians, policy makers, researchers, clinicians, and nongovernmental organizations would be valuable. The aims would be to carefully monitor the impact of detention practices on asylum seekers, and to examine the effect of any policy changes on their mental health and well-being after they are released into the community. There is a clear need for more research that focuses specifically on the unique needs of the family of the survivors so that those who provide services and set policies can better understand how the effects of severe traumatic life events may be long-enduring and far-reaching, extending well beyond the individual case.

REFERENCES

Antonovsky, A. (1987). *Unrevealing the mystery of health: How people manage stress and stay well.* San Francisco: Jossey Bass.

Bawa, U. (1995). Organized violence in apartheid South Africa: Children as victims and perpetrators. In Foundation for Children (Ed.), *Children: War and persecution, proceedings of the congress,* Hamburg, September 26–29, 1993 (pp. 182–190). Osnabrück, Germany: Secolo.

Cairns, E. (1996). *Children and political violence.* Oxford: Blackwell.

Canino, G., Lewis-Fernandes, R., & Bravo, M. (1997). Methodological challenges in cross-cultural mental health research. *Transcultural Psychiatry, 34,* 163–184.

Curran, P. S. (1988). Psychiatric aspects of terrorist violence: Northern Ireland, 1969–1987. *British Journal of Psychiatry, 153,* 470–475.

Dawes, A. (1989). The effects of political violence on socio-moral reasoning and conduct. In A. Dawes & D. Donald (Eds.), *Childhood and adversity: Psychological perspectives from South African research* (pp. 200–219). Cape Town, South Africa: Philip.

Eisa, J., & Nofel, E. (1993). *Screening for war exposure and posttraumatic stress disorder among children in Kuwait. Age 7–17.* Preliminary Report. Ministry of Education, Kuwait (in Arabic, mentioned in Pynoos, Kinzie, & Gordon, 2001).

Ekblad, S. (1993). Psychosocial adaptation of children while housed in a Swedish refugee camp: Aftermath of the collapse of Yugoslavia. *Stress Medicine, 9,* 159–166.

Ekblad, S. (1996). Diagnostik och behandlig av patienter med invandrarbakgrund. En ettårsuppföljning på en psykiatrisk öppenvårdsmottagning. (Diagnosis and treatment of patients with an immigrant background. A one-year follow-up at a psychiatric outpatient unit.) Institutet för Psykosocial Medicin/National Institute of Psychosocial Factors and Health. Avdelningen för stressforskning, Karolinska Institutet, WHO's Psykosociala Center, *Stressforskningsrapporter, 262.*

Ekblad, S. (2000). A survey of somatic, psychological and social needs of mass displaced refugees from the Kosova province while in Sweden. Institutet för Psykosocial Medicin (IPM). Avdelningen för stressforskning, Karolinska Institutet, WHO's Psykosociala Center, *Stressforskningsrapporter, 293.*

Ekblad, S. (2001). Health promoting introduction. A research project financed by the Swedish Integration Board (Dnr INT-33-00-2632, Dnr KI 1631/2001) and the European Refugee Fund (ERG 141/2001, Dnr KI 3341/2001).

Ekblad, S. (2001, fourth quarter). The impact of September 11 on refugees applying for asylum. *World Federation for Mental Health Newsletter,* 6–7.

Ekblad, S. (in press). A Swedish perspective on refugee adjustment, resettlement, acculturation and mental health. In F. Bemak, R. Chi-Ying Chung, P. Pedersen (Eds.), *Refugee Mental Health.* Westport, CT: Greenwood Publishing.

Ekblad, S., & Silove, D. (1998). *Proposal for the development of mental health and psychosocial services in refugee camps: 18 August 1998.* Geneva: United Nations High Commissioner for Refugees.

Garbarino, J., Kostelny, K., & Dubrow, N. (1991). What children can tell us about living in danger. *American Psychologist, 46,* 376–383.

Glod, C. A., Teicher, M. H., Martin, H., Hartman, C., & Harakal, T. (1997). Increased nocturnal activity and impaired sleep maintenance in abused children. *Journal of the American Academy of Child and Adolescent Psychiatry, 36,* 1236–1243.

Gordon, M. (2001). Domestic violence in families exposed to torture and related violence and trauma. In E. Gerrity, T. M. Keane, and F. Tuma (Eds.), *The Mental Health Consequences of Torture* (pp 227–245). New York: Kluwer Academic/Plenum.

Green, B. L., Korol, M., Grace, M. C., Vary, M. G., Leonard, A. C., Gleser, G. C., & Smitson-Cohen, S. (1991). Children and disaster: Age, gender and parental effects on PTSD symptoms. *Journal of the American Academy of Child and Adolescent Psychiatry, 30,* 945–951.

Harvey, M. R. (1996). An Ecological View of Psychological Trauma and Trauma Recovery. *Journal of Traumatic Stress, 9,* 3–23.

Herlihy, J., Scragg, P., & Turner, S. (2002). Discrepancies in autobiographical memories—implications for the assessment of asylum seekers: Repeated interviews study. *British Medical Journal, 324,* 324–327.

Janson, S. (2001). Barn och misshandel. En rapport om kroppslig bestraffning och annan misshandel i Sverige vid slutet av 1900-talet. (Children and abuse. A report on physical punishment and other abuse in Sweden at the end of the twentieth century.) Stockholm, SOU (Swedish Government Official Reports Series).

Janson, S. (2002). Våldet mot barn sker I den egna familjen. (Violence towards children takes place in their own family.) *PsykologTidningen, 3,* 8–9.

Kinzie, J. D., Sack, W., Angell, R., Clarke, G., & Binn, R. (1989). A three-year follow-up of Cambodian young people traumatized as children. *Journal of the American Academy of Child and Adolescent Psychiatry, 28*, 501–504.

Kinzie, J. D., Sack, W. H., Angell, R. H., Manson, S., & Rath, B. (1986). The psychiatric effects of massive trauma on Cambodian children: I. The children. *Journal of the American Academy of Child and Adolescent Psychiatry, 25*, 370–376.

Kozaric-Kovacic, D., Folnegovic-Smalc, V., Skrinjaric, J., Szajnberg, N. M., & Marusic, A. (1995). Rape, torture, and traumatization of Bosnian and Croatian women: Psychological sequelae. *American Journal of Orthopsychiatry, 65*, 428–433.

Laor, N., Wolmer, L., Mayes, L. C., Gershon, A., Weizman, R., & Cohn, D. J. (1997). Israel preschool children under Scuds: A 30-month follow-up. *Journal of the American Academy of Child and Adolescent Psychiatry, 36*, 349–356.

Lindencrona, F., Johansson Blight K., & Ekblad, S. (2001). System for promotion or as a barrier: A survey to health promotion potentials of reception of refugees in the community. Unpublished manuscript.

Lonner, W., & Ibrahim, F. A. (1996). Appraisal and assessment in cross-cultural counselling. In P. B. Pedersen, J. G. Draguns, W. J. Lonner, & J. E. Trimble (Eds.), *Counselling Across Cultures* (pp. 293–322). London: Sage Publications.

McLeroy, K. R., Bibeau, D., Steckler, A., & Glanz, K. (1998). An Ecological Perspective on Health Promotion Programs. *Health Education Quarterly, 15*, 351–377.

Montgomery, E. (1998). Refugee children from the Middle East. *Scandinavian Journal of Social Medicine, 54* (Suppl.), 1–152.

Muscroft, S. (Ed.). (2000). *Children's rights: Equal rights? Diversity, difference, and the issue of discrimination.* London: The International Save the Children Alliance.

Psychologists for Social Responsibility homepage (http://www.psvsr.com/IPN.htm).

Punamäki, R-L. (1988). Historical-political and individualistic determinants of coping modes and fears among Palestinian children. *International Journal of Psychology, 23*, 721–739.

Pynoos, R. S., Frederick, C., Nader, K., Arroyo, W., Steinberg, A. M., Eth, S., Nunez, F., & Fairbanks, L. (1987). Life threat and posttraumatic stress in school-age children. *Archives of General Psychiatry, 44*, 1057–1063.

Pynoos, R. S., Kinzie, J. D., & Gordon, M. (2001). Children, adolescents, and families exposed to torture and related trauma In E. Gerrity, T. M. Keane, and F. Tuma (Eds.), *The mental health consequences of torture* (pp. 211–225). New York: Kluwer Academic/Plenum.

Shaw, M., Dorling, D., & Davey Smith, G. (1999). Poverty, social exclusion, and minorities. In M. Marmont & R. Wilingson (Eds.), *Social Determinants of Health* (pp. 211–239). Oxford: Oxford University Press.

Silove, D. (1996). Torture and refugee trauma: Implications for nosology and treatment of posttraumatic syndromes. In F. L. Mak & C. C. Nadelson (Eds.), *International Review of Psychiatry* (Vol. 2, pp. 211–232). Washington, DC: American Psychiatric Press.

Silove, D. (1999). The psychological effects of torture, mass human rights violations, and refugee trauma. *The Journal of Nervous and Mental Disease, 187*, 200–207.

Silove, D., & Kinzie, J. D. (2001). Survivors of war trauma, mass violence, and civilian terror. In E. Gerrity, T. M. Keane, & F. Tuma (Eds.), *The mental health consequences of torture* (pp. 159–174). New York: Kluwer Academic/Plenum.

Silove, D., Ekblad, S., & Mollica, R. (2000). The rights of the severely mentally ill in post-conflict societies. *The Lancet, 355,* 1548–1549.

Silove, D., Steel, Z., McGorry, P., Miles, V., Drobny, J. (2002). The impact of torture on post-traumatic stress symptoms in war-affected Tamil refugees and immigrants. *Comprehensive Psychiatry, 43,* 49–55.

Silove, D., Steel, Z., & Mollica, R. (2001). Detention of asylum seekers: assault on health, human rights, and social development. *The Lancet, 357,* 1436–1437.

Somerfield, M. R., & McCrae, R. R. (2000). Stress and coping research: Methodological challenges, theoretical advances, and clinical applications. *American Psychologist, 55,* 620–625.

Southwick, S., Friedman, M. J. (2001). Neurobiological models of posttraumatic stress disorder. In E. Gerrity, T. M. Keane, and F. Tuma (Eds.), *The mental health consequences of torture* (pp. 73–87). New York: Kluwer Academic/Plenum.

Steel, Z., & Silove, D. M. (2001). The mental health implications of detaining asylum seekers. *Medical Journal Australia, 175,* 596–599.

Stuber, M. L., Nader, K., Yasuda, P., Pynoos, R. S., & Cohen, S. (1991). Stress responses after pediatric bone marrow transplantation: Preliminary results of a prospective longitudinal study. *Journal of the American Academy of Child and Adolescent Psychiatry, 30,* 952–957.

Sultan, A., & O'Sullivan, K. (2001). Psychological disturbances in asylum seekers held in long term detention: A participant-observer account. *Medical Journal Australia, 175,* 593–596.

United Nations Children's Fund (UNICEF) (1995). *War-time survey of exposure, posttraumatic stress reactions, and depression among children and adolescents. Report of UNICEF Psychological Program for the ex-Yugoslavia region.*

United Nations High Commissioner for Refugees (UNHCR). (2000). *The state of the world's refugees: Fifty years of humanitarian protection.* New York: Oxford University Press.

Vesti, P., & Kastrup, M. (1995). Refugee status, torture, and adjustment. In J. R. Freedy & S.E. Hobfoll (Eds.), *Traumatic stress: From theory to practice.* New York: Plenum Press.

Zimbardo, P. G. (2001, November). Opposing terrorism by understanding the human capacity for evil. *Monitor on Psychology,* 48. (APA's president-elect on why the efforts to prevent future terrorist acts must begin with understanding the root causes of the hatred against America.)

NOTE

This chapter was supported by European Refugee Fund (ERF 141/2001). I would like to extend my warmest thanks to Steve Wicks, for his great help in transforming the text into readable English.

3

Children and Trauma: An Overview of Reactions, Mediating Factors, and Practical Interventions That Can Be Implemented

Teri L. Elliott

Helping children and adolescents recover from the negative emotional consequences of a traumatic event is a critical role for parents, teachers, and trauma mental health specialists. Historically, children have been exposed to both natural disasters, such as floods and earthquakes, and those initiated by man. Examples of the latter include wars, terrorist attacks, and the recent spate of school-related incidents in the United States. While these events have captured national and international attention, they are but a small sample of traumatic events that children experience.

Each year children are subjected either directly or indirectly to a wide range of tragedies, such as auto accidents, interpersonal violence, and catastrophic events. For many children, witnessing the aforementioned acts is as painful as when an adult experiences them directly. In order to assist children who have experienced a traumatic event, this chapter will address reactions, mediating factors, and interventions to help in their recovery; it is intended for individuals, families, and professionals who support children in the healing process.

People commonly refer to events as traumatic when actually they may not reach that level of severity. Each year millions of children are exposed to critical events, such as natural disasters or the loss of a parent, but not all of these children will become traumatized. This chapter will provide a working definition of what constitutes a traumatic event and examine factors that contribute to the impact of critical events by addressing four areas: 1) a brief review of the typical distress reactions associated with traumatic events, 2) an age-specific outline of children's reactions and responses to critical events, 3) mediating variables that make a critical event more or less impactful, and, finally, 4) suggestions as to how adults may assist children as they move forward in their lives following a traumatic event.

WORKING DEFINITIONS

The presumption in clinical psychology is that traumatized people can benefit from psychological support or therapy. Moreover, while everyone may benefit from psychological support, given the limited mental health resources available it is often necessary to know where one's assistance is most needed. In addition, in order to enhance communication among practitioners as well as between care providers and clients, clear definitions of what constitutes a traumatic or critical event[1] and trauma are imperative.

People frequently use the word "traumatized." We often hear someone say he or she is traumatized because of missing an important deadline or breaking up with a partner. Adolescents may say they were traumatized because they were not allowed to attend an all-night party, and children may complain that they are being traumatized if they have to do their homework before being allowed to play. However, do these circumstances truly constitute a traumatic event? In order to answer this question, we must first define and differentiate between the terms *traumatic event* and *trauma*. While numerous definitions exist in the literature, this chapter will consider an event traumatic if it fulfills three conditions.[2]

First, a traumatic event must be sudden, unexpected, or non-normative. Examples of sudden or unexpected events such as flash floods and automobile accidents are quite easy to identify, but non-normative events are often more difficult to ascertain. The word *norm* refers to something that is considered the standard or model. In this situation, it refers to a standard of conduct or a way of behaving that society as a whole feels must be followed. By including *non-normative* in this working definition of traumatic events, our definition covers experiences or situations that may occur regularly in the life of the child, but can still be very damaging. Examples include repeated assaults such as incest or child abuse.

For adults, an event will be considered traumatic if it "overwhelms" the individual's "perceived" ability to cope with it. The two key words here are *overwhelm* and *perceived*. A traumatic event is thought to overwhelm an individual's normally effective coping skills (American Psychiatric Association, 1994; Mitchell & Everly, 1997). This condition does not always apply to children. Children, especially young children, interpret events in part by using their caregivers' reactions to such events as a model for determining whether the world is safe or unsafe. If the child's family offers a message of hope and personal action that can be taken by the child or the family, the event is more likely to be managed and the child does not become overwhelmed. For instance, in a war zone a family may view bombing as a controlled attack on an enemy and hence feel less threatened than if they perceive bombing as a direct threat to their personal or familial safety. If an individual feels that he or she is able to cope with an event, even a horrific event like murder of a loved one, he or she will likely manage. This does not mean that the event is easy to handle or that the healing process will be effortless. It means that the individual feels he or she has the strength to cope with the horrible situation and therefore it is not defined as traumatic.

The third condition is that the impacted individual's central psychological needs, beliefs, and frame of reference are violated (Janoff-Bulman & Frieze, 1983; McCann & Pearlman, 1990). In adults, these central convictions are deeply ingrained and caregivers rarely think of their belief systems until forced to. While these beliefs often change from culture to culture, some principles appear to be globally accepted. For example, it is likely a global belief that children should live longer than their parents. In addition, parents often believe that responsible parenting will protect their children from senseless accidents or acts of violence. These beliefs, that bad things will not happen to good children, may be illusory but they provide a sense of safety and comfort. Traumatic events shatter this feeling of safety (Herman, 1992; Janoff-Bulman & Frieze, 1983; McCann & Pearlman, 1990) and parents are forced to confront the limits of their powers of protection. Consequently, a traumatic event forces the individual to consciously or unconsciously revise his or her frame of reference (Herman, 1992). Parents can become disillusioned and are vulnerable to a host of doubts about their ability to protect their children.

Along these lines, if adults are asked to describe themselves, they often refer to the roles they hold, such as father, coach, employee, etc. A man in his forties may describe himself as a father, a Little League baseball coach, and an engineer. However, what happens to this man if his only child dies in a car crash? Does he still consider himself a father? Will he still coach Little League baseball and include this role in his life? A woman in her early twenties may describe herself as a sister and an athlete. If she is paralyzed in a car accident, will she still consider herself an athlete? However, this change in the sense of roles is not necessarily true for children. While children tend to perceive changes in their roles, their youth often allows them to accommodate these fluctuations with greater ease than adults.

For example, one can look at the process a child undergoes when he or she redefines his or her self-description after losing an only sibling in an accident. The child may initially define himself or herself as a sibling, but ultimately is confronted with the challenge of reevaluating his or her status as sibling. Disturbances in an individual's core beliefs can be highly disruptive to that individual's sense of self and the stability he or she feels in his or her environment. Older children may be forced to reevaluate the world around them and their role in it. They may question their faith, their ability to care for themselves, and even their desire to live in a world that appears to be unjust.

If an event or the witnessing of an event meets all three of these conditions, then it will match this chapter's working definition of what constitutes a traumatic event. Nevertheless, this still leaves us with the question of what is trauma? *Trau-*

ma has both a medical and a psychological definition. In medical terms, *trauma* often refers to a serious or critical body injury. In psychological terms and for the purposes of this chapter, *trauma* is defined as a response to a traumatic event that is experienced through thoughts, feelings, and senses. It can take a multitude of forms, including many of the symptoms described in post-traumatic stress reactions. Trauma is associated with significant distress and a sense of helplessness, which is often accompanied by a shift in the individual's view of the world around him or her as well as his or her view of themselves. This distress is demonstrated by emotional and behavioral reactions, which in most individuals abate with time. Finally, although these reactions are a natural response to an extreme event, if not appropriately addressed they can have long-term negative effects.

TYPICAL REACTIONS TO TRAUMATIC EVENTS

It is difficult to know what to do when it seems as if your whole world is falling down around you. The impact of traumatic events is painful and feels overwhelming. People express their thoughts and feelings about what they have experienced in many ways. There is no "right" way to express pain and confusion. However, people can become frightened by their own emotions. They may think that what they are feeling is too much or not enough, or even not natural. It is important to know that struggling with difficult, confusing, and painful emotions is a natural part of the recovery process. While individuals may not be able to avoid traumatic events in their lives, they can enhance their coping skills by becoming educated about the typical responses to traumatic events. Sometimes just knowing what to expect can bring relief. While each individual will respond to the traumatic event in a unique manner, there are some relatively common experiences.

A Sense of Helplessness

A common reaction to a traumatic event is feeling helpless (Herman, 1992) and out of control. By definition, the traumatic event has overwhelmed the individual's coping skills and he or she may feel as if he or she has lost control of his or her life. It is common to feel as if nothing one does matters or will make a difference in one's emotional state or in the world in general.

Sadness and Depression

Individuals may feel so sad that they fear never being able to feel happy again. They may lose interest in previously enjoyable activities. One result of severe sadness is a decrease in the individual's energy level and in his or her ability and/or desire to focus and set goals. When combined with a sense of helplessness, it can be very difficult for the impacted person to garner enough emotional resources to fight a growing sense of disillusionment and inadequacy.

Fear, Confusion, and Anxiety

Individuals, especially children who may not understand exactly what has happened, are often afraid that the traumatic event will reoccur. The confusion that often surrounds critical events can be anxiety-provoking. A family may be concerned about how they will survive living in a refugee camp, or how they will find a new home after a flood. Children may be fearful of being abandoned, especially if they had been separated from their caregivers during the traumatic event. They may also be worried about family members and friends who may still be missing. In particular, children who have experienced the loss of one parent are frequently in terror of losing their other parent.

In addition, impacted individuals may have previously seen the world as a "just" place. They may now feel unsafe and fearful. They may feel as if they no longer understand the world or know how to keep themselves and their family safe. This loss of a sense of safety and security can be very frightening for the whole family.

Relief at Being Alive

Sometimes individuals feel so happy to be alive that nothing else seems to matter. This can cause people to relinquish their long-term goals and "live for the moment." While this may sound appealing, it can cause future problems. Children may need to be motivated to continue going to school. They may have a tendency to engage in unhealthy activities such as smoking, alcohol or drug use, or unsafe sex. It is important for caregivers to address these changes in behavior and to help the child see the connection to the traumatic event.

Guilt

Guilt is a very common reaction for children after a traumatic event (Parson, 1996; Pynoos et al., 1987). It is natural for individuals to feel as if they should have been able to prevent the traumatic event or at least have made it less severe. They may also feel as if they should have been the person affected. These are common feelings. Once the immediate danger has passed, it is often easy for an individual to think of things he or she "could have" or "should have" done. However, in reality, people often have very little control over what happens during a critical event.

In addition, many people will not allow themselves to move on because they feel the need to punish themselves or would consider it disrespectful to the memory of the deceased (Parson, 1996). They often do this by not allowing happiness to enter their lives and, by doing so, they identify with the deceased individual's inability to experience life.

Anger and Irritability

Children may be very angry with people who have died. They may feel as if they have to deal with this horrible situation alone. In addition, it is common for individuals to feel angry with people trying to help them. Children may feel that no one understands their situation or that people are not being helpful enough. Overall, individuals often find that after a traumatic event they have a quick temper and find themselves becoming angry over little things. This can be exacerbated since critical events are often followed by a tremendous amount of bureaucracy. If a family has lost their place of residence, they may lose considerable control over their daily routines. A family impacted by a flood may have to fill out numerous forms or spend large parts of their day waiting in lines to accomplish such basic tasks as registering for disaster relief, obtaining cleaning supplies, or locating temporary accommodations. Adults and children alike need to have a sense of control over their lives, and when this is removed it can be stressful. In these situations, anger and irritability may be directed toward members of their family, and early evidence suggests an increase in levels of child abuse and domestic violence after a traumatic event (Adams & Adams, 1984; Norris, 2001).

Difficulty Sleeping

Individuals impacted by a traumatic event often feel as if they never get enough sleep. It is common for them to have difficulty falling asleep. In addition, some find that they wake up frequently during the night or very early in the morning and then have trouble falling asleep again. Nightmares or bad dreams are especially common in children and are one indicator that the child may be feeling frightened and anxious. It is common for children to become temporarily afraid of the dark or afraid of sleeping alone. Adults may feel the same way.

Physical Reactions

Following a traumatic event, some individuals express their stress physically and can feel weak or ill. If a child or an adult is evidencing physical symptoms, it is important to consult a physician to establish that there is nothing medically wrong. However, stomach problems and headaches, or other physical symptoms with no observable physical cause, can be signs of post-traumatic event distress. These symptoms may be due to feelings of guilt, fear, anger, or sadness. While these physical responses are quite common, it is essential for caregivers to understand that even if they are not due to a physical cause they are real and need to be addressed.

Heightened Startle Response

Individuals may find that after a traumatic event they have a heightened startle response, and they may jump at nearly every unexpected noise. What occurs is that the body is on maximum alert and prepares itself to react quickly to any threat. These symptoms tend to fade with continuous experience in a safe environment.

Difficulty Concentrating and Thinking

After a traumatic event, people often find it difficult to concentrate on a specific task or to complete tasks they used to find easy. Individuals often become easily distracted and find themselves ruminating about the critical event. Sometimes the entire family may be struggling with this same difficulty. Adults may find that they need to repeat instructions or requests, especially for children. As a caregiver, one must understand the child's lack of responsiveness. If this is new behavior, it may be that the traumatic situation has overwhelmed the child and consequently he or she has less energy for other things.

Boredom

This can be a significant stress factor. After a traumatic event, individuals may be living with circumstances, such as being confined in a shelter that requires periods of inactivity, that can lead to boredom and frustration. There may be significant stretches of time where there is nothing to do, further disrupting a child's familiar routines. Children may not know when to go to school, when dinner will be served, or when and where they can play. This may prompt restlessness and misbehavior.

Unpredictable Emotional Reactions, Isolation, and Traumatic Reminders

A child doing chores or playing may suddenly start crying for no apparent reason. A young girl in a temporary school may lash out at a classmate. These sudden emotional reactions are often connected to a traumatic reminder. *Traumatic reminders* are cues or stimuli in the environment that prompt the individual to suddenly remember the traumatic event in vivid detail, and they are often associated with intense feelings such as fear and anger. This experience can be very upsetting for the child and his or her family. To avoid these strong memories and emotions, children may attempt to escape reminders of the traumatic event. Children may isolate themselves from people as well as situations. This can be particularly damaging for children who are still developing socially and emotionally. In order to assist the child in his or her recovery process, it is important to help isolate the *trigger(s)*. Once a trigger has been identified, it is possible to process the emotional connection and hence regain a sense of control.

Each individual interprets and remembers the traumatic event in an idiosyncratic manner. Consequently, different triggers can exist for people who experienced the same traumatic event. Some of the more common triggers are sensory images associated with the event, anniversary dates of the traumatic event, and traditional special events.

A mother was extremely worried about her son when he began crying inconsolably whenever his father, who was a farmer, came in from feeding the animals.

This response started shortly after a firefighter saved him during a flood. Since the child loved his father, and was fine at other times, his parents were at a loss as to what was causing this extreme distress. After much exploration, it was determined that the firefighter had carried the boy in such a way that his head was hanging down. From this position, the child's view was of the fireman's large black rubber boots, which were very similar to the boots worn by the child's father when feeding the animals. The sight of these boots was acting as a trigger and prompting the child to remember the event and to re-experience many of the feelings from that time. Sensory cues such as this can activate memories of the traumatic event years later.

Anniversary dates after the event can reawaken painful memories in children. It is important to provide them with additional support and nurturing throughout this time.

Traumatic events often result in a loss or a series of losses. The death of a family member or destruction of the family home is a tremendous loss, and there is often an outpouring of sympathy and support. This may not be the case with other losses—such as cherished photo albums, a father's watch, or a treasured doll—that, while less readily identifiable, may also have profound effects. Shortly after a traumatic event, it is common to hear people proclaim that they are "fine" and just thankful that no one was hurt or killed. While these sentiments are often accurate, as time passes material losses can and do reawaken many of the painful and confusing feelings associated with the traumatic event. These losses are often most deeply felt on the next occasion of a traditional special event. These can include the first time a child plays baseball without the lucky sweatshirt that was destroyed in a fire or the first holiday without grandma's heirloom china. Sometimes children's distress over possessions can be hard for adults to understand. The loss of a small doll may seem insignificant to a parent when the family has lost their home. Nevertheless, to a child, the two losses may feel similar.

In sum, all of the experiences described above can cause individuals to feel a sense of helplessness. Children may react in ways similar to adults, but they also have unique ways of experiencing and reacting to traumatic situations, as outlined in the following section.

REACTIONS THAT ARE SPECIFIC TO CHILDREN

To assess the impact of traumatic events on children, we must keep in mind that children process and respond to traumatic events differently at different stages of development (Pynoos, Steinberg, & Wraith, 1995). Several factors related to a child's reaction to the traumatic situation should be noted. 1) Parental anxiety appears to influence children's reactions (Sugar, 1989) as children take their cues from the adults around them. 2) In the first year after a critical event, teachers may be better at spotting trauma reactions than parents. A caregiver may be dealing with his or her own responses to the critical event and not have the emotional or cognitive ability to perceive the child's distress (Bowlby, 1980). In addition, caregivers usually want to believe that the child is coping adequately, and consequently either consciously or unconsciously miss the subtle signs of distress. 3) A child may experience difficulty seeing a caregiver in pain, which he or she may perceive as reactive to his or her stress. Consequently, children often become conditioned not to exhibit any signs of discomfort in front of their parents. The result is that children's difficulties are often observed first in school, where they can be interpreted as emotional or academic problems, but can also be seen as misbehavior. The latter may also be a way for children to avoid feeling and thinking about the traumatic event.

Knowledge of how a child responds to traumatic events will better prepare the caregiver to understand the child's behavior and hence assist in the recovery process. Consequently, in order to enhance the caregiver's ability to identify distress in children, an overview of common post-event emotional and behavioral changes in children will be explored in the next section.

Preoccupation With, Or Increased Interest In, Death

A traumatic event that includes death may prompt a child to become preoccupied with what it means to die. It is common for children to focus on the details of death and they may ask questions that make the caregivers uncomfortable. They may want to know what happens when someone dies or what happens to the person's body after they are dead. A child's questions are one indicator that he or she is trying to learn about what has happened and they can help him or her to come to terms with the loss.

With children who have had previous experiences with loss, there may be a rekindling of past feelings and memories about death or other losses. For example, if a child has lost a family member or person close to him or her, the current traumatic situation may cause him or her to re-experience the earlier loss and cause distressed feelings to resurface.

Problems in Schoolwork and a Decline in School Performance

It is common for children to become distractible and have trouble concentrating after a traumatic event. Intrusive imagery may disrupt concentration, with a subsequent decrease in school performance. In addition, children may no longer believe in a future (Terr, 1983), and hence feel there is no reason to study or learn new things (Parson, 1996).

Regressive Behavior

It is common for children who are overwhelmed by a traumatic situation to act younger than they had before the crisis. Developmental skills may be temporarily impaired. Recently mastered skills are particularly vulnerable under stress. For instance, there may be a loss or slowdown in language acquisition. More dramatically, a six-year-old who used to be toilet trained may now start urinating in his or her sleep. Older children may now evidence separation fears and feel afraid to be left alone. These are natural reactions for children and are usually temporary.

Children may also lose the capacity to control their aggression and their capacity to comfort themselves. This may be in direct response to the content of the traumatic event or it may appear as a generalized loss of control. As children mature, they learn to self-soothe. After a traumatic event, this ability may be negatively impacted and the child may no longer be able to manage the day-to-day frustrations of childhood. They may feel quite fragile and need additional support. This can be especially difficult for the family that feels the child is putting additional demands on its time and energy. These children are not trying to be difficult and may not even realize that they are acting differently. While this resurfaced need for external assistance may strain the stamina of an already stressed parent, it is usually a temporary condition. As time passes, and the child learns to handle the traumatic event, his or her behavior matures once again.

Post-Traumatic Play

Play is an integral part of children's lives and is thought to be enjoyable for them (Terr, 1981). *Play* is how they learn about and organize the world and make sense of the new information they are learning on a daily basis. In addition, play allows children to achieve a sense of mastery over imaginary or real frustrations (Terr, 1981; Varkas, 1998). Consequently, in an attempt to understand a traumatic event, children often put aspects of the situation into their play. After the war in Bosnia, one Bosnian child was often found playing "graveyard." While seeing this type of game can be unsettling for adults, it is important to allow children to use play as a way to process what has happened. As they play the same game repeatedly, they often come to feel as if they have more control over the situation. They find a way to understand and master the event, and it will bother them a little less each time.

In *post-traumatic play*, the enjoyment that characterizes ordinary play is absent and instead there is a sense of anxiety and discomfort. A child may seem "stuck" and the play continues in an anxious and unchanging manner, apparently providing no relief (Herman, 1992; Terr, 1981; Varkas, 1998). The child is not conscious of the connection with the traumatic situation (Varkas, 1998). Outside assistance in processing the event may be necessary, and consulting a mental health professional may be helpful.

CHILDREN'S UNDERSTANDING OF TRAUMATIC EVENTS IS DIFFERENT AT ALL AGES AND STAGES OF DEVELOPMENT

While this section is broken into distinct age groupings, it is important to note that these are just convenient separations. As with adults, each child is unique and will understand, process, and react to a traumatic event in an idiosyncratic manner. In addition, children can only understand a situation with the skills they have. As they mature, they often need to re-examine a traumatic event that happened years earlier in order to gain a more complete understanding and to incorporate the event into their current view of the world. Consequently, while these age groups are developmentally and logically arranged, they are meant as an organizing tool, and their boundaries are fluid. In addition, children will not experience or display all of the behaviors and symptoms listed. Many of the symptoms that are listed in one age group may also exist in other age groups. With this in mind, symptoms distinctive to particular age groups are highlighted in the following discussion.

Birth to Two-and-a-Half Years

Although infants lack the vocabulary to share their feelings, it does not mean that they do not have memories about the traumatic event (Terr, 1991). They may remember the smells, sounds, or even particular sights of the event. They usually do not have the cognitive or emotional maturity to understand the traumatic event, so they look to their parents and caregivers for cues about how frightening or safe the world is (Bowlby, 1980). Since infants cannot express their trauma linguistically, they often demonstrate uncharacteristic crying and inconsolability. They may want to be held continually and can be very hard to soothe. With infants, one often sees increased separation fears and clinging behavior. A heightened startle response and sudden rigidity of the body are also common. Disruptions in sleeping patterns and regressive behavior in toilet training and in language acquisition may also occur.

Two-and-a-Half to Six Years

As children mature through this age range, the likelihood that they have accurate verbal and pictorial memories of the traumatic event increases (Monahon, 1993; Terr, 1991). These children may feel overwhelmed by the traumatic event. At this age, children tend to focus on their own pain and needs. They may be quite concerned about who will take care of them and can demonstrate separation anxiety when their trusted caregivers leave. It may be difficult for them to understand that others around them, including their family, friends, and neighbors, may also be struggling with the traumatic event. Children of this age can be quite narcissistic and have little ability to empathize with others.

Sleep disturbances including nightmares, night terrors, and sleepwalking can occur. It is also common for young children to become fearful about being alone in the dark, and consequently bedtime can become a difficult process.

Temporary regression to younger behavior is normal. Children may also demonstrate noticeable anxiety and show a tendency to withdraw. They may stop engaging in previously enjoyed activities. Traumatic reminders also play a role in this behavior (Pynoos, Goenjian, & Steinberg, 1998; Pynoos, Steinberg, & Wraith, 1995). In order to reduce stress, children (and adults) often avoid situations and people who elicit memories of the traumatic event(s). As previously mentioned, if not resolved, this type of phobic behavior can have a long-term negative impact on children's development.

Young children do not understand that death is permanent and may feel as if events are reversible. Children may talk about people who have died as returning soon. This is a critical area for caregivers to recognize and address. Religious and spiritual faith can often assist with healing, but it is important to help children understand the finality of death. If "heaven" or "the afterlife" is portrayed as a wonderful place where grandmother is now living, a child may decide that he or she wants to go there as well. One young boy decided that he would die and go to heaven to visit his grandfather, but then come back in time for his soccer game. Children's unrealistic understanding of death can lead to confusing patterns of behavior. Consequently, this can be a taxing time for caregivers. In addition, children often ask the same questions repeatedly. While it can be frustrating, these questions are the child's way of understanding and processing the event. Each time a question is answered, children understand the situation just a little more.

Magical thinking occurs in children prior to their understanding of how events in the real world transpire, and when a young child does not understand a situation, he or she often uses magical thinking to fill in the gaps. This can be problematic, since children can make illogical connections and elaborations. Consequently, their imagined version of the situation can be more frightening than the actual event. This can be especially true for children who blame themselves and their behavior when something "bad" happens. While angry outbursts are not unusual in children, if they become associated with subsequent traumatic event(s), the child may feel responsible. For example, if a child is upset and yells, "I hate you, you're the meanest father in the world," and then a tornado strikes the family's home, the child may feel that his or her rage caused the tornado. While it is usually quite clear to the caregiver that the child did not cause the traumatic event, it is critical to clarify the matter for the child. Unfortunately, children often do not verbalize their fears. Hence, it is important for caregivers to listen carefully to them to ascertain if the child has any misunderstandings of the traumatic event. If such issues are not adequately addressed, the child may suffer from a painful sense of guilt. While traumatic events are often not understandable even from an adult perspective, it is important to help a child develop a realistic understanding of what has transpired.

Six to Eleven Years

Children in this age range have a better understanding of death. Anxiety and fearfulness, including concerns about the critical event reoccurring, are obvious signs of stress. Behavioral or mood changes are common, as are sleep disturbances and loss of enjoyment in previously pleasurable activities. Children may also focus on details surrounding the traumatic event and have less energy for other activities. Difficulty concentrating due to intrusive imagery and preoccupation may negatively influence their social interactions and school performance.

Children still need to find answers for a multitude of questions, and they ask related questions repeatedly. Children who have been removed or forced from their home may ask when they are going home or how long they will have to stay in the shelter or refugee camp. These can be difficult questions since the answers may be unknown. However, it is helpful to listen, respond to the child's questions with age-appropriate answers, and try to share whatever is known about the situation. Children at this age can appreciate being part of the information-sharing process.

In an attempt to deal with the critical event, children and adults may repeatedly retell the traumatic story (Galante & Foa, 1986). In the sharing of their experience, children are able to discharge some of their anxiety about the situation and find some self-importance in the listeners' comments. With each repetition, these children process the event in more detail. Similar to traumatic play, if the retelling persists without apparent relief or change, the child may be experiencing significant difficulty and need external assistance.

Children's emotions may fluctuate rapidly. One minute they may appear calm and act as if nothing is bothering them, and then suddenly they may become intensely emotional. Children have a wonderful ability to survive, but stimuli in the environment (traumatic reminders/triggers) may remind them of the traumatic event and prompt them to feel a surge of emotions.

Similarly to adults, children may feel multiple emotions at any one time. Sometimes they may feel angry or sad or sometimes both at once. Children in this age group are particularly vulnerable to feelings of responsibility and may feel as if they are failures because they were not able to prevent or stop the traumatic event. Although it may appear illogical to adults, children often feel responsible for events over which they had no influence.

In addition, traumatic events can be so disturbing that adults and children react in ways that make them feel ashamed. It is important to provide an opportunity for children to share their thoughts, including those that may be embarrassing. If feelings of self-blame persist, they can fester and prompt long-term dissatisfaction and self-doubt (Pynoos et al., 1987). It is important to help children understand that during a traumatic event people often act in ways that appear illogical or inappropriate.

Eleven Years Through Adolescence

As children mature, they often exhibit a mixture of both childish and more adult reactions to traumatic situations. In addition, as children become young adults, they gain a more complete understanding of the finality of death, which can make the loss of a loved one even more frightening.

Adolescents may feel the need to take on adult responsibilities. This may be an accurate interpretation since a redistribution of roles is often required in the aftermath of traumatic events. For instance, death or relocation can separate families, and adolescents may need to take on the role of caregiver for their younger siblings. Adolescents may suddenly have to care for themselves. On the positive side, by helping caregivers, older children and adolescents gain a sense of usefulness and control. Caregivers can help this process by supporting their efforts and by acknowledging the difficulty of going from childhood to adulthood in such a short period of time. On the other hand, adolescents should not be overwhelmed with new responsibilities. It is important to provide a safe place for them to act like the adolescents they really are. "Young adults" still need time to be children.

Although adolescents often value their privacy and independence, in times of dire stress such as armed conflict or relocation they may suddenly not want to be alone. They may stay near their living quarters and spend unusual amounts of time with their parents or caregivers. This may occur because the adolescent now sees the world from a different perspective and a previous sense of invulnerability may have been damaged. In contrast, some adolescents who survive dangerous situations may feel a heightened sense of invulnerability and imagine that they have some sort of special protection. This can often result in them engaging in danger-ous activities and taking more risks. For example, they may take more chances in obtaining necessary goods through acts such as theft or they may engage in taunt-ing behavior toward more powerful elements in their community.

With inadequately monitored conditions, such as shelters and refugee camps, adolescents may be at more risk than younger children. Adolescent girls may be at increased risk for sexual attacks. In addition, adolescents are often sought by com-bating forces to reinforce their armies and consequently are at greater risk to be taken out of the control of their family and thrust into the world of war and adult-hood.

MEDIATING FACTORS THAT CAN INFLUENCE THE EFFECT OF TRAUMATIC EVENTS

Many factors influence how people react to traumatic situations. Although an entire family may have been exposed to the same traumatic event, none of them will have exactly the same experience during or after the event. It is therefore important to understand the conditions surrounding the event, those that existed before the event, and those that existed afterward. These are critical in determining how severely impacted the individual will be. When assessing children's reactions to traumatic events, it is important to consider personal characteristics as well as the characteristics of the situation and the post-event environment.

Personal Characteristics of the Impacted Individual

Age

As previously discussed, age and stage of development play a large role in how children interpret, process, and respond to traumatic events. One important variable is a child's beliefs about death. As children mature, they progress from viewing death as a reversible process to viewing death as final. In addition, their sense of control moves from idiosyncratic magical thinking to a more universal understanding. It may also be the case that, unlike adults, who actively engage in denial, children may experience less psychic numbing due to their active remembering of the event through daydreaming (Terr, 1985). In general, the more care a child is given during the course of a traumatic situation, the less overwhelmed he or she is likely to become, and this influences how vulnerable or resilient the child may ultimately feel.

Parental Reactions Toward the Event

Children's reactions are intimately connected with those of their caregivers (Newman, 1976; Pynoos & Nader, 1988; Wasserstein & La Greca, 1998). Since children have less experience with the world, they often look to their caregivers and other adults for indications of how to react to novel situations, and how a family copes with a traumatic event influences how children in the family will respond.

Premorbid Conditions

Traumatic events do not occur in isolation. They are just one part of the child's life and consequently must be explored and understood in that context. Each stressor in the child's life—whether it is living in poverty, a tornado, or an upcoming history exam—requires emotional energy. One way to view this is through a math analogy using "coping units." If a child has twenty coping units and living with poverty requires ten, the tornado requires eight and the history exam requires one, the child has one extra coping unit and thus has the emotional resources to cope with the demands of their environment. On the other hand, if living with poverty requires ten coping units, the tornado requires twenty, and the history exam requires one, the child is eleven units short and is likely to be overwhelmed. While this is a very simple way of looking at premorbid issues, the simplicity allows for clarity. Individuals with special needs, including such challenges as a physical or emotional disability or previous loss, often have a more difficult time handling the aftermath of a traumatic situation. For example, if a child has an attachment disorder, physical disability, or has recently lost a family member, transferred to a new school, or had previous displacements, a new challenging event may prove to be more unsettling than one might have initially anticipated.

It is easy to understand that children who already have an abundance of stressors in their lives—whether poverty, child abuse, or illness—are more likely to be overwhelmed by the most recent traumatic event, and hence are at increased risk for long-term problems.

Characteristics of the Traumatic Event

Type of Traumatic Event

Traumatic events are often complex and can be caused by an intricate mixture of variables that further interact with personal and environmental factors. In the beginning of this chapter, a traumatic event was defined as any event that was either unexpected or non-normative, overwhelmed the individual's perceived coping skills, and disrupted the individual's frame of reference and central psychological beliefs. This definition allows inclusion of a wide range of events from individual accidents (e.g., dog bites) to interpersonal violence (e.g., child abuse), to natural disasters (e.g., floods), to "man-made" disasters (e.g., terrorist attacks) and it places value on the impacted individual's *perception* of the event. There are many different ways of classifying and categorizing critical events (Berren, Beigel, & Ghertner, 1980; Berren, Santiago, Beigel, & Timmons, 1989; Gist & Lubin, 1999; Raphael, 1986), and while it is beyond the scope of this chapter to discuss all of the options, a simple example can illustrate the complexity of the task.

It would seem that the distinction between "natural" and man-made traumatic events is clear, with natural disasters being caused by forces of nature and man-made disasters being caused by anything other than nature, but this is deceptive. Man-made disasters can be further divided into acts of omission and acts of commission (Berren et al., 1989). For example, a flood that destroys a community would likely be considered a natural disaster, but what if human error at the dam (act of omission) or an intentional act of sabotage (act of commission) caused the flood? While this demonstrates that classification can be complex, it is only the tip of the iceberg. In order to fully understand the differences among events, it is important to differentiate between single and chronic events, interpersonal and community events, sudden and predictable events, and accidental and intentional events, just to name a few. In addition, within each classification, the level of exposure, duration of the event, and range of impact are just a few of the variables that would also need to be considered. Predicting the mental-health consequences of an event based solely on the type of event is virtually impossible.

With this in mind, brief comments about the duration of the event, the suddenness of the event, and the range of impact of the event are offered.

Duration

In general, longer-lasting events are more likely to have negative effects. It is also important to again note that there is a difference between single and chronic events.

Suddenness

Events that are sudden and unexpected are often more difficult to handle. This may be because the sudden nature of the event precludes a sense of control. Catastrophe signifies a dramatic loss of control (Herman, 1992), and this is important because of the apparent connection between a sense of loss of control and helplessness and the known relationship between helplessness and depression (Seligman, 1975). In addition, if children do not feel as if they have control over the event, concerns about reoccurrence may negatively impact their mental health (Terr, 1979).

Range of Impact

In determining the effect of a traumatic event, it is important to consider both the personal and the environmental impact. As the personal severity of the loss increases, so does the negative impact on mental health (Murphy, 1986). For example, loss of a loved one is more likely to result in mental health problems than loss of property. In addition, impacted individuals are part of a larger community and, as the disruption expands, recovery may be hampered.

Proximity

In general, the closer a child is to a traumatic event, either physically or emotionally, the more difficult the situation (Newman, 1976; Pynoos et al., 1987; Pynoos & Nader, 1989). It is more burdensome for a child who had direct experience with a traumatic event than for a child who may have only heard about or identify with the situation. For example, it is more difficult for a child who has witnessed a school shooting than for a child who only heard the shots. In a similar fashion, a child who has a direct emotional connection to the event will also tend to be more severely impacted. For example, a child who was not at school during the shooting but knew someone injured is more likely to experience distress than a child who did not know anyone involved.

Intentionality

When a traumatic event is caused deliberately, such as an act of terrorism, impacted individuals are likely to experience a sense of injustice or of being unfairly targeted. In addition, there may be a strong desire for revenge or retaliation. Studies have shown that acting on this anger can increase negative affect rather than decrease it (Hamblen, 2002).

Loss

If the event involves loss, it is more difficult to manage. Obviously, the loss of a loved caregiver is difficult. There are a variety of other losses that can also make the situation more difficult to manage, such as loss of a familiar school and supportive community if the neighborhood is destroyed or if the child is displaced. As previously discussed, the loss of cherished heirlooms or special toys may also complicate the recovery process.

Post-Event Environment

The conditions following the traumatic event are also influential. When trying to ascertain or predict the severity of a child's distress, it is important to evaluate the environmental and community conditions, the influence of the media, and existing social support structures.

Post-Event Environmental Conditions

When people leave their homes to escape a traumatic event such as a natural disaster or are forced to leave their homes because of an event such as a military or paramilitary intrusion, their distress about the situation is likely to increase. When an individual is uprooted from his or her home, there may also be concerns about necessities, such as having adequate shelter and sufficient food and water. Having inadequate supplies of such items as diapers or clean clothes or a lack of bathing facilities also places stress on the individual.

Fear of the unknown is a tremendous worry. If families become separated, there is concern for missing members. Children may worry that their caregivers, family, or friends have been hurt or killed. Young children often hold a central belief that their caregivers will keep them safe. When separated, they are likely to become frightened, but—perhaps even more importantly—they may temporarily lose faith in their caregiver's ability to protect them.

Community Conditions

Having a location where people who share similar language, beliefs, and values can associate is helpful. If a family has been displaced, its members may have little or no private space to process the event and share concerns with loved ones. It is also important that people have access to accurate and timely information concerning the situation.

Media Involvement

In understanding and recovering from a traumatic event or events, the media has the potential for both a negative and a positive influence. It is often the case that the media enters a situation of conflict, whether it is a natural disaster or terrorist attack, and presents the situation in a manner that may or may not be representative of the individuals' experiences. The media's choice of what to emphasize can slant or bias news coverage. In addition, depending on the intensity and duration of reporting, impacted individuals can feel either ignored or intruded upon. The media may also represent the event or events in a manner that seems disrespectful to cultural or religious beliefs and values.

On the positive side, the media also has the ability to foster awareness of an event in the larger community and can assist in generating physical and material assistance for the impacted individuals. In addition, the media can be tremendously helpful in providing much-needed information about safety issues, details of the event, location of relief agencies, and even suggestions on how to recover from the event. It can be beneficial to develop an ongoing collaborative working relationship with the media in order to enhance positive and helpful coverage.

Assistance or Support Conditions

Another crucial mediating variable is the child's support system. The support system includes not only the child's family and friends, but—depending on the traumatic event—it may also include larger communities such as the neighborhood, country, and possibly the entire international community. Again, the individual's perception plays a central role here. For example, if a strong and supportive social network surrounds an adolescent, he or she is likely to feel more reassured and able to cope with the events at hand. However, if that same adolescent either does not perceive the support to be available or would not reach out to that support, then the support structure is considerably less effective.

When impacted individuals are recovering from a large-scale event, many relief agencies can play a central role. It is essential that relief workers respect the beliefs and values of the population being served. While this sounds obvious, it is often not adequately implemented. For example, it is not sufficient to have relief workers take a class on diversity and cultural sensitivity. They must be supervised in order to ensure that adequate services are equitably provided to all impacted individuals and groups, including groups that may be in the minority or suffer from discrimination.

In addition, an impacted individual may feel as if he or she has no control over his or her own life and that the relief workers are making all the decisions without asking or considering his or her thoughts and wishes. When control is removed from an individual, this further complicates an already stressful and painful situation.

It is important to keep in mind that personal, event, and post-event variables are dynamic and interact with one another. Consequently, the entire context of the traumatic event must be assessed in order to gain a thorough understanding of the impact on the child.

HOW WE CAN ASSIST CHILDREN AS PARTICIPANTS IN THEIR LIVES

Throughout history, children have been exposed to traumatic events, and they have demonstrated a tendency to be resilient and recover with time. Nonetheless, emotional support and guidance can be helpful in the recovery process. Empowering families and natural support systems is likely to have the most positive influence in a child's recovery from traumatic events. As previously discussed, children often look to adults for cues about how dangerous an event is or how to respond. Caring adults can assist children in the recovery process by maintaining a supportive and consistent presence. In addition, it is important to limit children's exposure to additional traumatic scenes.

The following is a brief exploration of possible interventions that can be implemented after a traumatic event.

During and Immediately After a Critical Event

A child's worst fear is often not knowing or understanding what is happening around him or her. Whenever possible, reunite children with their families and allow families to be the conduits of information to their children. If families are unavailable, provide age-appropriate knowledge of the situation and the future plans for the children and their families.

When physically possible, guide children away from seriously wounded individuals at the site of the traumatic event and assist children in avoiding areas of impending danger. Emergency workers and available adults should attempt to create a safe haven where children can be protected from intrusive media and inquisitive strangers. It is important to remember that this time can be very distressing for children, so the utmost sensitivity is required. Reassure the child that people are working to control the situation, but avoid making false promises or unfounded predictions that everything will be fine.

While all children can benefit from support at this time, it may be necessary to identify those children who are having more severe reactions to the event. Children showing symptoms such as extreme anxiety, uncontrollable shaking, and/or erratic and dangerous behavior should be kept with a protective and supportive adult. For those children experiencing less distress, it may be helpful to engage them in some form of helping behavior. A simple task like helping to stack blankets or caring for younger children can help children regain a sense of control.

While reassurance is helpful and needed, it is also important to respect children's needs. Children's traumatic event history is usually unknown to first-responders, and additional care must be taken to be sensitive to children's physical and emotional boundaries.

Once the Acute Danger Is Over

In traumatic situations not involving familial violence, parents or caregivers are often the most accessible support system for children. In age-appropriate language and detail, the adults can explain what has happened and listen to the children's responses. Without pressure, encourage them to share their feelings and thoughts. Wait for questions, allowing children to attempt to formulate their own path through the events. Like adults, children come to understand the event over time, so the process of questioning and explaining may continue for some time. When working with younger or less-verbal children, assisting them in labeling their feelings is an important activity. Reassure them that they are cared about and loved. One way to do this is by respecting their reactions. Allow them to cry or sit silently. Do not overreact if they have angry outbursts or display signs of withdrawal. If regressive behavior occurs, do not be punitive or insinuate that they are acting like "a baby." If children are fearful about their caregivers being hurt, they may worry excessively each time the parent leaves. Caregivers can reduce this fear by being consistent in their comings and goings and by providing clear messages about when they will return. If bedtime has become an anxiety-provoking experience, a nightlight or extra bedtime story may be helpful.

Sometimes children may feel as if they are to blame for an event. They often will not verbalize this fear, so it is important to raise this issue directly and not wait for the child to initiate the topic. Even if the child had contributed to the event—for example, by playing with matches and causing a house fire—it is important to maintain perspective and differentiate between accidents and intentional acts of hostility. Children will respond more openly to attempts at understanding their role in the situation rather than being assigned blame by an adult.

Foster a sense of control and allow time for recovery. Engage children in age-appropriate decision-making, such as a discussion of what to have for dinner. Given the possibility of intrusive imagery and disruptions in concentration, a time-limited reduction in responsibilities may be appropriate. It is important to explain the reasons for this change in expectations, and addressing the traumatic events from the family's perspective rather than solely from that of the child may be useful at these times. A return to the family's normal routines should occur as quickly as possible. This will reassure children that their parents are once again in control and can provide an increased sense of protection and safety.

Children should not be made to feel as if they are the only ones experiencing distress, and they benefit from observing adults who are managing the situation. While it is important not to lose control in front of children—by sobbing inconsolably, for example—it is also important to demonstrate that having feelings about the event is natural.

The School System

School personnel often work with parents to help children recover from a traumatic event (Garmezy, 1986; Gordon, Farberow, & Maida, 1999; Slaikeu, 1990). Teachers or school counselors may be the first to notice a change in a child's behavior. It is common for school personnel to recognize a child's negative actions, such as aggression, regressive behaviors, and withdrawal. It is often less noticeable when the child increases his or her positive actions and suddenly becomes the "perfect" student. While there is certainly nothing wrong with good behavior, a significant change can indicate the child is experiencing distress. A child who feels responsible for a traumatic event may use magical thinking and believe that if he or she is good enough, the situation will heal itself. It is important at these times to engage the child in discussion about feelings and assist him or her in connecting new behavior to the precipitating event.

Developing and practicing a disaster response plan prior to a critical event can help in the recovery process and promote appropriate interventions. In large-scale critical events, the entire school system should be involved. Schools are often seen as centers of communities, and as such community members often look to them for guidance and support during times of crisis. In addition, working in a school setting can avoid the stigmatization that is often associated with mental health centers (Pynoos & Nader, 1989). A disaster response plan also allows the school community to prepare itself prior to the event. The school community can strategize and rehearse different courses of action, educate itself about the normal responses to traumatic events, and prepare for the unexpected, fostering a greater sense of control and preparedness.

Since school staff may be experiencing stress reactions, their needs must be met in order for them to have the emotional resources to assist with the children's needs. It may be useful to have group meetings to process the traumatic event and plan how to handle the children's return to school.

Children and adolescents may also benefit from group discussions about the event. Therapeutic groups should allow children not only to share their feelings surrounding the event, but also to share ways of coping with the situation. This can promote a sense of control and mastery. While discussion is useful, it may be detrimental to have those most seriously impacted in the same group as children who may have only heard about the events. It is also important to keep rumor and event distortion to a minimum and address them as they develop.

It is critical to listen to those impacted by the event with an open mind. For example, after a tornado had devastated an entire community, a group of children discussed the event, and one child talked about waking up to find dead bodies on the family farm. This seemed very unlikely, so the child's teacher took steps to reassure the rest of the children that this was not the case. Unfortunately, the teacher was mistaken; a graveyard had been disturbed and the child's tale was accurate.

These group discussions should be conducted in conjunction with a trauma mental health specialist. Some schools have disaster or critical incident response teams that can assist with this process; others can consult with disaster mental health specialists for guidance.

All interventions should be sensitive to different cultural expectations and reactions (Parson, 1996). A child who avoids eye contact may not be withdrawn but rather showing appropriate respect as dictated by his or her culture. Some cultures may not support talking about the event, and consequently the use of other expressive modalities must be considered. Emotional protection is intricately tied to the child's culture and values learned from his or her family (Parson, 1996). Consequently, it is helpful to have a detailed understanding of the different cultural groups before a critical event occurs so that appropriate resources can be developed and easily accessed in times of need.

SUMMARY

Children of all ages need time to overcome the fear and confusion generated by traumatic events. Like most adults, they are only able to process a small piece of the experience at any one time. By examining each piece slowly, they are able to avoid becoming overwhelmed by their worries and emotions. Caregivers can assist by helping children remember that they are valued, needed, and loved. It is important for family and friends to be aware that recovery from traumatic events can be a slow and painful process. It is also true that while humankind is amazingly resilient, the process of recovery is not a straightforward, linear event. Since traumatic reminders can trigger a reawakening of painful memories and feelings, those involved in assisting children or adults with recovery must be alert to all signs and symptoms of distress. It is important for children and adults to know that an indirect road to recovery is part of the process and is not due to a personal flaw, nor is it an indication that they are not healing from the traumatic event. If it is not understood as a normal part of recovery, children and adults may feel as if they are starting over in their healing process and this can be extremely discouraging.

Healing from a traumatic event and working through the myriad of feelings and emotions can be a difficult process. As individuals involved in a child's life, we have the desire is to protect, yet we often feel helpless in the face of all the obstacles. Caregivers can feel overwhelmed with their own experiences and feel as if they have nothing left for the child. It is important to remember that this is not the case! In times of uncertainty, children need to feel loved and cared for, and just being with them can be helpful.

Ideally, we should be able to keep children safe from traumatic events, but this is not always possible. This chapter was written to assist all individuals involved in children's lives to help them move past the traumatic event and be able to lead happy and productive lives with the strength and support to overcome past and future challenges.

REFERENCES

Adams, P. R., & Adams, G. R. (1984). Mount Saint Helens's ashfall: Evidence for a disaster stress reaction. *American Psychologist, 39,* 252–260.

American Psychiatric Association (1994). *Diagnostic and statistical manual of mental disorders* (4th ed.). Washington, DC: Author.

Berren, M. R., Beigel, A., & Ghertner, S. (1980). A typology for the classification of disasters. *Community Mental Health Journal, 16,* 103–111.

Berren, M. R., Santiago, J., Beigel, A., & Timmons, S. (1989). A classification scheme for disasters. In R. Gist & B. Lubin (Eds.), *Psychosocial aspects of disaster* (pp. 40–58). New York: John Wiley & Sons.

Bowlby, J. (1980). The place of loss and mourning in psychopathology. In *Attachment & loss: Loss, sadness and depression.* New York: Basic Books.

Galante, R., & Foa, D. (1986). An epidemiological study of psychic trauma and treatment effectiveness for children after a natural disaster. *Journal of the American Academy of Child Psychiatry, 25,* 357–363.

Garmezy, N. (1986). Children under severe stress: Critique and commentary. *Journal of the American Academy of Child Psychiatry, 25,* 384–392.

Gist, R., & Lubin, B. (Eds.). (1999). *Response to disaster: Psychosocial, community, and ecological approaches.* Philadelphia: Brunner/Mazel.

Gordon, N. S., Farberow, N. L., & Maida, C. A. (1999). *Children & disasters.* Philadelphia: Brunner/Mazel.

Hamblen, J. (2002, February 22). *What are the traumatic stress effects of terrorism?* Retrieved March 12, 2002, from http://ncptsd.org/facts/disasters/fs_terrorism.html.

Herman, J. L. (1992). *Trauma and recovery.* New York: Basic Books.

Janoff-Bulman, R., & Frieze, I. H. (1983). A theoretical perspective for understanding reactions to victimization. *Journal of Social Issues, 39,* 1–17.

McCann, I. L., & Pearlman, L. A. (1990). *Psychological trauma and the adult survivor: Theory, therapy and transformation* (1st ed., Vol. 21). New York: Brunner/Mazel.

Mitchell, J. T., & Everly, G. S. J. (1997). *Critical incident stress debriefing: An operations manual for the prevention of traumatic stress among emergency services and disaster workers* (2nd rev. ed.). Ellicott City, MD: Chevron.

Monahon, C. (1993). *Children and trauma: A guide for parents and professionals.* San Francisco: Jossey-Bass.

Murphy, S. A. (1986). Status of natural disaster victims' health and recovery 1 and 3 years later. *Research in Nursing and Health, 9,* 331–340.

Newman, J. C. (1976). Children of disaster: Clinical observations at Buffalo Creek. *The American Journal of Psychiatry, 133,* 306–312.

Norris, F. H. (2001, October 10). *Disasters and domestic violence.* Retrieved February 2, 2002, from http://www.ncptsd.org/facts/disasters/fs_domestic.html.

Parson, E. R. (1996). "It takes a village to heal a child": Necessary spectrum of expertise and benevolence by therapists, non-governmental organizations, and the United Nations in managing war-zone stress in children traumatized by political violence. *Journal of Contemporary Psychotherapy, 26,* 251–286.

Pynoos, R. S., Frederick, C., Nader, K., Arroyo, W., Steinberg, A., Eth, S., et al. (1987). Life threat and posttraumatic stress in school-age children. *Archives of General Psychiatry, 44,* 1057–1063.

Pynoos, R. S., Goenjian, A. K., & Steinberg, A. M. (1998). A public mental health approach to the postdisaster treatment of children and adolescents. *Child and Adolescent Psychiatric Clinics of North America, 7,* 195–210.

Pynoos, R. S., & Nader, K. (1988). Psychological first aid in treatment approach to children exposed to community violence: Research implications. *Journal of Traumatic Stress, 1,* 445–473.

Pynoos, R. S., & Nader, K. (1989). Prevention of psychiatric morbidity in children after disaster. In D. Shaffer, I. Philips, & N. Enzer (Eds.), *Prevention of mental disorders, alcohol, and other drug use in children and adolescents* OSAP Prevention Monograph-2, pp. 225–271. Rockville, MD: U.S. Department of Health and Human Services.

Pynoos, R. S., Steinberg, A. M., & Wraith, R. (1995). A developmental model of childhood traumatic stress. In D. Cicchetti & D. Cohen (Eds.), *Developmental psychopathology: Risk, disorder, and adaptation* (Vol. 2, pp. 72–95). New York: John Wiley & Sons.

Raphael, B. (1986). *When disaster strikes: How individuals and communities cope with catastrophe.* New York: Basic Books.

Seligman, M. (1975). *Helplessness: On depression, development and death.* San Francisco: Freeman.

Slaikeu, K. A. (1990). *Crisis intervention: A handbook for practice and research* (2nd ed.). Boston: Allyn and Bacon.

Sugar, M. (1989). Children in a disaster: An overview. *Child Psychiatry and Human Development, 19,* 163–179.

Terr, L. C. (1979). Children of Chowchilla: A study of psychic trauma. *The Psychoanalytic Study of the Child, 34,* 547–623.

Terr, L. C. (1981). "Forbidden Games": Post-traumatic children's play. *American Academy of Child Psychiatry, 20,* 741–760.

Terr, L. C. (1983). Chowchilla revisited: The effects of psychic trauma four years after a school-bus kidnapping. *The American Journal of Psychiatry, 140,* 1543–1550.

Terr, L. C. (1985). Children traumatized in small groups. In S. Eth & R. S. Pynoos (Eds.), *Post-Traumatic Stress Disorder in Children* (pp. 47–70). Washington: American Psychiatric Press.

Terr, L. C. (1991). Childhood traumas: An outline and overview. *American Journal of Psychiatry, 148*, 10–20.

Varkas, T. (1998). Childhood trauma and posttraumatic play: A literature review and case study. *Journal of Analytic Social Work, 5*, 29–51.

Wasserstein, S. B., & La Greca, A. (1998). Hurricane Andrew: Parent conflict as a moderator of children's adjustment. *Hispanic Journal of Behavioral Sciences, 20*, 212–225.

NOTES

1.   Throughout this chapter, the terms "traumatic event" and "critical event" will be used interchangeably.

2.   While these three conditions are commonly accepted as aspects of the traumatic event–trauma response complex, this grouping of conditions is not a standard in the field of disaster or trauma psychology. This grouping may also not be unique to this author, yet an extensive search of the literature, Internet material, and personal communication with experts in the field of psychology, could not determine where this grouping was originally developed.

4

The Terror of Torture: A Continuum of Evil

J. E. (Hans) Hovens and Boris Drozdek

INTRODUCTION

It may be in the genes of humans that hate and pain are more prominent in our history than love. It may also be understandable in the struggle for life that it is more likely to conquer one's perceived opponent than trying to cooperate. In any event, since humans first roamed the world they have inflicted pain on each other, and only sociological and cultural refinements over hundreds of years have led to a lessening of harsh methods and the adoption of sublimated acts, such as the games of football and soccer.

Instruments and techniques for torture have been described since ancient times. In Chinese history, wooden instruments were used to restrict prisoners. Ropes, twigs, and sticks were frequently employed. The most important physical punishment was carving prisoners in the face or body with a knife and putting ink in the wounds. Cutting off a nose, a foot, or the penis was not uncommon. Other methods included breaking ribs, suspension by the hair or the back, starvation, sleep deprivation, being forced to sit on a bed of nails, nailing the fingers, and filling the nose with water. Capital punishments included Hai, in which the victim was pulped into a sort of human jam; Fu, slicing the victim into small pieces of meat; Heng, boiling or frying the prisoner; and Huan, tying the prisoner to five horses that were forced to run in different directions (Li & Hu, 1994).

Kerrigan (2001) distinguishes a number of broad categories in torture techniques. He cites locking prisoners up in (extremely small) cells; chaining them in different ways; methods of stretching, such as the rack; suspensions; applying pressure, such as thumb screws; burning or boiling; torture with water, such as being forced to drink or being drowned; using animals, such as allowing bees to sting to death victims who are smeared with honey; beatings; and cutting and piercing. All these techniques have been applied in one way or another for centuries. Except for the use of electrical currents, which were introduced in the nineteenth century, and the use of psychotropic drugs, introduced in the twentieth century, basic torture techniques have not changed over the centuries. In other words, just about everything that could be imagined has been used to inflict pain on other human beings in the course of human existence.

Historically, torture comes in three variations. The first one is deliberately inflicted pain as punishment for a crime. The biblical proverb "an eye for an eye and a tooth for a tooth" seems to apply here. This holds that evil should be punished by a way that is congruent with the harm done. In recent years, we have seen that cutting off hands for theft is frequently used in countries that have *shari'a*-based law. The death penalty, as a capital punishment, is still not abolished in eighty-six countries, and, in 2000, at least 1,457 prisoners were executed in twenty-seven countries (Amnesty International, 2001). Eighty-five prisoners were executed in the United States in 2000, and 17 in the state of Texas alone in the year 2001 (Texas Department of Criminal Justice, 2002).

Farrington (1996) gives us a detailed historical overview of punishment and torture through the ages. In the Middle Ages, a thief could lose his[1] hand; a poacher risked losing his legs if he trespassed on another person's land. Failing to attend church in the times of King Henry VIII could cost one's ears. At the same court, an act was passed that one who committed poisoning would be boiled alive. The ingenuity of finding parallels in punishment to crimes is stunning. Not only was pain pursued, but disgrace and shame were also the fate of the criminal; the crime would be made visible to the community. For example, prostitutes had their noses slit into the eighteenth century (Kerrigan, 2001).

Although we consider these punishments nowadays as unnecessary cruel, it should also be realized that executions were a kind of theater for the public. Well known are the crowds at the guillotine who watched the executions during the French Revolution. Farrington (1996) writes: "[T]he spectacle of death summoned eager audiences, which numbered well into the thousands. People flocked to watch a poor fellow or wretched woman writhe in agony at the end of a rope . . . Execution days were a public holiday. Mothers took their children to teach them a lesson for life . . . Hawkers joined the throng to sell their wares, including food and drink for the spectators." Elias (1978/1969), in his work on the development of society, remarks that when public executions were abandoned, crowds liked to watch a substitute for life executions, such as the public burning to death of cats.

In the course of time, punishment for crimes in Western societies has evolved to more humane sentences, which are predicated on the idea that punishment should primarily be intended to prevent a repetition of crime instead of be revenge for it. Nevertheless, it is well known that guards or police officers frequently misuse their power and abuse prisoners in horrifying ways. For example, one patient mentioned that she was detained on false grounds in one of the former Soviet republics and that the arresting officers incited one of the other prisoners, a man with a known venereal disease, to rape this patient while they watched. The experience was extremely traumatic for the patient, but was not torture in a formal sense; it was severe abuse of power.

The second variation on torture is using torture techniques to extract the "truth" or a "confession" from a subject. Kerrigan (2001) remarks that torture was used to test the purity of truth just as a touchstone could be used as a test for the purity of gold. Although today we believe that someone who is tortured is willing to agree on anything, the Greeks and Romans thought that truth was something impersonal, which was locked up in the body and would come out under severe pain. Our philosophy about truth may have changed to a more individualistic perspective instead of perceiving it to be something with a value of its own, but this does not mean that the application of extreme pain reveals no truth.

Perhaps there is truly sense in persecutors applying torture. Torture in this sense is not something that is done easily. In 1486, Jacobus Sprenger and Heinrich Kramer (1968) published *Malleus Maleficarum* (*The Hammer of Witchcraft*), the textbook on the medieval procedure of inquisition to be followed to obtain confessions in witchcraft cases. In the *Malleus Maleficarum,* it is pointed out what the judge should look for in the torture chamber and how the torture should proceed: "If, after keeping the accused in a state of suspense, and continually postponing the day of examination, and frequently using verbal persuasions, the judge should truly believe that the accused is denying the truth, let them question her lightly without shedding blood." If this does not work, the torture becomes more painful. If the witch confesses under torture, "she should then be taken to another place and questioned anew, so that she does not confess only under the stress of torture." If she then refuses to confess the truth, new torture instruments are brought to her and, if necessary, the torture is continued. One notices the remarkable reference to the judge's strongly believing the guilt of the accused.

Similar advice is given in the interrogator's manual on torture from the Tuol Sleng extermination center in Cambodia (see Peters, 1996): "[T]he purpose of torture is to get their responses. It is not something we do for fun. We must hurt them so that they respond quickly. . . . It is not something that is done out of individual anger or for self-satisfaction. So we beat them to make them afraid, but absolutely not to kill them." Torture is not seen as an end unto itself but as a supplementary measure. But here, there is no room for doubt: The accused is guilty and should confess as soon as possible.

Finally, the third variation of torture was its application to prevent unrest or put down uprisings. If opposition leaders are brought to death in horrific ways, resistance will be subdued. The Assyrians (2500 B.C.) knew this. If there was unrest in a conquered country, they flayed their leaders or pegged them out in the sun to dry on the city walls (Kerrigan, 2001). The current president of Iraq, Saddam Hussein, uses similar techniques to prevent uprisings in his country: someone who is willing to kill his own sons-in-law for treason and leave his daughters widows will do anything to anyone to retain power. An Iraqi torture survivor, whose fingernails were extracted during the process of torture, told us that the most severe torture method to which he was submitted was the secret service showing him a movie of his family while they were shopping, while they told him that filming the family was not difficult, nor would it be difficult to run them over with a car.

DEFINITIONS OF TORTURE IN THE TWENTIETH CENTURY

The practice of state-organized violence, including torture, constitutes a worldwide epidemic (Basoglu, 1993). Torture is practiced with the knowledge of governments in 70 of the world's 183 countries (Genefke, 1993, 1994), and only 104 countries in the world have ratified the United Nations Convention against Torture (International Rehabilitation Council for Torture Victims, 1998). With respect to the refugee population worldwide, between 5 percent and 35 percent, or 1.6 million to 5 million people, have been tortured (Baker, 1992). The fight to make torture a visible phenomenon is largely a fight for democracy (Genefke, 1993).

The first declaration in which torture is mentioned and discussed is the 1948 United Nations Universal Declaration of Human Rights (see United Nations, 1996). In Article 5, it states, "No one shall be subjected to torture or cruel, inhuman or degrading treatment, or punishment." This declaration was adopted in the aftermath of World War II. The desire that the world after the war should be different, without disregard and contempt for human rights, was reflected in the declaration. The hope was to create a world in which people could enjoy freedom of speech, religion, and belief; a world without fear, distress, and suffering (Rasmussen, 1990). The declaration, however, offered no guidance on what was to be understood by the term *torture*. Its definitions were to some extent elastic, and interpretation changed with time (Rodley, 1987).

The simplest—and broad—definition of torture was adopted later by Amnesty International (1973): "Torture is the systematic and deliberate infliction of acute pain by one person on another, or on a third person, in order to accomplish the purpose of the former against the will of the latter."

Later, the World Medical Association, in its Tokyo Declaration in 1975, adopted a similar definition: "Torture is defined as the deliberate, systematic or wanton infliction of physical or mental suffering by one or more persons acting alone or on the orders of any authority, to force another person to yield information, to make a confession, or for any other reason" (see Amnesty International, 1994). This declaration serves as a guideline for the medical profession concerning torture and other cruel, inhuman, or degrading treatment or punishment in relation to detention and imprisonment. It also clearly defined the ethical position of physicians facing the issue of torture. "A physician cannot participate, lend advice or support to any activity that may cause torture or cruel or inhuman treatment and punishment to any person, or be in the premises or institution where it may be conducted or threatened" (Amnesty International, 1994).

The World Medical Association definition differed from the United Nations Declaration mainly in that there were no exclusions, and there was no attempt to clarify cruel, inhuman, or degrading treatment. The United Nations Declaration stated that torture does not include pain or suffering arising from, inherent in, or accidental to lawful sanctions to the extent consistent with the Standard Minimum Rules for the Treatment of Prisoners, and that torture constitutes an aggravated and deliberate form of cruel, inhuman, or degrading treatment or punishment (see United Nations, 1996).

Discussing this topic in his monograph on medical aspects of torture, Rasmussen (1990) states that it is not possible to include the suffering of a torture victim in a definition of torture. However, it is important to realize that a torture victim is a defenseless person, on whom one or more persons, who have power, inflict physical or psychological damage (Wagner & Rasmussen, 1983). Also, a definition of torture leaves open the question of the treatment no longer consisting of torture, but of cruel, inhuman, or degrading treatment. Grey areas exist that need an investigation on a case-by-case basis in order to develop a common understanding of what constitutes cruel, inhuman, or degrading treatment. The United Nations Standard Minimum Rules for the Treatment of Prisoners serve as important international guidelines. In order to concentrate the different efforts in the fight against torture, a rather strict definition is essential, suggests Rasmussen (1990).

No definitions of torture or cruel, inhuman, or degrading treatment or punishment were included in 1950 in the European Convention on the Protection of Detainees from torture and from cruel, inhuman, or degrading treatment or punishment (see Rasmussen, 1990). The Commission of Human Rights had, however, examined several cases of alleged torture and declared whether torture or maltreatment that was contrary to the declaration had been inflicted. The best-known cases were examinations of torture allegations in Greece in 1968 and in Northern Ireland in 1976 (Amnesty International, 1984; Rodley, 1987). The Northern Ireland case illustrated the difficulties in distinguishing between torture on the one hand and inhuman and degrading treatment on the other. The European Human Rights Commission found that the interrogation techniques used (hooding, wall-standing, subjection to continuous noise, and deprivation of sleep, food, and drink) could be classified as torture, while the European Court of Human Rights judged that cruel, inhuman, and degrading treatment had been committed, and thus reversed the ruling by the commission. The court decided that the interrogation process described was a maltreatment, but not torture. Amnesty International used maltreatment instead of torture in the report of an international mission to Northern Ireland in 1977 (Mikaelsen & Pedersen, 1979).

In 1984, the United Nations, in the Convention against Torture and Other Cruel, Inhuman, or Degrading Treatment or Punishment, adopted in Article 1 the following definition:

> For the purpose of this Convention, the term "torture" means any act by which severe pain or suffering, whether physical or mental, is intentionally inflicted on a person for such purpose as obtaining from him or a third person information or a confession, punishing him for an act he or a third person has committed, or is suspected of having com-

mitted, or intimidating or coercing him or a third person, or for any reason based on discrimination of any kind, when such pain or suffering is inflicted by, or at the instigation of, or with the consent or acquiescence of a public official or other person acting in an official capacity. It does not include pain or suffering arising only from, inherent in, or accidental to lawful sanctions. (United Nations, 1996)

This legal definition applied only to nations and restricted the definition to government-sanctioned torture. It did not include cases of torture such as mutilation or whipping, practiced in some countries as a lawful punishment, nor did it include torture practiced by different gangs or hate groups. According to Mossallanejad (2000), this definition

does not address state and religiously sanctioned forms of torture, which are prevalent in many parts of the world. In Iran, Saudi Arabia, Sudan, Bangladesh, and some other countries, the law permits flogging people who drink alcohol or do not observe the dress code of the government. Men and women, especially women, are stoned to death for the crime of adultery. Governments turn ordinary people into torturers by inciting them to throw stones at the victims. They are told to bury men up to their bellies and women up to their breasts and start throwing stones; they are instructed to choose stones that are neither too small nor too large, in order to prolong the victims' agony. This type of torture is a part of the criminal code of some fundamentalist countries. Another religiously sanctioned form of torture is the act of suttee: the burning alive of a widow on a funeral pyre alongside the dead body of her husband. With the rise of Hindu fundamentalism in India, there have been reports of the revival of suttee. Although this extreme form of torture can be a voluntary sacrifice on the part of the widow, most of the time women are forced by the community or priests and/or tricked into believing they will not feel pain. There is no prosecution against people who are involved in this monstrous act, and who reap super-profits out of the ashes of these women. What is worse is the total silence of the international community.

Another serious gap in the Article 1 definition of torture, according to Mossallanejad (2000), was the invisibility of women, who are not only tortured the same way men are, but also subjected to gender-related forms of torture such as female genital mutilation, dowry murder, rape, domestic violence, or childhood marriage.

The United Nations Convention reintroduced the concept of grades, when making a distinction between torture as severe pain or suffering, and cruel, inhuman, or degrading treatment (also called maltreatment). In an epidemiological study or in an advocacy report, this difference is of utmost importance. At the same time, it is almost impossible to define it from a subjective or an objective point of view (Gurr & Quiroga, 2001). "However, given that cruel and inhuman treatment is also contrary to international law, attempting to set clear borders between the two is probably a futile and potentially misleading task," suggest Welsh and Rayner (1997).

Some other aspects were not included in the United Nations definition. While the definition stated that the aim of torture is always to make victims confess and to obtain information, it forgot its other aims of breaking down the identity and the personality of the victim (Elsass, 1997), taking revenge, and creating anxiety and spreading terror in the community (International Rehabilitation Council for Torture Victims, 1998). A formerly strong person, after being broken through physical and psychological torture, will be sent back into community, in order to serve as an example of what will occur if one has other political ideas, ethnicity, etc. The purpose of torture is to silence the torture victims and those who think alike (International Rehabilitation Council for Torture Victims, 1998).

Throughout the years, a number of other declarations considering torture have been published. The Vienna Declaration and Programme of Action of 1993 (see United Nations, 1996) pointed out such issues as provision of assistance to victims of torture, eradication of torture, and prosecution of those responsible for torture. Several developing countries reacted to this declaration by claiming that the real problem was one of development. As a means to end torture, they preferred development aid to equalize economic differences over humanitarian aid. The Western world's focus on torture in developing countries has been called an act of indulgence in order to obscure the fundamental problem of economic inequality between rich and poor countries (Elsass, 1997). In 1998, the United Nations chose June 26 to commemorate the International Day in Support of Victims of Torture worldwide.

The World Health Organization working group in 1986 introduced the concept of "organized violence"; it was defined as:

> The inter-human infliction of significant, avoidable pain and suffering by an organized group according to a declared or implied strategy and/or system of ideas and attitudes. It comprises any violent action that is unacceptable by general human standards, and relates to the victims' feelings. Organized violence includes "torture, cruel, inhuman or degrading treatment or punishment" as in Article 5 of the United Nations Universal Declaration of Human Rights (1948). Imprisonment without trial, mock executions, hostage-taking, or any other form of violent deprivation of liberty also falls under the heading of organized violence. (van Geuns, 1987)

This broader definition included other victims of violence, in addition to survivors of torture. The definition included government repression and terrorist group violence. Torture is a tool of political and social control. It is also used to immobilize political or social activists by intimidation or the infliction of serious psychological damage or, more widely, to induce in a population a sense of terror (Welsh & Rayner, 1997). Torture is an instrument of power and is used in different contexts. Dictatorships and authoritarian regimes use it as a way of creating general anxiety in society and suppressing the opposition. In this context, torture encourages the development of what Barudy (1989) calls a "repressive ecology": a state of generalized insecurity, terror, lack of confidence, and rupture of social relations.

In new democracies, torture is a remnant of authoritarian regimes and is a means of individual abuse of power used by military or law enforcement personnel. In armed conflicts, torture of enemies, both soldiers and civilians, is used as a strategic means to expand power and territory, and to suppress opposition and national minority groups (International Rehabilitation Council for Torture Victims, 1998).

CHARACTERISTICS OF TORTURE

"Torture is among the most gruesome of human manifestations, particularly because it does not have its origin in animals, primitive man, or pre-culture. On the contrary, it is planned and it stems from social order. It is a display of force, the aim of which is to break an individual's judgment. Consequently, it breaks down parts of the victim's personality. The greatest challenge to the torture survivor is therefore to remain a human being under these inhumane conditions" (Elsass, 1997).

In their recent study covering the effects, cost-effectiveness, sustainability of, and participation in torture rehabilitation, Gurr and Quiroga (2001) described the unique characteristics of torture:

- Torture is a perverted form of human interaction that involves at least two persons, the torturer and the victim. The interaction is characterized by extreme degradation, humiliation, and dehumanization. Torture's third partner, as Elsass (1997) points out, is the witness.
- The torturer inflicts severe pain or psychological suffering on the victim.
- The torturer–victim relationship is one of the most intimate that can arise between strangers (Simpson, 1993). This relationship is also asymmetric (Doerr-Zegers, Hartman, Lira, & Weinstein, 1992), meaning that the torturer has physical control over the victim, who is defenseless (handcuffed, blindfolded, and/or physically and mentally debilitated). This situation creates a relationship of extreme dependency and helplessness that permits the psychological manipulation of the victim.
- The relationship is characterized by its anonymity (Doerr-Zegers et al., 1992). The torturer and the victim do not know each other. The name of the torturer is a fictitious one. Because the head of the victim or torturer head is covered, each cannot identify the other or

establish eye contact. This planned depersonalized relationship could explain in part the violence of the interaction.

- The victim is trapped in a double-bind situation (Lira, Baker, & Castillo, 1990). He has been deprived of all rights as a human being and is forced to choose between two equally impossible options. He has to cooperate with the torturer, by giving confidential information and the names of comrades, or he has to suffer more pain and possible death.

Torture is often targeted at leaders of opposition groups or political parties fighting for democracy, but other groups such as union leaders, journalists, and human rights, student, or ethnic minority leaders can become victims as well. Besides that, torture can occur in a nonpolitical context, and ethnic minorities, asylum seekers, drug users, criminal suspects, marginalized groups, or victims in war zones can be afflicted, too.

OBJECTIVES AND GOALS OF TORTURE

Torture has its defined goals and purposes. Authoritarian governments use torture as a political tool to suppress dissidents. In that context, torture is planned and implemented by state officers as a form of political ritual that belongs to the ceremonies through which power is manifested (Foucault, 1979). It is a ritual to produce the truth, the truth in the absence of the accused; that is to say, to produce a confession from an individual subjected to torture about his comrades (or companions) (Gurr & Quiroga, 2001). Other goals of torture are to destroy psychological defenses and the personality of the victim, and to create an atmosphere of fear and terror in the community. Sometimes the latter goal is also the only one.

From psychotherapeutic work with victims of torture, we have learned that another important goal of torture is to break down the victim's humanity and sense of what is right and wrong (Elsass, 1997). Being subjected to torture, a victim may become so weak that he will confess and inform against his close family or friends.

According to Gurr and Quiroga (2001) torture has been used:

- At the level of individuals, as punishment, with the intention to dehumanize the victim, through a systematic method of infliction of severe pain and psychological suffering, and without killing the victim. Its intent is to destroy his dignity by humiliating him through the most macabre forms of harm. Besides the severe pain or suffering inflicted upon the person, the issue is also the prolonged psychological tension that victims experience between resisting and the possibility of betraying their country, community, family, and friends. The scars, especially the psychological ones, last a lifetime. (Mossallanejad, 2000)

- To destroy the victim's identity by forcing him to give confidential information and names, becoming a traitor to his ideology and comrades. At the same time some authors (see, e.g., Mossallanejad, 2000) find that obtaining information, as a goal of torture, is an illusion. Torture may lead to more defiance and intransigence on the part of the victim, who comes to view his suffering as a virtue.

- To obtain a false confession to convict the victim of an unlawful criminal act. The confession is the result of breaking the prisoner's will and is an expression of submission.

- In some extreme cases, to transform the victim into a collaborator, which is the maximum expression of identification of the victim with the aggressor. Sometimes, in the context of torture, a victim breaks down and confesses not only what he knows, but also what he does not know. The victim will give everything because he wants the torture to stop. This attempt to give what one does not have is the same structural situation that characterizes the insistent, one-sided demand for love.

- At a social level, as a method to intimidate dissident groups, with the objective of preventing the population from expressing opposition toward government policies. The intent is to create fear with a subliminal message: Political action carries risk of torture and possible death.

Confessions of torture victims confront those who are willing to listen to them with the evil of aggression and violence that is part of the common human potential. Witnesses of these confessions feel their own core beliefs or basic assumptions (Janoff-Bulman, 1983; McCann & Pearlman, 1990) are being attacked and realize that the world is not a good place to be in, that the world is not always just, and that one cannot always have a sense of mastery over one's life. Because of this, one does not always want to listen to the stories of torture survivors and be aware of the existence of torture. One uses different words and terminology in order to neutralize the impact of violence; hence talk of "ethnic cleansing" and not of massacres and killings. This leads to the formation of a "conspiracy of silence," as Danieli (1980) named the phenomenon in relation to the Holocaust. Everybody knows that torture exists, but we do not talk about it and we continue to act as if torture is a very exclusive and rare phenomenon.

TORTURE METHODS

Torture is a technique, and not an extreme expression of rage. It must produce a certain degree of pain in certain parts of the body or the psyche, which may be measured exactly. It is not applied indiscriminately but calculated according to detailed rules and protocols. The number of lashes of the whip, the position of the body hanging from the wrist with the tip of the toes touching the floor, the number and parts of the body where electrical shocks are applied, etc. The purpose is to carry pain almost to the infinite without killing the victim (Gurr & Quiroga, 2001). In order to achieve this, different professionals, including medical personnel, assist torturers. Torture is often unpredictable, and victims do not have signals regarding either when they will be tortured or when they will be submitted to violence within a given torture session (Basoglu & Mineka, 1992).

Rasmussen (1990) published the most detailed paper we have on the medical aspects of torture. This paper also includes the methods used. The most recent classifications of torture methods are those from Mossallanejad (2000) and Gurr & Quiroga (2001). They make a distinction between physical and psychological methods of torture, as follows.

The physical methods of torture are numerous and varied. The most frequent methods are beating and mutilation, such as the breaking of bones, extraction of nails and teeth, or amputation of body parts. Electric torture is applied to sensitive organs such as the genitals and rectum. Whipping happens on the soles, hands, and back with instruments such as cables, batons, whips, and sticks. Submersion, suffocation, and suspensions, like attaching both hands to a bar, or one leg, or handcuffing both hands together at the back by force, are also frequently used. Burning, while the victim is naked and tied with his hands and legs to the bars of a steel bed frame, is one of the most dangerous forms of torture and has resulted in the death of many victims. In this case, torturers push the victim's abdomen in a way that his buttocks touch an open flame set beneath the bed. The burning continues for two to three seconds. Other methods are damaging internal organs, such as by forcing the victim to urinate on open electricity wires of a boiler, which leads to a damaging of the urethra without visible scars, and sexual assault.

Psychological methods include such techniques as induced exhaustion and debility through food, water, and sleep deprivation; isolation, such as in being blindfolded in solitary confinement; monopolization of perception by restriction of movement during detention or manipulation of the environment by putting victims in darkness, having them face bright lights, or having them listen to crying sounds; and threats of death, which sometimes are extended to their family. Occasionally victims experience sham executions, i.e., the victims are blindfolded and taken to the execution site, all pre-execution formalities are carried out, but the shots are aimed into the air. Other methods include kidnapping and execution of members of the victim's family; leaving the victim in a state of limbo, i.e., putting the victim into a state of readiness for torture and prolonging the waiting time; forced ingestion of noxious substances; and witnessing the torture of another prisoner or of family members, which is among the most traumatic experiences.

Torturers normally use a combination of physical and psychological techniques against their victims.

The experts from Research Centre for Torture Victims (Vesti, Somnier, & Kastrup, 1992) make a distinction between the weakening—i.e., teaching the victim to be helpless, inducing exhaustion, and creating intense fear—and the personality-destroying techniques, such as inducing anxiety, guilt, shame, repentance, and loss of self-esteem. They have also put the torture techniques into five categories:

- Deprivation techniques, such as mental deprivation—including social, sensory, and perceptual deprivation—and deprivation of fundamental bodily needs, as for sleep, food, hygiene, or health services.

- Coercion techniques, such as impossible choices and incongruent actions, humiliations, threats, and blind obedience to rules, using force to experiment with stimuli and situations that are uncommon and may be harmful to the victim's personality, such as eating feces, urinating upon others, or glorifying the authorities.

- Communication techniques, such as counter-effect and double-binding techniques; use of disinformation; distortion of perception; or conditioning of new reflexes.

- Techniques that abuse pharmacology and psychiatric institutions; victims are defined as "mentally ill" and submitted to psychiatric treatment in a hospital. Hallucinogenic or drugs with pain-inducing compounds are used.

- Sexual torture techniques, such as direct instrumental violence to the sexual organs, sexual violence using animals, or sexual acts performed by other human beings.

Agger (1989) wrote:

> Sexual torture seems to be very traumatic, as it is characterized by a confusing and complex ambiguity containing both libidinal and aggressive components, against which the victim has difficulty maintaining a psychological defense. The victim's and the torturer's sexual structure is involved in the psychodynamics of this interaction, and the victim experiences the torture as directed against his sexual body-image and identity with the aim to destroy it.

Rape as a form of sexual torture "may have manifold effects: such abuses may pose a mortal threat to the victim; erode the survivor's self-concept and feelings of integrity; disrupt marital functioning as a consequence of injury, stigma, and unwanted pregnancy; and, as an instrument of 'ethnic cleansing,' constitute a massive threat to the identity, culture, and religious fabric of the whole community" (Silove, 1999).

Women are at higher risk of sexual torture and subsequent sexual difficulties (Allodi & Stiasny, 1990; Lunde & Ortmann, 1990). While sexual torture of women takes advantage of shame and guilt in connection with sexuality, and cultural norms about the "right" kind of femininity, the torture of men provokes active sexuality; activates castration anxiety, homosexual anxiety, and identity feeling; and makes use of the fear of not being a "real' man (Agger, 1989).

The prevalence of sexual torture among torture victims seems to be very high. Obtaining information about this from victims is especially difficult due to the culturally imposed stigma and social consequences of being a sexual torture victim. The prevalence of sexual torture varies from 80 percent to 94 percent in women and from 56 percent to 66 percent in men (Lunde & Ortmann, 1990; Meana, Morentin, Idoyaga, & Callado, 1995).

Although many torture methods are universal and are used in most parts of the world, some techniques are very specific to certain countries, such as the use of electric shocks and hanging in the Middle East, abuse of psychiatric services and medication in Russia (Bloch & Reddaway, 1985), falanga (severe beating on the soles of the feet) in Greece, or whipping in the Middle East and Africa.

When listening to torture victims, one realizes that classifications of torture techniques are arbitrary and of academic importance. For the survivors it is sometimes very difficult to delineate what the aim of a certain method was and where the damage took place—in their bodies or in their souls (Valdes, 1975). However, it seems that psychological methods of torture are the most difficult to survive. As Gilligan (1996) wrote, "The death of the self is of far greater concern than the death of the body."

A STORY OF A TORTURE VICTIM

Warning: The story below has been added to illustrate the terror of torture and to make clear that torture happens all around the world. It is not an uncommon story for psychotherapists who work with refugees and who are willing to listen to them. The reader, however, should be warned that it is horrifying material, and that this section can be skipped without losing the general context of the chapter.

I.S. is a 43-year-old Bosnian Muslim, a civilian, married, and father of three children. He is a farmer. His armed Serbian neighbors caught him in the field while he was farming the land. Insulting him and threatening him with a gun pointed at his temple, they forced him to take off his pants and underwear. They then placed his penis on a log and drew the blunt side of a knife over it, telling him that there will never be any more "Muslim children." At that moment, I.S. urinated and defecated out of fear. A deep scar on his penis is still visible and he has difficulties urinating and getting an erection.

After that, he was taken to a main square in a village where other non-Serbian neighbors were already waiting. The men were separated from the women, and they were told that they would be exchanged for Serbian soldiers and that their wives and children would join them later. On three occasions the prisoners were driven around in trucks for the exchange to take place. Each time, however, they were told that the exchange would not occur because the Muslims had given up on their own people. The fourth time, I.S. was taken to a Serbian detention camp. There he spent four months.

The detention camp was an old factory warehouse. Five hundred men crowded the former production hall. There was not even enough room to find a sleeping place on the concrete floor. During the daytime, detainees were forced to perform different types of labor. In the camp, they spent most of the time in the hall with their heads down and their hands behind their backs. Every day one of the guards would approach a randomly chosen prisoner and order him to collect a certain amount of money from other prisoners within a short period. Since most of the prisoners, including I.S., had been caught by surprise, they had no money with them. When the chosen prisoner had not collected the required amount, he would be slaughtered or shot to death the same evening, often in front of other prisoners. Prisoners only occasionally received very small quantities of food and water. They had to eat a red, hot soup with a few beans in it, or a slice of bread, and had to finish eating within two to three minutes. As none of the prisoners dared to go to the toilet outside the hall, out of fear of being beaten every time they went outside, they all urinated in the same place. I.S. did not use the toilet at all during the first ten days and consumed almost no food and water. At that time, he thought that the whole world had forgotten him and his fellow prisoners. There was no communication with the world outside the camp. At this time, no one in the world seemed to know anything about the detention camps in Bosnia-Herzegovina.

I.S. was forced to witness rape scenes. All prisoners had to take their clothes off. Then the guards would choose two of them, mostly a father and his son, or two brothers, who were threatened with death and forced to commit fellatio and have anal sex with each other. Besides this, one of the chosen prisoners would be forced to bite off the other prisoner's genitals and eat them. At other times, they were forced to pull each other's genitals with a rope until they tore off. All prisoners were forced to witness such scenes, and if they dared to turn their gaze away, they were shot. I.S. did not dare to turn his head when his uncle was slaughtered. Afterward he was forced to carry the body to the dump yard. Up to now, he can still hear the sound of thyroid cartilage being cut. This sound resembles the sound of walking on freshly fallen snow. In the winter, when it snows, I.S. does not go outside because he does not want to remember his uncle's death.

Like all the half-starved and exhausted prisoners, I.S. was later forced to do very hard labor on the estates of the Serbian farmers. The Serbs also exposed him to maltreatment. Passersby and children would hit him with sticks and other blunt objects, or throw stones at him. Each prisoner who refused to do this forced labor was killed.

After a period of three months, teams from the International Red Cross and a U.S. diplomat arrived in the camp. I.S. hoped that the truth about the camps would become public and that the conditions in the camp would improve at least a little. Prisoners were, however, forbidden to complain about the treatment in the camp. In addition, guards dressed like prisoners and mixed with them in order to be able to control the prisoners' statements more easily. Furthermore, the translators who were assisting the official missions were Serbs. In front of them, prisoners were afraid to tell the truth.

After spending five months in the detention camp, I.S. was exchanged for a Serbian soldier. Throughout the whole detention period his only thought had been to survive and to see his family again. After being released, he spent about a month in a United Nations High Commissioner for Refugees reception center in Croatia and was then sent to the Netherlands. After his arrival, he developed symptoms of acute post-traumatic stress disorder. Eight months after his release from the detention camp, he started individual psychotherapy.

He suffered from flashbacks and intense psychological distress at exposure to events that resembled aspects of the traumatic events. He made active efforts to avoid activities that could arouse recollections. He experienced a feeling of detachment, a restricted range of affect, and a sense of foreshortened future. He also suffered from persistent symptoms of increased arousal, including sleeping problems, irritability, concentration difficulties, hypervigilance, and stomach pains. However, he did not suffer from nightmares.

PHYSICAL, PSYCHOLOGICAL, AND SOCIAL SEQUELAE OF TORTURE

Physical Sequelae

Infliction of severe physical suffering is one of the methods torturers use to break their victims. Torturers want to avoid responsibility for the violence, and thus they try to avoid visible body marks and scars that can be a consequence of the torture. This is the reason why, for documenting physical sequelae of torture, special skills and knowledge are needed.

Survivors present a variety of symptoms of different body-systems that have been reviewed in several publications (Allodi et al., 1985; Cathcart, Berger, & Knazan, 1979; Cunningham & Cunningham, 1997; Goldfeld, Mollica, & Pesavento, 1988; Rasmussen, 1990). Most of these papers give only a listing of symptoms and signs but no diagnoses. Some of the symptoms seem to be the result of somatization rather than of physical trauma (Gurr & Quiroga, 2001). This makes the linking of physical symptoms to torture experiences even more difficult.

Physical torture produces a group of acute symptoms and visible signs. The amount of chronic or late sequelae is related to the type and intensity of the method applied.

In his monograph on medical aspects of torture, Rasmussen (1990) describes symptoms and signs of torture immediately after infliction of violence and at the time of a later medical examination. He presents his findings according to the organ.

According to this study, a majority of victims report acute skin lesions immediately after torture, mostly because of being beaten, burned, or submitted to electrical shocks. These acute symptoms usually disappear, except for lesions following burning and electrical shocks.

The cardiopulmonary system can be affected most commonly by blunt trauma of the chest. In these cases chest fractures, hemo- or pneumothorax, acute lung symptoms, and chest pain can be documented. Acute lung infections and tuberculosis can be also present because of bad living conditions in the prison.

Gastrointestinal symptoms are not very specific, and they are usually caused by blunt trauma. Hematemesis, weight loss, alteration in defecation, vomiting, and pain or bleeding of the perineal region are documented.

In the musculoskeletal system, special torture methods leave specific acute marks. These are described for different forms of suspension or falanga. Falanga produces an acute closed-compartment syndrome in the foot. Besides this, fractures following severe beating are reported.

Neurological symptoms are very frequent, but are not specific. The most frequently reported ones are headache, loss of concentration and attention, and memory disturbances. Loss of consciousness related to head trauma or other causes, head injuries, and acute and chronic peripheral nerve symptoms are documented as well. The majority of the peripheral nerve symptoms are related to pressure at the wrists from tight binding ropes or handcuffing.

Mild closed-head injuries can lead to long-term problems, such as post-concussive syndrome (the symptoms have similarities to post-traumatic stress disorder and psychosomatic symptoms), and an increased incidence of mood disorders, obsessive-compulsive disorder, and psychosis (see also Lishman, 1998).

Urological and genital symptoms are usually present at the time of torture, and are difficult to document later. The most common complaints are hematuria and dysuria, caused by direct trauma of the genital and renal region, or by living conditions in the prisons.

Gynecological symptoms can be related to sexual or other torture methods. Pain in the lower abdomen, uterine bleeding (sometimes fear-induced), inflammatory symptoms, and menstruation irregularities are among common documented signs.

Otorhinolaryngological lesions were mainly associated with hearing and were caused by special torture methods like "telefono," i.e., the simultaneous beating of both ears with the palms of the hands. It is suggested that the mechanism is similar to that after blast injuries.

Ophthalmological symptoms are mostly reported at the time of torture, and rarely later. They usually consist of short-term visual disturbances caused by blindfolding.

Long-lasting dental symptoms are due mainly to affection of the gingiva. Examination of masticatory muscles is recommended since fibrositis has been described very frequently in victims of torture (Rasmussen, 1990).

Most of the symptoms and signs resolve spontaneously or under the influence of therapy. However, in a number of victims, a residual effect of short or long duration persists, mainly chronic pain, skin scars, neurological and orthopedic deficits, and clinical or radiological evidence of bone fractures. Very few late skin scars are characteristic except those from burns, cigarette burns, burns from corrosive fluids, and scars from a tight rope (Gurr & Quiroga, 2001). Victims of trauma and survivors of torture are also at increased risk of infectious diseases, cancer, cerebrovascular accidents, and heart problems (Goldman & Goldston, 1985).

Psychological Sequelae

Torture aims to distort the victim's sense of self-esteem and personal identity (Fischman, 1998). Psychological damage in victims of torture is complex and goes far beyond diagnostic categories known and defined in current classifications of psychiatric disorders. Description of psychological damage by torture is only partially covered by the diagnostic criteria for post-traumatic stress disorder (PTSD) (American Psychiatric Association, 1994), which include re-experiencing symptoms (recollections, nightmares, and flashbacks), avoidance of stimuli associated with the trauma, numbing of general responsiveness, and symptoms of increased arousal, such as difficulties concentrating, irritability, outbursts of anger, hypervigilance, and exaggerated startle response. The range of symptoms seen in torture survivors is much wider (McIvor & Turner, 1995).

Psychological damage in victims of torture can be better conceptualized as complex post-traumatic stress disorder (Herman, 1992). Besides suffering "classic" PTSD symptoms, these victims also suffer from changes in core beliefs or basic assumptions (Janoff-Bulman, 1983; McCann & Pearlman, 1990), have developmental arrests, show symptoms of dissociative disorders, or have lasting changes in personality.

Basic assumptions that are damaged or changed are feelings of safety, trusting others, predictability in life, and having control over one's own life and future. Also, survivors of torture may no longer believe that the world is a benevolent place, that they are worthy, or that there is justice in the world. Their sense of what is right and what is wrong may become confused. Those tortured and traumatized at younger age are especially at risk of becoming stuck in the process of personality development. Dissociative disorders may also develop and persist in victims of extreme traumatizations. Using dissociation (altering of consciousness) at the time of traumatization (peritraumatic dissociation) for protection against the impact of a traumatic event seems to be associated with bad prognosis in chronic PTSD (Marmar et al., 1994). These individuals can function after trauma without suffering from re-experiencing for quite a long period, but when dissociation stops functioning as a defense mechanism, they suffer from a significant and usually dramatic decline of their functioning. There is a lively scientific discussion going on about lasting changes in personality of trauma victims. It is observed that chronic PTSD frequently goes together with a whole spectrum of personality changes, such as borderline, paranoid, or obsessive-compulsive traits, but the question remains whether these changes are caused by traumatization or an adaptation of the victim's personality to damaged core beliefs and other chronic post-traumatic stress symptoms (Southwick, Yehuda, & Giller, 1993). However, Reid and Strong (1988) concluded that torture never reaches its ultimate goal—the total destruction of the personality.

Lansen (1994), describing damage after extreme traumatization, such as with torture, broadens the concept even more. He describes in survivors a clinically difficult-to-classify personal suffering, for which diagnoses of depression or dysthymia are not satisfactory, and for which sometimes the diagnosis "existential emotional syndrome" is used. Also, a severe affect regression, with reduced tolerance, anhedonia, and alexithymia; proneness to new traumatization by seemingly innocuous or even normal life events; and permanent alteration of the internal representational world by elementary patterns of aggression and victimization, may be present.

In its most extreme forms, traumatization can lead to psychotic regression; super-ego changes, as in the form of "identification with the aggressor"; extreme introversion and resignation, the so-called Mussulman stage (Ryn, 1990); or "conservation-withdrawal" (Lansen, 2000). In the latter case, the victim does not participate in life, conserves only a minimum amount of energy to stay alive, tries to avoid any activity in order to remain invisible, and avoids any further danger.

According to different studies, post-traumatic disorders are predicted by the severity of the trauma (van Putten & Yager, 1984), the amount of family support victims received (Figley, 1986), social support and resources available (Gorst-Unsworth & Goldenberg, 1998), and the victim's personal coping strategies with active reappraisal and re-analysis of the traumatic situations (Wolfe, Keane, Kaloupek, Mora, & Wine, 1993). The meaning of torture and trauma is very important in determining the effect on an individual, and this meaning is shaped by religious, cultural, and political beliefs (Holtz, 1998). While some authors (e.g., Fornazzari & Freire, 1990) find that involvement in social and political activities prior to torture does not seem to protect the victims from the sequelae of torture, others (e.g., Basoglu et al., 1994) suggest that prior knowledge and preparedness for torture, strong commitment to a cause, immunization against traumatic stress as a result of repeated exposure, and, again, strong social support appear to have protective value against PTSD in torture survivors.

Besides effects of torture on the individual, there are also effects on the victim's immediate family. Closeness and intimacy of the marriage relationship and the sexual relationship can be damaged, with increased irritability, domestic violence, intergenerational conflicts, problems in child rearing, or overcompensating partners trying to restore a certain balance within the relationship. Also, trauma can be transmitted across generations and cause damage in children who grow up in families where one or more members have been traumatized.

Social Sequelae

Torture leads to a psychological, physical, social, and economic breakdown. Torture victims may lose their physical and mental health as described, but they are also likely to lose work, study, status, family, and credibility. They may be confronted with suspicion and social isolation in their community. On top of that, when they decide to leave their homeland and to seek asylum and safety in another country, they get a chance to start a "new life," but they face even more losses, such as their regular social network. Torture, therefore, must be seen not only as a very important life event, but also as the cause of many others (Turner & Gorst-Unsworth, 1993).

In contrast with the above-mentioned concepts, which perceive trauma as an individual-centered event bound to the soma or psyche, there is a different conceptualization of traumatic experiences in terms of a dynamic interaction between a victim and a surrounding society (Summerfield, 1995). According to this concept, trauma is above all a social and not a medical problem. As Summerfield (1995) writes: "Some torture victims seek psychological help, but all of them want social justice." In other words, extensive focus only on physical and psychological sequelae of torture may lead to the medicalization of a social problem.

Torture and killing of individuals may also have a striking effect on the social and political life of a community. A climate of generalized terror and fear can result in the internalization and privatization of terror and fear (Gurr & Quiroga, 2001). The families of victims of organized violence have to mourn their loss in private (Padilla & Comas-Diaz, 1987). They are afraid to share their experiences, sometimes even with family members. They are afraid of collaborators of the regime. In some countries, families are even forbidden to bury in official graveyards members who have died in prisons after being tortured. In such a climate, the political action of the opposition can be frozen, and governments or different groups remain in power.

PREVENTION OF TORTURE

Prevention of torture can be carried out in the short and long term, and on a national and international level. Different organizations, such as Amnesty International and the United Nations, and various experts have given concrete examples of experiences in prevention (Akukwe, 1997; Amnesty International, 1994; Basoglu, 1993; Gurr & Quiroga, 2001; Harding, 1989; Madariaga, 1996; Mollica, 1992; Rasmussen, 1990; United Nations, 1996).

Short-term prevention consists of immediate measures that can be taken, such as increasing public awareness through the media (Madariaga, 1997), putting the United Nations under greater pressure for more effective action against countries with poor human rights records, or examining foreign policies for their direct or indirect contribution to the problem of human rights (Basoglu, 1993). There is a need for closer cooperation among national governments, international organizations, and nongovernmental organizations.

Long-term prevention should target the underlying causes of torture. Torture might be eradicated in the world with a more balanced distribution of wealth, as well as the recognition of basic human rights. Therefore, global economic, social, and political reforms are required (Basoglu, 1993).

Primary prevention at the national and local level can be based on the work of national medical organizations and local doctors (Rasmussen, 1990). They can create awareness within the community and can monitor and report cases of torture.

Unfortunately, in some countries medical personnel working against torture and promoting human rights are at great risk of being imprisoned, tortured, or charged with subversive activities. Human Rights Watch used to publish an annual world-wide report of human rights monitors who had been persecuted (Human Rights Watch, 1987). In the countries where they exist, rehabilitation of torture institutions or programs can have an important role, too. Nongovernmental organizations that champion human rights are very active around the world, and their work is of utmost importance at the local and national level. Religious institutions are also one of these local powers; the Catholic Church in Latin America is a good example.

Gurr and Quiroga (2001) suggest the following areas of possible action on the national and local levels:

- Ratification of international human rights covenants and protocols, and particularly the Convention against Torture and the International Criminal Court.

- Implementation of the international human rights covenants in the national legislation.

- Promotion of the revision of penal and judicial codes.

- Promotion of the establishment of regular visits to places of detention by independent observers to study the conditions there and the treatment of prisoners, to prevent acts of torture.

- Promotion of support for community complaints, reporting, and appeals against torture practices.

- Promotion of the effective investigation of torture allegations and the prosecution of those responsible, and revocation of any amnesty law that protects violators of human rights laws.

- Documentation and denunciation of human rights violations. Medical documentation of cases of torture should follow clear guidelines that ensure independence and confidentiality of the examination. Amnesty International has published some basic principles to provide a framework to carry out such examinations, or to assess the quality of investigations done by governments and courts (Amnesty International, 1997).

- Promotion of the creation of a strong network of local nongovernmental organizations, and the use of the mass media, when possible, to denounce violations, encourage social mobilization, and lobby for the respect for human rights.

- Education and training of law enforcement personnel and the military involved in the investigation and supervision of the detained. Education and training of members of the judicial system.

- Education and training of health professionals and students on human rights, the medical and psychological sequelae of torture, and treatment.
- Education of members of the Immigration Department who are involved in deciding requests of political asylum of survivors of torture.
- Education of the public to create awareness and mobilization on human rights.
- Documentation and research of human rights violations, the medical and psychological consequences of torture, treatment effectiveness, cost efficacy of treatments, and different rehabilitation approaches to maximize effectiveness in that particular environment.

Primary prevention at the international level is in hands of international nongovernmental organizations and governmental organizations, including the United Nations, Amnesty International, and the World Health Organization. In 1983, Amnesty International called on all governments to implement the so-called 12-Point Programme for Prevention of Torture (see Amnesty International, 1994):

1. Official condemnation of torture.
2. Limits on incommunicado detention.
3. No secret detention.
4. Safeguards during interrogation and custody.
5. Independent investigations of reports of torture.
6. No use of statements extracted under torture.
7. Prohibition of torture in law.
8. Prosecution of alleged torturers.
9. Training procedures for officials involved in custody, interrogation, or treatment of prisoners.
10. Compensation and rehabilitation.
11. International response.
12. Ratification of international instruments.

One year later, in 1984, the United Nations approved the Convention against Torture and Other Cruel, Inhuman or Degrading Treatment or Punishment (see United Nations, 1996). The convention established a committee of ten experts, the Committee against Torture, which was given the task of reviewing implementation of the convention. Also, the United Nations places obligations on governments to provide international cooperation and assistance to support the realization of human rights. One of the ways to do that is the fact-finding missions that investigate alleged human rights violations on the spot.

Besides the above-mentioned organizations, there is a growing number of international organizations working in advocacy for and treatment of torture survivors. Their work still needs better coordination on the international level. However, a couple of international networks are already functioning and promoting the primary prevention of torture. A few examples are the Association for the Prevention of Torture, headquartered in Geneva; the International Rehabilitation Council for Torture Victims network in Copenhagen; and the International Society for Health and Human Rights.

Finally, governments that support the cessation and prevention of torture need to demonstrate that clearly to other governments. Effective ways to do this are providing resources for the treatment of torture survivors and related activities in other countries, and basing humanitarian or other aid on respect for human rights and on cessation of torture in the recipient country.

REHABILITATION OF TORTURE VICTIMS

Torture-related rehabilitation services have traditionally been divided into two groups: rehabilitation services in countries where torture is, or was, practiced (home country services) and rehabilitation services in countries of resettlement (host country services) (Chester, 1990; Cunningham & Silove, 1993; Jaranson, 1995, 1998; van Willigen, 1992).

Rehabilitation services in countries where torture is, or was, practiced face many problems. Their staff is often at risk and may become victims of violence or torture. In a community where torture is a daily practice, helping victims of political violence is interpreted as helping the opposition, and further violence is sanctioned. This is the reason why these services often require the protection of a powerful and respected international organization in order to be able to function efficiently. The staff is usually multidisciplinary and composed mostly of volunteers or activists working for minimal reimbursement. In the majority of cases, the work is focused on advocacy, legal help, and social support, as conditions are not satisfactory for psychological assistance of torture victims. Financial support for these services is very limited.

Rehabilitation services in countries of resettlement have better conditions than those in home countries, especially when they are set up in countries where torture is not practiced. However, resources for psychological and medical assistance are seriously limited by other priorities for the victims, such as the need for legal assistance or practical resettlement help. Most programs accept torture survivors regardless of their legal status in the country, while others accept only legal residents. Some programs work with translators; others accept only torture victims speaking the language of the country of resettlement. The International Rehabilitation Council for Torture Victims publishes on a regular basis a very good overview of treatment and rehabilitation services throughout the world. In some countries, such as Sweden, Denmark, Australia, and the Netherlands (Drozdek, 2001), services for torture victims are quite well developed. Currently, there are interesting developments going on in the field of treatment services, including combined verbal and nonverbal treatment of torture victims (de Winter, 2001; Drozdek, 2001; Orth, 2001).

WHAT WE KNOW ABOUT TORTURERS

There are hardly any studies on torture perpetrators. The most complete and relevant ones, which have helped us gain insight into the creation of a torturer, are those written by Lifton (1986), Haritos-Fatouros (1988), Gibson (1990), and Staub (1990).

Lifton (1986) concludes that the Nazi doctors were able to develop a "second personality" that did the murderous acts, and that under certain conditions almost everybody will comply with demands for exterminations as were required by the Nazi regime. Staub (1990) also believes that almost anybody can become a torturer. Maybe only those individuals with very strong identities and strong universal moral values can resist the pressure. Torturers are not "sick" or extremely deviant individuals, as we like to perceive them. It is very provocative to realize that almost all people can commit violent acts against others. One study (Kren & Rappaport, 1980) showed that no more than 10 percent of German SS members were clinically considered "abnormal." A "sick" individual whose motivation to torture is only gratification of his sadistic wishes, or feelings of power, is too unreliable to be counted on by authorities to follow orders (Gibson, 1990).

Both the characteristics of a person and the context are important factors in the creation of a perpetrator of torture. Important personality characteristics seem to be positive orientation to authority; obedience of rules; enjoyment of military activities; strong belief in ideology; negative evaluation of other human beings; strong identification with one's own group, which is very different from other groups in society that are devalued and excluded from the range of applicability of moral values (Staub, 1980); and self-concepts that easily give rise to the need to defend or elevate the self (Staub, 1990). Torturers must also disengage themselves morally from the acts they are committing. This can be achieved by moral restructuring; psychological justification of acts they commit; euphemistic labeling of atrocities, which diminishes their responsibility; dehumanizing victims; and blaming victims for what happens to them (Bandura, 1990).

Contextual aspects include a range of cultural and societal characteristics, such as a history of scapegoating of a certain subgroup of the community; stimulation of respect for authority in society; a monolithic, uniform culture or social organization; undefined cultural self-concepts that balance between a belief in superiority and underlying self-doubt; and an ideology that designates an enemy (Staub, 1990).

In her study of Adolph Eichmann, Arendt (1964) described this well-known perpetrator of the Nazi regime. Her description is a good portrait of a torturer and summarizes some of the above-mentioned facts. "He [Adolph Eichmann] left no doubt [during his testimony at his Jerusalem trial] that he would have killed his own father if he had received an order to that effect. . . . He remembered perfectly well that he would have had a bad conscience only if he had not done what he had been ordered to."

OVERCOMING TORTURE

It is clear that torture should not go unnoticed when working to heal a society and its individuals. How should the torturer be treated in this healing process? After World War II, the Nuremberg Trial process indicted Nazi leaders and tried them as war criminals. During this process, twelve were sentenced to death, three to life imprisonment, four to imprisonment for ten to twenty years, and three were acquitted. At the Tokyo international tribunal, seven Japan war leaders were sentenced to death and seventeen to life imprisonment. Similar tribunals are currently being held at Arusha in Tanzania in relation to the 1994 genocide in Rwanda, and at The Hague, Netherlands, in relation to the 1992–1995 war in Bosnia. These tribunals may give people the feeling that justice has been done, but at the same time it is clear that many lower-level war criminals and torturers are not being prosecuted.

In other countries, such as Argentina and Chile, torturers received amnesty. It is extremely hard to understand how victims should forgive those who tortured or committed other crimes to humanity when there is no clear verdict. How should people deal with their own pains when those who inflicted those pains seem to have escaped punishment?

It may not be in the interests of societies or countries to dwell too long on their history of repressing the population. It may also be questionable whether victims ever can forgive what has happened to them, although it may be true that time heals some wounds. Such healing of wounds by time is primarily instigated by states or countries that do not have any personal interests; countries realize that they have to cooperate with each other and start maintaining economic interests in each other; the economy appears to lead a normalization of relations in about two to three generations.

Instead of waiting, South Africa tried a completely different approach with the so-called Truth and Reconciliation Commission (Tutu, 2000). The commission received about twenty thousand statements. Ten percent of the witnesses were offered the opportunity to testify in public. In the hearings, the commission acknowledged the fact that truth is not only factual, but also has aspects of personal experience. According to Tutu (2000), the testimony of police officers and their confessions to torture made clear how cruel the former government had been. It is believed that the openness of the commission and the testimonies have been very helpful in overcoming the former cruelties. Whether this is truly the case, time will tell. In any case, it must be stated that this endeavor has been courageous because this commission, for the first time as far as we know, did not accept that only time can heal.

REFERENCES

Agger, I. (1989). Sexual torture of political prisoners: An overview. *Journal of Traumatic Stress, 2,* 305–318.

Akukwe, C. (1997). Torture in the 21st century: The need to move from the focus on programmes and services to strategic prevention issues and policy development. *Torture, 7,* 82–87.

Allodi, F., & Stiasny, S. (1990). Women as torture victims. *Canadian Journal of Psychiatry, 35,* 144–148.

Allodi, F., Randall, G. R., Lutz, E. L., Quiroga, J., Zunzunegui, M. V., Kolff, C. A., Deutsch, A., & Doan, R. (1985). Physical and psychiatric effects of torture: Two medical studies. In E. Stover & E. O. Nightingale (Eds.), *The breaking of bodies and minds: Torture, psychiatric abuse and the health profession.* New York: W. H. Freeman.

American Psychiatric Association (1994). *Diagnostic and statistical manual of mental disorders* (4th ed.). Washington, DC: Author.

Amnesty International (1973). *Report on torture.* London: Duckworth.

Amnesty International (1984). *Torture in the eighties.* London: Amnesty International Publications.

Amnesty International (1994). *Ethical codes and declarations relevant to the health professionals: An Amnesty International compilation of selected ethical texts* (3rd rev. ed.). London: Amnesty International Publications.

Amnesty International (1997). Principles for the medical investigation of torture, and other cruel, inhuman or degrading treatment. In *Amnesty International Report 1997.* London: Amnesty International Publications, USA.

Amnesty International (2001). Web site against the death penalty. www.web.amnesty.org/rmp/dplibrary.nsf. Accessed January 19, 2002.

Arendt, H. (1964). *Eichmann in Jerusalem: A report on the banality of evil.* New York: Viking Press.

Baker, R. (1992). Psychosocial consequences for tortured refugees seeking asylum and refugee status in Europe. In M. Basoglu (Ed.), *Torture and its consequences: Current treatment approaches.* Cambridge, England: Cambridge University Press.

Bandura, A. (1990). Mechanisms of moral disengagement. In W. Reich (Ed.), *Origins of terrorism: Psychologies, ideologies, theologies, states of mind* (pp. 161-191). New York: Cambridge University Press.

Barudy, J. (1989). A programme of mental health for political refugees: Dealing with the invisible pain of political exile. *Social Science and Medicine, 28,* 715–727.

Basoglu, M. (1993). Prevention of torture and care of survivors: An integrated approach. *Journal of the American Medical Association, 270,* 606–611.

Basoglu, M., & Mineka, S. (1992). The role of uncontrollable and unpredictable stress in post-traumatic stress responses in torture survivors. In M. Basoglu (Ed.), *Torture and its consequences: Current treatment approaches.* Cambridge, England: Cambridge University Press.

Basoglu, M., Paker, M., Paker, O., Ozmen, E., Marks, I., Incesu, C., Sahin, D., & Sarimurat, N. (1994). Psychological effects of torture: A comparison of tortured with nontortured political activists in Turkey. *American Journal of Psychiatry, 151,* 76–81.

Bloch, S., & Reddaway, P. (1985). Psychiatrists and dissenters in the Soviet Union. In E. Stover & E. Nightingale (Eds.), *The breaking of bodies and minds: Torture, psychiatric abuse and the health profession.* New York: W. H. Freeman.

Cathcart, L. M., Berger, P., & Knazan, B. (1979). Medical examination of torture victims applying for refugee status. *Canadian Medical Association Journal, 121,* 179–184.

Chester, B. (1990). Because mercy has a human heart: Center for victims of torture. In P. Suedfeld (Ed.), *Psychology and torture.* New York: Hemisphere Publishing.

Cunningham, M., & Cunningham, J. D. (1997). Patterns of symptomatology and patterns of torture and trauma experiences in resettled refugees. *Australian and New Zealand Journal of Psychiatry, 31,* 555–565.

Cunningham, M., & Silove, D. (1993). Principles of treatment and service development of torture and trauma survivors. In J. P. Wilson & B. Raphael (Eds.), *International handbook of traumatic stress syndromes.* New York: Plenum Press.

Danieli, Y. (1980). Countertransference in the treatment and study of Nazi Holocaust survivors and their children. *Victimology, 5,* 355–367.

de Winter, B. (2001). Psychomotor therapy for asylum seekers: Possibilities and pitfalls. In M. Verwey (Ed.), *Trauma and empowerment.* Berlin: VWB.

Doerr-Zegers, O., Hartman, L., Lira, E., & Weinstein, E. (1992). Torture: Psychiatric sequelae and phenomenology. *Psychiatry, 55,* 177–184.

Drozdek, B. (2001). Can traumatized asylum seekers be treated? In M. Verwey (Ed.), *Trauma and empowerment.* Berlin: VWB.

Elias, N. (1978/1969). *Ueber den prozess der zivilisation, I, II.* Frankfurt am Main, Germany: Suhrkamp Taschenbuch Verlag AG.

Elsass, P. (1997). *Treating victims of torture and violence.* New York: New York University Press.

Farrington, K. (1996). *History of punishment and torture.* New York: Hamlyn.

Figley, C. R. (1986). Traumatic stress: The role of the family and social support system. In C. R. Figley (Ed.), *Trauma and its wake* (Vol. 2). New York: Brunner/Mazel.

Fischman, Y. (1998). Metaclinical issues in the treatment of psychopolitical trauma. *American Journal of Orthopsychiatry, 68,* 27–38.

Fornazzari, X., & Freire, M. (1990). Women as victims of torture. *Acta Psychiatrica Scandinavica, 82,* 257–260.

Foucault, M. (1979). *Discipline and punish: The birth of the prison.* New York: Vintage Books.

Genefke, I. (1993). Torture by those in power: The most efficient weapon against democracy. In L. Wisaeth & L. Mehlum (Eds.), *People, traumas and crises.* Oslo, Norway: Universitetsforlaget.

Genefke, I. (1994, May 6). Listen to the victims of evil. *Weekendavisen.*

Gibson, J.T. (1990). Factors contributing to the creation of a torturer. In P. Suedfeld (Ed.), *Psychology and torture.* New York: Hemisphere Publishing.

Gilligan, J. (1996). *Violence: Our deadly epidemic and its causes.* New York: Putnam.

Goldfeld, A. E., Mollica, R. E., & Pesavento, B. H. (1988). The physical and psychological sequelae of torture: Symptomatology and diagnosis. *Journal of American Medical Association, 259,* 2725–2729.

Goldman, H. H., & Goldston, S. E. (1985). *Preventing stress related psychiatric disorder.* Washington, DC: U.S. Government Printing Office.

Gorst-Unsworth, C., & Goldenberg, E. (1998). Psychological sequelae of torture and organised violence suffered by refugees from Iraq: Trauma-related factors compared with social factors in exile. *British Journal of Psychiatry, 172,* 90–94.

Gurr, R., & Quiroga, J. (2001). Approaches to torture rehabilitation: A desk study covering effects, cost-effectiveness, participation, and sustainability. *Torture, 11* (Supp. 1), 7–35.

Harding, T. W. (1989). Prevention of torture and inhuman or degrading treatment: Medical implications of a new European convention. *Lancet, 8648,* 1191–1193.

Haritos-Fatouros, M. (1988). The official torturer: A learning model for obedience to the authority of violence. *Journal of Applied Social Psychology, 18,* 1107–1120.

Herman, J. L. (1992). Complex PTSD: A syndrome in survivors of prolonged and repeated trauma. *Journal of Traumatic Stress, 5,* 95–109.

Holtz, T. H. (1998). Refugee trauma versus torture trauma: A retrospective controlled cohort study. *Journal of Nervous and Mental Disorders, 186,* 24–34.

Human Rights Watch (1987). *The persecution of human rights monitors: A worldwide survey.* New York: Human Rights Watch.

International Rehabilitation Council for Torture Victims (1998). *Status on torture.* Copenhagen, Denmark: IRCT.

Janoff-Bullman, R. (1983). The aftermath of victimisation: Rebuilding shattered assumptions. In C. R. Figley (Ed.), *Trauma and its wake* (Vol. 1). New York: Brunner/Mazel.

Jaranson, J. M. (1995). Government-sanctioned torture: Status of the rehabilitation movement. *Transcultural Psychiatric Research Review, 32,* 253–286.

Jaranson, J. M. (1998). The science and politics of rehabilitating torture survivors: An overview. In J. M. Jaranson & M. K. Popkin (Eds.), *Caring for victims of torture.* Washington, DC: American Psychiatric Press.

Kerrigan, M. (2001). *The instruments of torture.* New York: Amber Books Ltd.

Kren, G. M., & Rappaport, L. (1980). *The Holocaust and the crisis of human behaviour.* New York: Holmes and Meier.

Lansen, J. (1994, January 19). *Treating victims of persecution and torture: The importance of supervision.* Introduction to the Research Centre for Torture Victims, Copenhagen, Denmark.

Lansen, J. (2000). Verlating bij slachtoffers van vervolg en marteling. In A. Boerwinkel & W. Heuves (Eds.), *De kunst van het verliezen: Over verlating en verlatenheid.* Amsterdam, Netherlands: Boom.

Li, B., & Hu, P. (1994). Torture has long roots in Chinese history. *Torture, 4,* 108–110.

Lifton, R. J. (1986). *The Nazi doctors: Medical killing and the psychology of genocide.* New York: Basic Books.

Lira, E., Baker, D., & Castillo, M. I. (1990). Psychotherapy with victims of political repression in Chile: A therapeutic and political challenge. In J. Gruschow & K. Hannibal (Eds.), *Health services for the treatment of torture and trauma survivors.* Washington, DC: American Association for the Advancement of Science.

Lishman, W. A. (1998). *Organic psychiatry* (2nd ed.). London: Blackwell Science.

Lunde, I., & Ortmann, J. (1990). Prevalence and sequelae of sexual torture. *Lancet, 336,* 289–291.

Madariaga, C. (1996). Torture prevention as a public health problem. *Torture, 6,* 86–89.

Madariaga, C. (1997). Prevention of torture in the IRCT network: Survey performed on 26 rehabilitation centers. *Torture, 7,* 104–108.

Marmar, C. R., Weiss, D. S., Schlenger, W. E., Fairbank, J. A., Jordan, B. K., Kulka, R. A., & Hough, R. L. (1994). Peritraumatic dissociation and posttraumatic stress in male Vietnam theater veterans. *American Journal of Psychiatry, 151,* 902–907.

McCann, L., & Pearlman, L. A. (1990). Vicarious traumatization: A framework for understanding the psychological effects of working with victims. *Journal of Traumatic Stress, 3,* 131–149.

McIvor, R. J., & Turner, S. W. (1995). Assessment and treatment approaches for survivors of torture. *British Journal of Psychiatry, 166,* 705–711.

Meana, J. J., Morentin, B., Idoyaga, M. I., & Callado, L. F. (1995). Prevalence of sexual torture in political dissidents. *Lancet, 345,* 1307.

Mikaelsen, L., & Pedersen, C. (1979). *Menneskerettighederne: Et internationalt problem.* Copenhagen, Denmark: Danske Unesco-nationalkommission.

Mollica, R. F. (1992). The prevention of torture and the clinical care of survivors: A field in need of a new science. In M. Basoglu (Ed.), *Torture and its consequences: Current treatment approaches.* Cambridge, England: Cambridge University Press.

Mossallanejad, E. (2000). Torture at the threshold of the new millennium. *Torture, 10,* 36–40.

Orth, J. (2001). Between abandoning and control: Structure, security and expression in music therapy with traumatized refugees in a psychiatric clinic. In M. Verwey (Ed.), *Trauma and empowerment.* Berlin: VWB.

Padilla, A. M., & Comas-Diaz, L. (1987). Miedo y represion politica en Chile. *Revista Latinoamericana de Psicologia, 19,* 135–146.

Peters, E. (1996). *Torture.* Philadelphia: University of Pennsylvania Press.

Rasmussen, O. V. (1990). Medical aspects of torture: Torture types and their relation to symptoms and lesions in 200 victims, followed by a description of the medical profession in relation to torture. *Danish Medical Bulletin, 37* (Supp.), 1–88.

Reid, J. C., & Strong, T. (1988). Rehabilitation of refugee victims of torture and trauma: Principles and service provision in New South Wales. *Medical Journal of Australia, 148,* 340–346.

Rodley, N. (1987). *The treatment of prisoners under international law.* Oxford, England: Clarendon Press.

Ryn, Z. (1990). Between life and death: Experiences of concentration camp mussulmen during the holocaust. In *Genetic, Social, and General Psychology Monographs* (Vol. 116), 1–36. Washington, DC.

Silove, D. (1999). The psychosocial effects of torture, mass human rights violations, and refugee trauma. *Journal of Nervous and Mental Disease, 187,* 200–207.

Simpson, M. A. (1993). Traumatic stress and the bruising of the soul. In J. P. Wilson, & B. Raphael (Eds.), *International handbook of traumatic stress syndromes.* New York: Plenum Press.

Southwick, S. M., Yehuda, R., & Giller Jr., E. L. (1993). Personality disorders in treatment-seeking combat veterans with posttraumatic stress disorder. *American Journal of Psychiatry, 150,* 1020–1023.

Sprenger, J., & Kramer, H. (1968). *Malleus maleficarum* [The Hammer of witchcraft] (M. Summers, Trans.). London: Folio Society. (Original work published 1486)

Staub, E. (1980). Social and prosocial behavior: Personal and situational influences and their interactions. In E. Staub (Ed.), *Personality: Basic aspects and current research*. Englewood Cliffs, NJ: Prentice-Hall.

Staub, E. (1990). The psychology and culture of torture and torturers. In P. Suedfeld (Ed.), *Psychology and torture*. New York: Hemisphere Publishing.

Summerfield, D. (1995). Addressing human response to war and atrocity: Major challenges in research and practices and the limitations of Western psychiatric models. In R. J. Kleber, C. R. Figley, & B. P. R. Gersons (Eds.), *Beyond trauma: Cultural and societal dynamics*. New York: Plenum Press.

Texas Department of Criminal Justice (2002). www.tdcj.state.tx.us/statistics/stats-home. htm. Accessed January 19, 2002.

Turner, S. W., & Gorst-Unsworth, C. (1993). Psychological sequelae of torture. In J. P. Wilson, & B. Raphael (Eds.), *International handbook of traumatic stress syndromes*. New York: Plenum Press.

Tutu, D. M. (2000). *No future without forgiveness*. London: Random House.

United Nations (1996). *Human rights 1945–1995*. United Nations: Blue Book Series.

Valdes, H. (1975). *Diary of a Chilean concentration camp*. London: Gollancz.

van Geuns, H. (1987). The concept of organized violence. In *Health hazards of organized violence: Proceeding of a working group*. Netherlands, April 22–25, 1986. Rijswijk: Ministry of Welfare, Health, and Cultural Affairs.

van Putten, T., & Yager, J. (1984). Post traumatic stress disorder. Emerging from the rhetoric. *Archives of General Psychiatry, 41*, 411–413.

van Willigen, L. H. M. (1992). Organisation of care and rehabilitation services for victims of torture and other forms of organized violence. In M. Basoglu (Ed.), *Torture and its consequences: Current treatment approaches*. Cambridge, England: Cambridge University Press.

Vesti, P., Somnier, F., & Kastrup, M. (1992). *Psychotherapy with torture survivors*. Copenhagen, Denmark: RCT/IRCT.

Wagner, G., & Rasmussen, O. V. (1983). *Om tortur*. Copenhagen, Denmark: Hans Reitzels Forlag.

Welsh, J., & Rayner, M. (1997). The "acceptable enemy": Torture in non-political cases. *Torture, 7*, 9–14.

Wolfe, J., Keane, T. M., Kaloupek, D. G., Mora, C. A., & Wine, P. (1993). Patterns of positive readjustment in Vietnam combat veterans. *Journal of Traumatic Stress, 6*, 179–193.

NOTE

1. In this chapter, where we write in an unspecified way "he," one should also read "she."

5

State Terrorism:
When the Perpetrator Is a Government

Marc Pilisuk and Angela Wong

The suicide attacks on the World Trade Center were the first tragedy of this magnitude to be perpetrated by a small group of individuals. The bombs that exploded over Hiroshima and Nagasaki claimed many more civilian lives, but until September 11, 2001, one might have taken all the individual mass murderers, all the serial killers the world has known, and found their victims to number in the hundreds. Even with the September 11 event, the more dramatic numbers of victims of terror are killed by sources other than deranged or obsessed individuals or criminal bands. The real mass murderers produce victims by the thousands and tens of thousands, many times dwarfing the tragic losses from the attack on the World Trade Center. These murderers are on the loose. They are called governments.

The behavior of governments is not frequently construed to be the province of psychology. But the ways in which people in the decision-making circles of governments think and act are governed by the same principles that explain behavior in other contexts. The explanatory constructs, to which we will return, are attitudes regarding inequality, relative deprivation, impunity (from the consequences of one's actions), dehumanization of outsiders (particularly dissenters), the mindset of domination, and the pursuit of interests inspired by decision theory (and unfettered by principles).

DEFINING TERRORISM AND STATE TERRORISM

The term *terrorism* first gained visibility as a description of purposeful and planned acts by a government, rather than of wanton acts of rage by individuals. The Jacobins' rule of France in the late eighteenth century introduced a "reign of terror." Robespierre noted that "Terror is nothing but justice—prompt, severe and inflexible" (Nunberg, 2001, p. C5). The inflexible guillotine severed the heads of 1,200 people, including Robespierre's, in the years that followed. Another horrendous example occurred in the Zulu state from 1816 to 1828, when 2 million people were killed in an effort to enforce complete submission to the rule of one man, Shkar (Walter, 1972).

The idea of terrorism as a justifiable political strategy was used again by the Russian revolutionaries who assassinated Czar Alexander in 1881 and by the Zionist organization Lehi (the Stern gang) against British rule in Palestine in 1946. The term has lost acceptability as a rationale for killing. Groups such as the Irish Republican Army and the Ulster Defense Association are likely to use it only to describe the activities of the other group. That tradition of accusation has persisted in many of the world's poor and exploited areas, referring to terrorism on the part of the colonial powers or the puppet governments they support. Meanwhile, colonial governments use the term to refer to those who confront their control through revolutionary struggles for independence. The more positive term "freedom fighters" has been used to apply both to indigenous leaders of revolutionary movements and, somewhat deceptively, to mercenaries paid to help overthrow governments.

Some have tried to distinguish terrorism from warfare by limiting the term to specific violent acts. Bombing buildings, assassinating leaders, destroying access to food or water, or shooting people in warfare are not easily distinguished, however, from the same acts used more sporadically by nongovernmental groups. The use of the term to describe nonviolent protest, the spreading of computer viruses (cyberterrorism), the rampages of a disturbed high school student, or the actions of antiabortion extremists has confused the topic. The term is used loosely by the general public to apply to a spectrum of various forms of violence, ranging from random acts to those that are politically oriented (Kleff, 1993). Clearly, the term is manipulated by government officials, academics, private-sector entrepreneurs, the media, the identified targets of terrorism, the perpetrators of terrorist acts, and the general public in order to serve their own purposes. A lack of consistency in use generates confusion and inhibits both the understanding of terrorism and acting upon it in ways that would hold hope for its prevention (Han, 1993; Lador-Lederer, 1993).

We start with a working definition of terrorism that combines two elements: planned political purpose and civilian targets. First, terrorism is "the (calculated) use of violence for political goals" (Kleff, 1993, p. 15). The perpetrator's motive— violence as part of a political agenda—is paramount. Terrorism in this view is not random violence. This definition, however, is broad enough to include both the assassination of political leaders and declarations of war. One helpful distinction deals with the targets of violence. "Terrorism is a form of violence (or warfare) directed primarily against civilians, rather than the uniformed military, police forces or economic assets. It is used by both governments (against their own people or other countries) and insurgents" (O'Neill, 1993, p. 77). In 1775, Sir Edmund Burke, a fierce critic of the excesses of the French Revolution, cautioned his colleagues in the British Parliament not to treat the insurgent colonies as parties to be suppressed but rather as legitimate partisans of a struggle to be free (Burke, 1775). Surely if targeting civilians is a defining characteristic, then the dropping of atomic bombs on Hiroshima and Nagasaki would qualify as state terrorism. War has undergone tremendous changes. The proportion of civilian casualties jumped markedly from World War I to World War II, and by the time of the Vietnam War civilian casualties vastly outnumbered the deaths of servicemen. It is entirely possible that modern technology has turned the conduct of war into a form of terrorism. The term "low-intensity conflict" and the methods employed in such a conflict have little to distinguish them from the definition of terrorism. Under our two-part definition, activities planned for a political purpose and directed against civilians are considered to be terrorism.

Terrorist acts performed against a totalitarian government, or any government that controls its media, may be either widely publicized or totally concealed, at the government's discretion. In fact, governments do use charges of terror conducted by adversaries as an excuse for their own systematic and official terror. Terror as practiced by a government is frequently conducted with elaborate mechanisms for concealment. This was true in the cases of Nazi Germany and of the Soviet Union under Stalin. When it happens, the casualties are difficult to estimate, particularly during the time when they are occurring (O'Kane, 1996).

This account of state terrorism is restricted to purposeful actions by governments that commit violence upon civilians or noncombatants. Such activities are not justly attributed to a single government, nor are the actions of governments that do practice such activities typically distinguishable from the influences that provoke or support such activities. State terrorism is found among nations with vastly different cultural and political forms. In the arena of support and provocation for state terrorism, the most common and most egregious perpetrator, by any fair accounting, is the United States. The United States as a nation has more extensive interests in the economic affairs of other countries and provides greater support to governments friendly to these interests than does any other nation. This influence includes support for terrorism by governments. We believe the cases presented will support this thesis with clarity.

Our purpose, however, is not to cast blame, but rather to ask what actually makes possible the forms of state terrorism that we observe. There are two patterns worth noting: 1) violent attacks upon citizens by their own governments without legitimate judicial determination of criminal activity; 2) efforts of governments to gain or to maintain control over the people, territories, and resources of *other* nations by violent means but without an official declaration of war (Amnesty International, 1993).

The term *desaparecido* became part of the human rights vocabulary in 1966 in Guatemala to describe people who vanished after being taken into custody by government officials, or with the acquiescence of government officials, and of whom the authorities claimed no knowledge. A second type of terrorist activity is the extra-judicial execution—an unlawful killing performed at the behest of a government without the individual being found guilty of any crime. Such political killings are frequently performed by governments either directly or indirectly through paramilitary groups. The ingenuity of the barbarity commonly involved suggests the complete impunity of the perpetrators. It also reveals the underlying goal of intimidation of dissent. Trade unionists, human rights activists, community leaders, lawyers, and teachers are frequent targets. But other frequent victims are bystanders, street children whose hunger and homelessness is bothersome, or people who simply are in the wrong place at the wrong time (Amnesty International, 1993).

This chapter seeks to find a pattern among those forms of state terrorism that have claimed the largest number of victims. Not reviewed here are three major examples of terrorism by states, i.e., the Soviet Union under Stalin, Germany under Hitler, and U.S. actions against the Native Americans for more than a century. According to a "Terrorism and Human Rights" progress report prepared by Kalliopi K. Koufa, Special Rapporteur, United Nations:

> State terrorism in the form of "regime" or "government terror" is characterized by such actions as the kidnapping and assassination of political opponents of the government by the police or the secret service or security forces or the army; systems of imprisonment without trial; persecution and torture; massacres of racial or religious minorities or of certain social classes; incarceration of citizens in concentration camps; and, generally speaking, government by fear. . . . This type of bureaucratized terror intimidates, injures and abuses whole groups, sometimes whole nations, and it is the type of terrorism that historically and today produces the most harm. . . . A further point that deserves particular mention is the role of the law in the reification and legitimacy of "regime" or "government terror". In fact, "regime" or "government terror" is exercised according to the law that the public authorities have themselves created. (Koufa, 2001, pp. 43, 45, 46)

China's violent assault on practitioners of Falun Gong presents a clear example of such actions by a nation (Human Rights Watch, 1999). But the number of such regimes is great.

The U.S. government has shown concern about terrorism since the 1980s. Elite groups chosen to study the phenomenon have focused on governments that use their resources to kidnap U.S. diplomats or businessmen or to destroy U.S. military facilities or personnel. The United States Senate Subcommittee on Security and Terrorism (1985) released a detailed report prepared by the Center for Strategic and International Studies at Georgetown University. Its definition of terrorism suggests an emphasis on certain types of activities, i.e., those intended to "undermine selectively the policies, the psycho-social stability and political governability of pluralistic states with representative governments" (p. xiii). Written before the demise of the USSR, the report focuses on efforts by the USSR or Soviet bloc states to assist militant groups in their efforts to harm Western democracies, in particular the United States. It lists 104 terrorist groups in many nations and lists as well the activities that have been attributed to them. In the vast majority of cases, the attacks have been against U.S. military personnel, U.S. embassies, or U.S. businessmen. The work has been updated by a contract research organization, but the emphasis remains the same: on groups that use violence against U.S. military and business interests (Terrorism Research Center, 2001). The role of U.S. military personnel (or of U.S. corporate interests) in so many parts of the world and the reason why such individuals are targets are not questioned.

The report includes secret documents showing that Palestine Liberation Organization leaders had received training in the USSR, Hungary, and China. It also presented a copy of a top-secret report by the Iranian minister of national guidance indicating that a number of dedicated groups, willing to give their lives, were being mobilized into brigades to fight violators of the orthodox Muslim faith, such as the Shah of Iran and Saddam Hussein of Iraq; also mentioned were the Americans seen to be their sponsors. These documents show a concerted effort by a militant group to use violent means to further its interests. The report summarizes a view of terrorism that takes as a given the right of the United States to determine which states must be attacked before calling a violent activity "terrorist"; they must be "representative democracies" as judged by the United States (Terrorism Research Center, 2001). The report also ignores the United States' history of overthrowing elected democracies that sought to limit exploitation by U.S.-based corporations of their countries. Chile (1973), Guatemala (1954), and the Dominican Republic (1963) are examples. The report fails to evaluate whether the various terrorist groups' grievances are legitimate or whether the people among whom such groups find support have been so oppressed as to have no peaceful way to address their concerns, which would have been the case in South Africa under apartheid and the U.S. colonies under British rule. Finally, the report fails to look into the historical, cultural, and economic circumstances by which the great powers have come to enjoy the benefits of exploiting poorer ones, often using military means to achieve these ends. A look at several cases of state terrorism reveals a more complex picture than that presented by the report.

STATE TERROR IN CAMBODIA

The government as a source of terror reached dramatic proportions in Cambodia under the Khmer Rouge between April 1975 and January 1979. The number of people executed will never be known, but estimates range from 400,000 to 3 million out of a population of 7.7 million (Barron and Paul, 1977; Chomsky and Herman, 1979; Keesing's, 1984; Ponchaud, 1978; Vickery 1985). Despite the numbing quality of statistics, the differences in numbers are important, as each individual death is a horrific tragedy and should be counted.

One element leading to the emergence of the Khmer Rouge was the unwilling-ness of the United States to accept a neutral government in Southeast Asia during the period of the Vietnam War (Chomsky & Herman, 1979; O'Kane, 1996). The popular Prince Sihanouk had sufficient support to withstand any serious challenge from guerrilla forces that had been part of the fight for independence against French colonial rule. The coup d'état that overthrew the Sihanouk government in 1970 brought in military rule under General Lon Nol, who enjoyed U.S. support and was viewed as a pawn of the United States. The National United Front of Cambodia (NUFC) combined Sihanouk and Khmer Rouge forces in opposing him. The Viet Cong provided military supplies to this coalition while the United States supplied the puppet regime until its collapse in 1975 (O'Kane, 1996).

Richard Dudman, a U.S. war correspondent who was captured in the fall of Phnom Penh, evaluated the U.S. intervention:

> The constant and indiscriminate bombing, an estimated 450,000 dead and wounded civilians, to say nothing of the military casualties, and the estimated 4 million refugees were almost inevitable results of the short U.S. invasion of Cambodia and the consequent proxy war that ended in defeat for the U.S. as well as for the client regime in Phnom Penh. (cited in Chomsky & Herman, 1979, p. 165)

Between March and August of 1973, 40,000 tons of bombs were dropped on Cambodia each month (Ponchaud, 1978; Vickery, 1985). The bombing and ground fighting together destroyed crops, forests, transportation, and factories and forced massive movement of people from rural areas to cities. Approximately 3 mil-lion refugees fled the fighting zones for urban areas controlled by Lon Nol, where they survived on rice supplied by the United States.

The opposition NUFC defeated Lon Nol and took power in April 1975. The Khmer Rouge had consolidated its military power in the countryside and Sihanouk was to return only briefly, the following year, to tender his resignation. In January 1976, a new constitution renamed the country "Democratic Kampuchea." A 250-seat National Assembly was elected. Pol Pot was named prime minister, and Khieu Samphan became president of the State Presidium (O'Kane, 1996). Samphan, in his doctoral dissertation at the University of Paris in 1959, had presented a case for making the Cambodian economy self-reliant by increasing agricultural productivity as a base for industrial development. He considered 80 percent of the urban popu-lation, even then, to be unproductive and believed they should be relocated to do agricultural work. Samphan's theory was to be put into practice immediately; peas-ant refugees to the cities were sent back to the country to plant a new crop of rice before the ending of U.S. supplies could result in famine. The forced evacuations were brutal, and the economic plan was unsuccessful. Hunger was widespread despite evidence that people of all ages were forced to work from twelve to sixteen hours a day, and despite statements to the contrary by Khmer officials (O'Kane, 1996; Sagar, 1989).

By March 1976, the National Assembly had dropped into obscurity (Carney, 1989). The administrative and legal arms of government disappeared and neither laws nor decrees were issued. Khmer Rouge rule was secret, and through terror. Some regional military groups continued to oppose the Khmer Rouge forces and were suppressed. In a plan similar to one that had been used by the United States in Vietnam, suspect village leaders were deposed and replaced by Khmer Rouge loyalists. Angkar, or "organization on high," provided a justification to commandeer vehicles, to order people out of hospitals, and to kill. Purges and massacres were commonplace. At their center was the Tuol Sleng School in Phnom Penh, which was converted for purposes of interrogation, torture, and execution. Records found when the Khmer Rouge fled showed that many of its victims included Khmer Rouge supporters (Hawk, 1989; Quinn, 1989). Of 14,499 people held there, only four survived. Norkobal, the secret police system, replicated the death machine in the provinces with far greater numbers of executions. Some 66,000 bodies were found in three provinces in 1981. In 1982, 16,000 bodies were found in the Kampot province alone in 386 mass graves, with uncounted numbers buried in the 1,400 mass graves elsewhere in the province (O'Kane, 1996).

There was certainly an extremist and revivalist ideology at work. There was also an ideology sanctioning absolute behavioral domination and control. Terror was intended to strip away all vestiges of an individual's beliefs or connections that give meaning to life. The avowed aim was to create, from the malleable and atomized individuals who remained, a new classless society, without money or property, living in "perfect harmony." In the "Black Book," leaders revealed a longstanding fear of foreign invasion and made repeated references to Cambodia's former glory during the Angkor Empire (800–1400). They promised to liberate ethnic Khmers from provinces in Vietnam and Thailand. Purges in the provinces were particularly harsh on Muslims, Buddhists, Catholics, and Vietnamese (Sagar, 1989).

State terrorism continued until military groups opposed to the Khmer Rouge were joined by 100,000 Vietnamese troops in overthrowing the genocidal regime of Pol Pot in 1979 and replacing it with the People's Republic of Kampuchea. The legacy includes a country with a 61 percent illiteracy rate and a reported 47 percent of its children suffering from malnutrition (*The 2001 World Development Indicators*, 2001).

THE CASE OF COLOMBIA

In Colombia's cities, "social cleanup operation" is the official term for a night in which police or their collaborators murder drug addicts, homosexuals, prostitutes, vagrants, street children, and the mentally ill. In the larger cities—Medellin, Cali, Barranquilla, and Bogota—the assailants often gun down victims from motorbikes or trucks. At other times groups are rounded up and forced into trucks, their bodies (often mutilated) found later in rubbish containers or on the roadside. Accurate figures on such killings are difficult to determine. Many of the victims are un-known, and most deaths go unregistered and unreported. One human rights group recorded 298 murders by death squads in the eight months of a study in 1992 (Amnesty International, 1993). Despite the fact that, to inflict such terror, Colom-bian police use their arms (i.e., police weapons that are U.S.-supplied), U.S. aid has continued to support the Colombian government.

The term "democra-tatorship" is used by Eduardo Galeano to describe the Colombian amalgamation of democratic forms and state terror. (Galeano, a native of Uruguay, is well known in Latin America as a brilliant author who writes in opposition to imperialism operating in that region.) In a continent severely marred by human rights abuses, Colombia has compiled the worst record (Giraldo, 1996). Assistance in both training and arming the Colombian military has come from Britain, Israel, and Germany, but particularly from the United States. Father Javier Giraldo, director of the Commission of Justice and Peace, published a report that documented atrocities during the first part of 1988. These included 3,000 politi-cally motivated killings, 273 of which occurred in "social cleansing campaigns." Political killings averaged eight a day. People were murdered in their homes and in the streets, or they just disappeared. During the 1988 electoral campaigns, 19 of 87 mayoral candidates from the one independent political party were assassinated, along with more than 100 other candidates. The Central Organization of Workers, a trained union coalition, had lost over 230 members since 1986 (Comision Inter-Congregacional, 1995; Giraldo, 1996).

In July 1989, the U.S. State Department announced subsidized sales of military equipment to Colombia "for anti-narcotics purposes." The announcement noted that "Colombia has a democratic form of government and does not exhibit a con-sistent pattern of gross violations of internationally recognized human rights." The Washington Office on Latin America actually cited Father Giraldo's report and added, "The vast majority of the people who disappeared in recent years are grass-roots organizers, peasant or union leaders, leftist politicians, human rights workers, and other activists." By 1989, the Colombian branch of the Andean Commission of Jurists reported that political killings had increased to eleven per day (Giraldo, 1996).

Gradually through the 1980s, U.S. participation in the Colombian war against its own population increased. Between 1984 and 1992, six thousand Colombian soldiers were trained under the U.S. military education and training program. Pres-ident Cesa Javiria was favored by the Clinton administration for the position of secretary general of the Organization of American States. He was considered "for-ward-looking in building democratic institutions in a country where it was some-times dangerous to do so" (cited in Giraldo, 1996). War against the guerrillas and narco-trafficking operations is the official State Department explanation for U.S. involvement. These groups were blamed for all of the violence. In 1989, President George H. W. Bush announced the largest shipment of weapons ever authorized under the Emergency Provisions of the Foreign Assistance Act. The arms went not to the national police, who have the responsibility for countering narcotic opera-tions, but to the army.

Much of the killing in Colombia has been in the areas of greatest inequality, perhaps as a means of imposing silence. The top 3 percent of the landed elite own more than 70 percent of the arable land, while 57 percent of the poorest farmers subsist on fewer than 3 percent. Unable to satisfy basic subsistence needs, 40 percent of the population live in absolute poverty and 18 percent are unable to meet basic nutrition needs. The Colombian Institute of Family Welfare estimates that 4.5 million children under the age of fourteen—half of the country's children—are hungry (Chomsky, 1996). But Colombia is a nation of enormous resources. It is considered one of the healthiest and most flourishing economies of Latin America (Martz, 1991). Latin American scholar John Martz writes in *Current History* that Colombia is the triumph of capitalism in a society with democratic structures. It is a model of "well-established political stability" (Martz 1994).

From 1988 to 1995, 67,378 Colombians were assassinated, an average of 23.4 per day. The number of victims of political violence in this Colombian "democracy" far exceeds the combined number of political killings in Uruguay, Argentina, Brazil, Bolivia, and Chile during their years under military dictatorship. The Truth and Reconciliation Commission in Chile registered 2,700 politically motivated murders during the seventeen years of its brutal military dictatorship. This horrible statistic is nonetheless far less than the number of cases reported annually in Colombia for each year between 1986 and 1995 (Giraldo, 1996). Kidnappings by the Revolutionary Armed Forces of Colombia have continued as have the massacres by right-wing paramilitary groups such as the United Self-Defense Forces of Colombia (AUC in Spanish), which continues, even after agreements to desist, to conduct massacres of villagers (Wilson, 2001).

Colombia's government has favored privatization, and major World Bank projects favoring export agriculture have resulted in the country now importing much of its food from abroad. Two million internally displaced Colombians are homeless, unemployed, and have no government support. Coffee plantations provide only low-wage and seasonal employment.

Colombia's local farmers, disproportionately Afro-Colombians, were put out of the business of growing corn, yucca, and other agricultural products by low-cost imports. They were displaced in every area except one, coca. The farmers can earn 50 cents for a gram that will earn Mafia distributors $50 for the same amount. As a result, farmers have become the target of Plan Colombia, a $1.3 billion aid package, 75 percent of which goes to military and police activity. Much of this is to fumigate the farms (in order to kill coca plants), although coca production increased threefold in the eight years after the operation began (Giraldo, 1996). Even coca-free farms have been fumigated (Giraldo, 1996). The big beneficiaries of the antidrug program are Sikorsky (maker of helicopters), Lockheed Martin (radar surveillance), Monsanto (pesticides), and the strongest promoter, Occidental Petroleum, which sees military action as a way to secure both oil exploration and a pipeline through forest areas that have been the long-term home of indigenous groups. The U'wa, a tribe with pre-colonial origins, are being eliminated by attacks on their villages, confiscation of farmland, and contamination of water. People who try to organize the displaced farmers, either before they leave the countryside or after they find sweatshop work, are in jeopardy; recently, one union organizer was killed every day (Giraldo, 1996), and support for the military and paramilitary groups responsible for this activity has only increased to the present time. The psychological mechanisms of dehumanization and psychic numbing contribute to the continued justification for killing large numbers of people.

THE CASE OF PERU

Following years of exploitation of Peru's natural mining and agricultural resources, as well as state policies that favored wealthy elite and foreign investors, two revolutionary groups gained popularity in Peru. The Sendero Luminoso has been a catalyst for violent attacks against both civilians and government officials, with the intent of overthrowing the Peruvian government. The MRTA (Movimiento Revolutionario Tupac Amaru) has focused on bombings and kidnappings. The strategy of the insurgents has been partly successful because of centuries of governmental neglect of the rural poor.

In an impoverished economy, the drug trade in coca has flourished. Drug traffickers pay both Sendero's and the government's military forces for protection. The government's response has been the use of civil patrols that have been associated with violent abuses of the rights of civilians since they were first formed in 1982. In civil patrols, villagers are lured by pay or by threats to take part in violent activities against those suspected of opposition to the government. The Fujimori government, with U.S. support, embraced a counterinsurgency strategy, relying on these patrols, thereby drawing the population, including the children, into the conflict. The militarization of rural Peruvians invited Sendero retaliation, and the military evades any duty to protect the population. In addition to the civil patrols, the police ignore or support the activities of trained death squads. Torture is well documented, as are restrictions on the freedom of information, the assassination of journalists, and attacks on human rights monitors (Americas Watch Report, 1991).

In 1991, President Fujimori signed a bilateral anti-narcotics agreement with the United States. The U.S. Congress adopted the law but with particular human rights conditions in order to be sure that the United States will not be identified with human rights violations of countries receiving aid. The U.S. State Department, ignoring its own country's report on human rights practices for 1990, defended the Peruvian government's human rights practices. The report indicated

> credible reports of summary executions, arbitrary detentions, torture and rape by the military as well as less frequent reports of such abuses by the police . . . Credible reports of rape by elements of the security forces in the emergency zone were so numerous that such abuse can be considered a common practice condoned—or at least ignored—by the military leadership. The constitutional rights by persons detained by

the military are routinely ignored. (cited in Americas Watch Report, 1991, p. 38)

Subsequent military assistance came with provisions to assist the development of military courts in Peru. The practice virtually guarantees impunity of military officers involved in human rights violations. Impunity for behavior reduces the constraints that support standards of human decency. Once the military claims jurisdiction over a case, the civilians must give up the case. U.S. assistance for judicial reform would be better served by enhancing the civilian judicial system.

THE CASE OF GUATEMALA

Before and during most of the Second World War, Guatemala was a typical banana republic. It was ruled by a military elite and was oppressive toward its indigenous Mayan majority. From 1944 through 1954, Guatemalans elected the most democratic and populist government in the nation's history. In 1954, the U.S. Central Intelligence Agency participated in the overthrow of the democratically elected Socialist government under President Jacobo Arbenz Guzman. A mercenary army led by Colonel Carlos Castillo Armas (organized and supported by the CIA) staged the coup. It was labeled a "liberation," but in fact it returned Guatemala to military rule (Wise & Ross, 1964).

After the invasion, the government systematically destroyed the country's former communist and social democratic leadership. Peasants, labor activists, and intellectuals by the hundreds were subjected to detention, torture, and sometimes death. Many were forced into exile or to withdrawal from political activity. Any sign of opposition was vilified and labeled Communist. The Guatemalan case was one of the best documented through collaboration of the International Center for Human Rights Investigations and the American Association for the Advancement of Science (Ball, Kobrack, & Spirer, 1999).

This military action marked the start of one of the most horrible examples of state terrorism. The CIA solicited Miguel Ydigoras Fuentes, who had left the country and was living in exile in El Salvador. Ydigoras later wrote of his encounter with the CIA:

> They wanted me to lend assistance to overthrow Arbenz. When I asked their conditions for the assistance I found them unacceptable. Among other things I was to favor the United Fruit company and the International Railways of Central America; to destroy the railroad workers union; to establish a strong-arm government, in the style of Ubico. (Wise & Ross, 1964, p. 183)

The success of the Cuban revolution in overthrowing the Batista dictatorship was a reminder to Guatemalans of the popular government they once had and of the fact that military strongmen could be defeated. But when Cuba confiscated holdings of foreign firms and offered repayment at the low value the firms had used to avoid taxes, the United States began to step up its threat, not only against Cuba but also against all of Latin America.

General Fuentes was the Guatemalan president from 1958 to 1963. His government was corrupt and unpopular. An attempted coup by military officers, some trained in the United States, marked the beginning of Guatemala's revolutionary movement for democracy as well as the creation of the counterinsurgency state (Moss, 1972). Large demonstrations and strikes by students, labor, and middle-class opponents demanded that President Fuentes step down. They increased following fraudulent congressional elections. Government response included the shooting of student leaders in 1961–62. This convinced many Guatemalans that peaceful protest would not work. Officers from the unsuccessful coup joined in support of the PGT workers party. In 1963, another army coup (Centro Internacional para Investigaciones [CIIDH & GAM], 1999; McClintock, 1985), supported by the U.S. government, brought former Defense Minister Colonel Enrique Peralta to the presidency.

Elections were promised again in 1966. Twenty-eight members of the PGT, lured out of hiding by hopes of a fair election, disappeared; their bodies were never found. When Mendez Montenegro, a university law professor, was elected president, he was forced to sign a decree granting the military the right to fight against its opponents without interference from civilian authorities. U.S. military advisors supervised the bombing of villages, and government forces were responsible for the killing or disappearance of many civilians. Estimates of civilian deaths between 1966 and 1968 varied from 2,800 (Melville & Melville, 1971) to 8,000 (Jonas, 1991). Under U.S. guidance, the army organized a powerful military force and a network of counterinsurgency surveillance that would continue for more than thirty years. It would be used both to battle guerrillas and to control, in brutal fashion, the civilian population. Paramilitary death squads carried out much of this activity. Some were security forces dressed in civilian clothes. Others were private thugs of the extreme right. The secret nature of these groups created terror but also gave the police and the army an opportunity to deny responsibility (Black, 1984).

In 1970, the army candidate, Colonel Carlos Arana, became president. He had created the counterinsurgency plan to exterminate the guerrillas and their supporters. A state of siege was declared. Legal protests against a corrupt government contract with a Canadian nickel-mining concern were met with mass arrests, and the University at San Carlos was occupied. Death squad attacks against law school professors and other leaders followed. Killings and disappearances exceeded those of the late 1960s. After the leadership of the outlawed labor group, the PGT, were tortured and killed, opposition subsided, but not before the formation of the National Front Against Violence. This group of university students, church groups, opposing political parties, and workers called for human rights and constitutional rule (Aguilera Peralta & Imery, 1981). Arana's handpicked successor, Defense Minister Lugged Garcia, trying to gain public acceptance after a fraudulent election, permitted a measure of labor and popular organizing. State violence declined for a brief time, and a group of K'che and Ixil Indians found the courage to come to Guatemala in 1980 to protest the kidnapping and murder of nine peasants. They were joined by a student group but were not well received. Their legal advisor was assassinated outside police headquarters, and when they occupied the Spanish Embassy, the police attacked, trapped them inside, and watched both protestors and hostages burn to death (Blanck & Castillo, 1998; CIIDH & GAM, 1999).

Guerrillas began to harass the army and then retreated to the mountains. Typically they had substantial civilian support, since the guerrillas had worked closely with the peasant population, from which many of them had come. Increasingly, the military viewed unarmed villagers as participants in the insurgency. "Operation Ashes" clearly stated the government's program of mass killings and burning of houses, crops, and farm animals, and the scorching of entire villages (Americas Watch, 1982). The mass killings included children, women, and the elderly in a strategy that General Rios Montt called "draining the sea that the fish swim in." During almost four years under President Lucas Garcia, the government was responsible for more than 8,000 killings and disappearances in what Amnesty International labeled a "government program of political murder" (Amnesty International, 1989). Ethnic factors were central, since the majority Mayan population were viewed as less than human and suffered casualties in even greater proportion than their number in the population. General Rios Montt took power in a military coup in 1982. The U.S. Congress, which had cut off military aid to Guatemala in 1977, switched to restore aid at President Reagan's request. The aid came with assurances that the general could fight the war as he saw fit, without concern for human rights and without fear of losing the funding. With extensive military support from the United States, the military effort escalated. In remote villages the policy was toward overkill, beheading victims or burning them alive, smashing the heads of children on rocks, and commonly raping women even when pregnant (Amnesty International, 1982; Falla, 1983; Nairn, 1983). In the fourteen months of Montt's rule, 10,000 documented killings or disappearances occurred, although press censorship reduced the reporting of these at the time (Ball, Kobrack, & Spirer, 1999). The proportion of unnamed victims rose dramatically from the previous era. Nonetheless, President Reagan described Rios Montt, in December 1982, as "a man of great personal integrity and commitment who is totally dedicated to democracy" (Schirmer, 1998, p. 33).

The killings, torture, and kidnappings became fewer but more targeted and selective under the regimes that followed. The remarkable efforts of peasant women in Guatemala and of students have helped to bring some attention and efforts at accountability to an appalling case of state terrorism.

THE CASE OF IRAN

CIA intervention in Iran illuminates the power and the aims the agency has pursued. Iran has deposits of copper and coal and holds 13 percent of the world's oil reserves, much of it yet untapped. Its rivers hold an almost unlimited potential for hydroelectric power. It supports the population of about 40 million people on a landmass that has 1,000 miles of common border with states of the former Soviet Union. Amid these resources, much of the population remains in poverty. It is poverty that has persisted through long periods of U.S. assistance that has run into hundreds of millions of dollars. In the early 1900s, a European cartel, the Industrial Bank of Persia, was organized to finance the Anglo-Iranian Oil Company. The German banking house of J. Henry Schroeder & Co. was a partner in the cartel. On the American board of directors of this German company sat Alan Dulles, who was later to head the CIA. The legal counsel for Anglo-Iranian Oil was Sullivan Cromwell, a New York law firm in which Alan Dulles and his brother John Foster Dulles (secretary of state under Eisenhower) were partners. In 1951, the Shah of Iran named as his premier Mohammed Mossadegh, a strong spokesman for nationalism and economic development. The immensely popular Mossadegh quickly took action to bring profits from Iranian oil to the people of Iran. He announced the expropriation of Anglo-Iranian Oil and the nationalization of Iran's oil fields. At stake for Anglo-Iranian were assets valued in the billions, in the form of resources that it had exploited for fifty years. Anglo-Iranian refused to permit its technicians to work the oilfields, and other Western companies joined to effect a virtual boycott of Iranian oil. Iran was helpless, and the economy careened toward bankruptcy (Pilisuk, 1972; Tully, 1962).

Mossadegh then wrote to President Eisenhower, indicating that unless he received American aid for Iran's financial troubles, he would be forced to ask for help elsewhere—meaning the Soviet Union. The president delayed while the CIA put pressure on the Shah to oust Mossadegh. An American agent then paid a visit to the Shah, who suddenly announced that he was replacing Mossadegh as premier with Major General Fazollah Zahedi, a member of the overly inflated Iranian police force. But by the time the Colonel of the Imperial Guards, whose duty it was to serve notice to Mossadegh, performed this task, Mossadegh had gathered an army of supporters. They arrested the colonel, and the Shah hastily left for Rome.

Undaunted, the American agent supervised the careful spending of more than $10 million by the CIA in Tehran over the next few days. Within four days, a large impromptu circus parade, common in the streets of Tehran, suddenly became an organized mob chanting "Long live the Shah" and "Death to Mossadegh." The crowd joined in and, at the height of the confusion, troops loyal to the Shah attacked Mossadegh's supporters. After nine hours of bitter fighting, Mossadegh's troops were surrounded and forced to surrender. The Shah was flown home from Rome and Major General Zahedi became premier. The assistance once sought by Mossadegh now flowed in at an average rate of $5 million a month (Tully, 1962). The manipulation by the CIA in this instance reveals the mindset of domination, wherein the attainment of power is considered an end that justifies such practices.

The Shah and other Iranian officials soon became men of extreme wealth, and the Shah maintained a standing army larger than that of West Germany. After the coup, an international consortium signed a twenty-five-year renewal pact with the Iranian government. Anglo-Iranian Oil Company (which became the British Petroleum Oil Company) got 40 percent of the oil being extracted, and a group of American companies divided 40 percent, with the remainder going to Royal Dutch Shell and Compagnie Française des Pétroles. The details of the contract were not made public because, according to Secretary of State Dulles, such information "would affect adversely the foreign relations of the United States . . . and would almost certainly revive the former antagonisms and detract from the benefits of the consortium formula" (Nirumand, 1969, pp. 100–104). Expectations of benefits to the consortium were, and continue to be, amply fulfilled. The control of Iranian oil, and hence of the Iranian economy, has remained in its hands. Some Iranians supported the Shah's opening to the West and the secular reforms regarding education and vocational opportunity for women in this Muslim nation. The benefits to most Iranians, however, have left something to be desired.

The Iranian government, under popular pressure, introduced land reforms in 1961, but these affected only a quarter of the needy Iranian peasants. Those assisted were saddled with exorbitant mortgages that negated the benefits of land ownership. The landlords, meanwhile, were compensated for the parcels of land taken from them. As a bonus, they were given the opportunity to become shareowners in formerly government-owned enterprises. Widespread illiteracy, estimated by the Iranian government at 85 percent in 1962, still remained in Iran after the reforms of the Shah (Nirumand, 1969). Hunger and malnutrition continued to be critical problems. At the same time, political dissent among university students was brutally suppressed, and students were arrested and beaten by the hundreds, tortured, and murdered for their political views (Nirumand, 1969). Income distribution and class structure did not change, and the Iranian peasant remained in the miserable condition that Mossadegh had once tried to address.

Amid hostility to the West, a revolution of the orthodox mullahs rose to recreate a religious state in 1979 under the Ayatollah Khomeini. Khomeini had little regard for Western domination, and the famed hostage crisis helped to bring an end to the Carter administration. The Iranian movement to avenge the overthrow of the nationalist government in Iran and to restore religious rule in the Muslim world grew among the Shi'ites, a sect that saw itself as a persecuted minority and was elevated by Khomeini as "vanguard of the oppressed and innocent masses crushed under foot all over the world" (quoted in Taheri, 1987, pp. 7–8). The group was quite powerful in Lebanon, where it staged many of its violent actions, escalating them after the Israeli occupation. Factional strife had destroyed the capacity of the Lebanese government either to resolve or to repress fighting. Through Hezbollah, Shi'ites backed the Muslim sector. The U.S. policy, directed by Secretary of State George Shultz, sought to force Lebanon into a peace treaty with Israel in opposition to the desires of much of its population and despite the threats of neighboring Syria. The U.S. military presence provided a rallying point for suicide attacks upon soldiers and embassies. Attacks led to reprisals seemingly without end, the most egregious being the massacres at Sabra and Shatila by Christian militias while the occupying army, under General Ariel Sharon's command, stood passively by.

Rather than one single group, Islamic Jihad served more as an ideological coordinating center in Iran with other groups often carrying on operations independently in Turkey, Kuwait, Egypt, and Saudi Arabia (Hoffman, 1990). Within Iran, the battle raged between the more extremist faction and those more pragmatic groups with which Khomeini himself was associated. Iran suffered huge loses in the war against Iraq, and the accidental shooting down by the United States of an Iranian plane carrying 290 passengers created a sense of caution in the Iranian government about openly staging violent attacks. Iran, since Khomeini's death, has held democratic elections in which 80 percent of the mostly young population vote. Despite education that is heavily influenced by the religious state, the vote has usually favored moderate leaders. Still, the mission of fighting back against the secular and oppressive West and the creation of armed networks of militants had brought a new life to militant and oppressed leaders (Hoffman, 1990).

The government of Iran has sought to assist Islamic fundamentalist movements beyond its borders. A top-secret document from the Islamic Republic of Iran laid out directions for carrying out unconventional warfare in enemy territory. The document clearly accuses Middle Eastern governments of being pawns of either Russia or the United States and declares it the duty of Muslims to aid in sacrifices, including suicidal missions, to bring about a return to the religious state. Another document from an al-Qaeda training manual warned members of its various cells about the countries—Israel, Jordan, Egypt, Syria, and Saudi Arabia—that employed torture against them and offered advice on how to withstand it (Haddock, 2001).

The British and American actions in the Middle East, and the Soviet efforts as well, do not excuse the state-sponsored acts of terrorism that were inspired by the Iranian government. They do, nevertheless, help to explain it. Iran can do little to reap the benefits of its resources so long as the United States and Western Europe have alternative sources of oil from Saudi Arabia, Kuwait, and the United Arab Emirates, as well as Latin America and Indonesia. We have witnessed a century of the creation and maintenance of governments responsive to the needs of the great powers, but unresponsive to the history, the religious differences, and the material needs of their own people. The revolutionary Islamic movement has been a source of several acts of state terrorism. But it has, in some cases, been abetted by United States.

AFGHANISTAN AND THE TALIBAN

Secret military aid by the CIA to Afghan militants drew the Soviets into an invasion of Afghanistan in 1979. Then the CIA and Pakistan's ISI (Inter Services Intelligence) launched the largest covert operation in CIA history. Their purpose was to magnify Afghan resistance to the Soviets and expand it into an Islamic *jihad*, a holy war that would turn Muslim countries within the Soviet borders against the communist regime, with hope of eventually destabilizing it. When the covert assistance began, it was meant to make Afghanistan the Soviet Union's version of America's Vietnam. That was not, however, the only outcome. Over the years of that war, the CIA, through the ISI, funded and recruited close to 100,000 radical *mujahideen* from forty Islamic countries as soldiers for a U.S. proxy war. Few if any of the *mujahideen* soldiers were aware that their *jihad* was being fought on behalf of the United States (Arundhati, 2001).

The Russians withdrew in 1989, after ten years of brutal conflict. They left behind a civilization reduced to rubble. Civil war in Afghanistan continued. The effects of the *jihad* were seen in Chechnya, Kosovo, and eventually in Kashmir. The CIA continued to provide money and military equipment throughout the war. But the cost of maintaining continuous warfare in a poor country was great. In order to raise more money the *mujahideen* ordered farmers to plant opium and taxed the sales. The ISI set up hundreds of heroin laboratories in Afghanistan. Within two years of the CIA's action, the Pakistan–Afghanistan borderland had become the world's largest producer of heroin. It has remained the primary source of heroin sold on American streets. The training and arming of militants have been supported by annual profits, said to be between $100 billion and $200 billion (Levine & Levine, 1993).

The Soviet withdrawal left behind their supporters in the Kabul regime, along with stocks of Scud missiles, heavy arms, jet bombers, tanks, and advisors and KGB agents. The American support of the *mujahideen* left heavy arms and Iranian, Pakistani, and CIA agents working with conflicting tribal groups. The country was strung with land mines. For purposes other than self-interest, the world walked away from the plight of Afghanistan (Lohbeck, 1993). The United States and countries neighboring Afghanistan continued to press for an Afghan government that was favorable to their own interests, but there was no effective international relief. The United States essentially deserted Afghanistan after it was no longer fighting the Soviet Union.

The Taliban was a marginal sect of hard-line fundamentalists. By 1995, with the help of funding from the ISI, it had fought its way to power in Afghanistan. It was supported by several political parties in Pakistan. The Taliban, still not in control of all of Afghanistan, unleashed a reign of terror that followed from its cult-like ideology. Its first victims were women in the areas of Taliban control. It removed women from government jobs and shut down schools for girls. It then enforced the oppressive *shari'a* laws. Under these edicts, women said to be "immoral" are stoned to death and widows guilty of being adulterous are buried alive (Arundhati, 2001). None of these facts was sufficient to prevent the United States from cutting a further deal with the Taliban. Six months before the suicide bombings of the World Trade Center, the Bush administration provided assistance to the Taliban as part of its own crusade, the militarization of the war on drugs (Scheer, 2001). The legacy includes a country with a 64 percent illiteracy rate, a reported 48 percent of its children suffering from malnutrition, and a life expectancy of 46 years (The 2001 World Development Indicators, 2001).

The cases selected leave out the historic examples of state terrorism of Germany under Hitler and the Soviet Union under Stalin. They omit the genocidal extermination of indigenous people in the Americas, and the tragic state terrorism in Algeria (Sandhu, 2001), Nigeria, Rwanda, Sudan (Onishi, 2001), Chad, Sri Lanka, and East Timor. Each case has its own complex history. Yet all show the involvement of official U.S. policy that would be consistent with the theme that follows.

THE MINDSET OF DOMINATION

Humans are not unlike other mammals in their dislike for killing other members of their species. It takes a particular form of detachment to engage in the calculated planning to inflict violence. The target group must be mentally distinguished in a process that has been described as dehumanization (Bernard, Ottenberg, & Redl, 1965) and as psychic numbing (Falk, Kolko, & Lifton, 1971; Lifton and Markusen, 1980). Once the "enemy" is detached and defined as an adversary, the nature of the act against such a dehumanized enemy changes. It becomes a move in a preconceived plan to win against an opponent deemed to have the same objective of winning in mind. The mindset changes to one that has been studied in the theory of rational choice, or game theory. A game in this formal sense includes any situation in which the adversaries are identified, the possible moves and countermoves are defined in the rules, and the payoff or outcome results from these moves. The theory helps to categorize various types of games or conflicts and to use the power of mathematics to identify optimal moves. In the theory, one does not question why one tries to win or to maximize one's winnings, nor do the risks or losses matter except in the context of winning. The elegance of the theory is rarely employed, but the *Realpolitik* school of political science repeats the assumptions of the theory, that nation states are the players and that each chooses its moves to maximize its benefits in competition with others (Pilisuk, 1982; Rapoport, 1964).

Henry Kissinger, secretary of state under Richard Nixon, was asked about the values being adhered to in American foreign policy. His reply: "We have no values, only interests" (Hitchens, 2001). This permits a range of truly horrific choices for how one addresses obstacles to these interests. Identifying enemies is central. The principle is stated clearly in Curt Wolf's *United States Policy and the Third World.* The goal is not economic or social development but the denial of communist control. The tactics used may run from "confiscation of chickens, razing of houses or destruction of villages" to any other military harshness. They are justified if they serve "to penalize those who have assisted the insurgents" (Wolf, 1967, p. 66).

Torture has been a common part of such efforts to penalize the insurgents. It is used purposefully to force people to name other suspects or allegedly to extract confessions. That latter purpose is in fact a cover, since confessions so obtained are hardly believable. The real function is to instill fear among a larger group. The use of torture was discussed in a 1994 conference on state terror organized by Jesuits in San Salvador. The point was made by Israeli Doctor Ruchama Marton, who investigated the use of torture in her home country, that the methods are primarily to produce a culture of "silence induced by fear. Fear is contagious and spreads to other members of the oppressed group, to silence and paralyze them. To impose silence through violence is torture's real purpose, in the most profound and fundamental sense" (cited in Chomsky, 1996, p. 13).

Torture is, however, a practice specifically banned by international law.

> Article 3 of the Geneva Conventions of 1949 prohibits mistreatment of persons taking no active part in hostilities, including combatants who have laid down their arms or have been placed on hors de combat for any reason. Specifically prohibited are: violence to life and person, in particular murder, mutilation, torture; humiliating or degrading treatment; the passing of sentences or carrying out execution without previous judgement pronounced by a regularly constituted court affording guarantees of due process. (Americas Watch Report, 1991, p. 25)

Similarly, the U.S. constitution and several others prohibit cruel and unusual punishment.

Where states try to rationalize torture, the argument is put forward that it may be necessary for the prevention of an even greater crime. Harvard law professor Alan Dershowitz is reported to have suggested a mechanism, in the wake of the September 11, 2001, tragedy, through which U.S. judges could approve domestic "torture warrants" if they are convinced that such tactics could thwart an imminent attack (cited in Haddock, 2001, p. D1). The practice was used by the British in an effort to stop the nighttime shootings by Sinn Fein and the IRA, and by Israel to put an end to terrorists driving trucks filled with dynamite into buildings. Both efforts to use torture failed to deter further violence, and probably served to increase it. Once unleashed, the practices cease to be an abstraction. Denial of water, forcing people to eat food with excrement, murdering a victim's family one by one in front of the person, sodomizing the suspect's children, applying electrodes to genitals and nipples, soaking heads in bags of vomit, searing flesh, stuffing live rats into vaginas and anuses, beating the bottoms of feet with truncheons, forcing people to watch the rape of their children while being suspended naked from a crossbeam—all of these have been used. The level of fear, brutality, and lifelong effects can best be appreciated by examining the voices of survivors (Sanford, 1997). Torture crosses the line of morality by treating people as objects. It erodes the foundation of liberty—the respect for the human dignity of each and every person (Levendosky, 2001). Without that, there is no telling where the unleashed brutality will extend.

Some of the origins of this policy that justifies the use of force to promote interests can be found in a discussion by Gerald Haines (historian of the CIA) of the U.S. domination of Brazil in 1945. The policy assumed that out of self-interest the United States "assumed responsibility for the welfare of the world-capitalist system" (cited in Giraldo, 1996, p. 14). In 1965, Secretary of Defense Robert McNamara informed the national security advisor that "in the Latin American cultural environment," the military must be prepared to "remove governmental leaders from office, whenever in the judgement of the military, the conduct of these leaders is injurious to the welfare of the nation" (cited in Giraldo, 1996, p. 11). According to this view, it is the military that is entitled to determine the welfare of the nation, rather than the vast majority of mostly poor peasants and working people in the country, if that should be in U.S. interests.

Bruce Russet notes that consultants and officials who advise on military policy present themselves as avoiding value judgments in their pursuit of rigorous conclusions. But they do in fact make a critical value judgment in favor of survival and stability of the existing order. They consider no risks that would entail changing the system or revising the function that the system serves; their concern is with stability and survival without regard to *what* survives. "This unconcern with the purpose of America by those who guide its policies is the tragedy of our country and our profession" (Russet, 1970, p. 81).

Playing the strategic game can have long-term, unintended consequences, as the situation in Afghanistan illustrates. While it is often assumed that the extensive U.S. military aid to the militant *mujahideen* in Afghanistan was provided in response to a Soviet attack, statements by U.S. officials reveal that *the aid was given earlier in order to provoke Soviet military action.* The ten-year war that followed killed more than 100,000 Soviet soldiers and more than a million Afghanis. It left a decimated country embroiled in a bitter civil war with millions of people dependent upon UN and NGO (nongovernmental organization) relief operations to keep from starving. From the viewpoint of a U.S. strategic advisor, the operation was successful.

An interview with Zbigniew Brzezinski, the national security advisor to President Carter, reveals the mindset of the strategic gamester at the beginning of the U.S. support for the *mujahideen* in Afghanistan. Robert Gates, a former CIA director, had written in his memoirs that military assistance to the *mujahideen* in Afghanistan was given even before there had been any indication of armed threat from the Soviet Union. Brzezinski was asked if he had a role in the decision. His reply:

> Yes. According to the official version of history, CIA aid to the Mujahadeen began during 1980, that is to say, after the Soviet army invaded Afghanistan, 24 Dec 1979. But the reality, secretly guarded until now, is completely otherwise: Indeed, it was July 3, 1979 that President Carter signed the first directive for secret aid to the opponents of the pro-Soviet regime in Kabul. And that very day, I wrote a note to the president in which I explained to him that in my opinion this aid was going to induce a Soviet military intervention. (*Le Nouvel Observateur,* 1998)

Brzezinski was then asked about whether he had any regrets about encouraging this covert military assistance given his awareness that the Soviets might find this secret aid to the militant group a reason for a larger war. His reply:

Regret what? That secret operation was an excellent idea. It had the effect of drawing the Russians into the Afghan trap and you want me to regret it? (*Le Nouvel Observateur*, 1998)

It is worthwhile to note that Soviet casualties of that war were high, but higher still were those of the Afghanis. Civil war has persisted long after the Soviet withdrawal. Years of violent conflict left this tribal society in destitute condition, with unusable land scattered with land mines. The group that gained military power through that war has since been associated with a number of acts of terror against the United States and with a repressive domestic rule. It also provided some nurturance to a fundamentalist crusade within Muslim nations ranging from Indonesia to Pakistan, and throughout the Middle East and much of Africa. With food production diminished, the cash crop used by competing warlords was opium. As the situation of Colombia illustrates, the U.S. militarization of the war on drugs was able to override human rights atrocities in the decision to provide aid to the Colombian military. The irony is that America was unaware, in the Taliban case, that it was financing a future attack against itself. As recently as six months before the suicide attack on the World Trade Center, the United States provided financial aid to the Taliban as part of its own crusade to address the drug problem militarily and to gain support for a pipeline for oil (Scheer, 2001).

The CIA has consistently over the years distorted its own intelligence information in order to provide support to Congress and to the administration for policies that the government was intent on pursuing. The strongest documentation for this can be found in the work of John Gentry (1993), a former analyst of the CIA's directorate of intelligence in which he is especially critical of Robert Gates, the CIA director under President George H. W. Bush. In many instances, the covert action schemes involving terrorist actions have violated even the scholarship available to the CIA itself. Perhaps the most egregious illustration of training future terrorists on the part of the United States, however, may be seen in a training school in Georgia.

For the past fifty-five years, the United States has been running a training camp for military and police officers in Fort Benning, Georgia, whose victims, through acts of terrorism, greatly outnumber the people killed by the attack on New York, the embassy bombings, and the other atrocities laid, rightly or wrongly, at the door of al-Qaeda. The camp is the School of the Americas, or SOA (renamed Western Hemisphere Institute for Security Cooperation, or WHISC, in January 2001).

Since 1946, SOA has trained more than 60,000 Latin American police officers and soldiers. Its graduates include many of the continent's most notorious torturers, mass murderers, dictators, and state terrorists. Hundreds of pages of documentation compiled by the group SOA Watch (Bourgeois & Panetta, 2001) show that Latin America has been torn apart by SOA alumni.

In June 2001, Colonel Byron Lima Estrada, a former student at the school, was convicted in Guatemala City of murdering Bishop Juan Gerardi in 1998. Gerardi was killed for helping to write a report on the atrocities committed by Guatemala's "D-2," the military intelligence agency run by Lima Estrada with the help of two other SOA graduates. D-2 arranged the "anti-insurgency" campaign that obliterated 448 Mayan Indian villages and murdered tens of thousands of their people. Recall the genocidal regimes of Lucas Garcia, Rios Montt, and Mejia Victores. Forty percent of the cabinet ministers who served these regimes studied at SOA (Monbiot, 2001).

A United Nations Truth Commission on El Salvador released in 1993 the names of military officers who had committed the worst atrocities of the civil war. Two-thirds of them had been trained at SOA. This group included Roberto D'Aubuisson, the leader of El Salvador's death squads; the men who killed Archbishop Oscar Romero; and 19 of the 26 soldiers who murdered the Jesuit priests in 1989. In Chile, other SOA graduates ran Augusto Pinochet's secret police and his three principal concentration camps. One of them helped to murder Orlando Letelier and Ronni Moffit in Washington, D.C., in 1976 (School of Americas Watch, 2001).

Panama's Manuel Noriega and Omar Torrijos were graduates of SOA. Two Argentina dictators, Roberto Viola and Leopoldo Galtieri, were graduates, as were Peru's Juan Velasco Alvarado and Ecuador's Guillermo Rodriguez. Other beneficiaries of the training included the leader of the Grupo Colina death squad in Fujimori's Peru; four of the five officers who were in charge of the notorious Battalion 3-16 (which controlled the death squads in Honduras in the 1980s) and the commander responsible for the 1994 Ocosingo massacre in Mexico (Monbliot, 2001).

The pursuit of interest without principle has included major assistance with narcotics trafficking. Senator John Kerry, following testimony during the Iran-contra hearings, took note of the testimony indicating that the U.S. government, including the potential criminal implications of two presidents, had been involved in flooding the United States with narcotics. "Our system of justice has been perverted; [our covert agencies] had converted themselves into channels for the flow of drugs into the United States" (Kerry, cited in Levine & Kavanau-Levine, 1993, p. 3). Michael Levine notes:

> For decades the CIA, the Pentagon, and secret organizations like Oliver North's Enterprise have been supporting and protecting the world's biggest drug dealers. Those brave freedom fighters in Afghanistan, the Mujahadin, supply a major portion of heroin used in the United States. The Contras and some of their Central American allies like Honduras have been documented by DEA as supplying us with at least 50 percent of our national cocaine consumption. They were the main conduits to the United States for Colombian cocaine during the 1980s. The rest of the drug supply for the American habit came from other CIA-supported groups, such as DFS (the Mexican equivalent of the CIA), the Shan United Army in the Golden Triangle of Southeast Asia, or any of the scores of other groups and/or individuals like Manuel Noriega. (Levine & Kavanau-Levine, 1993, p. 463)

The complementary side of that problem is that millions of people in poor countries who have been displaced by the global economy—Bolivia, Peru, Colombia, Afghanistan, Turkey, Taiwan, Ghana, Nigeria, Iran, India, Pakistan, Mexico, and Southeast Asia—depend upon the $200 billion a year that Americans spend on illegal drugs for money to pay for food and clothing for their children (Levine & Kavanau-Levine, 1993).

TOWARD A THEORY OF STATE TERRORISM: INEQUALITY, "RELATIVE DEPRIVATION," IMPUNITY, AND THE DEHUMANIZATION OF DISSENTERS

Why then do governments engage in gross terrorism? The answer is complex. First, governments' ability to inflict terror depends on weapons and training in how to use them. The arming of any group increases the potential for terror. Second, when the military is unaccountable to civilian authority, terrorism is more likely. Third, the dehumanization of opposing groups makes their brutal treatment more likely. Fourth, when states remain in power by means of fear, they treat all dissent as a threat. Fifth, violent acts beget further violence, creating a cycle of retribution that is carried on often over generations. Finally, the domination of the world's resources and wealth by a few at the expense of the poverty of others creates an incentive for revolutionary change that may be tapped by leaders for violent actions and that may be used by governments as an excuse for state terror.

One underlying factor in terrorism lies in the role played by governments in justifying the gross inequalities of wealth and power. This inequality has grown to astounding proportions with the onset of economic globalization (Korten, 1998; Pilisuk, 2001). The January 2001 CIA report on future trends noted these consequences of globalization: ". . . regions, countries, and groups feeling left behind will face deepening economic stagnation, political instability, and cultural alienation. They will foster political, ethnic, ideological and religious extremism, along with the violence that often accompanies it" (cited in Roth, 2001, p. 18). Rather than seeking to constrain or redirect the globalization process, the report assumes continuation of the destructive process and views the resultant violence as something to be contained. That is consistent with the mission of protecting the interests of an expanding capitalism. In developed nations such as the United States, gross inequality is viewed as a legitimate outcome of the market, and the increasing centralization of corporate global forces is seen as inevitable. Also in developed countries, political rights are often sufficient to allow dissenters to express their views even if they lack the power or the wealth to address their needs. In most of the less-developed world, which by contrast is still facing economic and military colonialism, governments lack such legitimacy and remain in power through police control over opposing groups. The colonial pattern creates the need to protest. Such groups may protest violently or nonviolently. Government attempts to eliminate nonviolent protest will drive people to acts of defiance. The dissenters may be dedicated to the principles of peaceful change or they may be disciples of leaders who urge violence. In either case, state leaders share the perceived need to suppress attempts by discontented groups to overthrow them.

One insight into the origin of such oppositional groups comes from a theory of *relative deprivation*. This is the idea that people rate their level of distress not in absolute terms but relative to some group or some time that they hold as a standard for comparison (Stouffer, 1949). The theory notes that large cult movements occur frequently where there has been a relative loss of status and of living standards for a group of people. The loss is relative to what is recalled as better times and is frequently accompanied by a revivalist message, a messianic belief in a return to the glories of a prior time. One such movement spread among Native American tribes of the western United States toward the end of the nineteenth century. It envisioned a rolling back of the white settlers who had usurped the land and a return of the buffalo. Other examples are seen in the Melanesian "cargo cults," the aborigines' rituals in Australia, and La Fiesta de los Tastones in Guadalajara, Mexico. All of these promised a ritualistic return to values at a time before being dehumanized by colonial status (Najera-Ramirez, 1997; Sharp, 1976; Wallace, 1956). The beliefs do not necessarily call for violence, but they do call for a pervasive, sometimes fanatic, devotion to a particular view.

In Cambodia and again in Iran and Afghanistan, we see illustrations of relative deprivation. Each showed elements of an ideology recalling a former time of grandeur. In Cambodia, in Guatemala, and in Iran the perpetrators of major suffering came to power after a history in which domination by foreign governments had been a source of visible oppression. In these cases, they had observed firsthand the emerging privileges and wealth of a small group amid deepening poverty for others. And in all of the cases discussed, states had amassed weapons from foreign governments.

State terrorism is aimed largely at groups seeking a change in their conditions. The conditions for wanting revolutionary change appear to be: a feeling that one is oppressed; a sense that conditions are worse now than they were at some previous time; a belief that the current powers of government are not addressing the problem; and leaders who indicate the possibility of empowering people to achieve something better. These conditions are now widely experienced on an international level. They help to explain why vast, nonviolent protests have managed to upset meetings of the World Trade Organization in any city in the world in which it chooses to meet. The tactics of those desiring revolutionary changes are typically peaceful. They turn violent when they have weapons and training in the use of violence, and when they are not allowed to express their dissent peacefully. One further contributor to the use of violent activities comes when people have responded to leaders who convince them that their most cherished values are under attack, that such an attack justifies a violent response, and that those seeking peace are cowards or traitors, and when opinion leaders encourage the dehumanization of the enemy.

Clearly the matter of state terrorism occurs among nations that are communist or capitalist, have religious or secular governments, or have either elected governments or dictatorships. Equally clearly, terrorism, once begun, taps a potential for its further use, both to prevent retribution and to attain retribution.

State terrorism is used to resist the advocates of revolutionary change. It comes about when military or police forces have power that is unaccountable to civilian authority, when governments need to cover up the trail of their own misdeeds, and when governments have the resources to control by inducing terror and targeting scapegoats. It is frequently disclaimed by its practitioners, who use the threat of violence to silence their critics. Whatever its cause, violence tends to beget further violence. Victims of violence are a threat for further retribution. And violence by those with power sets the moral standard that violence conducted for a cause is proper. State terrorism is not only brutal as a form both of killing and of silencing dissent. It also teaches vast populations that inflicting violence is a manner of action approved by legitimate governmental authorities despite their awkward attempts to deny this. A true war on terrorism is not an effort to gain retribution against one group of its practitioners. It calls for a confrontation with the conditions that cause governments to condone or to conduct terrorism. It calls also for a realization that principles of decency, caring, and justice, rather than markets and power, are the real interests of all of us.

REFERENCES

Aguilera Peralta, G., & Imery, J. R. (1981). *Dialecta de la Tierra in Guatemala*. San Jose, Guatemala: EDUCA.

Americas Watch (1982). *Human rights in Guatemala: No neutrals allowed*. New York: Americas Watch.

Americas Watch Report (1991, September). *Guatemala: Slaying of rights activists, impunity prevail under new government*. Washington, DC: Americas Watch.

Amnesty International (1982). *Guatemala: Massive extrajudicial executions in rural areas under the government of General Efrain Rios Montt*. London: Author.

Amnesty International (1989). *Guatemala: Human rights violations under civilian governments*. London: Author.

Amnesty International (1993). *Getting away with murder: Political killings and "disappearances" in the 1990s*. New York: Amnesty International Publications.

Arundhati, R. (2001, September 29). The algebra of infinite justice. *Guardian*, p. 1.

Ball, P., Kobrack, P., & Spirer, H. F. (1999). *State violence in Guatemala, 1960–1996: A quantitative reflection*. Washington, DC: American Association for the Advancement of Science.

Barron, J., & Paul, A. (1977). *Peace with horror*. London: Hodder and Stoughton.

Bernard, V. W., Ottenberg, P., & Redl, F. (1965). Dehumanization: A composite psychological defense in relation to modern war. In M. Schwebel (Ed.), *Behavioral science and human survival*. Palo Alto, CA: Science and Behavior Books.

Black, G. (1984). *Garrison Guatemala*. New York: Monthly Review Press.

Blanck, E., & Castillo, R. M. (1998). El palacio de las intrigas. *Cronica* (Guatemala).

Bourgeois, R., & Panetta, L. (2001). School of assassins. *Yale Latin American Review*. http://www.soaw-ne.org/articles.html

Burke, E. (1775). Speech on the conciliation with America, March 22, 1775. Cited in G. M. Welling (1996), *The American Revolution: An HTML project.* University of Groningen, Netherlands (February 15, 1999). http://odur.let.rug.nl/~usa/D/1751-1775/libertydebate/burk.htm

Carney, T. (1989). The organization of power. In K. D. Jackson (Ed.), *Cambodia 1975–1978: Rendezvous with death* (pp. 79–107). Princeton, NJ: Princeton University Press.

Centro Internacional para Investigaciones en Derechos Humanos (CIIDH) and Grupo de Apoyo Mutuo (GAM) (1999). En pie de lucha: Organizacion y represion en la Universidad de San Carlos, Guatemala 1944–1996. In P. Ball, P. Kobrack, & H. F. Spirer (1999), *State violence in Guatemala, 1960–1996: A quantitative reflection.* Washington, DC: American Association for the Advancement of Science.

Chomsky, N., & Herman, E. S. (1979). *After the cataclysm.* Nottingham: Spokesman.

Chomsky, N. (1996). The culture of fear. In J. Giraldo, *Colombia, the genocidal democracy* (pp. 7–16). Monroe, ME: Common Courage Press.

Comision Inter-Congregacional de Justicia y Paz (1995). *Data bank.* Guatemala City: Author.

Falk, R. A, Kolko, G., & Lifton, R. J. (Eds.) (1971). *Crimes of war: A legal, political-documentary, and psychological inquiry into the responsibility of leaders, citizens, and soldiers for criminal acts in wars.* New York: Random House.

Falla, R. (1983). *Masacre de la Finca San Francisco, Huehuetenango, Guatemala.* Copenhagen, Denmark: International Work Group for Indigenous Affairs.

Gentry, J. A. (1993). *Lost promise: How CIA analysis misserves the nation.* Lanham, MD: University Press of America, Inc.

Giraldo, J. (1996). *Colombia: The genocidal democracy.* Monroe, ME: Common Courage Press.

Haddock, V. (2001, November 18). The unspeakable. *San Francisco Chronicle,* pp. C1, D6.

Han, H. H. (Ed.) (1993). *Terrorism and political violence: Limits and possibilities of legal control.* New York: Oceana Publications Inc.

Hawk, D. (1989). The photographic record. In K. D. Jackson (Ed.), *Cambodia 1975–1978: Rendezvous with death* (pp. 209–214). Princeton, NJ: Princeton University Press.

Hitchens, C. (2001). *The trial of Henry Kissinger.* New York: Verso.

Hoffman, B. (1990). *Recent trends and future prospects of Iranian sponsored international terrorism.* Santa Monica, CA: Rand Corporation.

Human Rights Watch (1999, July 22). U.N. asked to intervene to protect Falun Gong's rights. *China Human Rights Watch Report.* http://www.hrw.org/press/1999/jul/china2207.htm

Jonas, S. (1991). *The battle for Guatemala: Rebels, death squads and U.S. power.* Boulder, CO: Westview Press.

Keesing's Contemporary Archives, 1975–1993. London: Longman.

Kleff, R. (1993). Terrorism: The trinity perspective. In H. H. Han (Ed.), *Terrorism and political violence: Limits and possibilities of legal control.* New York: Oceana Publications Inc.

Korten, D. (1998). *Globalizing civil society: Reclaiming our right to power.* New York: Seven Stories Press.

Koufa, K. (2001, June 27). *Terrorism and human rights.* United Nations Economic and Social Council, Commission on Human Rights, Sub-Commission on the Promotion and Protection of Human Rights.

Lador-Lederer, J. J. (1993). Defining "terrorism": A comment. In H. H. Han (Ed.), *Terrorism and political violence: Limits and possibilities of legal control.* New York: Oceana Publications Inc.

Levendosky, C. (2001, November 18). Tortured logic. *San Francisco Chronicle,* p. D6.

Le Nouvel Observateur (France) (1998, January 15–21), 76.

Levine, M., & Kavanau-Levine, L. (1993). *The big white lie: The deep cover operation that exposed the CIA sabotage of the drug war.* New York: Thunder's Mouth Press.

Lifton, R. J., & Markusen, E. (1980). *The genocidal mentality: Nazi Holocaust and nuclear threat.* New York: Basic Books.

Lohbeck, K. (1993). *Holy war, unholy victory: Eyewitness to the CIA's secret war in Afghanistan.* Washington, DC: Regnery Gateway.

Martz, J. D. (1991, February). Colombia at the crossroads. *Current History, 90,* 69–75.

Martz, J. D. (1994, March). Colombia: Democracy, development, and drugs. *Current History, 93,* 134–138.

McClintock, M. (1985). *The American connection: State terror and popular resistance in Guatemala.* London: Zed Press.

Melville, T., & Melville, M. (1971). *Guatemala: The politics of land ownership.* New York: Free Press.

Monbiot, G. (2001, October 30). America's terrorist training camp: What's the difference between Al Qaeda and Fort Benning? *The Guardian,* p. 17.

Moss, R. (1972). *Urban guerillas: The new face of political violence.* London: Robert Temple Smith.

Nairn, A. (1983, April 11). Guatemala bleeds. *The New Republic.*

Najéra-Ramírez, O. (1997). *La fiesta de los Tastoanes: Critical encounters in festival performance.* Albuquerque: University of New Mexico Press.

Nirumand, B. (1969). *Iran: The new imperialism in action.* New York: Monthly Review Press.

Nunberg, G. (2001, October 28). Terrorism: The history of a very frightening word. *San Francisco Chronicle,* p. C5.

O'Kane, R. H. T. (1996). Terror as government and its causes, Cambodia, April 1975–January 1979. In R. H. T. O'Kane (Ed.), *Terror, force, and states: The path from modernity.* Cheltenham, England: Edward Elgar.

Onishi, N. (2001, October 13). Sudan government tops list of those causing agony for oil. *New York Times.*

O'Neill, B. E. (1993). The strategic context of insurgent terrorism. In H. H. Han (Ed.), *Terrorism and political violence: Limits and possibilities of legal control.* New York: Oceana Publications Inc.

Pilisuk, M. (1972). *International conflict and social policy.* Englewood Cliffs, NJ: Prentice-Hall.

Pilisuk, M. (1982, November). Games strategists play. *The Bulletin of the Atomic Scientists, 38,* 13–17.

Pilisuk, M. (2001). Globalism and structural violence. In D. J. Christie, R. V. Wagner, & D. D. Winter (Eds.), *Peace conflict and violence: Peace psychology for the 21st century* (pp. 149–157). Upper Saddle River, NJ: Prentice Hall.

Ponchaud, F. (1978). *Cambodia year zero*. London: Allen Lane.

Quinn, K. M. (1989). Explaining the terror. In K. D. Jackson (Ed.), *Cambodia 1975–1978: Rendezvous with death* (pp. 215–240). Princeton, NJ: Princeton University Press.

Rapoport, A. (1964). *Strategy and conscience*. New York: Harper and Row.

Roth, G. (2001, November 10). All politics is local. *San Francisco Bay Guardian*, p. 18.

Russet, B. M. (1970/1973). Report from Iron Mountain. In K. E. Boulding (Ed.), *Peace and the war industry* (2nd ed., pp. 79–81). New Brunswick, NJ: Transaction Books.

Sagar, D. (1989). Historical survey. In M. Wright (Ed.), *Cambodia: A matter of survival* (pp. 9–70). Harlow, England: Longman.

Sandhu, A. (2001). Algerian conflict: An exercise in state terrorism. *Journal for the Study of Peace and Conflict*, pp. 1–15.

Sanford, V. (1997). *Mothers, widows and guerilleras: Anonymous conversations with survivors of state terror*. Uppsala, Sweden: Life and Peace Institute.

Scheer, R. (2001, May 22). Bush's Faustian deal with the Taliban. *Los Angeles Times*, p. B15.

Schirmer, J. (1998). *The Guatemalan military project: A violence called democracy*. Philadelphia: University of Pennsylvania Press.

School of Americas Watch (2001). http://www.soaw.org

Sharp, N. (1976). *Millenarian movements: Their meaning in Melanesia*. Department of Sociology, School of Social Sciences, La Trobe University, Bundoora, Vic. 3083, Australia.

Stouffer, S. A. (1949). *The American soldier: Studies in social psychology in World War II* (Vols. 1–2). Princeton, NJ: Princeton University Press.

Taheri, A. (1987). *Holy terror: The inside story of Islamic terrorism*. London: Sphere Books.

Terrorism Research Center. (2001). *Terrorist group profiles*. http://www.terrorism.com/terrorism/links.html.

Tully, A. (1962). *CIA: The inside story*. New York: William Morrow & Co.

The 2001 World Development Indicators CD-ROM (2001). World Development Indicators CD-ROM Version. International Bank for Reconstruction and Development/World Bank. From University of California, Berkeley Library Network CD-ROM.

United States Senate Subcommittee on Security and Terrorism (1985). *State-sponsored terrorism*. Report prepared for the use of the Committee on the Judiciary, United States Senate. Washington, DC: U.S. Government Printing Office.

Vickery, M. (1985). *Cambodia, 1975–1982*. London: Allen and Unwin.

Wallace, A. F. (1956). Revitalization movements. *American Anthropologist, 58*, 2.

Walter, E. V. (1972). *Terror and resistance: A study of political violence*. New York: Oxford University Press.

Wilson, S. (2001, October 12). Paramilitary troops massacre villagers in Colombia. *Washington Post*, p. A29.

Wise, D., & Ross, T. (1964). *The invisible government*. New York: Random House.

Wolf, C. (1967). *United States policy and the Third World: Problems and analysis*. Boston: Little, Brown.

Wright, M. (Ed.) (1989). *Cambodia: A matter of survival*. Harlow, England: Longman.

6

The Emotional Injuries of Indirect Trauma

Lourens Schlebusch and Brenda Ann Bosch

South Africa in the last decade has been epitomized by a transformed social order and unprecedented political developments. The unthinkable occurred when the political order changed through peaceful negotiations from apartheid (official racial segregation) to a full democracy. Unfortunately, this transformation did not preclude an escalation in violence, with resultant trauma. It therefore seems appropriate in this chapter to examine aspects of the South African situation in regard to the universal features of the psychology of terrorism, given the country's legacy of trauma in both the apartheid and post-apartheid eras against the backdrop of international terrorism.

It has been strongly argued that dealing with stress and trauma solutions requires a collective multi-dimensional approach (Schlebusch, 1998, 2000). Violence and crime resulting in stress and trauma remain major public issues in South African society (Baird, 1999; Barolsky, 1999; Landman, 2000; Louw, 1999; Shaw, 2000) whether they occur in families, the community, institutions, or society at large and whether they result in direct or indirect exposure. The 1998 National Victims of Crime Survey revealed a pervasive quality of violence in South African society indicative of a high level of interpersonal conflict (Barolsky, 1999). According to the latest Crime Intelligence Analysis (Green, 2000), there is a seven-in-ten chance that South Africans will have their property stolen and a one-in-ten chance that they will be a victim of serious violent crime. This gives rise to elevated levels of trauma. Human trauma, being as old as humanity, is rooted in interaction, on interpersonal, group, or collective levels—locally, nationally, and internationally.

Elevated stress, with its consequent myriad of health problems, forms an indisputable part of this equation (Schlebusch, 1998).

TRAUMA-PRODUCING BEHAVIORS

Trauma-producing behaviors (TPBs) can take many forms, the violence referred to above being one. Terrorism manifests in another form of trauma. Acts of terrorism (including bioterrorism, such as anthrax-contaminated mail) spread fear and anxiety to people even far removed from where the acts occur. Terrorism is an abnormal and unthinkable act, and people are horrified by it. Injury by terrorism carries with it a stigma for the victim that can leave him or her feeling abandoned, ashamed, and isolated.

Any TPB resulting in trauma can be construed as legitimate or illegitimate, depending on individual legal systems and specific beliefs. Violence leading to trauma is mostly a learned response, and desensitization to this can result from social learning. Thus, it can be perpetuated intergenerationally; for example, children who are victims of prolonged exposure to trauma become desensitized to violence. This can result in their repeating patterns of violence to resolve conflict or to satisfy political and/or religious motivations. Furthermore, a TPB is often countered by another TPB, and repressive violence leads to reactive violence. An example is the trauma and aggression that often manifest in sport, especially in certain contact sports such as rugby, boxing, and wrestling. Another example is driving behavior. South African road accident statistics and casualties are alarming, and support the notion that trauma in South Africa has extended to this area. Road rage is on the increase (as is air rage), and many incidents of violence are not merely "accidental"; acting out aggression on the road, stoning of vehicles, drive-by shootings, and mob TPBs directed at motorists form part of this repertoire.

Membership in families and in larger organizations such as schools and religious affiliations and later in political and occupational affiliations is important in the socialization of children. Such membership shapes beliefs about trauma. Children learn to participate in the groups to which they belong and to internalize and adhere to the values, norms, and practices that regulate conduct within a particular group. In this process, discipline is a prominent socializing feature, but such discipline can also be exercised through acts that produce trauma, either physically or psychologically resulting in further traumatization. Similarly, children can learn TPBs as a form of expression. A poignant example comes from the fact that in traditional armies, young adults are the recruits. In many liberation struggles, children are robbed of their childhood as recruits of war, as often seen in Africa and recently elsewhere in the world.

State-sanctioned acts of TPBs, such as war and laws of repression, are in themselves portrayed as legitimate to control conduct that is perceived to be acting against the interests of the state. Further, legal TPBs are formally taught by the military and, in South Africa (as elsewhere in the world), countless people have either died in incidents of political trauma or (if they have survived) have been severely traumatized.

EFFECTS OF TRAUMA: HUMAN RIGHTS VIOLATIONS

A clear example of the above is evident in the responses of individuals seen at the Truth and Reconciliation Commission (TRC) hearings in South Africa (Pillay & Schlebusch, 1997). The TRC was established as part of the post-apartheid transformation process in South Africa, to deal with the historical facts of and future prevention of human rights abuses and associated trauma in that country. Rather than functioning as a confrontational or retributive organ, it aimed to restore relationships between the state and/or other perpetrators and victims of violence, and to give people the opportunity to be psychologically healed by providing a facility and platform to deal with their anguish and trauma. The TRC commenced its work on December 15, 1995. As a result of a request that clinical psychologists from the authors' department assist the TRC with psychological support services, we were provided with an immense clinical opportunity and scope for research in the psychology of stress-related trauma resulting from gross human rights violations. This took place at the first hearing in Durban (a major harbor city on the east coast of South Africa). Clinical psychologists from our department worked with individuals and/or with victims' families, debriefing and/or providing supportive psychotherapy and follow-up psychological treatment where indicated (Pillay & Schlebusch, 1997).

The types of violations to which victims were exposed (directly or indirectly), as reported by the individuals and/or families (who were sometimes witnesses), included forced removals and separation from loved ones as a result of not being permitted to live or work in certain areas; killings; attacks; torture; bomb blasts; death of loved ones in detention; and major political and personal harassment. Furthermore, we observed that testifying and relating their experiences at the TRC hearings was not necessarily "cathartic" for those concerned and in fact reopened and/or exposed festering psychological wounds and contributed to secondary trauma, not only in the witnesses but among the TRC staff, the media representatives covering the proceedings, and the public.

ISSUES AND PSYCHOPATHOLOGY

However, since a denial of their suffering by the previous political system was a major issue for victims that exacerbated underlying psychopathology, they did feel a sense of relief that their suffering was "finally being acknowledged and recognized" and because the TRC hearings offered an opportunity to express the wrong they had suffered. The fact that the guilt and self-blame that many had developed was acknowledged was an important part of the healing process. Recognizable psychological disorders were evident in all witnesses, except one (who had had prior psychological treatment). The most common were chronic post-traumatic stress disorder (PTSD), other anxiety disorders, and mood disorders, although some witnesses psychologically decompensated into an acute psychosis afterward, requiring hospitalization. Other common symptoms included "freezing" (being locked into the period of experiencing the trauma in order to cope with integrating changes and new experiences, both positive and negative, that had taken place since); the inability to feel anger; flashbacks; snapshot memories (recalling vividly and with precise detail, not only the incidents, but clothing, color, sounds, etc., of objects and situations associated with traumatic incidents); avoidance of people out of feelings of "embarrassment" (i.e., about being violated and traumatized); and verbal tiredness (verbal expressive fatigue).

Subsequent to the hearings, most of the witnesses voluntarily contacted the psychologists who had been involved, for further treatment either as individuals or as families. Patients initially most often assumed the role of "rescuer or martyr" in the family, and often failed to deal with their own personal issues—instead taking care of the family's problems. They also had problems coping interpersonally. Ultimately, treatment for some involved hospital admission and appropriate medication. It was also necessary to provide psychological expertise and support to TRC staff, which involved daily debriefing and weekly support groups. An interesting consequence was that the psychologists themselves also showed signs of "compassion fatigue" and needed support. We found the use of additional staff, with regular rotations, a useful method to deal with these latter responses.

EFFECTS OF TRAUMA: NATURAL DISASTERS

Further evidence of the indirect effects of trauma is seen in the responses to natural disasters. A study by the senior author (Schlebusch, 1987) of reactions to trauma following one of the worst natural disasters in South African history, which left the province of Kwa-Zulu Natal devastated, revealed interesting results. Heavy rains started lashing the province on Friday, September 25, 1987. Major downpours lasted for several weeks, followed by intermittent rain for several more days. The province was officially declared a disaster area by the state president on the evening of September 30, 1987, when he appealed for donations to a Disaster Relief Fund established by the state. The death toll in the floods was estimated at more than three hundred. Thousands of homes were destroyed or damaged, and at least sixty thousand people were left homeless. Many factories were flooded, large areas were strewn with debris, and most major industrial activities ground to a halt. Numerous roads and bridges were swept away and transport, communications, health services, and food and water supplies were severely disrupted, resulting in thousands of people being unable to get to work.

More than one billion rands' worth of damage was done to the province's economy, with insurance claims topping millions of rands a day. Stringent water restrictions were implemented in those areas of Durban that still had a water supply. Durban is a holiday mecca and one of Africa's busiest ports. Authorities appealed to shippers to make use of Maputo harbor (in the neighboring country of Mozambique) where possible, following disruptions of imports and exports. The death and devastation of those few days was so widespread that few people in the province were not affected in some way, and the entire nation was moved by their plight. In the midst of the chaos and destruction, stories of heroism, courage, bravery, and humanitarian support emerged.

Psychological reactions to the disaster were found to be exceedingly stressful based on a post-factum analysis of the difficulties experienced in some of the events described above, and with reference to local and international research findings. Major effects on short- and long-term mental health equilibrium were noted, and a number of mechanisms were involved in the dynamics of the psychological effects, including suffering loss (of health, property, loved ones, etc.) and feelings of having played a passive role during the event. The closer the individual was to the epicenter of the disaster, the greater the feelings of involvement.

However, involvement was affected further by individual feelings of separation from the community in which the disaster occurred, or from the victim thereof, or both. Thus, depending on the extent and magnitude of the disaster, psychological boundaries developed between the microcommunity (those directly involved) and the macrocommunity (the suburb, city, region, or nation). There was a lesser psychological barrier between the victims and the community in the former instance, whereas in the latter situation the shoppers, workers, or inhabitants experienced feelings of victimization and psychological separation from the community.

Follow-up work showed that the survivors of the 1987 Kwa-Zulu Natal flood disaster experienced a range of psychological symptoms including phobic symptoms, irritability, acute and post-traumatic stress disorders, and depression, which contributed to alcohol-related substance abuse disorder, marital problems, unemployment, absenteeism, and frequent job changes. Reactions to the disaster occurred in stages commensurate with other research findings. These are similar in some ways to reactions following terror attacks and included:

- The *recoil stage*, in which victims often present as numbed and apathetic, or show acute panic reactions or inappropriate apathetic and automatic behavior.

- The *post-disaster Utopia phase*, which occurs soon after a disaster and is characterized by victims being more helpful and cooperative in their social relations, often even resolving old quarrels, until this state of benevolence dissolves, sometimes fairly rapidly. A prime example of this is the mutual support and resourcefulness that was demonstrated by people of all persuasions in the Kwa-Zulu Natal flood disaster, when major differences between people were set aside in their willingness to help.

- The *post-impact/aftermath phase*, which can be identified by the presentation of prolonged psychological reactions characteristic of some of the disorders mentioned earlier, requiring early identification and treatment.

EFFECTS OF TRAUMA-PRODUCING BEHAVIORS

In our experience, TPB effects can surface either immediately or can be delayed for weeks, months, or years. Desensitization can become a coping behavior, with denial of the existence of feelings about the event or the plight of others involved. Emotional blunting occurs as a result. These symptoms can themselves become problematic if prolonged and can lead to a kind of moral atrophy in which the individual no longer questions the TPB because moral principles no longer apply, and there is a sense of being absolved of the responsibility of making personal moral choices. In such circumstances, when assessing the legitimacy of actions, people learn to look to official definitions of actions or authorization of actions rather than to their human consequences. This extends the notion of learned helplessness to include *moral* helplessness.

Illegitimate TPBs can be directed at people (individually or in groups) and at property. Examples include interpersonal violence/terror such as murder, manslaughter, aggravated assault, rape, robbery, burglary, larceny, and other illegal conduct. Group and intergroup TPBs may be racially, religiously, ethnically, or politically defined, especially when there are incompatible attitudes, beliefs, and values between and within such different groups. They can cross international boundaries when external wings of political or religious groups from one country precipitate trauma in other countries, and are often based on terrorism or insurgents, or on rallying psychological or financial support for their cause.

Violence/terror leading to trauma, since it is linked to a human need to be aggressive, has traditionally been associated with frustration in line with the well-known frustration-aggression hypothesis. However, the acknowledgement that aggression can be linked to a number of other factors has led to a more embracing understanding that includes powerful psychological, environmental, social, and biological stimuli. Examples are found in sociocultural factors within the broader society, such as are expressed in various norms, beliefs, values, social structures, and institutional arrangements, as well as in medical causes, pathological behavior, mental retardation, brain injury, and alcohol or drug abuse. Although more research is needed to bridge the gaps between behavioral and social sciences and brain research, the link between experience and neurophysiology has been demonstrated. For example, research on the biological aspects of stress, anxiety, depression, aggression, and substance abuse has yielded new insights, one of the most challenging being that life experiences can significantly affect brain chemistry as well as gene expression. Regarding violence, such expression can occur in both aggressor and victim.

Nevertheless, any TPB shares certain common characteristics, such as conflict, force, physical or mental power, fear, potential retaliatory trauma, a victim and a perpetrator, violence/terror as a form of communication, violation of the dignity and rights of those who fall prey to it, and invasion of the personal and the physical space of direct or indirect victims.

Although a TPB can occur in public or private, intergroup violence/terror usually occurs in or spills over into public settings. The privacy of a home lends itself to secrecy about abusive interactions, whereas when it becomes public, the community becomes involved and is affected.

The effect of TPBs on individuals and society can be overwhelming. It pervades the very fabric of existence and few remain untouched by it. If they are not directly involved, people are often indirectly drawn in by the mass media and the "fallout" caused by the sequelae of the trauma. Financial implications and the social and emotional stress of living in a violent environment, or witnessing it elsewhere, can be direct or indirect, because people respond differently to exposure to violence/terror depending on whether they participate in it or are affected indirectly. The psychological implications may manifest unobtrusively or overtly and may have short-term or long-term consequences.

Because TPBs usually contradict the commonly held values of personal, family, and societal well-being, and can result in human injury or harm, they are disruptive and can result in the extensive use of security arrangements in homes, in commercial, shopping, and industrial premises, and in travel (such as at airports). This detracts from the quality of life, affects lifestyles, and can result in serious psychopathology.

A critical response following TPBs is fear. Freedom from fear is one of the four basic freedoms proclaimed by U.S. President Franklin Delano Roosevelt. Fear of further trauma or violence/terror leads to restricted movement, polarization, psychological problems, dysfunctional interpersonal and intergroup relationships, disruption of social networks, and depletion of communities, whose members try to escape from trauma or the threats of trauma by fleeing from their neighborhoods or countries. Fear can be individual, localized, widespread, or pervasive in society. If the latter, it tends to affect everyone in that society, including those who were not directly exposed to the trauma. In such cases, everyone becomes a victim.

TPBs can lead to pervasive feelings of helplessness, guilt, withdrawal, sadness associated with loss, sleep disturbances, and a sense of loss of control over the situation. Other sequelae are feelings that one's fate is in the hands of others, feelings of powerlessness, depression, anxiety, anger, outrage, shame, humiliation, despair, self-blame, feelings of unfairness and injustice, feelings of frustration, feelings of disempowerment, fear of losing the ability to predict what will happen to one, learned helplessness, denial, numbness, and amnesia. Indirect trauma not only causes psychological disruption, it can dehumanize and alienate victims as a result of creating distrust in society, lowering morale, and stimulating social disorganization.

It is not unusual to encounter similar responses to direct trauma when assessing emotional injuries caused by indirect trauma. Shock, numbness, and confusion are common initial reactions. As shock wears off, intense grief and uncontrollable crying sometimes emerge, along with depression and feelings of loneliness associated with guilt. Those who were indirectly exposed to the traumatic disaster attempt to understand why this happened, and grieving families wonder why they lost a loved one. Some people find it easier to accept what happened if they can blame someone more visible, such as a government or themselves, in some way. Anger, resentment, and feeling outraged at the tragedy, the person or persons who caused the tragedy, or someone the individual believes could have prevented it, are commonly seen, as are feelings of panic. People may feel as if they are going crazy, particularly when they experience fear, and become easily startled or extremely anxious, either when leaving the home or when alone. It is common to manifest physical symptoms of distress, such as headaches, fatigue, nausea, sleeplessness, loss of sexual feelings, and weight gain or loss after a traumatic event. Also, the person may feel uncoordinated, experience muscle pain and chills/sweats, twitch/shake, and grind his or her teeth. Many individuals report that they are unable to function at the same premorbid levels or to return to their usual social activities. Executive functions are impaired and people may find it hard to think and plan; what they used to enjoy may now seem meaningless. It is well recognized that some individuals will have a delayed reaction, that is, will only react weeks or months later. These reactions are often with a perception that TPBs seem unreal and incomprehensible.

IMPLICATIONS AND APPLICATIONS FOR INTERVENTION

From our experiences, it is apparent that debriefing, supportive therapy, follow-up intervention, and the need for society and the system to acknowledge the suffering of victims are essential components of the processes of addressing and dealing with human rights violations. But this often opens a Pandora's box. We noted (Pillay & Schlebusch, 1997) that the trauma experienced by individuals and communities (both victims and perpetrators) in South Africa is much deeper and more pervasive than is generally realized. Consequently, it had to be addressed well after the life span of the TRC, placing a mammoth workload and responsibility on psychologists seeking to assist in the process of healing and reparation in the "New South Africa." This is probably true for all trauma that results from widespread, national TPBs, such as in the aftermath of terrorism.

REFERENCES

Baird, M. I. (1999). Blasting carjacking: Prosecution-led law enforcement. *Crime and Conflict, 16,* 37–40.

Barolsky, V. (1999). Victims and the police: The national victims of crime survey. *Crime and Conflict, 16*, 26–31.

Green, J. (2000, January 29). Violent crimes decrease in DKZ. *The Mercury*, p. 2.

Landman, K. L. (2000). Man the barricades: Gated communities in South Africa. *Crime and Conflict, 21*, 24–26.

Louw, A. (1999). Who suffers most? The national victims of crime survey. *Crime and Conflict, 16*, 32–36.

Pillay, B. J., & Schlebusch, L (1997). Psychological intervention to assist victims and others exposed to human rights violations in South Africa. *International Psychologist, 37*, 94.

Schlebusch, L. (1987). Psychological intervention following a community disaster. *Psychiatric Insight, 4*, 56–59.

Schlebusch, L. (1998). Recent advances in stress research and implications for health and well-being. In L. Schlebusch (Ed.), *South Africa beyond transition: Psychological well-being*. Proceedings of the Third Annual Congress of the Psychological Society of South Africa. Pretoria: Psychological Society of South Africa.

Schlebusch, L. (2000). *Mind shift. Stress management and your health*. Pietermaritzburg, South Africa: University of Natal Press.

Shaw, M. (2000). Theatre of terror: Responding to the Cape bombings. *Crime and Conflict, 21*, 5–10.

7

Unresolved Trauma:
Fuel for the Cycle of Violence and Terrorism

Timothy Gallimore

TRAUMA: A PSYCHIC WOUND

Trauma is an attack on the self. *Trauma* comes from the Greek word that means "to wound or to pierce." Traumatic events generally involve a threat of injury or death that causes the victim to feel intense fear, helplessness, loss of control, and impending annihilation. Trauma can occur following the experience or witnessing of military combat, natural disasters, terrorist incidents, serious accidents, or violent personal assaults such as rape. These events are outside the range of normal human experience. They cause physical or psychological injury that produces mental or emotional stress. In our universal search to derive meaning from our experiences, our psyche is sometimes wounded, pierced by our inability to mentally process the incongruous, unpleasant, unexpected, dramatic, and shocking events that come our way. The resulting psychological condition is trauma. Prolonged or repeated abuse can also cause trauma.

Humans react to traumatic events with the autonomic nervous system, or with basic reflexes. At the moment of the threatening experience, victims may freeze in terror, unable to escape the event; run away; or flee in panic to get away from the event. Or they may fight to avoid or end the threat.

The emotional symptoms of trauma are sadness, depression, anxiety, fear, irritability, anger, despair, guilt, and self-doubt. Victims may develop phobias, sleep disorders, eating disorders, and conduct disorders. Trauma victims may also experience mental confusion and become emotionally impaired and socially dysfunctional.

Clinical research shows that about 30 percent of trauma victims develop a psychiatric illness called post-traumatic stress disorder (PTSD), which may last a lifetime. According to the National Center for PTSD, the traumatic events most often associated with PTSD in men are rape, combat exposure, childhood neglect, and childhood physical abuse. For women, the most common events are rape, sexual molestation, physical attack, being threatened with a weapon, and childhood physical abuse.

General knowledge about trauma came out of concern for soldiers who developed PTSD after being exposed to the shock of military combat. There is documentation of the illness in historical medical literature starting with the Civil War, where a PTSD-like disorder was known as Da Costa's Syndrome. There are descriptions of PTSD in the medical literature on combat veterans of World War II and on Holocaust survivors. However, careful research and documentation of PTSD began in earnest after the Vietnam War.

The research shows that about half of all American veterans who served in Vietnam have experienced PTSD. The estimated lifetime prevalence of PTSD among these veterans is 30.9 percent for men and 26.9 percent for women. An additional 22.5 percent of men and 21.2 percent of women have had partial PTSD at some point in their lives (Kulka et al., 1990). Research on Persian Gulf War veterans show a PTSD rate ranging from 3 percent to 50 percent (Wolfe & Proctor, 1996). About 48 percent of soldiers in deployed units met criteria for PTSD, and they have a lifetime prevalence of 65 percent. According to one study, the psychological aftermath of war-zone participation in the gruesome task of handling human remains was profound (Sutker et al., 1994).

People with PTSD develop hyperarousal or a persistent expectation of danger. They have an indelible imprint of the traumatic experience that can be triggered years later by traumatic reminders that cause them to have "flashbacks" in which they relive the traumatic event. They may also display a numbing response to the trauma and enter an altered state of consciousness in which they disassociate or detach themselves from reality as a defense against the traumatic experience.

According to Herman (1997), overwhelming trauma robs us of our power and autonomy. Trauma breaches the attachments of family, friendship, love, and community, undermining the belief systems that give meaning to human experiences and violating the victim's faith in a natural or divine order. More importantly, trauma destroys identity, shatters the construction of self, and robs the individual of the basic human need for safety.

The salient characteristic of traumatic events is that they cause helplessness and terror. "The terror, rage and hatred of the traumatic moment live on in the dialectic of trauma" (Herman, 1997, p. 50). Trauma produces shame and guilt that are associated with being a victim of violence and abusiveness. We are all exposed to varying degrees of traumatic experiences, but not everyone becomes dysfunctional or traumatized because of those experiences. We learn to live with unhealed, deep emotional wounds as we go through our daily lives.

We live in a society that is organized around unresolved traumatic experience. . . . [T]he effects of multigenerational trauma lie like an iceberg in our social awareness. All we see is the tip of the iceberg that is above the surface crime, community deterioration, family disintegration, and ecological degradation. What lies below the surface of our social consciousness is the basis of the problem—the ways in which unhealed trauma and loss have infiltrated and helped determine every one of our social institutions. (Bloom & Reichert, 1998, p. 9)

Violence is the primary cause of this unhealed trauma.

VIOLENCE: THE URGE TO AVENGE

Violence is any relation, process, or condition by which an individual or a group violates the physical, social, and/or psychological integrity of another person or group. Violence seldom ends with the original violation of the victim. Violence is cyclical. Many injured individuals describe a need to avenge their hurt by retaliating against their assailants with even more violence than the victims experienced. This urge for revenge has been characterized as a basic human need. We seek revenge when we experience injustice and become outraged.

The act of avenging promotes trauma, as does the inability or powerlessness to avenge a perceived wrong or injury. Both victims and perpetrators of violence are exposed to trauma.

"Traumatized people imagine that revenge will bring relief, even though the fantasy of revenge simply reverses the roles of perpetrator and victim, continuing to imprison the victim in horror, degradation, and the bounds of the perpetrator's violence" (Minow, 1998, p. 13).

In addition to direct or individual, personal violence, there exist also collective or group violence and structural violence. Collective violence is often related to group or ethnic identity. Most forms of terrorism involve collective violence, in which there is a targeted outsider, an enemy identified as the "other." In what is called the violence of differentiation, the enemy is dehumanized by myth and propaganda in order for perpetrators to justify injuring and/or killing members of the target group. In pursuit of their identity needs, groups have committed mass violence of ethnic cleansing and genocide (Staub, 1999).

The structural barriers are an important part of the cycle of violence. Robbed of meaningful social roles, status, respect, and identity in the broader society, some disenfranchised individuals turn to violence and terrorism. All societies and their institutions have degrees of structural violence that are endemic. They produce deprivation and frustration that may drive some people to commit violence in order to meet their needs (Burton, 1997).

Structural violence perhaps explains the generational dysfunction in the lifestyles of families and identity groups. The parent-child relationship is governed by societal norms. It is a relationship of unequal status and power, as is the relationship between groups in society. Parents abuse their children and powerful groups take advantage of weaker groups. Violent youth who are victims of domestic violence often victimize others in their quest for revenge. These young perpetrators of violence are also traumatized by the violent acts they commit and by witnessing the injury they inflict on others. The mimetic theory of violence explains this cycle of "paying back" for the violence one experiences.

Mimetic Structures of Violence

The mimetic theory comes from the work of Rene Girard (1977), who hypothesized that violence is generated through scapegoating and mimetic desire. The premise of mimetic desire is that people imitate the actions of others who they admire. On first examination, it seems that victims of violence would hate, rather than admire, their assailants. However, the basic human need for power causes victims to desire the position of power that their victimizers occupy. Power and control become the objects of desire and victims identify in a positive way with that aspect of their aggressors. Victims become perpetrators in order to regain power. They model the behavior of their victimizers.

Studies show that adolescents who were abused or witnessed abuse are more likely to commit violent acts, including murder. A child who is abused imitates the violence that his family models for him. "It is accepted that violence is learned through modeling within the family" (Hardwick & Rowton-Lee, 1996, p. 265). In addition to the abuse that they suffer, children who witness unchallenged abuse at home or in the community learn that violence is normal and acceptable. "It further models aggression as a way of dealing with conflict and acting in interpersonal situations" (Staub, 1999, p. 187).

The mass media are additional significant structures of mimetic violence in American society. The bulk of media content serves primarily to model violence. Whether it is conflict-based news reporting or cultural/entertainment programming, the focus is on violence. Children absorb a steady diet of violent media content that encourages them to imitate violence and to develop a high tolerance for violence. Their heroes, role models, and objects of desire come largely from this content.

Collective violence also comes out of the rivalry between groups for desired objects—resources and power. "Thus, mimesis coupled with desire leads automatically to conflict" (Girard, 1977, p. 146) and conflict leads to violence. Possession of the desired object gives a sense of superiority, victory, revenge, honor, and/or vindication. When violence is introduced in a rivalry or conflict for an object of desire, violence is returned (imitated) but with increased intensity and severity. The violence becomes the focus of attention as it spirals out of control. "The mimetic attributes of violence are extraordinary—sometimes direct and positive, at other times indirect and negative. The more men strive to curb their violent impulses, the more these impulses seem to prosper. The very weapons used to combat violence are turned against their users. Violence is like a raging fire that feeds on the very objects intended to smother its flames" (Girard, 1977, p. 31).

The psychiatrist and author Frantz Fanon systematically examined this mimetic cycle of violence. Fanon was attempting to explain the violence that accompanied the liberation movement to end colonial rule in Africa and the Caribbean (Fanon, 1963, 1967). He found that those freed from colonial masters began imitating their oppressors. They were expressing a mimetic desire for the object (power) possessed by the model, who was both admired and hated at the same time. The victim hates the oppressor or aggressor for the injury inflicted on him, but he admires the oppressor because of his position of power and control. By imitating the violence of the aggressor, the victim sheds his victimization and satisfies his urge for revenge—not by attacking his aggressor, but by victimizing those perceived to be less powerful and less desirable than himself. Often the new victim is a member of the oppressed group to which he also belongs.

Human Needs and Violence

The basic human needs have been identified as meaning, identity/belonging or connectedness, material well-being, stimulation/creativity, self-actualization, self-determination, and security/safety. These needs are assumed to be universally inherent in human beings. Theorists argue that individual personal identity, the separation of the self from others, is the most fundamental need of all humans. Among the basic needs, meaning/justice, agency/self-esteem, recognition, and dignity/respect are said to be nonnegotiable identity needs. Identity needs are objects of mimetic desire. People will engage in conflict and extreme violence to satisfy these basic needs. That violence often triggers trauma because violence robs victims of the basic human needs that make us emotionally stable and psychologically functional.

Fear produces a need for security. Anger produces a need for meaning, including for justice. Depression is the root of the need for self-esteem (Sites, 1990). Meaning is the most significant human need and it is that basic need that is deprived when a person is traumatized. He cannot make sense of his traumatic experiences because they are out of the range of normal, predictable experiences. Their incongruousness challenges the mind because the traumatic events do not fit in the schema developed over time for processing experiences. Psychological and emotional dysfunction develops as a result. The manifestations are debilitating stress, disassociation, depression, disengagement from normal social relations, and loss of a sense of safety and knowledge of self.

Violence can be prevented by satisfying the need for security and identity. Otherwise, conflicts will develop over satisfiers of those needs. The needs that are met or satisfied by violence include revenge, power, security/self-defense, and the social need of belonging. Trauma and the personal violation caused by violence rob individuals of their basic need for safety, dignity, trust, connectedness, justice, and self-worth. In order to recover or heal, victims must rid themselves of the shame, guilt, helplessness, and vulnerability they experience from the traumatic event.

Trauma invokes the basic human need or urge to avenge to restore autonomy, self-esteem, dignity, and identity. Victims of trauma and violence externalize their injury/hurt by exacting revenge against the victimizing perpetrator or the hated "other." In those cases, "Violence is idealized to enhance self-esteem and as a defensive response to an individual's (or group's) sense of entitlement to revenge" (Volkan, 1997, p. 162).

Unresolved childhood trauma is common in youth with violent behavior. Shame and humiliation destroy self-esteem and a healthy identity. Anger, rage, and violence are the original defenses against shame. "Men who assault their wives experience high levels of chronic anger, high levels of chronic trauma symptoms, a tendency to externalize the cause of their violence, and an admixture of shame and guilt about their violence" (Dutton, van Ginkel, & Starzomski, 1995, p. 211).

There is a strong relationship between shame and anger. It has been called the "shame-rage spiral" (Scheff, 1987). Shame disturbs self-identity, and negative identity promotes self-hatred and violence. Fear, hate, and rage are produced by trauma, and traumatized people have the fuel for starting and continuing violent conflict.

Identity Disorder and Violence

Needs are inextricably bound to identity and identity formation. When basic needs are not met, it leads to frustration and ultimately to violence. Those who experience trauma from abuse, violence, and acts of terror develop identity disorders, self-hatred, and fatalism, and they can become suicidal. From the psychodynamic viewpoint, all violence may be attributed to "psychotic parts of the personality" (Kernberg, 1998, p. 198). In fact, "most cases of severe violence emerge within the broad spectrum of severe personality disorders, and are seen typically in cases of the syndrome of malignant narcissism, the antisocial personality, severe, chronic self-mutilation and suicidal behavior, and severe paranoid personality disorders" (Kernberg, 1998, p. 198).

Identity crisis and identity disorder are risk factors for violent youth. Low self-esteem and self-hatred are critical elements in violent youth. Young people who are preoccupied with fantasies of death and violence can develop a "morbid identity" that enables them to kill (Hardwick & Rowton-Lee, 1996). "Identity formation in very violent young people so far seems to have been given little specific attention. However, it is known in the abuse field that some survivors of abuse adopt a victim identity whereas others identify with the abuser and go on to be perpetrators of abuse and violence themselves" (Hardwick & Rowton-Lee, 1996, p. 270).

People join groups in order to participate in violence or to experience violence vicariously through their membership. They also find a positive identity in the group to replace their damaged personal identity (Staub, 1999, p. 187). Terrorist groups may serve several functions, but at their core is violence. The Ku Klux Klan is an example of a terrorist group that serves the benign psychological and social needs of its casual members. However, it is part of the white supremacy movement, whose goal is "power and domination; its history, rhetoric, and analysis direct it into violence; its language draws to it people who will be capable of violence, along with many other people. Without periodically re-earning its reputation for violence, the movement would disappear. Violence is a key to understanding the multiple meanings of the movement for different kinds of members" (Ezekiel, 1995, p. xxix).

Malignant Narcissism

Identity or personality disorders motivate trauma victims and others to commit violence. Their violence is an expression of the hurt they experienced, usually in childhood. "Narcissistic personality organization develops as a defensive adaptation to childhood hurts and humiliations as well as deficiencies in self-esteem" (Volkan, 1997, p. 247).

The malignant narcissist hurts or kills others in order to feel good about himself. Aggression builds his self-esteem by making him feel powerful and dangerous. Malignant narcissism might explain the destructive behavior of gang-bangers who perpetrate much of the violence in American urban centers. These psychologically damaged individuals seek aggressive triumphs to verify their self-worth. In conditions of poverty and oppression, the currency of status and value is the degree of raw power that a person can wield. It is to the advantage of the emotionally insecure to be perceived as dangerous and threatening. The level of fear that one can evoke in this environment is directly translated into personal respect because there are few other accepted positive measures of success. Although the pattern of violence produces external public status and respect, it is born from a deep sense of personal deficiency and self-hatred.

> Self-hate is converted into hatred of strangers. One's own deficiencies and inadequacies—the hated parts of one's self—are projected on the stranger, the foreigner, and attacked in him. The hate is directed at someone who supposedly threatens the substance of the self. The enemy-other is needed to stabilize one's self in a symbiosis of opponents. . . . It is an entanglement in which the other experiences what is meant for oneself. Unbearable conflicts, impulses which are defended against, destructiveness, and self-hate are projected onto the chosen enemy, who becomes the target of hostility. (Streeck-Fischer, 1999, p. 261)

TERRORISM: TARGETED VIOLENCE

Terrorism is a violent act, or other acts that threaten human life, and is meant to intimidate or coerce a government or segment of a civilian population to further the political or social objectives of the perpetrator. Those who organize formally or informally to plan and carry out systematic targeted violence are terrorists. Terrorists use bombings, shootings, kidnappings, hijackings, and other forms of violence primarily for political purposes. Their goal is to produce constant fear and the threat of injury or death in the target of their violence. Terrorism causes stress because of the continual uncertainty and danger of attack. Over time, this stress can cause trauma in the targets even if no attack is ever carried out.

The availability to and possession of guns by Americans contribute to fear and an ongoing low level of terrorism in daily life. Random acts of extreme violence terrorize residents and visitors in urban areas because of the unpredictability of their occurrence. Workplace violence and recent mass shootings add to this general fear of coworkers. A number of highly publicized shootings has increased fear of U.S. postal workers as a particular occupation group. "Going postal" is now a commonly accepted term for describing workplace shootings and a disproportionately violent response to a perceived wrong.

American terrorists are often motivated primarily by racial animus. To the extent that their terrorist actions are political, it is in advancing the idea that the races should not mix and that African Americans should be sent back to Africa. An extension of this racist motive is seen in acts of terror and ideological dogma against Catholics, Jews, and immigrants. Among American terrorists are right-wing fringe groups made up of white supremacists, white separatists, skinheads, neo-Nazis, and advocates against gun control. Domestic terrorists also include lone aggrieved individuals who are anti-government and against state power. Gang members, wannabes, and misguided youth infected with the racist poison of their peers and parents compose a third category of perpetrators of terrorism in the United States.

The Symbionese Liberation Army and the FALN Puerto Rican separatist group were among the few domestic terrorist organizations with an obvious political motive. These left-wing organizations were active in the 1960s and 1970s but disappeared with the end of the social unrest and protests that characterized that era in American history. The Black Panther Party may also have been considered a terrorist organization with political grounding. However, the FBI weakened the organization when it arrested or killed many of the Black Panthers at the end of the 1960s.

Terrorist Leaders

Some of the most villainous leaders of modern times have been victims of personal trauma. Politicians such as Joseph Stalin, Adolf Hitler, and Slobodan Milosevic had traumatic childhood experiences that rendered them damaged goods despite their rise to power. Although it is difficult to apply clinical concepts to complex global sociopolitical phenomena, some researchers have argued that traumatized leaders have projected their unresolved trauma onto a hated "other" and galvanized popular support for their campaigns of terror, mass murder, and genocide (Gilligan, 1996; Kernberg, 1998; Staub, 1999; Volkan, 1997).

As a child, Stalin suffered abuse, serious injury, and disease that disfigured him physically and damaged his self-esteem. Stalin became an embittered, shame-filled person possessed by the thought of avenging the humiliation and injustices of his youth. One researcher argues that Stalin's infamous purges and wars were "a restaging of previous traumas" (Ihanus, 1999, p. 71).

Stalin tried to boost his low self-esteem by projecting his rage onto enemies who vicariously carried "the burden of his self-hate and shame" (Ihanus, 1999, p. 75).

Adolf Hitler was abused, shamed, and humiliated by his father, who was described as "a clinical alcoholic who tyrannized his family" (Redlich, 1998, p. 8). Adolf stayed in his parents' bedroom until he was six or seven years old. He was subjected to "the common trauma of witnessing parental sexual intercourse in the shared bedroom" (Redlich, 1998, p. 14).

Hitler is infamous for advocating the superiority and purity of the Aryan race that was to make Germany great. However, records show that one of his grandfathers was of Jewish origin (Redlich, 1998, pp. 11–13). In light of his anti-Semitic ideology, Hitler's Jewish ancestry no doubt caused him emotional stress and affected his self-esteem. Researchers have concluded that the shame and humiliation he suffered at the hands of his father most likely caused Hitler's cruelty and quest for vengeance (Redlich, 1998, p. 14).

Others have argued that a national sense of shame and humiliation can also give rise to collective violence and group victimization. Hitler rose to power because he promised to undo the shame that Germans felt over previous military defeat. Hitler was able to galvanize national anger and shame of the symbolic defeat to perpetuate collective violence on the scale of genocide (Gilligan, 1996, pp. 66–69). Hitler said that shame, disgrace, and humiliation "should arouse the German people to a common sense of shame and a common hatred" of the Jews (Gilligan, 1996, p. 275).

Slobodan Milosevic, who also came from a dysfunctional family, used the shame of symbolic defeat to perpetrate mass violence. Milosevic is described by those who know him as an angry, aloof, and self-centered man who found solace from his personal hurts in the Serbian nationalistic crusade of ethnic cleansing that he conducted in the former Yugoslavia (Volkan, 1997, p. 67). Milosevic was successful in reviving the collective memory of his Serbian followers and using the chosen trauma of the group's historic defeat six hundred years earlier at the Battle of Kosovo as entitlement to avenge their loss. Like the Germans of Hitler's time, the Serbs were humiliated and powerless when Milosevic made his appeal to take vengeance by exterminating the other ethnic groups living among the Serbs in greater Yugoslavia.

We could also add Pol Pot of Cambodia and others to the list of narcissistic leaders who were responsible for the deaths and injury of untold millions. These are some of the more prominent international examples of traumatized individuals who orchestrated state-sponsored terrorism. On close examination, we find that the recent American terrorists also share this background of trauma and abuse that may have motivated them to kill and injure their fellow citizens. Hitler's racist ideology remains alive in the minds of recent American terrorists. It was especially influential with the two students who committed the mass murder at Columbine High School on April 20, 1999, the anniversary of Hitler's birth.

TRAUMA AND THE TERRORIST PERSONALITY

The history of childhood victimization and trauma is not confined to the notorious political figures of our times. Based on interviews with terrorist leaders in Northern Ireland, political psychologist Jeanne Knutson found that "all had been victims of terror themselves, all had experienced violations of their personal boundaries that damaged or destroyed their faith in personal safety" (Volkan, 1997, p. 160). These violations occurred in beatings or abandonment by parents, parental divorce, incest or other sexual abuse, and rejection by peer groups. The common element among all these terrorists was the experience of personal trauma during their formative years.

Based on my clinical hypothesis, the terrorist personality appears to develop from a painful and dysfunctional childhood in which the individual forms personality and identity disorders. The terrorist responds to his personal identity problems and attempts to strengthen his troubled internal sense of self by seeking power to hurt and by expressing entitlement to power. These psychologically damaged individuals seek power and sanction for their violent actions through membership in groups and organizations that give them a sense of shared identity in an attempt to replace their flawed personal identity.

Trauma tears a part a complex system of self-protection that normally functions in an integrated fashion (Herman, 1997). Trauma fragments the personality of its victims and drives them to the basic survival strategies of shock reflexes as a defense against the traumatic experience. The basic freeze, flight, or fight responses are limbic reflexes of a disassociative state that individuals enter in order to cope with traumatic experiences. The trauma victim may freeze in a state of numbness, flee from the threat in terror, or fight in a fit of rage in order to survive.

According to Pomeroy (1995), the "fragmented self" is exposed when trauma victims lose protection of the outer circles or boundaries of the self, leaving only the core shock reflexes of freeze, flight, and fight survival strategies. The antisocial or terrorist response to trauma originates from the shock reflex of rage. "If you don't have boundaries and you aren't able to fight, but you do have rage, then you become a terrorist" (Pomeroy, 1995, p. 97). People who have been traumatized are more likely to use violence to solve conflict and relieve stress. Theorists believe that trauma victims resort to violence because they have lost their sense of self. In turning to violence and terrorism, victims seek for a substitute identity and a substitute sense of power.

The practice of bullying (teasing, taunting, threatening, and hurting a weaker person) appears to be a significant trigger for retaliatory violence and acts of terrorism. It has been recognized that "victims of abuse, including bullying, can become perpetrators who themselves often feel as though they are primarily victims" (Hardwick & Rowton-Lee, 1996, p. 267). "Bullying contributes to the evolution of perpetrators into even more aggressive people" (Staub, 1999, p. 190). Many of the terrorists analyzed in this study were victims of bullying.

Those who experience trauma usually go through a stage of blaming themselves for allowing the traumatic event that happened to them. They also project their anger at the external perceived cause of their trauma. This struggle between the hated guilty self and the culpable assailant sets up the conditions for violence—violence against the self to end their emotional suffering or violence against others on whom they have projected their trauma. At the extremes, the trauma victim either commits suicide or homicide. Terrorists seek to kill the victimized aspects of themselves and the victimizing aspects of those they identify as aggressors or the cause of their suffering.

"Those who become terrorist leaders or their lieutenants have a psychological need to 'kill' the victimized aspects of themselves and the victimizing aspects of their aggressors that they have externalized and projected onto innocent others" (Volkan, 1997, p. 162). Streeck-Fischer (1999) also described this cycle of violence that arises out of self-hatred. Self-hate is changed to hatred for the victimizing "other." In this cycle, the rage from previous trauma is transformed into hatred. There develops a tension "between a hateful self and a threatening, hateful and hated object that needs to be controlled, to be made to suffer, to be destroyed" (Kernberg, 1998, p. 203).

Trauma victims sometimes join groups to rid themselves of their victimization and to repair their damaged self-image. They often are attracted to violent organizations like the Ku Klux Klan or the neo-Nazis because of their need to identify with a figure of power and success. Hitler and his Third Reich appeal to these individuals who see in them a powerful conqueror of Europe obliterating the hated enemy. Fascism appeals to feelings of powerlessness. Hitler rose to power by addressing a national sense of defeat, humiliation, isolation, and powerlessness of the Germans. Although their members seek power and safety in these organizations, "Fear is at the center of these groups, fear and a sense of isolation. Belonging to the group affords comradeship within struggle. The mythical 'white race' is the larger family for which these spiritual orphans long" (Ezekiel, 1995, p. xxv).

Some members of the white supremacist organizations develop the terrorist personality. These members form underground cells and become a "Klan within the Klan." The added secrecy and conspiracy of their cells satisfies the psychological needs of these individuals. Often the overriding need is to commit violent acts of revenge. The individual who acts is the real engine of the organization. He is the terrorist. "He believes the ideology literally, word for word—there is an Enemy, the Enemy is Evil. He believes that ideology because he wants it: He wants the grounds for radical action. He must have radical action. Violence is the language in which he can speak his message; his spirit needs the comradeship of the tight terrorist cell" (Ezekiel, 1995, p. xxxi).

AMERICAN TERRORISTS

We will now examine four instances of terrorism in America. They involve white supremacist organizations, a mentally ill individual, a right-wing political zealot, and young men who carried out mass shootings in their schools. Analysis of these terrorists shows some common themes in their childhood experiences. The common element among all these terrorists is unresolved trauma. They reported being filled with shame, humiliation, rage, and hatred. These are all elements in the mimetic cycle of violence as described earlier in this chapter.

Many of these victimized individuals sought membership and acceptance in terrorist groups to compensate for their identity disorders and low self-esteem. The racist ideology that the terrorist white supremacist groups espouse offers a venue for traumatized individuals to seek revenge for the abuse and bullying that they experienced. These similarities support my clinical hypothesis that unresolved trauma motivates victims to repeat the cycle of violence by becoming perpetrators in an attempt to avenge their victimization.

The KKK: Defending the USA

The Ku Klux Klan is the oldest and most persistent American terrorist organization. The Klan was, at one time, a state-sanctioned, if not state-sponsored, terrorist organization. In the 1920s, the Klan was the official law enforcement agency in many states, including Indiana. In most Southern states, Klan membership was the unofficial ticket to power and status. Those in political office and in the police ranks were Klan members or Klan supporters representing the Jim Crow segregation that was the legal order of the day.

The original Ku Klux Klan was organized at Pulaski, Tennessee, in May 1866 by ex-Confederate elements that wanted to maintain white supremacy in Southern communities after the Civil War. The Klan feared that outraged former black slaves would cause an insurrection. Dressed in flowing white sheets, their faces covered with white masks, and with skulls at their saddle horns, Klan members posed as spirits of the Confederate dead returned from the battlefields. Although the Klan was often able to achieve its aims by terror alone, it also used whippings and lynchings against blacks and political opponents.

"These lynchings were meant to terrorize the black population and keep it quiescent and under white control. Many of the victims were burned alive, chained to iron stakes that had been driven into the ground; others were hanged. The lucky ones were shot soon after the burning or the hanging began; there are many accounts, however, of desperate men crawling from the flames and being pushed back in. The newspaper accounts are grueling, the cruelty astonishing. Bodies were slashed; fingers were cut off. Often the victim's testicles or penis were cut off" (Ezekiel, 1995, p. 311).

In 1915, the Klan added to its white supremacy an intense nativism, anti-Catholicism, and anti-Semitism. It furnished an outlet for the militant patriotism aroused by World War I and it stressed fundamentalism in religion. Civil rights activities in the South during the 1960s helped to strengthen the Klan. The Klan had a resurgence of popular support in the early 1990s that culminated in the candidacy of Klansman David Duke for elected office in Louisiana.

The continued existence of the Klan and other white supremacist organizations demonstrates the deep roots that racism has in American culture. There are still three or four main Klan groups operating in the United States. There are about thirty neo-Nazi groups and more than a hundred active skinhead organizations. Together they were responsible for hundreds of assaults and 108 murders between 1990 and 1993, according to figures from various organizations that monitor these terrorist hate groups.

The Klan has slowly been merging with the other white supremacist organizations. What binds them together is the Christian Identity theology. This doctrine was imported from Europe. It posits that the Aryan peoples of Northern Europe—whites only—are the true chosen children of God, the lost tribes of Israel. This racist ideology teaches that only whites are human and the dark races or "mud people" resulted from whites mating with animals. Jews are seen as the evil spawn of Eve mating with the Serpent, or Satan. Christian Identity adherents argue that God has called his chosen people to North America so they can fulfill God's plan for them to dominate the earth, rule over the dark races, and fight to the death to eliminate the Jews.

While the motives for joining white supremacist groups may be many, researchers who have studied and interviewed members of the Klan, neo-Nazis, and skinheads have found that the white racist movement allows members to feel like victims who have been unjustly victimized. They want, and need, to belong to a group so that they can feel better about themselves and have the sense that they are part of a group that is acting for the greater good of the victimized group.

For several years, Raphael Ezekiel studied a neo-Nazi group in Detroit. He found that the group was made up of young urban whites who feared blacks because they bullied them in school and on the city streets. They faced violence and fighting to survive or defend their honor when teased or bullied in their racially divided city. The youngsters sought refuge in the terrorist group from the structural violence of urban poverty. Their lives were characterized by personal loss and trauma. All of them suffered the loss of a parent through separation, divorce, or death. They came from dysfunctional families in which they experienced violence from alcoholic and abusive parents. Every member of the group had experienced the trauma of childhood diseases or of being born with physical deficiencies.

The fundamental reason for joining the supremacist group was terror. "These were people who at a deep level felt terror that they were about to be extinguished. They felt that their lives might disappear at any moment. They felt that they might be blown away by the next wind" (Ezekiel, 1995, p. 156). Through membership in the group, they tried to find power over the perceived oppressor or threat to their survival. They were also seeking meaningful relationships and a sense of belonging to find their identity and build self-esteem.

The Unabomber: A Lone Ranger

Theodore Kaczynski represents the lone individuals who become terrorists because they are emotionally unstable. Kaczynski was a brilliant mathematician who graduated from Harvard University. He was on the faculty at the University of California–Berkeley before mental illness drove him to a hermit's existence in a small cabin in the wilderness of Montana. There he wrote his "manifesto," stating his goal to destroy the existing form of society. He claimed to be fighting against those who were corrupting America with technology. Between 1978 and 1995, Kaczynski conducted a campaign of terror by sending sixteen mail bombs to businesspeople and academics in seven different states. Nicknamed the Unabomber, he eluded police for seventeen years until his brother turned him in for a reward offered by the FBI. Kaczynski's bombs killed three people and injured twenty-three others. He is now serving four consecutive life sentences plus thirty years in federal prison.

Sally Johnson, chief psychiatrist and associate warden of health services at the Federal Correctional Institution in Butner, North Carolina, wrote a forensic report of Kaczynski's mental condition. He was diagnosed with paranoid schizophrenia. Johnson made her evaluation after interviewing Kaczynski, his family, and people who knew him. She also analyzed psychological tests and studied the Unabomber's journals, which document more than forty years of his life. The Ninth Circuit Court of Appeals in San Francisco ruled that the psychiatric report should be made public in order to provide a better understanding of the Unabomber's motivations. The events of his life discussed below were taken from that psychiatric report.

Kaczynski's life of trauma apparently started very early. As a result of an allergic reaction, he was hospitalized for several days when he was approximately nine months old. Kaczynski's mother reported that the hospitalization was a significant and traumatic event for her son because he experienced a separation from her. She described him as having changed after the hospitalization. He became withdrawn, less responsive, and more fearful of separation from her after that point. Kaczynski said that he was abused during childhood. He described the abuse as severe verbal psychological abuse. Kaczynski constantly sought an apology from his parents for emotionally abusing him.

Kaczynski identified two events in his life as being highly significant and triggering episodes of depression. The first was when he skipped directly from the fifth grade to the seventh. He said he did not fit in with the older children and that he endured considerable hostility, verbal abuse, and teasing from them. He said that, "By the time I left high school, I was definitely regarded as a freak by a large segment of the student body" (Johnson, 1998).

Kaczynski said that during high school and college, he would often become terribly angry and because he could not express that anger or hatred openly, he would indulge in fantasies of revenge. However, he was afraid to act on his fantasies, and described himself as having frustrated resentment toward school, parents, and the student body. During his college years, he also had fantasies of living a primitive life and envisioned himself as "an agitator, rousing mobs to frenzies of revolutionary violence" (Johnson, 1998).

The second pivotal incident came when he was twenty-five and a graduate student at the University of Michigan. Kaczynski sought psychiatric help after experiencing several weeks of intense and persistent sexual excitement involving fantasies of being a female. He decided to undergo sex change surgery that required a psychiatric referral. He set up an appointment with a psychiatrist at the university health center. While in the waiting room, he became anxious and humiliated over the prospect of talking to the psychiatrist about his problem. When the doctor arrived, Kaczynski did not discuss his real concerns, but rather claimed he was feeling some depression and anxiety over the possibility that he would be drafted into the military. Kaczynski describes leaving the office and feeling rage, shame, and humiliation over this attempt to seek evaluation.

Kaczynski said,

> As I walked away from the building afterwards, I felt disgusted about what my uncontrolled sexual cravings had almost led me to do and I felt—humiliated, and I violently hated the psychiatrist. Just then there came a major turning point in my life. . . . I thought I wanted to kill that psychiatrist because the future looked utterly empty to me. I felt I wouldn't care if I died. And so I said to myself why not really kill the psychiatrist and anyone else whom I hate. What is important is not the words that ran through my mind but the way I felt about them. What was entirely new was the fact that I really felt I could kill someone. My very hopelessness had liberated me because I no longer cared about death. I no longer cared about consequences and I said to myself that I really could break out of my rut in life and do things that were daring, irresponsible or criminal. (Johnson, 1998)

Kaczynski described the source of his hatred as social rejection and the "fact that organized society frustrates my very powerful urge for physical freedom and personal autonomy." He also described experiencing anger from other sources and then turning his hatred toward organized society.

McVeigh: The Neo-Nazi Patriot

Timothy McVeigh, the Oklahoma City bomber, committed the greatest act of terrorism ever perpetrated against Americans by an American. On April 19, 1995, McVeigh killed 168 people and injured 642 others when he blew up the Murrah Federal Building with a truck bomb. He had suffered war trauma during military service in the Persian Gulf. He was a victim of bullying and humiliation in his childhood. McVeigh also carried psychological scars from his parents' three separations and their eventual divorce.

McVeigh was on a crusade against the United States government, which he saw as a bully and a threat to the right-wing values he espoused. McVeigh contended that his terrorist act was in revenge for the government's killing of his right-wing compatriots at Waco and at Ruby Ridge. He maintained that he was a political martyr and said his death sentence was nothing more than state-assisted suicide. While on death row, McVeigh called himself a patriot who was fighting for the greater good against a bullying government. In defiance, he said he would invoke the text of the poem "Invictus" as a final statement before his execution. The poem talks of going "beyond this place of wrath and tears." He got his final wish on June 11, 2001, in an execution chamber at the federal prison in Terre Haute, Indiana.

In his fit of wrath and revenge, McVeigh chose April 19 for his attack, to coincide with the anniversary of the government's assault on the Branch Davidian compound in Waco, Texas, on April 19, 1993. McVeigh and his accomplices were associated with a right-wing militia group and were probably aware that the first shot of the Revolutionary War was fired on April 19, 1775, at the Battle of Lexington. A major issue in that war was the right to bear arms. McVeigh's attack was also coincidentally close to Hitler's birthday—April 20. Despite the racist political ideology that surrounded McVeigh's crusade, it was the boost to self-esteem that he found in the right to own and use weapons that led him on his path to being a patriot.

McVeigh's first encounter with a bully came on the Little League baseball field. The bully punched McVeigh and he fled to the family car to weep. He was humiliated and embarrassed in front of his team. The incident further injured his pride because he was not very athletic and he already felt a failure in the eyes of his father, who was an accomplished softball player. "But that humiliation on the Little League field—at the hands of a bully—was something he would remember forever. Over time, he would develop a seething hatred of bullies—or any person, institution or even nation that seemed to be picking on the weak" (Michel & Herbeck, 2001, p. 20).

Young McVeigh was close to his grandfather, who taught him how to handle guns, and the boy used his skills with firearms to build his self-esteem. McVeigh developed a fascination with guns and, when he got older, he built a shooting range in his backyard to hone his skills as a marksman. He became part of the gun culture and read gun magazines such as *Soldier of Fortune*. McVeigh saw an advertisement in the magazine that prompted him to buy *The Turner Diaries*. The book tells the story of a gun enthusiast who reacted to laws restricting firearms by making a truck bomb and destroying the FBI headquarters in Washington. The novel also promotes Hitler's racist ideology advocating the killing of blacks and Jews, whom Hitler considered inherently evil. McVeigh said he liked the book because of its support for the rights of gun owners and not because of its racist content (Michel & Herbeck, 2001, p. 39).

McVeigh soon tired of his life centered on shooting expensive guns. He joined the Army in May 1988. It was his experience as a soldier in the Persian Gulf War that traumatized McVeigh and so enraged him against injustice that he decided to take revenge on the U.S. government by bombing the federal building in Oklahoma City.

McVeigh rose through the ranks to become an Army sergeant. He was awarded the Bronze Star and the coveted Combat Infantry Badge. One of McVeigh's experiences while fighting in Iraq was to use a Bradley armored vehicle to bulldoze Iraqi soldiers and bury them alive in their trenches. Some accounts allege that McVeigh had to scrape the body parts of enemy soldiers off the tracks of his tank. A soldier who fought with McVeigh said their unit made ready for battle by chanting, "Blood makes the grass grow. Kill! Kill! Kill!"

After his discharge from the Army in 1992, McVeigh went to a Veteran's Administration hospital in Florida because he was horrified by memories of the Iraqi soldiers he had killed in the Gulf War. The staff turned him away because he sought counseling under an assumed name (Michel & Herbeck, 2001, p. 288).

In an interview with CBS Television, McVeigh placed emphasis on his experiences as a soldier. He said the war disillusioned him and deepened his anger against the government. He apparently hoped that the bombing of the federal facility would precipitate a civil war and ultimately the overthrow of the government by rightist militia forces. In the interview, McVeigh said his anger against the federal government was deepened by the killing of right-wing activist Randy Weaver's wife and son by federal agents at Ruby Ridge, Idaho, in 1992 and by the killing of some eighty members of the Branch Davidian religious sect in Waco.

Based on what is known about mimetic violence and the revenge motive, we could conclude that the Oklahoma City bombing was a result of untreated war trauma. When he attacked the Murrah Federal Building, McVeigh carried out a traumatic reenactment of the violence he experienced during the Gulf War.

The Columbine Massacre

On April 20, 1999, Dylan Klebold and Eric Harris shot to death eleven students and a teacher and wounded twenty-four other students at Columbine High School in Littleton, Colorado. They then killed themselves. The two eighteen-year-old gunmen were filled with hatred and rage. They planted pipe bombs and other explosives in the school in an attempt to destroy the building. Their homemade arsenal included forty-eight carbon dioxide bombs, twenty-seven pipe bombs, eleven propane containers, seven incendiary devices with more than forty gallons of flammable liquid, hand grenades, and two duffel bag bombs with twenty-pound liquefied petroleum tanks.

There has been some debate about the motives of the Columbine terrorists. However, police investigators concluded that Klebold and Harris planned the shooting as a suicide mission driven by their indiscriminate hate and their intention to wipe out most of their classmates and teachers. There is ample evidence that Harris and Klebold were bullied, ostracized, and alienated by their schoolmates.

Like Timothy McVeigh, the teenage gunmen also considered their attack on Columbine High School to be a "military operation" against a bully. War and the military fascinated both Klebold and Harris. The Columbine terrorists were preoccupied with violence. Harris kept a journal in which he raged against everyone, including minorities and whites. It even included ranting against racism. His diary opens with the telling phrase, "I hate the fucking world." Harris maintained a Web site that was replete with violent content. Two years before the attack, Klebold wrote in his journal that he would go on a "killing spree." Their class writing assignments focused on killing and on mass murderer Jeffrey Dahmer. The two also made a video for a class project in which they dramatized the shooting that they eventually carried out.

Harris apparently shared the anti-gun-control sentiments that McVeigh held. Harris wrote angry and profanity-filled comments in his journal criticizing the passage of the Brady Bill, which requires background checks and a waiting period before the purchase of a weapon. Harris was concerned that he would not be able to obtain a gun because of the law. He said he wanted the weapon for "personal protection." According to him, "It's not like I'm some psycho who would go on a shooting spree" (Dedman, 2000).

The Columbine killers also had racial and genocidal motives, as evidenced by the content of their diaries and their fascination with vengeful and hate-driven Nazi ideology. Harris's journal contained statements praising Hitler's "final solution." Their schoolmates said Klebold and Harris belonged to a group called the "Trench Coat Mafia." They worshiped Hitler and addressed each other in German. The two also wore swastikas and armbands proclaiming, "I hate people." Their classmates reported that the two played war games with cards and the winner gave the "Heil Hitler" salute.

In seeking to attract attention, terrorists carefully choose the date and place of their attack. Klebold and Harris chose April 20, Hitler's birthday, to carry out the Columbine massacre. They had originally planned the attack for April 19, the anniversary of the Oklahoma City bombing. They said in their writings that they intended to "top the body count" of McVeigh's bombing in their attack at the school.

Other School Shooters

Most of the other recent perpetrators of shootings in American schools also lacked the political motive or agenda typical of terrorists. These young people, almost exclusively males, experienced trauma and were driven by the desire for revenge against peers who bullied or humiliated them. Nine school shootings have occurred since the Columbine shooting. Another dozen were foiled when concerned students reported the planned attacks to police and school officials. There is evidence that aggrieved students may be mimicking the actions of the Columbine shooters. The trend has educators, parents, and students worried that the next terrorist attack may occur at their school.

Charles Andrew Williams is typical of these abused and enraged school shooters. "His schoolmates bullied him. His mother rarely saw him. His father neglected him. Even his friends taunted him—and may well have goaded him into his shooting rampage" (McCarthy, 2001, p. 24). When Williams told classmates at Santana High School that he was going to "pull a Columbine," they did not believe he would shoot his peers. "Two of his friends called him a 'pussy' and dared him to do it" (McCarthy, 2001, p. 24). He did it a few days later on March 5, 2001, when he killed two students and wounded thirteen others at the school in Santee, California.

The U.S. Secret Service published a report on school violence based on information about forty-one shooters, ages eleven to twenty-one, involved in thirty-seven school shooting incidents between 1974 and 2000. Data for the study was collected from journals and interviews with friends of the shooters and from the adolescents who were incarcerated (U.S. Secret Service, 2000, p. 2). The patterns and themes that emerged from the study mirror those present in the Columbine shooting and the other cases of terrorism discussed in this chapter.

Fantasy thoughts about revenge were a common motive mentioned, along with despair, hate, and rage. The students who turned on their peers had lost their hope and faith in people. Some wrote of desperation associated with aggressive acts. Kip Kinkel of Springfield, Oregon, wrote, "Hate drives me . . . I am so full of rage . . . Everyone is against me . . . As soon as my hope is gone, people die" (Dedman, 2000). On May 21, 1998, a day after he murdered his parents, Kinkel killed two students and wounded twenty-six others.

The Secret Service study found that two thirds of the attackers had been bullied and tormented by other children. The students who used guns at school did not just snap and kill on impulse. More than three fourths planned their attack in advance after airing grievances at school. More than half described revenge as a motive for their attack. The shooters were obsessed with violence and their self-esteem and identity became invested in getting even.

More than half of the shooters experienced extreme depression and anxiety. Three fourths had an important loss in relationships, a humiliating failure, or a loss of status with their peers before the shooting. They did not have the coping skills to deal with loss, shame, and embarrassment. Three fourths of the students had mentioned suicide or made suicidal gestures. Half threatened to kill themselves before the attacks and six killed themselves during the attack.

Time magazine published a comprehensive study of school shooters in its May 28, 2001, issue. A team of journalists analyzed the lives of twelve school shooters "who had terrified their classmates and periodically traumatized the nation since 1997" (Roche, 2001, p. 34). They were all males who committed their crimes when they were between eleven and eighteen years old.

The team of journalists interviewed some of the shooters, along with psychologists and law enforcement officials who evaluated them. They concluded that "almost all the shooters were expressing rage, either against a particular person for a particular affront or, more often, against a whole cohort of bullying classmates" (Roche, 2001, p. 34). One of the shooters told a psychiatrist that he felt going to prison would be better than continuing to endure bullying at school.

Evan Ramsey was bullied, demeaned, teased, taunted, and assaulted by his peers at Bethel Regional High School in Bethel, Alaska. On February 19, 1997, sixteen-year-old Ramsey took a shotgun to school and killed the principal and one student and wounded two other students. Ramsey was fueled by anger and the urge to avenge years of humiliation at the hands of his schoolmates. He admitted that he shot his schoolmates because he was "sick of being picked on in school."

The *Time* report quotes Park Dietz, a forensic psychiatrist who has interviewed numerous school shooters. Dietz said the shooters tend to have in common "some degree of depression, considerable anger, access to weapons that they aren't ready to have, and a role model salient in their memory" (Roche, 2001, p. 38). Dietz told a *Time* reporter that, so far, the role models for the shooters have "always been a mass murderer who has been given ample coverage in your magazine" (Roche, 2001, p. 38).

The journalists said that if the shooters were not suffering overtly from mental illness before their crimes, many of them clearly are now. Eight of the twelve convicted terrorists that *Time* interviewed have had some sort of mental disorder diagnosed since their crimes. These include depression, personality disorders, and schizophrenia. Most are plagued by nightmares and insomnia. For some, guilt and remorse about their crimes have added to their emotional problems. For all, the severed family relationships, isolation, and boredom of prison life are taking their toll.

Psychologists say that these young terrorists are likely to be suicidal for much of their lives and will suffer repeated flashbacks characteristic of the trauma that they inflicted on their victims who survived the attack or witnessed the killing of their peers. The cycle of violence and trauma is clearly seen in the trauma that these perpetrators are now experiencing in prison. If they were not traumatized before their crimes, they certainly were traumatized as a consequence of their crimes.

CONCLUSION: VIOLENCE, TRAUMA, AND TERRORISM

The American terrorists analyzed provide some support for the clinical hypothesis that unresolved trauma may play a significant role in the cycle of violence being carried out by terrorists. Abuse and childhood trauma are common to the terrorists analyzed for this study. Violence produces trauma. Trauma produces rage. Rage produces hatred. Hatred produces antisocial, violent, terrorist behavior. Victims create other victims. It is an unquenchable circle of fire that fuels itself.

By examining the personality of the perpetrator, we find evidence that unresolved personal trauma produces narcissistic and paranoid leaders who use historical group trauma, or chosen trauma, to move the masses to murder. Individuals who were victimized perpetuate the cycle of violence by seeking revenge for their psychological injuries. Rage over perceived injustice and the desire for revenge were the primary motives for the American terrorists examined in this study.

Youth who are going through identity formation are more susceptible to mimetic desire and mimetic violence. They imitate the violent actions of their abusive families, peers, and role models who influence and shape their identity. They also return (avenge) the violence they experienced in order to assert power and control over perceived weaker victims than themselves. Most of the young school shooters were victims of peer bullying. They imitated violence as a solution to their self-esteem and identity problems and as a satisfier of their basic needs.

Trauma, identity disorder, and low self-esteem lead to self-hatred. Violence is then directed against the hated self. Once the self is robbed of worth and value, numbing, disassociation, hopelessness, and fatalism set in. This leads to violence against the self (suicide) and violence against the "other" (homicide) who is also judged to be of no significance or worth. In one sense, perpetrators of violence kill themselves first and then they kill others. Their violence against others is an expression of their self-hatred and unresolved trauma.

REFERENCES

Bloom, S., & Reichert, M. (1998). *Bearing witness violence and collective responsibility.* New York: Haworth Press.

Burton, J. (1997). *Violence explained: The sources of conflict, violence and crime and their prevention.* Manchester, England: Manchester University Press.

Dedman, B. (2000, October 15). School shooters: Secret Service findings. *Chicago Sun-Times.* Retrieved March 1, 2001, from http://www.suntimes.com/shoot/find15.html.

Dutton, D., van Ginkel, C., & Starzomski, A. (1995). The role of shame and guilt in the intergenerational transmission of abusiveness. *Violence and Victims, 10,* 121–131.

Ezekiel, R. S. (1995). *The racist mind portraits of American neo-Nazis and Klansmen.* New York: Viking Penguin.

Fanon, F. (1963). *The wretched of the earth* (C. Farrington, Trans.). New York: Grove Press. (Original work published 1961)

Fanon, F. (1967). *Black skin white masks* (C. Markmann, Trans.). New York: Grove Press. (Original work published 1952)

Gilligan, J. (1996). *Violence: Our deadly epidemic and its causes.* New York: G. P. Putnam's Sons.

Girard, R. (1977). *Violence and the sacred* (P. Gregory, Trans.). Baltimore: Johns Hopkins University Press. (Original work published 1972)

Hardwick, P., & Rowton-Lee, M. (1996). Adolescent homicide: Towards assessment of risk. *Journal of Adolescence, 19,* 263–276.

Herman, J. (1997). *Trauma and recovery.* New York: Basic Books.

Ihanus, J. (1999). Water, birth and Stalin's thirst for power: Psychohistorical roots of terror. *The Journal of Psychohistory, 27,* 67–84.

Johnson, S. (1998, January 16). *Forensic evaluation of Theodore John Kaczynski.* Docket number CR S-96-256 GEB. San Francisco: Ninth Circuit Court of Appeals.

Kernberg, O. (1998) Aggression, hatred, and social violence. *Canadian Journal of Psychoanalysis, 6,* 191–206.

Kulka, R. A., Schlenger, W. E., Fairbank, J. A., Hough, R. L., Jordan, B. K., Marmar, C. R., & Weiss, D. S. (1990). *Trauma and the Vietnam War generation: Report of findings from the National Vietnam Veterans Readjustment Study.* New York: Brunner/Mazel.

McCarthy, T. (2001, March 19). Warning. *Time, 157,* 24–28.

Michel, L., & Herbeck, D. (2001). *American terrorist Timothy McVeigh and the Oklahoma City bombing.* New York: HarperCollins.

Minow, M. (1998). *Between vengeance and forgiveness: Facing history after genocide and mass violence.* Boston: Beacon Press.

Pomeroy, W. (1995). A working model for trauma: The relationship between trauma and violence. *Pre- and Perinatal Psychology Journal, 10,* 89–101.

Redlich, F. (1998). *Hitler: Diagnosis of a destructive prophet.* New York: Oxford University Press.

Roche, T. (2001, May 28). Voices from the cell. *Time, 157,* 32–38.

Scheff, T. J. (1987). The shame-rage spiral. A case study of an interminable quarrel. In H. B. Lewis (Ed.), *The role of shame in symptom formation* (pp. 109–140). Hillsdale, NJ: Erlbaum.

Sites, P. (1990). Needs as analogues of emotions. In J. Burton (Ed.), *Conflict: Human needs theory* (pp. 7–33). New York: St. Martin's Press.

Staub, E. (1999). The roots of evil: Social conditions, culture, personality, and basic human needs. *Personality and Social Psychology Review, 3,* 179–192.

Streeck-Fischer, A. (1999). Xenophobia and violence by adolescent skinheads. In *Trauma and adolescence* (pp. 251–269). Madison, CT: International University Press.

Sutker, P., Uddo, M. M., Brailey, K., Vasterling, J., & Errera, P. (1994). Psychopathology in war-zone deployed and nondeployed Operation Desert Storm troops assigned graves registration duties. *Journal of Abnormal Psychology, 103,* 383–390.

U.S. Secret Service (2000, October). *An interim report on the prevention of targeted violence in schools.* Washington: U.S. Secret Service National Threat Assessment Center.

Verlinden, S., Mersen, M., & Thomas, J. (2000). Risk factors in school shootings. *Clinical Psychology Review, 20,* 3–56.

Volkan, V. (1997). *Bloodlines from ethnic pride to ethnic terrorism.* New York: Farrar, Straus and Giroux.

Wolfe, J., & Proctor, S. (1996). The Persian Gulf War: New findings on traumatic exposure and stress. *PTSD Research Quarterly, 7,* 1–7.

8

The Retributional Terrorist: Type 4

Raymond H. Hamden

Terrorism can be defined as the use or threatened use of violence for political purposes to extort, intimidate, or coerce others into modifying their behavior. It is perpetrated by private individuals or small groups from the hegemonic strata against members of negative reference groups and enjoys the tacit approval if not the active participation of members of the security forces.

A terrorist is an individual who carries out or threatens to carry out acts of terror, for hire or not for hire. The act of harming or killing others, who are direct enemies or innocent victims, may be for monetary gain, gain of group principle, gain of personal principle, or any combination of these.

The literature on the specific types of terrorists featured in this chapter is sparse. Much of the information herein is based on the author's research and consultations while a visiting fellow (1986) at the Center for International Development and Conflict Management, University of Maryland–College Park, and in the years since. Clinical and forensic interventions were managed through the Human Relations Institute and Clinics, a Washington, D.C., psychology practice.

This information may be valuable for negotiators—knowing the type of terrorist with whom one is dealing can aid in the process. Various professionals in the world of forensics and political psychology may also find these matters of use—academically, practically, or both.

CONCEPTS AND PERCEPTIONS OF TERRORISTS

Commonly, terrorists are seen as psychopathic or having a religious or political cause. Yet, if we look at the individual players, we may see personal motives versus motives of principle. A common assumption is that terrorists use force or the threat of force instrumentally in a conscious and premeditated fashion because they misguidedly think that it will enhance the probability of achieving a certain political or religious goal or set of goals.

Psychologists may tend to see political or religious goals as an arena in which emotions originating elsewhere are stimulated and played out. So, the psychologist may ask, what nonpolitical frustrations or drives are at the base of the behavior? Berkowitz (1969) points out two basic variations on this theme. First is the situation in which an individual is suffering from the effects of very unpleasant present or past conditions (for example, from events that have caused pain, or frustrations). This will give rise to a "fairly specific internal inclination to be aggressive," which can be triggered by a political situation or event.

Berkowitz's second variation (1975) is that a person may merely be excited or aroused. This general, initially nonaggressive arousal can—under appropriate conditions—be channeled into political violence. The classic example is that of a large group of people that suddenly turns into an angry, violent mob.

Jeanne Knutson's research (1981) resulted in her belief that victimization is the motive force behind much political violence in the contemporary world. Victimization is a personally experienced injustice that the victim knows to be unnecessary and that creates a basic fear of annihilation. Discrete victimization events that have the strength to change the victim's perception of the world can cause the victim to act in defense of himself or herself and his or her group in order to reduce the chances for further aggression against the self, family, community, or all three.

Political psychologists are inclined to look at instances of the use of force or the threat of force in terms of these two perspectives: instrumental and expressive. Each act is usually based on some mixture of instrumental motivation and underlying psychological dynamics. Therefore, one must try to ascertain the particular mixture of underlying motives for acts of political violence.

The use of force or the threat to use force usually implies the use of some form of violence. The question of the origins and triggers of human violence has intrigued students of human behavior at least since the earliest days of written history. During the twentieth century, scholars have advanced a wide variety of theories of human aggressiveness. These can be roughly divided into three categories: (1) biological theories (psychophysiological, sociobiological, and ethological); (2) psychological and social-psychological theories (from Freudian theories to theories of situational conformity); and (3) the discipline of political psychology (which has generated many theories to better understand terrorism and international violence).

Knutson and Etheredge have joined thoughts in direct response to events in the political world of psychological understanding. Dollard (1939) and others have formed the basis for more politically oriented work. Ted Robert Gurr (1970) has developed a theory of revolutionary behavior based on frustration-aggression theory.

Freud, as well as Dollard and his associates and Etheredge (1979), focuses on what happens inside the individual. Situational conformity theory concentrates on what is happening in the microenvironment. Social learning theory, as well as Knutson's victimization theory, concentrates on the impact of both the microenvironment and the macroenvironment on individual behavior. Ethnocentrism focuses on the dynamics of the microenvironmental interactions within groups, as well as the macroenvironmental issues involved in the relationships between groups, which may consist of entire cultural or national collectivities.

All, to some extent, stress the importance of the personality-situation interaction. They can also be seen as making a significant contribution to the analysis of specific events involving the use or threat of force. One should see the whole issue of human aggressive behavior as involving a much more complex dynamic—microenvironment, macroenvironment, and the dynamics of the individual.

However, this chapter will only address the individual dynamics, the four types of terrorist—psychopathic, political ethnogeographic, religious ethnogeographic, and retributional. The "hired guns" are the individuals who seek satisfaction in the pathologically narcissistic need to control—the psychopathic terrorist. The "group-cause" terrorists can manifest through religious or political systems, or both—the ethnogeographic terrorist. In this chapter, the political ethnogeographic terrorist and religious ethnogeographic terrorist are discussed together. The person who had no history of pathology and was not inclined to membership in any particular group, yet suffered a deliberately planned major atrocity against self, family, community, or all, is the retributional terrorist.

The terrorist incidents (May 1, 1961, to September 11, 2001) listed in the Appendix are not qualified by terrorist type. Direct or indirect information on each person involved in these events would highlight the type of motivation and may enhance the negotiation process.

The psychology of the terrorist or terrorism-at-large is best understood when the holistic model is implemented. Although terrorism, torture, or any form of violence is inexcusable, there are explanations for acts of atrocity that need to be considered to foster an end to such unforgettable events.

CLINICAL AND FORENSIC PSYCHOLOGY INVESTIGATION

To learn about and understand the terrorist, we shall examine the personality profile of the individual—diagnosis, psychological defense mechanisms—and discuss how the knowledge gained from this examination can benefit the negotiation process.

The clinical information is critical in the negotiation process. Thinking as the perpetrator can be essential in developing a resolution to the conflict at hand. It is important to know the defense mechanisms highlighted in such individuals.

Psychological defense mechanisms are patterns of feelings, thoughts, or behaviors that are relatively involuntary and arise in response to perceptions of psychic danger. They are designed to hide or to alleviate the conflicts or stressors that give rise to anxiety (Vaillant, 1992).

Defense mechanisms are divided into categories by different theorists—narcissistic, immature, neurotic, and mature (Meissner, 1980); psychotic, immature, neurotic, and mature (Vaillant, 1992); and action, major image distortion, disavowal, narcissistic or minor image distortion, other neurotic, obsessional, and high adaptive-level (Perry, 1987).

The protocol of clinical and forensic intervention that leads to diagnosis and identifying defense mechanisms is the psychology interview and mental status examination.

Psychology Interview and Mental Status Examination

Psychological History

Identification. This is basically done by the examining professional, who requires the name, address of origin, and affiliations. This is usually provided by the referring government agency or the legal practice seeking expert representation for a client.

Chief complaint. This is where the professional inquires about what is troubling the terrorist and the reason he or she needs professional help.

History of present concern. This concerns the chronological background of the development of the person's behavior, cognition, emotions, and environment. The professional, however, should listen carefully to the symptoms and circumstances that led to the onset of these and to ascertain any premorbid personality characteristic or trait.

Family history. This is a very important source of information, to establish the environment the person grew up in as well as to elicit any evidence of psychological disorders.

Past personal history. This examines the individual's life from infancy to the present. It is divided into three stages: (1) early, middle, and late childhood, (2) adolescence, and (3) adulthood.

Sexual history. This determines whether the person has had any sexual disorders, or sexual misconduct, at any period or through different periods of life.

Medical history. This examines whether the individual has suffered or is suffering from any illness, disability, or disorder.

Social history. Here one records any reported or investigated evidence of military duty, legal problems involving imprisonment or arrests, or membership in organizations.

Psychological history. This examines the knowledge of all psychological conditions; this knowledge gives the ability to sift material and to know what information is missing and still must be obtained.

Mental Status Examination

This focuses on the individual's condition while being examined.

General description. This is done by observing the person's appearance, which gives a general idea about attitude and overall behavior—except if the person is jailed, in which case inmate attire would be expected.

Speech and stream of talk. This enables the examiner to determine whether the individual's tone is normal, rapid, or slow.

Emotional reaction and mood. This is to determine the person's reaction in different respects.

Perception. This is to examine the person's ability to perceive himself or herself, the world, and the appropriate relations between the two.

Thought content. This examines the rate of verbalized thoughts, to assess whether there is a paucity of ideas or seeming abundance. Abstract thinking is included to examine the ability to deal with different concepts.

Cognition. This examines the area of the sensorium-capabilities that include consciousness, orientation, memory, and intellectual tasks. Consciousness is evaluated by one's ability to concentrate. Orientation is usually assessed with respect to time, place, and person. Memory is evaluated from the point of view of recent memory and remote memory. Intellectual tasks are assessed by looking at the general fund of knowledge and intellectual functioning, reading and writing, judgment, and insight.

Furthermore, the professional must make a statement about *reliability*—that is, the tendency to minimize or exaggerate symptoms and the capacity to report situations truthfully.

Diagnosis

The Diagnostic and Statistical Manual of Mental Disorders, Fourth Edition, Text Revision (DSM-IV-TR) uses a multiaxial classification scheme consisting of five axes, each of which is covered in the diagnosis. Axis 1 includes all the disorders and conditions listed in *DSM-IV-TR* except the personality disorders and specific developmental disorders that are listed in Axis 2. Axis 3 includes physical disorders and conditions. Axis 4 relates to the severity of psychological stressors and Axis-5 rates the level of adaptive functioning during the past year.

THE PSYCHOPATHIC TERRORIST

In the *DSM-IV-TR* (American Psychiatric Association, 2000), the diagnosis of antisocial personality disorder highlights the following:

> The essential feature of Antisocial Personality Disorder is a pervasive pattern of disregard for, and violation of, the rights of others that begins in childhood or early adolescence and continues into adulthood. This pattern has also been referred to as psychopathy, sociopathy, or dissocial personality disorder. Because deceit and manipulation

are central features of Antisocial Personality Disorder, it may be especially helpful to integrate information acquired from systematic clinical assessment with information collected from collateral sources.

The pattern of antisocial behavior continues into adulthood. Individuals with Antisocial Personality Disorder fail to conform to social norms with respect to lawful behavior. They may repeatedly perform acts that are grounds for arrest (whether they are arrested or not), such as destroying property, harassing others, stealing, or pursuing illegal occupations. Persons with this disorder disregard the wishes, rights, or feelings of others. They are frequently deceitful and manipulative in order to gain personal profit or pleasure. A pattern of impulsivity may be manifested by failure to plan ahead.

Individuals with Antisocial Personality Disorder also tend to be consistently and extremely irresponsible. . . . They may be indifferent to, or provide a superficial rationalization for, having hurt, mistreated, or stolen from someone. These individuals may blame the victims for being foolish, helpless, or deserving their fate; they may minimize the harmful consequences of their actions; or they may simply indicate complete indifference. They generally fail to compensate or make amends for their behavior.

Child abuse or neglect, unstable or erratic parenting, or inconsistent parental discipline may increase the likelihood that Conduct Disorder will evolve into Antisocial Personality Disorder.

Case Example

This young man, 21 years of age, does not look at all like a criminal type or shifty delinquent. Tom looks and is in robust physical health. His manner and appearance are pleasing. . . . His immediate problem was serious but not monumental. His family and legal authorities were in hope that if some psychiatric disorder could be discovered in him, he might escape a jail sentence for stealing. . . .

Evidence of his maladjustment became distinct in childhood. He appeared to be a reliable and manly fellow but could never be counted upon to keep at any task or to give a straight account of any situation. He was frequently truant from school. . . . Though he was generously provided for, he stole some of his father's chickens from time to time, selling them at stores downtown. Pieces of table silver would be missed. These were sometimes recovered from those to whom he had sold them for a pittance or swapped them for odds and ends which seemed to hold no particular interest or value for him.

He lied so plausibly and with such equanimity, devised such ingenious alibis or simply denied all responsibility with such convincing appearances of candor that for many years his real career was poorly estimated. . . .

Though he often fell in with groups or small gangs, he never for long identified himself with others in common cause. Reliable information indicates that he has been arrested and imprisoned approximately fifty or sixty times. It is estimated that he would have been put in jail or police barracks for short or long periods of detention on approximately 150 other occasions if his family had not made good his small thefts and damages and paid fines for him. . . .

This case study depicts a typical cognitive and behavioral style of this personality-disordered character. From this, one can better understand the lack of emotional regards personified in the psychopathic individual.

Defense Mechanisms of Psychopathic Personalities

Denial. Psychotic denial of external reality. Unlike repression, it affects the perception of external reality. Seeing but refusing to acknowledge what one sees and hearing but negating what is actually heard are examples of denial and exemplify the close relationship of denial to sensory experience. However, not all denial is necessarily psychotic. Like projection, denial may function in the service of neurotic or even adaptive objectives.

Distortion. Grossly reshaping external reality to suit inner needs including unrealistic megalomania beliefs, hallucinations, wish-fulfilling delusions, and using sustained feelings of delusional superiority or entitlement.

Projection (narcissistic). Frank delusions about external reality, usually persecutory, including both perceptions of one's own feelings in another and subsequent acting on the perception (paranoid disorder).

Acting out. Direct expressions of an unconscious wish or impulse to avoid being aware of the accompanying affect. The unconscious fantasy, involving objects, is lived out impulsively in behavior, thus gratifying the impulse more than the prohibition against it. On a chronic level, acting out involves giving in to impulses to avoid the tension that would result from postponement of expression.

Rationalization. A mechanism in which the person devises reassuring or self-serving, but incorrect, explanations for his or her own or others' behavior.

Negotiations with Psychopathic Types

These individuals are narcissistic and unconcerned with the welfare of others. They are interested in their own personal benefits only. They can be hired to do "the job" with little or no interest in the cause; and they can kill with no remorse. To kill a hostage is of little concern, unless it directly affects the psychopathic terrorist.

THE ETHNOGEOGRAPHIC TERRORIST: RELIGIOUS OR POLITICAL

These two types display the same or very similar dynamics but for different causes. In explaining others' actions, professionals frequently commit the fundamental attribution error. That is, we attribute their behaviors so much to the inner dispositions that we discount important situation forces. The error occurs partly because our attention focuses on the person, not on the situation. A person's race or gender is vivid and attention-getting; the situational forces working upon that person are usually less visible.

> *Fundamentalism* is defined as a strict maintenance of traditional ortho-
> dox religious beliefs; a religious movement which developed among
> various bodies . . . based on strict adherence to certain tenets. (*The
> Oxford Reference Dictionary*, 1986)

Fundamentalism, by definition, is a movement that arises from an existing body of political or religious believers. It stresses the infallibility of the political premise or holy text in all matters of doctrine and faith, accepting it as a literal record of history; the basic underlying principles, the original and primary source of ideas, and the groundwork of a system. Fundamentalism is synonymous with essential and necessary laws and rules. Therefore, to the "believer," the law (fundamentalism) is indispensable.

This definition can be applied to political as well as religious fundamentalism. To understand the fundamental mindset, let us look at ourselves in terms of attribution theories. Pettigrew (1979) argues that attribution errors can bias people's explanations of group members' behaviors. We grant members of our own group the benefit of the doubt: "She donated because she has a good heart; he refused because he had to under the circumstances." When explaining acts by members of other groups, we more often assume the worst: "He donated to gain favor; she refused because she's selfish."

Defense Mechanisms of Fundamentalist Types

Introjection. With a loved object, introjection involves the internalization of characteristics of the object with the goal of establishing closeness to and constant presence of the object. Anxiety consequent to separation or tension arising out of ambivalence toward the object is thus diminished. Introjection of a feared object serves to avoid anxiety by internalizing the aggressive characteristics of the object, thereby putting the aggression under one's control. The aggression is no longer felt as coming from outside but is taken within and used defensively, turning the person's weak, passive position into an active, strong one. Introjection can also rise out of a sense of guilt, in which the self-punishing introject is attributable to the hostile-destructive component of an ambivalent tie to an object. The self-punitive qualities of the object are taken over and established within one's self as a symptom or character trait, which effectively represents both the destruction and preservation of the object. This is also called identification with the victim.

Passive-aggressive behavior. Aggression toward an object that is expressed indirectly and ineffectively through passivity, masochism, and turning against the self.

Projection (immature). Attributing one's own unacknowledged feelings to others; it includes severe prejudice, rejection of intimacy through suspiciousness, hypervigilance to external danger, and injustice collecting. Projection operates correlatively to introjection; the material of the projection is derived from the internalized configuration of the introject.

Schizoid fantasy. The tendency to use fantasy and to indulge in autistic retreat for the purpose of conflict resolution and gratification.

Reaction formation. A mechanism in which the person substitutes behavior, thoughts, or feelings that are diametrically opposed to his or her unacceptable ones.

Intellectualization. The individual deals with emotional conflicts, or internal or external stressors, by the excessive use of abstract thinking or generalizing to avoid experiencing disturbing feelings.

Negotiations with Fundamentalist Types

To negotiate better with the ethnogeographic types, know your own biases first. Learn to block them out, to maintain a clear and more objective role in negotiating. Issues of transference and countertransference are manifested here.

The ethnogeographic players work as part of a group. The group in itself enhances the goal to destroy "the common enemy." Their motto is "To die for the cause is an honor." Those who die with them, voluntarily or not, will also be rewarded in the afterlife, in youthful martyrdom, or both. So threats to kill or harm the terrorist are of no benefit to the negotiator.

Clinical experience with such persons and individual members of groups has suggested passive-aggressive characteristics. The symptoms of passive-aggressive personality disorder all revolve around the fact that the person with such a disorder sabotages efforts directed at getting him or her to work or socialize at an expected level.

Usually, such people think they are doing better work than they really are and get very angry when others make useful suggestions about how their performance might be improved. They tend to be critical of those in authority.

This person, or individual within-the-group, asks for help but then does not comply with the advice or evidence of cooperation.

THE RETRIBUTIONAL TERRORIST: TYPE 4

These are individuals who had no medical or psychological history of psychopathology. They may not have belonged to or favor any particular religious or political group or groups. Furthermore, they may not have entertained any notion of joining such. Yet, their home, community, family members, or all were destroyed by deliberately planned war, crisis, or terror on innocent and civilian locations.

The individual who survives an atrocity will seek revenge (punishment or injury inflicted in return for what one has suffered), through retaliation (to repay in kind or to make a counterattack) and revolt (to rise in rebellion; to be in a mood of protest or defiance). Retribution—"deserved punishment, requital, usually for evil done" (*The Oxford Reference Dictionary*, 1986)—becomes the focus for this person.

The retributional terrorist finds he or she has nothing to lose. He or she has lost everything of meaning in life. These terrorists will find justice by their own definition. However, the realization of isolation is clear when they are frustrated in reaching their target—the individual or group that caused them the grief.

These individuals are found to suffer from post-traumatic stress disorder. Post-traumatic stress disorder (PTSD) can strike anyone who survives a severe physical or mental trauma. The disorder has gained notoriety from the frequency with which it afflicts war veterans, but a much wider population, including children, is at risk. This population includes people who have been beaten, raped, tortured, or have witnessed gruesome accidents, catastrophes, or natural disasters.

Symptoms of PTSD can appear soon after the trauma or be delayed by months or years. But, eventually, people with the disorder begin to re-experience the traumatic event or the anxiety associated with it. The most dramatic symptoms are the distressing recollections, nightmares, or daytime flashbacks in which the trauma is "replayed."

Nightmares can be so severe that retributional terrorists awaken from sleep screaming. Flashbacks can include a dissociative state in which victims actually lose touch with reality.

Other symptoms include a kind of emotional anesthesia called psychic numbing, which leaves these individuals disinterested in the world around them. They may withdraw from family and friends, becoming increasingly isolated.

Retributional terrorists often try particularly hard to avoid situations that remind them of their traumas. Even minor similarities can trigger symptoms. Someone who has been severely assaulted by a policeman may, for instance, avoid watching television in the fear that a similar situation may be depicted. Someone who watched a friend drown may attempt to avoid seeing any body of water. This avoidance behavior can become so consuming that retributional terrorists are nearly housebound.

Some victims of PTSD report being extremely "touchy," easily startled, or easily moved to anger and violence. They can experience all the symptoms of panic disorder. PTSD also leaves people at risk for depression. Low mood, insomnia, difficulty concentrating, feelings of guilt, and bodily aches and pains are all common complaints.

In post-traumatic stress disorder, the traumatic event is quite prominent in the retributional terrorist's memory, not locked away in the unconscious. The disturbing memories are so easily triggered, in fact, that the mind initially seems to cushion itself against possible reminders. It accomplishes this through symptoms such as inattention to one's surroundings, emotional numbness, social withdrawal, and narrowing of one's range of thought. Retributional terrorists are also at great risk of turning to alcohol or illicit drugs in order to blunt their emotions.

Defense Mechanisms of the Retributional Type (with or without PTSD)

Controlling. Excessive attempt to manage or regulate events or objects in the environment in the interest of minimizing anxiety and solving internal conflicts.

Rationalization. Justification of attitudes, beliefs, or behavior that may otherwise be unacceptable by an incorrect application of justifying reasons or the invention of a convincing fallacy.

Anticipation. Realistic anticipation of or planning for future inner discomfort.

Intellectualization. The individual deals with emotional conflicts, or internal or external stressors, by the excessive use of abstract thinking or generalizing to avoid experiencing disturbing feelings.

Negotiations with the Retributional Terrorist

Negotiations with the retributional terrorist can best be served by reminding him or her that innocent people will be harmed, as his or her own innocent family or community was harmed. This fourth type uses hostages as instrumental victims for negotiation only, and does not prefer to harm them. These terrorists, however, care little for their own lives since they have little for which to live.

SUMMARY

Are there similarities among these four types of violators? Could one make a distinction between terrorists and "freedom fighters"? Certainly not in the case of the psychopathic type; but one could perhaps look at the two ethnogeographic types and the retributional type as "freedom fighters."

Frustrations, insults, and aggressive behavior heighten the aggressive tendencies of victimized people. Therefore, they may join a group—religious or political—that targets the same offenders and limits vengeance to the person, group, or nation that caused the atrocity that befell them. The groups can amplify aggressive reactions partly by diffusing responsibility (Gaebelein & Mander, 1978; Mikolic, Parker, & Pruitt, 1997).

In the laboratory, researchers can test and revise theories under controlled conditions. Real-world events inspire ideas and provide the venue for applying our theories. Today, the terrorist has no gender, age, or national limits.

As professionals seeking knowledge of such individuals, we must look at each holistically—cognitively, emotionally, behaviorally, physically—and at the effects of the environment on the total person. By effectively testing theories and learning real-world facts with open minds, professionals can make great strides in improving human understanding and fostering cooperation.

REFERENCES

American Psychiatric Association (2000). *Diagnostic and statistical manual of mental disorders,* 4th edition, text revision. Washington, DC: Author.

Berkowitz, L. (Ed.) (1969). *Roots of aggression.* New York: Atherton.

Berkowitz, L. (1975). *A survey of social psychology.* Hinsdale, IL: Dryden Press.

Dollard, J., Miller, N., Doob, L., Mowrer, O., & Sears, R. (1939). *Frustration and aggression.* New Haven, CT: Yale University Press.

Etheredge, L. (1979). Hardball politics: a model. *Political Psychology, I,* 3–26.

Gaebelein, J. W., & Mander, A. (1978). Consequences for targets of aggression as a function of aggressor and instigator roles: Three experiments. *Personality and Social Psychology Bulletin, 4,* 465–468.

Gurr, T. R. (1970). Psychology factors in civil violence. In I. K. Feierabend, R. L. Feierabend, & T. R. Gurr (Eds.), *Anger, violence, and politics: Theories and research.* Englewood Cliffs, NJ: Prentice-Hall.

Knutson, J. N. (Ed.) (1981). *Handbook of political psychology.* San Francisco: Jossey-Bass.

Meissner, W. W. (1980). Theories of personality and psychopathology: Classical psychoanalysis. In Kaplan, H. I., Freedman, A. M., & Sadock, B. J., (Eds.), *Comprehensive textbook of psychiatry* (3rd ed., Vol. I, pp. 631–728). Baltimore: William & Wilkins.

Mikolic, J. M., Parker, J. C., & Pruitt, D. G. (1997). Escalation in response to persistent annoyance: Groups versus individuals and gender effects. *Journal of Personality and Social Psychology, 72,* 151–163.

Oxford Reference Dictionary, The (1986). Oxford, England: Clarendon Press.

Perry, J. C., & Cooper, S. H. (1987). Empirical studies of psychological defenses. In J. O. Cavenar & R. Michel (Eds.), *Psychiatry* (Vol. I, pp. 1–19). Philadelphia: J. B. Lippincott, Basic Books.

Pettigrew, T. F. (1979). The ultimate attribution error: Extending Allport's cognitive analysis of prejudice. *Personality and Social Psychology Bulletin, 55,* 461–476.

Vaillant, G. E. (1992). *Ego mechanisms of defense: A guide for clinicians and researchers.* Washington, DC: American Psychiatric Press.

SUPPLEMENTARY BIBLIOGRAPHY

Berkowitz, L. (1969). Simple views of aggression: an easy review. *American Scientists, 57,* 372–383.

Bushman, B. J., & Anderson, C. A. Methodology in the study of aggression: Integrating experimental and nonexperimental findings. In R. Geen & E. Donnerstein (Eds.), *Human aggression: Theories, research and implications for policy.* San Diego: Academic Press.

Eldrige, A. F. (1979). *Images of conflicts.* New York: St. Martin's.

Farrell, R., & Swigert, V. (1978). Legal disposition of inter-group and intra-group homicides. *Sociological Quarterly, 19,* 565–576.

Fletcher, G. J. O., & Ward, C. (1989). Attribution theory and processes: A cross-cultural perspective. In M. H. Bond (Ed.), *The cross-cultural challenge to social psychology.* Newbury Park, CA: Sage.

Hamden, R. H. (1986). The retributional terrorist: Type 4. Research at Center for International Development and Conflict Management, University of Maryland–College Park.

Hewstone, M. (1990). The 'ultimate attribution error'? A review of the literature on intergroup casual attribution. *European Journal of Social Psychology, 20,* 311–335.

Hewstone, M., & Ward, C. (1985). Ethnocentrism and casual attribution in Southeast Asia. *Journal of Personality and Social Psychology, 48,* 614–623.

Human Relations Institute and Clinics (1983–1991) *Clinical cases in forensic psychology.* Unpublished. Washington, DC.

Jackson, J. S., Kirby, D., Barnes, L., & Shepard, L. (1993). Institutional racism and pluralistic ignorance: A cross-national comparison. In M. Wievorka (Ed.), *Racisme et modernité.* Paris: Editions la Decouverte.

Jaffe, Y., Shapir, N., & Yinon, Y. (1981). Aggression and its escalation. *Journal of Cross-Cultural Psychology, 12,* 21–36.

Karmen, A. (1984). *Crime victims: An introduction to victimology.* Monterey, CA: Brooks/ Cole.

Lagerspetz, K. M. J., Bjorkqvist, K., Berts, M., & King, E. (1982). Group aggression among school children in three schools. *Scandinavian Journal of Psychology, 23,* 45–52.

Maass, A., Milesi, A., Zabbini, S., & Stahlberg, D. (1995). Linguistic intergroup bias: Differential expectancies or in-group protection? *Journal of Personality and Social Psychology, 68,* 116–126.

Mitchell, C. R. (1981). *The structure of international conflict.* New York: St. Martin's.

Mullen, B. (1986). Atrocity as a function of lynch mob composition: A self-attention perspective. *Personality and Social Psychology Bulletin, 12,* 187–197.

Office of the Coordinator for Counterterrorism, Office of Public Affairs, U.S. Department of State. Washington, DC. www.state.gov/s/ct/. Accessed September 2001.

Paternoster, R. (1983). Race of victim and location of crime: The decision to seek the death penalty in South Carolina. *Journal of Criminal Law and Criminology, 74,* 754–785.

Pomper, G. N. (1970). *Elections in America.* New York: Dodd, Mead.

Staub, E. (1996). Altruism and aggression in children and youth: Origins and cures. In R. Feldman (Ed.), *The psychology of adversity.* Amherst, MA: University of Massachusetts Press.

Treiman, D. (1977). *Occupational prestige in comparative perspective.* New York: Academic Press.

APPENDIX: SIGNIFICANT TERRORIST INCIDENTS, 1961–2001

Information supplied by the Office of the Coordinator for Counterterrorism, Office of the Historian, Bureau of Public Affairs, U.S. Department of State.

1961–1982

First U.S. aircraft hijacked, May 1, 1961: Puerto Rico-born Antuilo Ramierez Ortiz forced at gunpoint a National Airlines plane to fly to Havana, Cuba, where he was given asylum.

Ambassador to Guatemala assassinated, August 28, 1968: U.S. Ambassador to Guatemala John Gordon Mein was murdered by a rebel faction when gunmen forced his official car off the road in Guatemala City and raked the vehicle with gunfire.

Ambassador to Japan attacked, July 30, 1969: U.S. Ambassador to Japan A. H. Meyer was attacked by a knife-wielding Japanese citizen.

Ambassador to Brazil kidnapped, September 3, 1969: U.S. Ambassador to Brazil Charles Burke Elbrick was kidnapped by the Marxist revolutionary group MR-8.

U.S. Agency for International Development adviser kidnapped, July 31, 1970: In Montevideo, Uruguay, the Tupamaros terrorist group kidnapped USAID Police adviser Dan Mitrione; his body was found on August 10.

"Bloody Friday," July 21, 1972: Irish Republican Army (IRA) bomb attacks killed 11 people and injured 130 in Belfast, Northern Ireland. Ten days later, three IRA car bomb attacks in the village of Claudy left six dead.

Munich Olympics Massacre, September 5, 1972: Eight Palestinian "Black September" terrorists seized 11 Israeli athletes in the Olympic Village in Munich, West Germany. In a bungled rescue attempt by West German authorities, nine of the hostages and five terrorists were killed.

Ambassador to Sudan assassinated, March 2, 1973: U.S. Ambassador to Sudan Cleo A. Noel and other diplomats were assassinated at the Saudi Arabian Embassy in Khartoum by members of the Black September organization.

Consul General in Mexico kidnapped, May 4, 1973: The U.S. Consul General in Guadalajara, Terrence Leonhardy, was kidnapped by members of the People's Revolutionary Armed Forces.

Domestic terrorism, January 27–29, 1975: Puerto Rican nationalists bombed a Wall Street bar, killing four and injuring 60; two days later, the Weather Underground claimed responsibility for an explosion in a bathroom at the U.S. Department of State in Washington.

Entebbe hostage crisis, June 27, 1976: Members of the Baader-Meinhof Group and the Popular Front for the Liberation of Palestine (PFLP) seized an Air France airliner and its 258 passengers. They forced the plane to land in Uganda, where on July 3 Israeli commandos successfully rescued the passengers.

Assassination of former Chilean diplomat, September 21, 1976: In Washington, exiled Chilean Foreign Minister Orlando Letelier was killed by a car bomb.

Kidnapping of Italian prime minister, March 16, 1978: Premier Aldo Moro was seized by the Red Brigade and assassinated 55 days later.

Iran hostage crisis, November 4, 1979: After President Carter agreed to admit the Shah of Iran into the United States, Iranian radicals seized the U.S. Embassy in Tehran and took 66 American diplomats hostage. Thirteen hostages were soon released, but the remaining 53 were held until their release on January 20, 1981.

Grand Mosque seizure, November 20, 1979: 200 Islamic terrorists seized the Grand Mosque in Mecca, Saudi Arabia, taking hundreds of pilgrims hostage. Saudi and French security forces retook the shrine after an intense battle in which some 250 people were killed and 600 wounded.

U.S. installation bombing, August 31, 1981: The Red Army exploded a bomb at the U.S. Air Force Base at Ramstein, West Germany.

Assassination of Egyptian president, October 6, 1981: Soldiers who were secretly members of the Takfir Wal-Hajira sect attacked and killed Egyptian President Anwar Sadat during a troop review.

Murder of missionaries, December 4, 1981: Three American nuns and one lay missionary were found murdered outside San Salvador, El Salvador. They were believed to have been assassinated by a right-wing death squad.

Assassination of Lebanese prime minister, September 14, 1982: Premier Bashir Gemayel was assassinated by a car bomb parked outside his party's Beirut headquarters.

1983

Colombian hostage-taking, April 8, 1983: A U.S. citizen was seized by the Revolutionary Armed Forces of Colombia (FARC) and held for ransom.

Bombing of U.S. Embassy in Beirut, April 18, 1983: Sixty-three people, including the CIA's Middle East director, were killed, and 120 were injured in a 400-pound suicide truck-bomb attack on the U.S. Embassy in Beirut, Lebanon. The Islamic Jihad claimed responsibility.

Naval officer assassinated in El Salvador, May 25, 1983: A U.S. Navy officer was assassinated by the Farabundo Marti National Liberation Front.

North Korean hit squad, October 9, 1983: North Korean agents blew up a delegation from South Korea in Rangoon, Burma, killing 21 persons and injuring 48.

Bombing of Marine barracks, Beirut, October 23, 1983: Simultaneous suicide truck-bomb attacks were made on American and French compounds in Beirut, Lebanon. A 12,000-pound bomb destroyed the U.S. compound, killing 242 Americans, while 58 French troops were killed when a 400-pound device destroyed the French base. Islamic Jihad claimed responsibility.

Naval officer assassinated in Greece, November 15, 1983: A U.S. Navy officer was shot by the November 17 terrorist group in Athens, Greece, while his car was stopped at a traffic light.

1984

Kidnapping of embassy official, March 16, 1984: The Islamic Jihad kidnapped and later murdered Political Officer William Buckley in Beirut, Lebanon. Other U.S. citizens not connected to the U.S. government were seized over a succeeding two-year period.

Hezbollah restaurant bombing, April 12, 1984: Eighteen U.S. servicemen were killed and 83 people were injured in a bomb attack on a restaurant near a U.S. Air Force base in Torrejon, Spain. Responsibility was claimed by Hezbollah.

Golden Temple seizure, June 5, 1984: Sikh terrorists seized the Golden Temple in Amritsar, India. One hundred people died when Indian security forces retook the Sikh holy shrine.

Assassination of Prime Minister Gandhi, October 31, 1984: The Indian premier was shot to death by members of her security force.

1985

Kidnapping of U.S. officials in Mexico, February 7, 1985: Under the orders of narcotrafficker Rafael Cero Quintero, Drug Enforcement Administration Agent Enrique Camarena Salazar and his pilot were kidnapped, tortured, and executed.

TWA hijacking, June 14, 1985: A Trans-World Airlines flight was hijacked en route to Rome from Athens by two Lebanese Hezbollah terrorists and forced to fly to Beirut. The eight crew members and 145 passengers were held for 17 days, during which one American hostage, a U.S. Navy sailor, was murdered. After being flown twice to Algiers, the aircraft was returned to Beirut after Israel released 435 Lebanese and Palestinian prisoners.

Air India bombing, June 23, 1985: A bomb destroyed an Air India Boeing 747 over the Atlantic, killing all 329 people aboard. Both Sikh and Kashmiri terrorists were blamed for the attack. Two cargo handlers were killed at Tokyo airport, Japan, when another Sikh bomb exploded in an Air Canada aircraft on a stopover en route to India.

Soviet diplomats kidnapped, September 30, 1985: In Beirut, Lebanon, Sunni terrorists kidnapped four Soviet diplomats. One was killed, but the others were later released.

Achille Lauro hijacking, October 7, 1985: Four Palestinian Liberation Front terrorists seized the Italian cruise liner in the eastern Mediterranean Sea, taking more than 700 hostages. One U.S. passenger was murdered before the Egyptian government offered the terrorists safe haven in return for the hostages' freedom.

Egyptian airliner hijacking, November 23, 1985: An EgyptAir airplane bound from Athens to Malta and carrying several U.S. citizens was hijacked by the Abu Nidal group.

1986

Aircraft bombing in Greece, March 30, 1986: A Palestinian splinter group detonated a bomb as TWA Flight 840 approached Athens Airport, killing four U.S. citizens.

Berlin Discotheque Bombing, April 5, 1986: Two U.S. soldiers were killed and 79 American servicemen were injured in a Libyan bomb attack on a nightclub in West Berlin. In retaliation, U.S. military jets bombed targets in and around Tripoli and Benghazi.

Kimpo Airport bombing, September 14, 1986: North Korean agents detonated an explosive device at Seoul's Kimpo Airport, killing five and injuring 29 others.

1987

Bus attack, April 24, 1987: Sixteen U.S. servicemen riding in a Greek Air Force bus near Athens were injured in an apparent bombing attack carried out by the revolutionary organization known as 17 November.

Downing of airliner, November 29, 1987: North Korean agents planted a bomb aboard Korean Air Lines Flight 858, which subsequently crashed into the Indian Ocean.

Servicemen's bar attack, December 26, 1987: Catalan separatists bombed a Barcelona bar frequented by U.S. servicemen, resulting in the death of one U.S. citizen.

1988

Kidnapping of William Higgins, February 17, 1988: U.S. Marine Corps Lt. Col. William Higgins was kidnapped and murdered by the Iranian-backed Hezbollah group while serving with the United Nations Truce Supervisory Organization (UNTSO) in southern Lebanon.

Naples USO attack, April 14, 1988: The Organization of Jihad Brigades exploded a car bomb outside a USO Club in Naples, Italy, killing one U.S. sailor.

Attack on U.S. diplomat in Greece, June 28, 1988: The defense attaché of the U.S. Embassy in Greece was killed when a car bomb was detonated outside his home in Athens.

Pan Am 103 bombing, December 21, 1988: Pan American Airlines Flight 103 was blown up over Lockerbie, Scotland, by a bomb believed to have been placed on the aircraft in Frankfurt, West Germany, by Libyan terrorists. All 259 people on board were killed.

1989

Assassination of U.S. Army officer, April 21, 1989: The New People's Army (NPA) assassinated Col. James Rowe in Manila. The NPA also assassinated two U.S. government defense contractors in September.

Assassination of German bank chairman, November 30, 1989: The Red Army assassinated Deutsche Bank Chairman Alfred Herrhausen in Frankfurt.

1990

U.S. Embassy bombed in Peru, January 15, 1990: The Tupac Amaru Revolutionary Movement bombed the U.S. Embassy in Lima, Peru.

U.S. soldiers assassinated in the Philippines, May 13, 1990: The New People's Army (NPA) killed two U.S. Air Force personnel near Clark Air Force Base in the Philippines.

1991

Attempted Iraqi attacks on U.S. posts, January 18–19, 1991: Iraqi agents planted bombs at the U.S. ambassador to Indonesia's home residence and at the USIS library in Manila.

1992

Kidnapping of U.S. businessmen in the Philippines and Colombia, January 17–21, 1992: A senior official of the corporation Philippine Geothermal was kidnapped in Manila by the Red Scorpion Group, and two U.S. businessmen were seized independently by the National Liberation Army and by Revolutionary Armed Forces of Colombia (FARC).

Bombing of the Israeli Embassy in Argentina, March 17, 1992: Hezbollah claimed responsibility for a blast that leveled the Israeli Embassy in Buenos Aires, Argentina, causing the deaths of 29 and wounding 242.

1993

Kidnappings of U.S. citizens in Colombia, January 31, 1993: Revolutionary Armed Forces of Colombia (FARC) terrorists kidnapped three U.S. missionaries.

World Trade Center bombing, February 26, 1993: The World Trade Center in New York City was badly damaged when a car bomb planted by Islamic terrorists exploded in an underground garage. The bomb left six people dead and 1,000 injured. The men carrying out the attack were followers of Umar Abd al-Rahman, an Egyptian cleric who preached in the New York City area.

Attempted assassination of President Bush by Iraqi agents, April 14, 1993: The Iraqi intelligence service attempted to assassinate former U.S. President George Bush during a visit to Kuwait. In retaliation, the United States launched a cruise missile attack two months later on the Iraqi capital Baghdad.

1994

Hebron massacre, February 25, 1994: Jewish right-wing extremist and U.S. citizen Baruch Goldstein machine-gunned Moslem worshippers at a mosque in West Bank town of Hebron, killing 29 and wounding about 150.

FARC hostage-taking, September 23, 1994: FARC rebels kidnapped U.S. citizen Thomas Hargrove in Colombia.

Air France hijacking, December 24, 1994: Members of the Armed Islamic Group seized an Air France flight to Algeria. The four terrorists were killed during a rescue effort.

1995

Attack on U.S. diplomats in Pakistan, March 8, 1995: Two unidentified gunmen killed two U.S. diplomats and wounded a third in Karachi, Pakistan.

Tokyo subway station attack, March 20, 1995: Twelve persons were killed and 5,700 injured in a Sarin nerve gas attack on a crowded subway station in the center of Tokyo, Japan. A similar attack occurred nearly simultaneously in the Yokohama subway system. The Aum Shinri-kyu cult was blamed for the attacks.

Bombing of the Federal Building in Oklahoma City, April 19, 1995: Right-wing extremists Timothy McVeigh and Terry Nichols destroyed the Federal Building in Oklahoma City with a massive truck bomb that killed 166 and injured hundreds more in what was up to then the largest terrorist attack on American soil.

Kashmiri hostage-taking, July 4, 1995: In India, six foreigners, including two U.S. citizens, were taken hostage by Al-Faran, a Kashmiri separatist group. One non-U.S. hostage was later found beheaded.

Jerusalem bus attack, August 21, 1995: Hamas claimed responsibility for the detonation of a bomb that killed six and injured more than 100, including several U.S. citizens.

Attack on U.S. Embassy in Moscow, September 13, 1995: A rocket-propelled grenade was fired through the window of the U.S. Embassy in Moscow, ostensibly in retaliation for U.S. strikes on Serb positions in Bosnia.

Saudi military installation attack, November 13, 1995: The Islamic Movement of Change planted a bomb in a Riyadh military compound that killed one U.S. citizen, several foreign national employees of the U.S. government, and more than 40 others.

Egyptian Embassy attack, November 19, 1995: A suicide bomber drove a vehicle into the Egyptian Embassy compound in Islamabad, Pakistan, killing at least 16 and injuring 60. Three militant Islamic groups claimed responsibility.

1996

Papuan hostage abduction, January 8, 1996: In Indonesia, 200 Free Papua Movement (OPM) guerrillas abducted 26 individuals in the Lorenta nature preserve, Irian Jaya Province. Indonesian Special Forces members rescued the remaining nine hostages on May 15.

Kidnapping in Colombia, January 19, 1996: Revolutionary Armed Forces of Colombia (FARC) guerrillas kidnapped a U.S. citizen and demanded a $1 million ransom. The hostage was released on May 22.

Tamil Tigers attack, January 31, 1996: Members of the Liberation Tigers of Tamil Eelam (LTTE) rammed an explosives-laden truck into the Central Bank in the heart of downtown Colombo, Sri Lanka, killing 90 civilians and injuring more than 1,400 others, including two U.S. citizens.

IRA bombing, February 9, 1996: An Irish Republican Army (IRA) bomb detonated in London, killing two and wounding more than 100 others, including two U.S. citizens.

Athens Embassy attack, February 15, 1996: Unidentified assailants fired a rocket at the U.S. Embassy compound in Athens, causing minor damage to three diplomatic vehicles and some surrounding buildings. Circumstances of the attack suggested it was an operation carried out by the 17 November group.

ELN kidnapping, February 16, 1996: Six alleged National Liberation Army (ELN) guerrillas kidnapped a U.S. citizen in Colombia. The hostage was released after nine months.

Hamas bus attack, February 26, 1996: In Jerusalem, a suicide bomber blew up a bus, killing 26, including three U.S. citizens, and injuring some 80 others, including three other U.S. citizens.

Dizengoff Center bombing, March 4, 1996: Hamas and the Palestine Islamic Jihad (PIJ) both claimed responsibility for a bombing outside Tel Aviv's largest shopping mall that killed 20 and injured 75 others, including two U.S. citizens.

West Bank attack, May 13, 1996: Arab gunmen opened fire on a bus and a group of Yeshiva students near the Bet El settlement, killing a dual U.S.–Israeli citizen and wounding three Israelis. No one claimed responsibility for the attack, but Hamas was suspected.

USAID worker abduction, May 31, 1996: A gang of former Contra guerrillas kidnapped a U.S. employee of the Agency for International Development (USAID) who was assisting with election preparations in rural northern Nicaragua. She was released unharmed the next day after members of the international commission overseeing the preparations intervened.

Zekharya attack, June 9, 1996: Unidentified gunmen opened fire on a car near Zekharya, killing a dual U.S.–Israeli citizen and an Israeli. The Popular Front for the Liberation of Palestine (PFLP) was suspected.

Manchester truck bombing, June 15, 1996: An IRA truck bomb detonated at a Manchester, England, shopping center, wounding 206, including two German tourists, and causing extensive property damage.

Khobar Towers bombing, June 25, 1996: A fuel truck carrying a bomb exploded outside the U.S. military's Khobar Towers housing facility in Dhahran, Saudi Arabia, killing 19 U.S. military personnel and wounding 515 persons, including 240 U.S. personnel. Several groups claimed responsibility for the attack.

ETA bombing, July 20, 1996: A bomb exploded at Tarragona International Airport in Reus, Spain, wounding 35 persons, including British and Irish tourists. The Basque Fatherland and Liberty (ETA) organization was suspected.

Bombing of Archbishop of Oran, August 1, 1996: A bomb exploded at the home of the French Archbishop of Oran, killing him and his chauffeur. The attack occurred after the archbishop's meeting with the French foreign minister. The Algerian Armed Islamic Group (GIA) was suspected.

Sudanese rebel kidnapping, August 17, 1996: Sudan People's Liberation Army (SPLA) rebels kidnapped six missionaries in Mapourdit, including a U.S. citizen, an Italian, three Australians, and a Sudanese. The SPLA released the hostages 11 days later.

PUK kidnapping, September 13, 1996: In Iraq, Patriotic Union of Kurdistan (PUK) militants kidnapped four French workers for Pharmaciens Sans Frontieres, a Canadian United Nations High Commissioner for Refugees (UNHCR) official, and two Iraqis.

Assassination of South Korean consul, October 1, 1996: In Vladivostok, Russia, assailants attacked and killed a South Korean consul near his home. No one claimed responsibility, but South Korean authorities believed the attack was carried out by professionals and that the assailants were North Koreans. North Korean officials denied the country's involvement in the attack.

Red Cross worker kidnappings, November 1, 1996: In Sudan, a breakaway group from the Sudanese People's Liberation Army (SPLA) kidnapped three

International Committee of the Red Cross (ICRC) workers, including a U.S. citizen, an Australian, and a Kenyan. On December 9, the rebels released the hostages in exchange for ICRC supplies and a health survey for their camp.

Paris Subway explosion, December 3, 1996: A bomb exploded aboard a Paris subway train as it arrived at the Port Royal station, killing two French nationals, a Moroccan, and a Canadian, and injuring 86 persons. Among those injured were one U.S. citizen and a Canadian. No one claimed responsibility for the attack, but Algerian extremists were suspected.

Abduction of U.S. citizen by FARC, December 11, 1996: Five armed men claiming to be members of the Revolutionary Armed Forces of Colombia (FARC) kidnapped and later killed a U.S. geologist at a methane gas exploration site in La Guajira Department.

Tupac Amaru seizure of diplomats, December 17, 1996: Twenty-three members of the Tupac Amaru Revolutionary Movement (MRTA) took several hundred people hostage at a party given at the Japanese ambassador's residence in Lima, Peru. Among the hostages were several U.S. officials, foreign ambassadors and other diplomats, Peruvian government officials, and Japanese businessmen. The group demanded the release of all MRTA members in prison and safe passage for them and the hostage takers. The terrorists released most of the hostages in December but held 81 Peruvians and Japanese citizens for several months.

1997

Egyptian letter bombs, January 2–13, 1997: A series of letter bombs with Alexandria, Egypt, postmarks were discovered at *Al-Hayat* newspaper bureaus in Washington, New York City, London, and Riyadh, Saudi Arabia. Three similar devices, also postmarked in Egypt, were found at a prison facility in Leavenworth, Kansas. Bomb disposal experts defused all the devices, but one detonated at the *Al-Hayat* office in London, injuring two security guards and causing minor damage.

Tajik hostage abductions, February 4–17, 1997: Near Komsomolabad, Tajikistan, a paramilitary group led by Bakhrom Sodirov abducted four United Nations military observers. The victims included two Swiss, one Austrian, one Ukrainian, and their Tajik interpreter. The kidnappers demanded safe passage for their supporters from Afghanistan to Tajikistan. In four separate incidents occurring between Dushanbe and Garm, Bakhrom Sodirov and his group kidnapped two International Committee for the Red Cross members, four Russian journalists and their Tajik driver, four UNHCR members, and the Tajik security minister, Saidamir Zukhurov.

Venezuelan abduction, February 14, 1997: Six armed Colombian guerrillas kidnapped a U.S. oil engineer and his Venezuelan pilot in Apure, Venezuela.

The kidnappers released the Venezuelan pilot on February 22. According to authorities, FARC was responsible for the kidnapping.

Empire State Building sniper attack, February 23, 1997: A Palestinian gunman opened fire on tourists at an observation deck atop the Empire State Building in New York City, killing a Danish national and wounding visitors from the United States, Argentina, Switzerland, and France before turning the gun on himself. A handwritten note carried by the gunman claimed this was a punishment attack against the "enemies of Palestine."

ELN kidnapping, February 24, 1997: National Liberation Army (ELN) guerrillas kidnapped a U.S. citizen employed by a Las Vegas gold corporation who was scouting a gold mining operation in Colombia. The ELN demanded a ransom of $2.5 million.

FARC kidnapping, March 7, 1997: FARC guerrillas kidnapped a U.S. mining employee and his Colombian colleague who were searching for gold in Colombia. On November 16, the rebels released the two hostages after receiving a $50,000 ransom.

Hotel Nacional bombing, July 12, 1997: A bomb exploded at the Hotel Nacional in Havana, injuring three persons and causing minor damage. A previously unknown group calling itself the Military Liberation Union claimed responsibility.

Israeli shopping mall bombing, September 4, 1997: Three suicide bombers of Hamas detonated bombs in the Ben Yehuda shopping mall in Jerusalem, killing eight persons, including the bombers, and wounding nearly 200 others. A dual U.S.–Israeli citizen was among the dead, and seven U.S. citizens were wounded.

OAS abductions, October 23, 1997: In Colombia, ELN rebels kidnapped two foreign members of the Organization of American States (OAS) and a Colombian human rights official at a roadblock. The ELN claimed that the kidnapping was intended "to show the international community that the elections in Colombia are a farce."

Yemeni kidnappings, October 30, 1997: Al-Sha'if tribesmen kidnapped a U.S. businessman near Sanaa. The tribesmen sought the release of two fellow tribesmen who were arrested on smuggling charges and the implementation of several public works projects they claimed the government promised them. They released the hostage on November 27.

Murder of U.S. businessmen in Pakistan, November 12, 1997: Two unidentified gunmen shot to death four U.S. auditors from Union Texas Petroleum Corporation and their Pakistani driver after they drove away from the Sheraton Hotel in Karachi. The Islami Inqilabi Council, or Islamic Revolutionary Council, claimed responsibility in a call to the U.S. Consulate in Karachi. In a letter to Pakistani newspapers, the Aimal Khufia Action Committee also claimed responsibility.

Tourist killings in Egypt, November 17, 1997: Al-Gama'at al-Islamiyya (IG) gunmen shot and killed 58 tourists and four Egyptians and wounded 26 others at the Hatshepsut Temple in the Valley of the Kings near Luxor. Thirty-four Swiss, eight Japanese, five Germans, four Britons, one French, one Colombian, a dual Bulgarian–British citizen, and four unidentified persons were among the dead. Twelve Swiss, two Japanese, two Germans, one French, and nine Egyptians were among the wounded.

1998

UN observer abductions, February 19, 1998: Armed supporters of late Georgian President Zviad Gamsakhurdia abducted four UN military observers from Sweden, Uruguay, and the Czech Republic.

FARC abduction, March 21–23, 1998: FARC rebels kidnapped a U.S. citizen in Sabaneta, Colombia. FARC members also killed three persons, wounded 14, and kidnapped at least 27 others at a roadblock near Bogota. Four U.S. citizens and one Italian were among those kidnapped, as well as the acting president of the National Electoral Council (CNE) and his wife.

Somali hostage-takings, April 15, 1998: Somali militiamen abducted nine Red Cross and Red Crescent workers at an airstrip north of Mogadishu. The hostages included a U.S. citizen, a German, a Belgian, a French, a Norwegian, two Swiss, and one Somali. The gunmen were members of a subclan loyal to Ali Mahdi Mohammed, who controlled the northern section of the capital.

IRA bombing, Banbridge, August 1, 1998: A 500-pound car bomb planted by the Real IRA exploded outside a shoe store in Banbridge, Northern Ireland, injuring 35 persons and damaging at least 200 homes.

U.S. Embassy bombings in East Africa, August 7, 1998: A bomb exploded at the rear entrance of the U.S. Embassy in Nairobi, Kenya, killing 12 U.S. citizens, 32 foreign service nationals (FSNs), and 247 Kenyan citizens. About 5,000 Kenyans, six U.S. citizens, and 13 FSNs were injured. The U.S. Embassy building sustained extensive structural damage. Almost simultaneously, a bomb detonated outside the U.S. Embassy in Dar es Salaam, Tanzania, killing seven FSNs and three Tanzanian citizens and injuring one U.S. citizen and 76 Tanzanians. The explosion caused major structural damage to the U.S. Embassy facility. The U.S. government held Osama bin Laden responsible.

IRA Bombing, Omagh, August 15, 1998: A 500-pound car bomb planted by the Real IRA exploded outside a local courthouse in the central shopping district of Omagh, Northern Ireland, killing 29 persons and injuring more than 330.

Colombian pipeline bombing, October 18, 1998: A bomb planted by the National Liberation Army (ELN) exploded on the Ocensa pipeline in Antioquia Department, killing approximately 70 persons and injuring at least 100 others. The pipeline is jointly owned by the Colombia state oil company Ecopetrol and a consortium including U.S., French, British, and Canadian companies.

Armed kidnapping in Colombia, November 15, 1998: Armed assailants followed a U.S. businessman and his family home in Cundinamarca Department and kidnapped his 11-year-old son after stealing money, jewelry, an automobile, and two cell phones. The kidnappers demanded $1 million in ransom. On January 21, 1999, the kidnappers released the boy.

1999

Angolan aircraft downing, January 2, 1999: A United Nations plane carrying one U.S. citizen, four Angolans, two Philippine nationals, and one Namibian was shot down, according to a UN official. No deaths or injuries were reported. Angolan authorities blamed the attack on National Union for the Total Independence of Angola (UNITA) rebels. UNITA officials denied shooting down the plane.

Ugandan rebel attack, February 14, 1999: A pipe bomb exploded inside a bar, killing five and injuring 35 others. One Ethiopian and four Ugandan nationals died in the blast, and one U.S. citizen working for USAID, two Swiss nationals, one Pakistani, one Ethiopian, and 27 Ugandans were injured. Ugandan authorities blamed the attack on the Allied Democratic Forces (ADF).

Greek Embassy seizure, February 16, 1999: Kurdish protesters stormed and occupied the Greek Embassy in Vienna, taking the Greek ambassador and six other persons hostage. Several hours later the protesters released the hostages and left the embassy. The attack followed the Turkish government's announcement of the successful capture of the Kurdistan Workers' Party (PKK) leader, Abdullah Ocalan. Kurds also occupied Kenyan, Israeli, and other Greek diplomatic facilities in France, the Netherlands, Switzerland, Britain, and Germany over the following days.

FARC kidnappings, February 25, 1999: FARC kidnapped three U.S. citizens working for the Hawaii-based Pacific Cultural Conservancy International. On March 4, the bodies of the three victims were found in Venezuela.

Hutu abductions, March 1, 1999: One hundred fifty armed Hutu rebels attacked three tourist camps in Uganda, killed four Ugandans, and abducted three U.S. citizens, six Britons, three New Zealanders, two Danish citizens, one Australian, and one Canadian national. Two of the U.S. citizens and six of the other hostages were subsequently killed by their abductors.

ELN hostage-taking, March 23, 1999: Armed guerrillas kidnapped a U.S. citizen in Boyaca, Colombia. The National Liberation Army (ELN) claimed responsibility and demanded $400,000 ransom. On July 20, ELN rebels released the hostage unharmed following a ransom payment of $48,000.

ELN hostage-taking, May 30, 1999: In Cali, Colombia, armed ELN militants attacked a church in the neighborhood of Ciudad Jardin, kidnapping 160 persons, including six U.S. citizens and one French national. The rebels released approximately 80 persons, including three U.S. citizens, later that day.

Shell platform bombing, June 27, 1999: In Port Harcourt, Nigeria, armed youths stormed a Shell oil platform, kidnapping one U.S. citizen, one Nigerian national, and one Australian citizen, and causing undetermined damage. A group calling itself "Enough Is Enough in the Niger River Delta" claimed responsibility. Further seizures of oil facilities followed.

AFRC Kidnappings, August 4, 1999: An Armed Forces Revolutionary Council (AFRC) faction kidnapped 33 UN representatives near Occra Hills, Sierra Leone. The hostages comprised one U.S. citizen, five British soldiers, one Canadian citizen, one representative from Ghana, one military officer from Russia, one officer from Kyrgyzstan, one officer from Zambia, one officer from Malaysia, a local Bishop, two UN officials, two local journalists, and 16 Sierra Leone nationals.

Burmese Embassy seizure, October 1, 1999: Burmese dissidents seized the Burmese Embassy in Bangkok, Thailand, taking 89 persons hostage, including one U.S. citizen.

PLA kidnapping, December 23, 1999: Colombian People's Liberation Army (PLA) forces kidnapped a U.S. citizen in an unsuccessful ransoming effort.

Indian Airlines Airbus hijacking, December 24, 1999: Five militants hijacked a flight bound from Kathmandu to New Delhi carrying 189 people. The plane and its passengers were released unharmed on December 31.

2000

Car bombing in Spain, January 27, 2000: Police officials reported that unidentified individuals set fire to a Citroen car dealership in Iturreta, causing extensive damage to the building and destroying 12 vehicles. The attack bore the hallmark of the Basque Fatherland and Liberty (ETA).

RUF attacks on UN Mission personnel, May 1, 2000: On May 1 in Makeni, Sierra Leone, Revolutionary United Front (RUF) militants kidnapped at least 20 members of the United Nations Assistance Mission in Sierra Leone (UNAMSIL) and surrounded and opened fire on a UNAMSIL facility, according to press reports. The militants killed five UN soldiers in the attack. RUF militants kidnapped 300 UNAMSIL peacekeepers throughout the country, according to press reports. On May 15 in Foya, Liberia, the kidnappers released 139 hostages. On May 28, on the Liberia and Sierra Leone border, armed militants released unharmed the last of the UN peacekeepers. In Freetown, according to press reports, armed militants ambushed two military vehicles carrying four journalists. A Spaniard and one U.S. citizen were killed in a May 25 car bombing in Freetown for which the RUF was probably responsible. Suspected RUF rebels also kidnapped 21 Indian UN peacekeepers in Freetown on June 6. Additional RUF attacks on foreign personnel followed.

Diplomatic assassination in Greece, June 8, 2000: In Athens, Greece, two unidentified gunmen killed British Defense Attaché Stephen Saunders in an ambush. The Revolutionary Organization 17 November claimed responsibility.

ELN kidnapping, June 27, 2000: In Bogota, Colombia, ELN militants kidnapped a five-year-old U.S. citizen and his Colombian mother, demanding an undisclosed ransom.

Kidnappings in Kyrgyzstan, August 12, 2000: In the Kara-Su Valley, the Islamic Movement of Uzbekistan took four U.S. citizens hostage. The Americans escaped on August 12.

Church bombing in Tajikistan, October 1, 2000: Unidentified militants detonated two bombs in a Christian church in Dushanbe, killing seven and injuring 70 others. The church was founded by a Korean-born U.S. citizen, and most of those killed and wounded were Korean. No one claimed responsibility.

Helicopter hijacking, October 12, 2000: In Sucumbios Province, Ecuador, a group of armed kidnappers led by former members of a defunct Colombian terrorist organization, the Popular Liberation Army (EPL), took hostage ten employees of Spanish energy consortium REPSOL. The kidnapped were five U.S. citizens, one Argentine, one Chilean, one New Zealander, and two French pilots who escaped four days later. On January 30, 2001, the kidnappers murdered American hostage Ronald Sander. The remaining hostages were released on February 23 following the payment of $13 million in ransom by the oil companies.

Attack on U.S.S. *Cole*, October 12, 2000: In Aden, Yemen, a small dingy carrying explosives rammed the destroyer U.S.S. *Cole*, killing 17 sailors and injuring 39 others. Supporters of Osama bin Laden were suspected.

Manila bombing, December 30, 2000: A bomb exploded in a plaza across the street from the U.S. Embassy in Manila, injuring nine. The Moro Islamic Liberation Front was likely responsible.

2001

Srinagar Airport attack, January 17, 2001: In India, six members of the Lashkar-e-Tayyba militant group were killed when they attempted to seize a local airport.

BBC studios bombing, March 4, 2001: A car bomb exploded at midnight outside of the British Broadcasting Corporation's main production studios in London.

ETA bombing, March 9, 2001: Two policemen were killed by the explosion of a car bomb in Hernani, Spain.

Bus stop bombing, April 22, 2001: A member of Hamas detonated a bomb he was carrying near a bus stop in Kfar Siva, Israel, killing one person and injuring 60.

Tel Aviv nightclub bombing, June 1, 2001: Hamas claimed responsibility for the bombing of a popular Israeli nightclub that caused over 140 casualties.

Hamas restaurant bombing, August 9, 2001: A Hamas-planted bomb detonated in a Jerusalem pizza restaurant, killing 15 and wounding more than 90.

Terrorist attacks on U.S. homeland, September 11, 2001: Two hijacked airliners crashed into the twin towers of the World Trade Center. Soon thereafter, the Pentagon was struck by a third hijacked plane. A fourth hijacked plane, suspected to be bound for a high-profile target in Washington, crashed into a field in southern Pennsylvania. More than 5,000 U.S. citizens and other nationals were killed as a result of these acts. President Bush and cabinet officials indicated that Osama bin Laden was the prime suspect and that they considered the United States in a state of war with international terrorism. In the aftermath of the attacks, the United States formed the Global Coalition Against Terrorism.

9

The Palestinian Suicide Bomber

Rona M. Fields, Salman Elbedour, and Fadel Abu Hein

The phenomenon of the suicide bomber has, in recent years, become an epidemic nightmare. How can an adversary effectively threaten someone who is trying to die for a cause? "Martyr warfare" is the opposite of soldiers' commitment to comrades and mission success. Suicide bombers are committed to their own deaths in missions intended to take with them as many as possible of their "enemy." The penalty of "death" for "political suicide" becomes an oxymoron when death is the objective of the subject.

Sacrificing oneself for a cause is not a new ideology. The ancient Celts went on hunger strikes outside the door of the person who had insulted them and thus shamed their adversary, usually before dying in the attempt. In the eighth decade of the last century, young Irishmen died on hunger strikes in British jails, as had their antecedents in 1916. This was their political martyrdom, contradicting their clergy's religious directives. In the Middle East, in Israel/Palestine, a more aggressive version of political suicide has become so commonplace as to obscure its relatively recent emergence in the bloody history of that place. But the Palestinians were anticipated by Lebanese Shi'ite Hezbollah and the Tamil Tigers several thousand miles away in Sri Lanka.

Is there a common mindset for individuals who commit political suicide and choose to kill themselves for one cause or another? The question has an etiology that originates in the social-political-cultural matrix, and the phenomenon evolves incorporated into the individual psyche through the institutions of society. The framework through which we are answering this question is driven from studies of the sociological context and from the psychodynamic profile of individuals who become members of paramilitary organizations. It also leads to the mind of the political suicider and finally to the developmental psychology of the suicide bomber.

This is a data-based study in contrast to others, which are anecdotal narrative. The data derive from individual psychological tests administered to more than a thousand children and adolescents ages six through sixteen collected in Northern Ireland, Israel, the West Bank, Gaza, Lebanon, and South Africa over a twenty-five-year span. The test batteries include the Thematic Apperception Test; the Story Sequence Analysis developed by Arnold (1962); the Spielberger (1985) State Trait Personality Index administered to members of paramilitaries and others; a Violence Distance Scale devised by Fields (1976); and the Tapp and Kohlberg questions of legal socialization based on a Piagetian model of cognitive/moral development (1971). Based on the hypotheses generated in these studies, a protocol evolved for the postmortem studies of Palestinian suicide bombers. These interviews were collated with demographic data collected from families and friends of Palestinian suicide bombers who committed their actions between 1993 and 1996.

FIGURE 1. INSTITUTIONS IN A SOCIETY
(SOCIAL CONTROL AGENCIES)

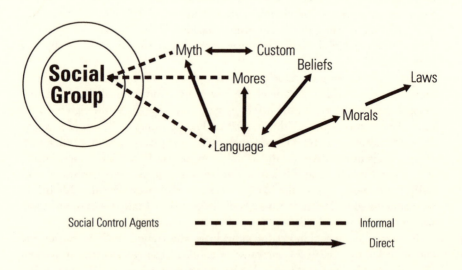

THE SOCIOLOGICAL CONTEXT

Violent societies develop in places and populations that are marginalized economically and institutionally. This can be a society or nation in which a colonial or postcolonial regime has imposed a legal system unrelated to the culture and belief systems of the indigenous population. Or it can be a portion of a society that is alienated by and from the legal system, cultural institutions, and economic supports of the larger society (see Figures 1 and 1a). Often in these populations there is a very high proportion of children and youths to adults. This portion of the society is not supported or engaged in the institutional nexus and therefore education and employment are not as accessible as are experiences outside the law. The marginalized indigenous population may, if there is cultural leadership that offers continuity and opportunity within their circumscribed society, develop alternative institutions. When that population is ghettoized, there is a better prospect for achieving this. Some examples are the Roman Catholic population in the north of Ireland, and the Shi'ite Muslim population in southern Lebanon. In both in-

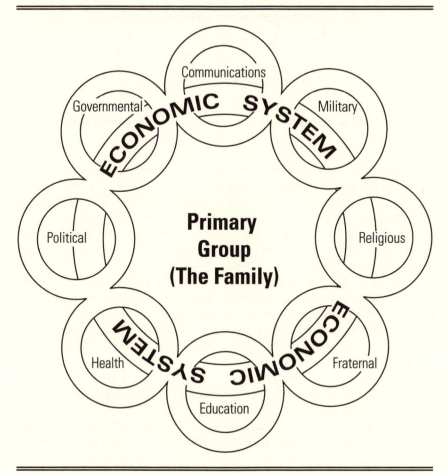

FIGURE 1A.

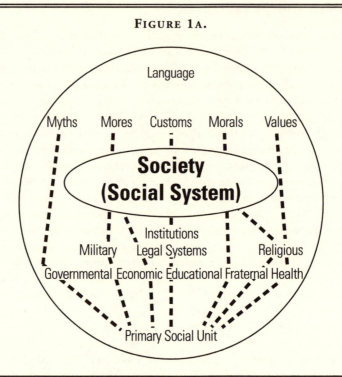

stances, the religious institution becomes the nexus for development of other institutions—education and health for example—that serve the needs of this identity group. Some of the literature on immigrant populations in Great Britain, notably the Pakistani immigrant community, remarks on the significantly better social and psychological adjustment of both the foreign-born and their British-born children in the segment of that community who live in ethnically homogeneous settings (Huyck & Fields, 1981).

In societies predicated on inclusion, in which the institutions and the legal system that underpins them are accessible, the goal is integration into the larger society and the imposition of their culture and value system on the newer arrivals. This has been the pattern in the United States and Canada with the remarkable exception of the marginalization of the Native Americans and the much-delayed integration of formerly enslaved African Americans.

Viewed through this paradigm, we can consider, as a dynamic process, the socialization of individuals and the interactions of the institutions with the economic and legal systems.

Legal socialization and moral development of the individual proceeds, as Piaget posits, through the continuing stimulation by the social and physical environment.

The growing child develops from the earliest stages of egocentric morality to the level of identity group morality, with its attendant retributive justice ideal of law. Emergence beyond this stage (usually ages eleven through fifteen) becomes a function of the capacity of the youngster to experience himself or herself in a variety of roles and institutions in the larger society. If experience is limited, as Piaget (1932) states, the individual will either go to prison or the barricades—in other words, become either an outlaw or a revolutionary. Furthermore, as he notes in later studies (1954), the individual under stress relapses into less and less mature modes of functioning.

In Northern Ireland, as long as the larger society was closed off by institutional prejudice against Catholics, along with their own religious, health, and educational institutions, the Catholic population evolved its own military and defense structures. When the political system opened to participation in the democratic process, dependence on the militias diminished and increasingly the Roman Catholic nationalist/republican population took to the ballot box instead of the bullet. Not so for the working-class Protestant population. Loyalists had never really been socially mobile nor had access to decision making in the political arena (Darby, 1976). As we shall see, in the mind of the individual who commits suicide as a political statement in this and other societies, this self-willed death may or may not be an aggressive act of retributive justice. Causing death as retribution on the "enemy" is the ultimate act of vendetta, but what distinguishes the suicidal aggressor is, of course, that the act of retribution consumes his or her own life as well.

In Lebanon, the legal system was adopted from the French colonial structure that preceded Lebanese independence. The indigenous society had been, prior to colonial rule, a subset of the Ottoman Empire and, of that, a sub-subset of Greater Syria. Of the various cultural groups within this society, the Shia Muslim minority was, with the exception of the Kurdish minority, at the social and economic bottom level. Even in the best of times, the rural Shi'ites of southern Lebanon were not served or incorporated into the military, fraternal, educational, and health institutions and systems of that region. Nor did they evolve their own such institutions to serve themselves. Their Christian and Sunni Moslem neighbors were, by contrast, well integrated and served by Lebanese and religious foundations. At the time of the Palestinian exodus at the creation of the State of Israel, many of the "camps" established for them by the United Nations Refugee Welfare Act (UNRWA; now known as the United Nations Relief and Works Agency) were in locations of poor Shia residences. Sabra and Shatela, bordering Beirut, for instance, were simply imposed on the shanty suburban sprawl originally executed for the impoverished rural Shi'ites who flocked to Beirut in an attempt to eke out a better living. It was little noticed by the Western world, but quite significant, that in the mid-1980s, when the Israelis and the Palestine Liberation Organization (PLO) had departed from the Beirut area, the remaining Palestinian population of the neighborhood continued to be massacred by then-ascendant Shia militias. Prolonged subjection to poverty and impoverishment in these camps did not unify these marginalized populations but rather increased conflict and violence between these two groups.

TABLE 1.
CORRECTIONS AMONG STPI STATE AND TRAIT SCALES FOR
MEMBERS OF A PARAMILITARY ORGANIZATION (N=28)

Scale	State Anxiety	State Anger	State Curiosity	Trait Anxiety	Trait Anger	Angry Temperament	Angry Reaction
State Anger	.34						
State Curiosity	.05	-.10					
Trait Anxiety	.56**	.09	-.45*				
Trait Anger	.00	.56**	-.03	.22			
Angry Temperament	-.21	.26	-.18	.20	.78***		
Angry Reaction	.22	.50**	.15	.17	.77***	.23	
Trait Curiosity	-.08	-.19	.76**	-.43*	.03	.01	.08

*   p < .05
**   p < .01
*** p < .001

SUICIDE BOMBERS OF THE *INTIFADA*

Measurement

This preliminary social history is essential for conceptualizing the context of what became known, in 1987 and again in 1999–2002, as the *intifada,* from which the Palestinian suicide bomber emerged. But the suicide bomber of 1999–2002 is no longer primarily traumatized youth or the disaffected adolescent who is susceptible to carry out political suicide acts. As political violence and social chaos continues through early childhood and into adulthood, there is a decrease in the capacity to fantasize (Fields, 1978) and thus to hope or imagine a better or different future. These youths' limited experience of roles and relationships and their recruitment into paramilitary organizations are reflected in a specific profile on the State Trait Personality Index (STPI) that is consistent across the different national and cultural populations included in this research. Among the 300 members of paramilitaries examined in this study, there is a range of personalities, on a normal curve of distribution much like the normative samples for development of the STPI. (The unique profile is illustrated in Table 1.) They are significantly high on State and Trait Anger, and although they range on Trait Guilt, they are significantly depressed on Guilt About Angry Expression. In short, they are very angry people who are quite able to experience and feel guilt about many things, but not about their Expression of Anger or Angry Behavior. They also exhibit significant State/Trait Curiosity. Apart from the State/Trait Curiosity score, there is the profile of Righteous Indignation, which connects with commitment to a cause. Their interest in novelty and risk taking marks them as individuals likely to engineer and embark on high-risk missions and novel ways of enacting and selecting their objectives. Connections with truncation at Level II, Retributive Justice or vendetta on the Tapp-Kohlberg measures of Legal Socialization/Moral Judgment suggest that these Righteously Indignant individuals and groups, with a propensity to novelty and risk taking, may engage in suicidal missions of vengeance or retributive justice (Fields, 1986) (see Table 2).

In earlier studies, most particularly "Predicting a Terror Vocation," published in the proceedings of the Stockholm Conference on Wartime Medical Services, Fields (1994) postulated a formula derived from psychological tests administered to child and adolescent populations at high risk for recruitment into paramilitary organizations and psychological tests administered to members of these organizations. The formula $T=SPV(LSII)(MI.SSA)$ incorporates the sociopolitical variable-place on the sociological circle multiplied by the quantity (scores on the Tapp-Kohlberg Measure of Legal Socialization at Level II) with the quantity (Motivation Index score derived from the Story Sequence Analysis of the TAT) (see Figures 2 and 3).

History

Beginning in 1975, studies of Palestinian children ages six through sixteen and their Israeli age peers, tracked annually in Israel and the occupied territories, show the commonalties and differences *within* the two populations as well as *between* the two. Until 1982, major differences among the Palestinian population separated children growing up in the UNRWA "camps" from those whose families lived in regular communities. There was also a measurable difference between Palestinian children living within Israel (Israeli Arab) and, most markedly, Palestinian children growing up in the enclaves known as refugee camps. Palestinian children in Nazareth, for instance, in many respects—particularly in Motivation for Achievement and political/legal socialization—scored similar to their Israeli Jewish age peers in Haifa, Tivon, and Kibbutz Amir. Many of these children had participated together in a summer camp experience in Bedford, Virginia, in which children from other cultures and countries were enrolled. Moreover, Palestinian children who were annually sampled in Beit Safafa, one of the many Arab villages that compose metropolitan Jerusalem, and children in Beit Hashitah, a kibbutz in the Jordan Valley, had more in common with each other than either group had with the Palestinian children living in Daheisha in the West Bank or Al Jalazon refugee camps.

TABLE 2.

	PAL '82	TK	BEL '71-2	BEL '73-4	PAL '82	TK	BEL '71-2	BEL '73-4
Why should people follow rules?								
Avoid negative consequences	75	50	60	82	4	13	50	90
Authority	30	5	27	20	60	—	25	15
Personal conformity	—	35	6	—	15	13	14	5
Social conformity	—	10	13	5	15	53	12	3
Rational/ Beneficial/ Utilitarian	—	5	—	—	—	27	4	—
Principled	—	—	—	—	—	—	—	—
Why do you follow rules?								
Avoid negative consequences	70	60	94	96	60	?	89	90
Authority	4	10	—	—	20	10	10	12
Personal conformity	—	20	—	—	10	40	10	—
Social conformity	—	—	—	—	10	40	10	5
Rational/ Beneficial/ Utilitarian	—	—	—	—	2	7	2	—
Principled	—	—	—	—	—	—	—	—
Can rules be changed?								
No	95	20	90	98	85	—	64	70
Yes	5	70	2	—	15	100	36	30

Are there times when it might be right to break a rule?

No, unqualified	80	55	95	95	60	7	70	80
Yes, unspecified	15	25	—	—	20	—	—	10
Morality of circumstances	5	20	5	5	20	73	25	10
Morality of rule	—	—	—	—	—	17	30	—

TK = Tapp and Kohlberg normative sample   **BEL** = Belfast sample   **PAL** = Palestinian sample
All questions except "Can rules be changed?" and "Are there times when it might be right to break a rule?" are multiple coded; therefore, percentages may total over 100 percent. Where answers were idiosyncratic or uncodable, the categories were omitted from the table. Level number indicates increasing cognitive maturity. (Adapted from Tapp and Kohlberg, 1971, p. 76)

But 1982–1983 marked a sharp turning point. In 1982, the Israel Defense Forces (IDF) launched their invasion of Lebanon. In June 1982, the IDF managed in less than a week to move north from its "Security Zone" all the way to Beirut and the Bekaa Valley. Their nominal mission was to push the Palestinian forces out of Lebanon and thus ensure the security of the northern part of Israel. The IDF air assault on Beirut, particularly, and the land assault on the cities, towns, and villages en route to Beirut, were widely covered by international media, particularly by television.

By 1982, there was a growing movement in Israel on the part of Israeli Arabs seeking recognition of their civil rights. The inequities in infrastructure between Jewish and Arab villages inside Israel had become a continuing irritation. Added to that, the expansion of Jewish settlements and appropriation of lands previously owned and farmed by Palestinians in the West Bank and Gaza—the expansion of Jewish settlement into Hebron, especially—had further intensified tensions. While the government of Israel and its security forces contended that the violence perpetrated on Israelis came in over the border from Lebanon and by means of weapons smuggled into the West Bank through PLO activists, there was a paucity of scholarly and public opinion studies of the Palestinian population, both inside Israel and in the occupied West Bank and Gaza.

Even as they began evolving their own institutions to serve needs neglected by the Israeli government and to compensate for their exclusion from Israeli institutions, the vacuum here was met through the nascent Islamist movement. As it had in southern Lebanon and in the Palestinian camps in Jordan, so, too, the Islamist groups inside Israel began providing free schools, clinics, and social services. The conservative government of Israel viewed the Islamists as a potential alternative for the allegiance of the Arab population and thus it supported their growth and activities financially and by simple recognition. In so doing, they overlooked the power of religion as a transformative experience that can carry the true believer beyond the ugliness and futility of everyday life in the Palestinian refuge camp. By the time of the Lebanon invasion by Israel army, the Islamist movement had become a visible political presence and by 1985 this was so in several of the universities of the West Bank and Gaza.

In September 1982, the IDF made their final push to Beirut and, having surrounded the Sabra and Shatela enclaves of refugee Palestinians after the PLO had departed, it allowed the Lebanese Phalangists under Ellie Hodeika to massacre thousands of Palestinian children and adult civilians. Worse yet was the testimony of survivors that Israeli soldiers blocked their attempted flight from the carnage. Thus the Phalangists and the IDF were, and continue to be, perceived by the Arab world as co-perpetrators in this historic bloodbath.

In 1982–1983, children in the Sabra and Shatela, Ein Hiloweh, and Mia Mia camps in Lebanon; and children in the Daheisha and Jalazon camps in the West Bank were examined using the Tapp-Kohlberg questions of legal socialization, the Story Sequence Analysis TAT (SSA-TAT), the State-Trait Personality Index, and the Fields Violence Distance schedule. These are the same tests that were used in previous annual evaluations in the same places, as well as in Beit Safafa, a Palestinian village in Jerusalem in which half the village had been on the Jordanian side prior to 1967 and in which prior testing had been done, and in Beit Hashitah Kibbutz. As in previous years, the sample size was twenty-six children in each place, ages 6 through 16, half boys, half girls. As was the case in these and other places, the Motivation for Achievement scores, according to the SSA-TAT, followed a skewed-to-the-left distribution in the Arab population and a normal curve of distribution in the kibbutz population (see Figures 2 and 3).

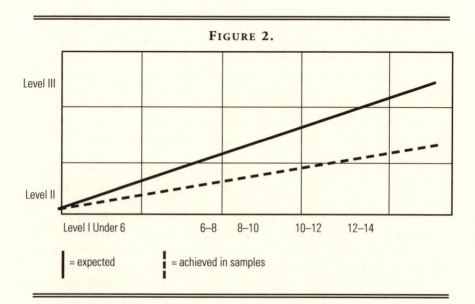

FIGURE 2.

Broken down into locations, however, the children in Beit Safafa and Beit Hashitah were more similar in Motivation Index score distribution along a normal curve. The same case held for the distribution on the Tapp-Kohlberg scale. Many of these children were progressing to Level III of Moral Judgment/Legal socialization albeit less sharply inclined toward Level III (Universal Justice) at ages 15 and 16 than the normative samples but with many more responses at the beginning phase of Level II than had been the case in Northern Ireland or among children in the Palestinian camps (see Table 2).

Similarly, on the Violence Distance questions, few of these children had ever seen anyone killed or dismembered or a bombing. In December 1982 and January 1983, however, the responses of children in Beit Safafa on all measuring instruments became different from those in Beit Hashitah for the first time. They reported scenes of devastation and human destruction and nightmares about it and, for the first time, all of the adolescents tested responded to the Tapp-Kohlberg questions at Level II, Retributive Justice. Their TAT stories indicated that they had been having nightmares and were experiencing themselves as victims of "the Jews." In Daheisha and Jalazon, these responses were even more dramatically and consistently evidenced. When the adults (teachers) in these communities were asked about these violent scenes, they commented, "They have watched it every day on television though it did not happen here!" Responses from Israeli Jewish children in kibbutzim and in cities were not different from earlier samplings. In fact, in 1983–1984, when a mutual recognition agreement between Israel and the Leba-

FIGURE 3.

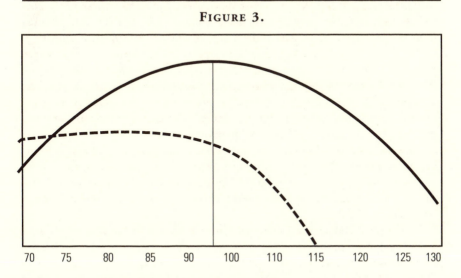

| 70 | 75 | 80 | 85 | 90 | 100 | 110 | 115 | 120 | 125 | 130 |

| = Expected distribution of MI scores under normal conditions

⋮ = Distribution of MI scores under conditions of violence

nese government was signed in Qiryat Shmona, the children, long accustomed to hiding in bomb shelters and experiencing raids on apartment complexes and schools, paraded singing in joyous celebration. In January 1983, the division between Arab and Jew in Israel was more pronounced. So also were the test scores and stories as compared with those previously collected.

In late 1982, following the massacre in Sabra and Shatela, Palestinian boys in the Lebanese camps were overwhelmed with feelings of survivor guilt, as reflected in their TAT stories and their commitment to vendetta on the Tapp-Kohlberg questions of legal socialization. But at the same time, State-Trait Personality Inventory (STPI) questions indicated they were feeling paralyzed, unable to act, and quite different in state from their trait responses. These boys expressed higher anger, both state and trait, and felt less guilty for expressing their rage. Unlike other samples, however, they had a very high state guilt score. If they were not feeling guilty about anger or angry behavior, they were feeling guilty about their perceived inaction in the face of overwhelming aggressive enemy force. They expressed anxiety about the vendetta in which they felt impelled to engage. This is a significant difference between these boys and the Palestinian boys in Israel and the West Bank camps.

Clearly, among the Palestinians inside Israel and those of the West Bank and Gaza, boys particularly identified with the events at Sabra and Shatela. Test data indicated that they felt no guilt, paralysis, or conflict about what to do. They were righteously indignant, according to the text. Their projective stories and Tapp-Kohlberg responses were specifically oriented to vengeance by any means necessary. In Ein Hollwe and Mia Mia in Lebanon, the girls had different responses. They had classic manifestations of post-traumatic stress disorder (PTSD) and withdrew from any reference to the events of the massacre. The girls talked about experiences during earlier massacres, when they were attacked. They attributed these earlier episodes to "the Jews," meaning the IDF. In Israel and the West Bank, however, the girls were only slightly less action-oriented than the boys (Fields, 1990). This vicarious identification with victimization presented a very significant factor in understanding intergenerational intercommunal conflict and the "politics of memory," which evolves into a pantheon of heroes and martyrs.

Between 1983 and 1989, annual and biannual sampling in southern Lebanon and Israel and the West Bank continued to provide data predicting an eventual violent uprising by these same youths. This was less the case among the Israeli Arabs, although they increasingly identified themselves as Palestinians living in Israel (Fields, 1986).

In 1986, Palestinian youths enacted a suicide mission in the airports of Rome and Vienna. They positioned themselves with automatic weapons to shoot to death helpless passengers and bystanders, all the while anticipating their own deaths. Two of the youths who participated were among those victims who were tested at Sabra and Shatela four years earlier. They had been readily recruited for missions that could only result in their death. They engaged as secular nationalists. There were no indications, when they were tested in 1982, that they identified with religious *jihad.* Nor was this action or the many acts that followed during the 1980s ever identified as religious violence in the terms defined by Juergensmeyer (2000).

During the same period, Shia Lebanese youths were also recruited for suicidal missions. There were differences between them and the Palestinians. Most significantly, the Palestinians were secularists. The Shia Lebanese youths were instructed by religious leaders and were committed to defend their land and even dying in *jihad* as martyrs. A few young women were among those who carried out suicide bombings against the IDF and their Lebanese allies, the Southern Lebanese Army (SLA). Content analysis of their martyr statements and of videos indicates their vendetta intentions and their conviction that their deaths would glorify and fiscally indemnify their parents as well as their cause—freeing southern Lebanon from foreign-Israeli—occupation. During the last half of the 1980s, as formerly secular southern Lebanon became increasingly polarized by confessional group identity, Hezbollah became the alternative institutional system for Muslims and used its influence to make a theocracy along the lines of the Iranian sponsors of the movement. Meanwhile the SLA and its Israeli allies established a panoply of social benefits for the Christians. In Gaza, because of its teeming overpopulation, poverty, and underserved population, the religious revival spread more rapidly as a coping strategy than on the West Bank. The single institution of higher education in Gaza was notable for its religious student population, while the University of Bir Zeit, in the West Bank, was characterized by its secular and nationalist student body. Al Najah University in Nablus, West Bank, became dominated by the religious student organizations.

Israeli arrests, detentions without trial, and demolitions of houses and olive groves fueled disaffection. These acts also increased identification with the victimized and further polarized and fractionated these societies. The growth of the Islamist movement matched a parallel increase in the population of Orthodox Jews in Israel, particularly in the establishment of West Bank settlements. The mid-1980s were most remarkable for the rapid emergence of Messianic religiosity among Jews, Muslims, and Christians in the Middle East and especially in pockets of the greatest impoverishment.

Life Conditions: Specific and General Aspects

It was no accident that the first *intifada* erupted in Gaza. The network of alternative institutions had been well established and the population there was the most disaffected of any, as well as the most confined. Most were refugees from other places in "Palestine" who viewed themselves as having lost their "homeland" with the establishment of Israel. Health conditions deteriorated, and the problem of the "invisibility" of the Palestinian people in the international arena became a self-concept that continues to be a problem. The standard of living is dismal: 96 percent do not own their homes, 89 percent have no sitting room, and 86 percent have no bathrooms. The average refugee family has a house with 1.55 bedrooms, and more than half of the Palestinians live in refugee camps (Yahya, 1991). The conditions of the camps intensified anxieties and touched off the spark that typically generates when "psychological tensions . . . boil up in human groups like lava under the earth's crust" (Farsoun & Landis, 1990).

Children and youth experience very little social nurturing under these circumstances. They mature in an atmosphere of disequilibrium and stress best described as a "war of all against all." The closing of schools, confinement without charges, the destruction of homes, torture, and detention of children by the Israeli authorities became daily lessons for children. For those able to avoid direct confrontation, soaring unemployment, poor living conditions, checkpoints, and searches by the Israeli military worked their way into children's psyches, creating a situation in which moral development stalls (Elbedour, Baker, & Charlesworth, 1997). A child's psychic energy is consumed in the nexus of fears: fear of being rejected by peers, impotence in the face of danger, lack of necessities, and constant doubt about one's own safety. Today, these children's personalities have already been molded by their war experience without their being fully aware of it. Fear, worry, and helplessness have dominated their formative years. When parents fail to act as protectors, society as a whole is fragmented in the eyes of the child and the boundaries between children and parents widen and become characterized by suspicion. The link of guilt and shame/blame can be considered the spark that flamed the protest of Palestinian youth and adolescents called "The Uprising." Palestinian children and youth tend to blame themselves and experience shame and guilt for not having done enough to save their parents or free their occupied land (Elbedour, 1992). According to these findings, the phenomenon is no less true in Gaza than it was for the boys who survived Sabra and Shatela (Fields, 1989).

Whatever the explanation, if these victims continue to live without facing and coping with their traumatization, they may become part of the system of victim-victimizers. As early as 1963, Curtis expressed concern about the connection between childhood trauma and adult violence. According to Curtis, abused and maltreated children "become tomorrow's murderers and perpetrators of other crime [*sic*] of violence, if they survive" (p. 386). Children and youth who suffer trauma because of warlike conflicts or physical maltreatment often manifest or hide higher degrees of anger, aggression, and rage. More disturbing, Elbedour, Bastien, and Center (1997) found that the Israeli-Arab conflict has "relatively impoverished individual identities" and strengthened group identity at the expense of individual identity. One direct outcome is that children who are in the initial process of de-individuation will use aggression in an attempt to reindividuate themselves. This history of political victimization and the feeling of being "unsafe" have allowed individuals to rely on violence as their method to work out conflicts and problems of social living and have diminished perception of risk, spurred a tendency to exert aggression, and lowered expectations for the future.

A Palestinian mother, without the benefit of training in psychology, describes the connection to childhood traumatic experience in the West Bank and Gaza resulting from occupation in this way:

These children are the *intifada* and they have been hurt deeply. . . . If there is no solution, these children will one day throw more than stones because their hatred is great and they have nothing to hope for. If hope isn't given to them, they will take it from others. They will react with violence. We fear they will take the knives from our kitchens to use as weapons. They have no rules. They do not understand laws. They are going to be wild in the streets. If the world doesn't help us, we will be helpless to control our children. (Roy, 1989, p. 78)

Intractable Problems

Political and Psychological Aspects

The Israeli-Palestinian conflict has dominated the psychological lives of inhabitants of this region for decades (Abu-Lughod, 1990; Elbedour, 1992). Elbedour (1998) found clinically elevated levels of psychopathology in 18 percent to 20 percent of the Palestinian children assessed. In their study, Thabet and Vostanis (1999) found a prevalence of 41 percent of moderate/severe symptoms of PTSD among Palestinian children from Gaza.

Of the two thousand casualties of the first *intifada*, nearly three hundred were children under the age of sixteen. Twenty-five thousand Palestinian children were treated for injuries, more than six thousand were victims of tear gas or gunfire, and 159 lost their lives during the first year of the *intifada* (Nixon, 1990). Palestinian children were exposed to punitive measures against their families, including deportations, evacuations, curfews, and restrictions on moving. These measures led to the complete collapse of an already weakened economy, with an estimated 40 percent to 50 percent unemployment (Collins, 1991).

The political discourse used by both Palestinians and Israelis not only perpetuates the conflict, but contributes significantly to the formation of individuals' group identities. Each group has adopted a nationalist discourse predicated on an assumption of superiority over the other group and on the goal of the other group's eventual subordination (Lerner, 1989). This discourse is, in each case, part of an ideological framework that has politicized interpersonal relations among ordinary people in the private sphere as well as in the public sphere. These circumstances, compounded by the real threat of violence, heighten each individual's sense of belonging and commitment to his or her group and, because of the strength of such affiliations, the feelings and thoughts of the group are taken on as the individual's own (Elbedour, Bastien, & Center, 1997; Mahjoub, 1989). The support offered by the group ideologies works both for and against the group. On the one hand, it enables members of each group to withstand the hardships of the political conflict and provide a solid resource for children (Punamaki, 1996); on the other hand, it creates a climate of violence and hostility between the two groups that in turn constitutes a psychological as well as physical danger for the children in the long run. Growing numbers of Israelis and Palestinians are beginning to recognize the self-defeating nature of this pattern, especially since the first *intifada*. Concern over this issue is reflected in an editorial that appeared in *Hadashot* on October 22, 1990, warning both sides of the long-term consequences of pursuing a violent resolution to the conflict: "The Palestinian leaders who call for murder and revenge bury (*kovrim*) their people's hopes in streams of blood, and for that they will be held accountable. On our side (Israeli) those who promote a policy of 'only by force,' in effect bury (*kovrim*) our chances to live here in peace and security" (Gabriel, 1992). This self-reflective attitude, however, is relatively new, and its influence limited. Hostility and aggression are still the dominant modes of interaction between the two groups, and the impact of the peace movement has yet to be felt on the levels of violence to which children are exposed on a daily basis. Under such circumstances, the ability of the Palestinian and Israeli children to empathize with and understand each other (their role-taking abilities) continue to be limited.

Religious Aspects and Growing Alienation

Religious interpretations of the past inflect such expressions as each group attempts to justify the negation of the other's claim (Gabriel, 1992). The rage that is the response of the collective psyche is funneled through individuals and directed outward in many forms, including suicidal attacks against the other group. Extremists on each side not only serve as the conduits for the most extreme expressions of collective emotions, but also provide the political ideologies, in their most pure form, that help to drive the behavior of the rest of the group. Palestinian inhabitants of the region, in reaction to Jews' justification that the land was promised to them by God, found their religious right and justifications for their tenure of the land. According to Koranic verses, a man who dies defending his invaded property/land is martyred.

A martyr's death also is not a cause for mourning but for respect and celebration. Political and religious revisions of history, and interpretations of present situations based on such revisions, exacerbate the conflict with fanatic intensity. For example, the Hebron massacre by Goldstein (Elbedour, Baker, & Belmaker, 1999) was motivated not only by nationalistic agendas but by religious fanaticism. Such historical and religious forces have shaped the conscious and unconscious lives of civilians on both sides, heightened their sense of vulnerability, and adversely conditioned children's attitudes toward the outgroup and their approach to life in general. These outcomes can be seen in children's play: "pretend" tear gas (cups of sand) and make-believe demonstrations (Elbedour, 1992).

In the 1990s, the Oslo Peace Process and the accords signed by Prime Minister Yitzhak Rabin and Chairman Yasir Arafat sparked new hope and the beginning of confidence in improved human rights and welfare for suffering families, as well as strengthening the economy (Elbedour, 1992, 1998). But for a large proportion of Palestinians, particularly in Gaza and West Bank refugee camps, this hope fell far short of the reality. As stated above, in Gaza, 70 percent of the 860,000 inhabitants are identified as refugees (Yahya, 1991). More than 50 percent still live in "permanently temporary" shantytowns. Both within and outside these camps, children and youth continued to be victims or witnesses of official and unofficial violence. Despite these constraints, the level of political violence between 1993 and 1999 was lower in the Israel–Palestinian territory than in any other contested polity in the world. But it was during this period that suicide bombings committed by adolescents and youths sharply escalated. They are yet another example, as were the Goldstein massacre at the Tomb of the Patriarchs and finally the assassination of Rabin, of the growth of extremist fanaticism motivated by "religious" messianicism. Frequently attributed to rejectionists on both sides, these suicidal and homicidal acts were fueled by antecedent events during the *intifada* and protest against the compromises required in the peace process (Sprinzak, 1991).

As Fields's data (1984, 1986, 1990a, 1990b) indicated a growing gulf among Palestinians and Arabs inside Israel, there was also, less well-documented in her data, a growing gulf between Israeli Jews. The orthodox religious elements who fought other Jews on issues of Shomer Shabbat (observance of the Sabbath); the urban secularists, the religious settler movement; the kibbutzniks; the Jews of Oriental origins in the Border new cities; the immigrants from Eastern Europe and the immigrants from Ethiopia and other African countries; the educated professionals and the growing tech-business bourgeoisie—all these no longer represented the united Zionist Pioneer ideology. A growing number of soldiers refused service in Lebanon and the Peace Movement blossomed in the perceived human rights depredations by the IDF during the 1987 *intifada*. This revulsion spread and formed a solid base for Israeli participation in the Oslo accords. The prosperity derived from the peace process was experienced mostly by those who were already middle class and educated. Kibbutzim neighboring Tel Aviv sold their land and disbanded because the land was more valuable for extending the city than for growing crops.

Even the establishment of the Palestinian Authority in Gaza failed to revive the already collapsing Palestinian economy. There were few jobs for laborers, and greater restrictions. Transit between Gaza and the West Bank required considerable Israeli bureaucratic procedures. The availability of electricity, water, and other essentials continued to be manipulated by the IDF and denied as punishment for episodes of protest. Land appropriations for settlements continued. The prosperity of peace especially eluded the Palestinians in the camps in Gaza. Ironically, this period also became the staging ground for the emergence of political suicide on a larger scale than ever before among Palestinians. The legal and economic displacements illuminated by this process exacerbated the impact of the classic colonial imposition of a foreign legal system on an indigenous population that compelled the latter to marginalization and alienation (see Figures 1 and 1a).

Measures of Personality

Merari (1994) claims that it is impossible to diagnose or characterize members of terrorist groups as abnormal or as possessing any particular types of personality. Fields's studies also emphasize the "normality," both statistically as a group and clinically as individuals. Efforts to find common distinguishing personality features and "profiling" may have failed because the experts attributed psychopathologies to those who were identified as "terrorists" (Robins & Post, 1997). They also anecdotally profiled "suicide terrorists" based on individuals imprisoned and so identified by their captors. For instance, Post (2001) refers to his "sample" of Palestinian suicide bombers as individuals imprisoned and so identified by Israel (thus evidently unsuccessful if their aim was suicide). Twenty years earlier, Knutson (1980–1981) identified as Irish terrorists men imprisoned in England for that offense. This kind of post hoc profiling presents obviously serious sampling errors. The deadly consequences when intelligence agencies rely on these methodologically flawed predictive profiles are tragically manifested in the events of September 11, 2001, and other deadly domestic attacks. The only valid measurements are psychological instruments, well normed and standardized, and obtained and compiled on members of such organizations acting on their deadly intentions. Although the STPI profiles described above provide a very brief, albeit universal, personality profile, these data correspond with findings utilizing other measurements (Fields, 1986). The social and political context in her data depict limited personal life experiences as predictive of susceptibility for recruitment into a militant group. Furthermore, individual subjective interpretation of immediate experience combines with perception of an act as "good" (motivation is the perception of something being "good for action" and hence a person moves toward it) (Arnold, 1962). This predicates political murder(s)/suicide. Such a paradigm is ontological as well as etiological; it is also sociological and psychological. Of more than a thousand Irish members of paramilitary groups, only two—one Loyalist and the other Republican—identified themselves as "terrorists." Not coincidentally, both were ex-British Army. The language of self-identification disallows the negative implications of identification as a "terrorist." In fact, Arabs and Muslim communities define Palestinians who committed political suicide acts as freedom fighters or martyrs—*Shaheed.*

Other literature presents hypotheses that may be applied to a group like Hamas's members who commit political suicide. Charlesworth, Elbedour, and Hein's study (1997) focused on Palestinian suicide bombers who completed their missions between September 1993 and February 1996. This sample acted between the two *intifadas,* at the direction of Oslo rejectionist organizations. One of the objectives of this study was to determine if, in any way, these individuals constituted a homogeneous group. In order to accomplish this objective, the authors studied life history and clinical variables. Several different instruments were used to identify characteristics of these political suicides that would warrant further exploration. This procedure systematically assessed this population. While Fields conducted longitudinal studies over more than two decades, widely casting a clinical net and monitoring development in the classic developmental research model, Charlesworth, Elbedour, and Hein selected individuals who had completed their suicide missions but for whom the authors had no prior psychological test data. Like Fields's study, this study views a social group individually through clinical measures. Unfortunately, the sample size is relatively small. Therefore, the amount of clinical data generated is provocative but inconclusive.

THE BOMBER GROUP

The nine subjects were all males between nineteen and twenty-five years of age at the time they died in attacks on Israeli targets. All had participated earlier on the front lines during the first *intifada*. Such confrontations resulted in thousands of arrests and the death and wounding of thousands of Palestinians and several hundred Israeli military personnel and noncombatants as well as damage to Palestinian civilian property. As previously stated, these casualty figures are derived from Nixon (1990), who noted that 7 percent of the total population of children in Gaza and the West Bank (approximately twenty-five thousand) suffered physical injuries as a result of violence and confrontations with the Israeli army in the first two years of the uprising. The use of tear gas also produced victims. The World Health Organization reported that 1,448 of the tear gas victims in Gaza and the West Bank in 1989 were children under the age of six. As we might expect in a population that is exposed to violence on an almost daily basis, the *intifada* politicized the attitudes and behaviors of everyone, including those who became political suicides. In this setting at this time, 1989, under these poor conditions, there was the strongest probability that average and brighter-than-average adolescents and youth would score high in State and Trait Anger, lack feelings of guilt about their angry behaviors, and be unusually high in State and Trait Curiosity. All of these psychological dimensions predicting a Terror Vocation (Fields, 1984, 1986, 1990a, 1990b). The *intifada* played a significant role in the preparation and motivation of the bombers' subsequent behaviors. A review of nine suicide bombers who committed their acts during this period of relatively low terror incidents reveals the following psychological and social information:

- Bomber 1 drove a car loaded with explosives into an Israeli military convoy (no civilians were present). There has been no official statement of the number of dead and injured, nor the amount of physical damage.

- Bomber 2 followed another bomber into a street crowded with soldiers and civilians, and after the latter detonated his explosives, waited until police and military gathered before detonating his explosives. Twenty-three Israeli (military and civilians) were wounded.

- Bomber 3 walked into an Israeli police station and detonated his explosives. Four policemen were killed.

- Bomber 4 tried to enter a large commercial building, failed, and walked instead into the street and detonated his explosives. Sixteen Israeli military and civilians were killed and about thirty injured.

- Bomber 5 rode a bicycle into a cluster of soldiers in a convoy and detonated his explosives. Three soldiers were killed and an unspecified number were wounded.

- Bomber 6 drove a car loaded with explosives, but before he reached his target, an Israeli army vehicle, his car exploded.

- Bomber 7 drove a car loaded with explosives into a truck in a passing military convoy; one soldier was killed, ten others were injured.

- Bomber 8, presumably preceding Bomber 2 above, walked into a street crowded with Israeli soldiers and civilians and detonated his explosives. Twenty-three individuals were killed and forty injured.

- Bomber 9 walked to a cluster of Israeli soldiers standing by a convoy and detonated his explosives. Three soldiers were killed, four were wounded.

The control group: In addition to the nine bombers, nine control subjects were interviewed. The controls were males of roughly the same age as the bombers, came from similar socioeconomic backgrounds, and purportedly had similar experiences to the latters' during the *intifada*. Controls were selected by asking each bomber's family to nominate three male friends of the bomber who had the same background and characteristics as the target subject. Selection of the nine specific controls was determined randomly from the twenty-seven prospective subjects. Four family members (mother, father, sister, and brother) and two male friends of each suicide bomber were interviewed, using several normed questionnaires. These interview questions were aimed at shedding light on the bomber's personality, psychological state, and life experiences. The same procedure was carried out with each control subject.

The bombers ranged between 19 and 25 years of age (mean = 21.4 years). Bombers' schooling ranged between 6 and 14 years (mean = 12.5 years). No bomber, except the one who had 6 years of school, had a work history of any great length. The number of members of bombers' families ranged from 12 to 17 (mean = 14.2).

The socioeconomic standing of all nine families ranged from very low to average for the area. The estimated family annual income (seven families reporting) was from $3,000 to $7,800 (mean = $4,828 annually).

Given mean number of members per family of 14.2 and mean income per family of $4,828, a rough estimate of annual income per family member is $340.

Sibling numbers: Bombers' brothers (eight families reporting) ranged from 2 to 10 (mean = 6.4). Bombers' sisters (eight families reporting) ranged from 2 to 9 (mean = 5.1). All bombers but one (who was the youngest) ranked in the middle of the sibling order.

All nine bombers experienced the *intifada* in Gaza. Fifty-six percent (five) of the nine bombers were injured during the *intifada*. Eighty-nine percent (eight) of the nine were imprisoned, three once, four twice, one on three separate occasions. The eight who were in prison were tortured, one very severely. During the first *intifada*, the homes of 89 percent (eight) of the bombers were entered by Israeli special commando forces. Five of the eight families of the suicide bombers were beaten and humiliated when their homes were entered, and the mothers and sisters were abused (psychologically if not physically) in front of other family members by soldiers.

Coopersmith's scale of self-esteem (1981) was one of the instruments used for postmortem evaluation of the subjects. Self-esteem is defined as liking and respect for and accepting oneself. The scale has considerable flexibility in measuring various aspects such as physical, mental, moral, in schools, at work, etc. Items to be answered—for example, as "like him" or "unlike him"—include "Things usually bother him," "He has a low opinion of himself," "He often wishes he was someone else," and "There are many times when he would like to leave home." Higher scores are indicative of high self-esteem. On this measure there are no significant differences between the means for bombers and for controls. However, the scores overall correspond with the Lundeberg, Fox, Brown, and Elbedour (2000) study using other measures that found that Palestinians' level of confidence exceeded that of the Israeli group; the scores of the Israeli group were also significantly higher than those of other groups (e.g., American). Compared with other groups, when questioned about their choices on multiple-choice questions, Palestinian children were more likely to be convinced that their answer was correct regardless of evidence to the contrary. This seems indicative of either very high self-esteem or extreme defensiveness. Thus the Coopersmith scores indicating high self-esteem may in fact reflect the defensiveness of feelings of inadequacy that are a consequence of attributions of negative or lachrymose identity.

The Achenbach Child Behavior Checklist was used (shortened to twenty items, which collectively measure different aspects of behavior problems). Sample items listed below were to be answered 0 = Not true, 1 = Somewhat true, 2 = Very true or often true:

- Argues a lot.
- Confused or seems to be in a fog.
- Disobedient at home.
- Doesn't eat well.
- Shy or timid.
- Unhappy, sad, or depressed.
- Worries.

The mean number of items (weighted) for the bombers equaled 9.11, the mean for the controls equaled 5.60 (T test=3.52, p < .05). Unlike some of the other parameters, this difference is statistically significant. The bombers showed a significantly higher frequency of reported behavior problems than the controls. This contrasts with the generalized statements (see below) regarding a lack of significant educational or social behavioral indices of pathology.

Given that the maximum weighted score is 40 for each subject, means of 9.11 and 5.60 appear quite low. However, since we have no norms for Palestinian youth in Gaza, it is not possible to interpret these findings in terms of a wider picture. Nevertheless, the difference between bombers and controls is statistically significant and deserves further inquiry into the items that contribute to this difference. The major question running through all studies of those who commit acts of political suicide is what differentiates them from the larger population of marginalized, disadvantaged, impoverished, and humiliated individuals and groups. These data are insufficient for conclusions, but quite provocative.

Given that the six interviewees answered the same questions concerning the nine political suicides, and an additional six interviewees answered the same questions concerning the nine controls, it is possible to establish a large number of indices of agreement between them.

Questionnaire session II was conducted later for the purpose of adding more demographic and life history information on the bombers to that collected in Questionnaire I. Other purposes were to check the reliability of the data collected on the bombers in the first interview, and to obtain new information on the response of the communities (both the subject's community and the government) to the suicide attack. Also sought were the family's personal opinions about the bombers' motives and suicide communities' response and additional information on the bombers' motives. The additional data was also collected through interviews of family members (mother, father, sister, and brother) and two male friends of each suicide bomber using several questionnaires. These interview questions aimed to shed light on the bombers' personality, psychological state, and life experiences.

BEHAVIORAL AND PSYCHOLOGICAL CHARACTERISTICS OF THE BOMBERS

Eight of the nine bombers were described by family and friends as very religious. Five expressed a desire at one time or another to meet God and to defend their land through martyrdom. Eight bombers were described as very likable guys, devoted to their communities, or noted for helping friends and other community members and, in one case, defending and helping the community's weaker members.

Three bombers were described as peaceful, nonaggressive and/or calm, and were clearly not pathological. Neither did they suffer from psychological or educational problems. Three were especially described as average, normal guys, one of whom loved life, another of whom was generally happy, and two of whom loved to work. (These descriptions are at variance with the scores on the Achenbach.)

Five bombers were described as being frustrated and depressed at times. One was described as usually serious. And one was described as especially depressed because his family had no money for him to pursue graduate studies and because the Israeli army did not permit him to leave Gaza to pursue his education in the West Bank. None of the bombers drank, took drugs, or engaged in antisocial behavior against the community.

Interviews were conducted individually and, because of their length, were carried out during two separate sessions, one in the morning and one in the late afternoon or evening. Family members were informed of the objective of the study by the interviewer, who was a prominent clinical psychologist in the Gaza community.

Again and again, it became apparent from these interviews that family and communities recognized suicide bombers as heroes and freedom fighters.

- Bomber 1: His family was shocked and greatly saddened, and immediately called for a wedding or wedding-like celebration (to observe that the bomber was wedded to God on entering Paradise). The community responded by celebrating and giving condolences and moral support to the family, also rejoicing that the bomber had entered Paradise. No gifts or any form of material support or money was given to the family by anyone.

- Bomber 2: His family called for a wedding (as above), and friends came and shot (presumably small arms) into the air as a sign of respect and joy at the bomber's achievement of Paradise through martyrdom. The community responded with condolences. No gifts or any form of material support or money was given to the family by anyone. No burial was possible.

- Bomber 3: Over a traditional period of twelve days following the bomber's death community members came to the house to offer condolences. The bomber's father, however, was arrested and taken to the police station to identify his son's body. The police required that the body be buried in the middle of the night with no more than ten persons present.

- Bomber 4: Although greatly saddened, the community called for a wedding with much joyful singing because the bomber was in heaven. The family received no compensation, gifts, etc., from anyone. No burial was conducted because only the bomber's head was found and the authorities did not return it to the family.

- Bomber 5: The family called for a wedding with women singing, etc. The family received no compensation from anyone. The remains of the bomber's body were turned over to the family by the Palestinian Authority. The burial was attended by a great number of people.

- Bomber 6: The family received many community members who came to give condolences and to congratulate the family on their son entering Paradise through martyrdom. The bomber's body was turned over at a border checkpoint in the middle of the night. The Palestinian Authority allowed only fifteen people to attend the burial.

- Bomber 7: The family was approached by many community members. There was much singing. Many members appeared to offer condolences. No compensation or gifts were given to the family. No burial took place because no body was turned over to the family.

- Bomber 8: The family called for a wedding, with much joyous singing but also much pain. The family received no gifts, remuneration, etc. No burial took place because the bomber's body was blown to bits.

- Bomber 9: There was a great joyous community outpouring, accompanied by much shooting into the air as signs of great respect. No one was observed to display outward grief. The family received no gifts, remuneration, etc. The bomber's body was badly mangled, but his head and face were intact. The latter was held up to view (presumably on top of body wrappings) during the burial procession.

All families gave more than one motive or reason. What is reported here is a composite of their responses.

Five families said the bomber was very religious and motivated to carry out a holy war against the oppressor/occupier. Three said the bomber was very religious and hence motivated also by religious reasons. One did not mention religion. However, seven families (including the one that did not mention religion) said the bomber was not afraid of death since he was seeking Paradise through freedom martyrdom.

Seven said the bomber responded (through his action) to the injustices (occupation, daily harassment, economic exploitation, suppression, etc.) perpetrated by the Israeli occupation.

Eight of the nine said the bomber reacted out of hatred for Israeli Jews who suppressed his people and occupy his homeland. The same eight bombers reportedly acted out of love for their people, to defend and liberate them.

The actions of eight bombers were said to have been triggered in response to the death or expulsion of other martyrs or of Hamas members in general by the Israelis.

Five said the bomber was frustrated, very unhappy, and depressed by the situation of the Palestinians under the occupation. No family reported that the bomber acted for material gain for his family or community.

One family noted that the bomber acted in response (presumably revenge) to his prison experiences.

Political suicide may have started in the course of the *intifada,* but continued after the first *intifada* was officially concluded. In political terms, these suicides are the behavioral manifestation of some individuals who see no hope from the Oslo accord. In a psychological and social context, the results of this study suggest that political suicide is an outgrowth of a subjective individual response to prolonged social distress related, in this group, to the occupation. Situational factors are more likely than pathological personality to precipitate these acts. These results also suggest the increasing impact of the media as an antecedent for many of these suicide attacks. Problems are exacerbated when media and identity group membership endorse a moral objective in attacking the enemy without fear of social disapproval.

In all cases in this study, community and family members called for a wedding, with women singing, etc. In some cases, the burial was attended by many people, and respect and honor of the attacker and his deed reflected in street posters, in graffiti, or on the radio. There was a great joyous community outpouring. Not only did families call for a wedding (as above), but friends came and shot into the air as a sign of respect at the bomber's achievement (the advancement of nationalist struggles). Finally, the easy targets selected for suicide attacks reflect the sense that alternative methods of struggle are unavailable.

While this approach to such studies makes it possible to point to social trends that lead people to the use of extreme violence, homicide through suicide, it provides little information about why a specific individual turns to this type of violence while others with similar demographics and experience do not. Possible suggestions or explanations indicate potentially important reasons for commuting acts of political suicide. First, there is the combination of personally experienced traumatic events, which challenge coping abilities. All nine subjects themselves had been subjected to violence and were particularly vulnerable to threats against their safety and their physical and psychological well-being. For example, in the course of the *intifada* period the bombers witnessed or experienced, directly or indirectly, injury (five of the nine bombers), imprisonment (eight of the nine were imprisoned, three once, four twice, one on three separate occasions). Some were tortured, most many times, one very severely, as the findings demonstrate. Loss of family members and close friends and punitive measures by the army against their families, including deportations and evictions, were reported. Economic and social stress were evident in nearly all cases, and this heightened the sense of burden and inflated feelings of helplessness and despair.

None of these individuals was working when he made his choice for this action. The socioeconomic standing of all nine families ranged from very low to average for the area, reporting from $3,000 to $7,800 (mean = $4,828 annually). The imposition of curfews and restrictions on trade and movement have "led to a complete collapse of an already weakened economy and an estimated 40 to 50 percent unemployment" (Collins, 1991). The distress resulting from unresolved PTSD shatters the survivor's sense of coping and leads to the perception of suicide as a solution to suffering, and of death as attractive. Fields used the titled "Terrorized Into Terrorist" for several of her reports on studies of terrorized children (1986, 1989, 1992).

Religion and its transformative power override anxiety about death. The most salient finding that discriminates the bombers from non-bombers is the high incidence of religiosity, as the interview data suggested. Theological-spiritual victory over death is the Messianic conviction. The belief in afterlife Paradise as both a relief from the hardships of real life and as a reward for sending others to damnation is not a new thesis. In fact, it dates back to the third to eighth centuries in Christianity and Islam. Maltsberger and Bute (1980) argue that persons seek death as an escape from the internal persecutor and in search of rebirth. Dislocated individuals tend to adopt totalistic ideologies, whose function is similar to that of paranoid systems. Totalistic ideologies succeed in attracting believers to the valley of death because the explanation of everything in life by means of a single simplistic concept provides a stable anchor that frees them from uncertainty and reduces their insecurity. The fact that most totalistic ideologies succeed in overcoming death in one way or another also reduces the believer's death anxiety. At times of complex and complicated conflicts, true believers tend to search for an immediate, unquestioned solution that brings peace. The view that the believer will be sent to heaven and the guilty to hell aids in this. In this polar perception, sending the guilty to hell turns the death of the perpetrator into a holy act. The findings of this study point to the function of religion as motive as well as protective factor. This seems to be a common denominator in the background of political suicides. This idea is supported by De Wind (1968), who points out that belief in an afterlife sometimes reduces anxiety (p. 304).

The five types of symbolic immortality identified by Lifton (1967) are internal standards by means of which life is extended and a sense of continuity and meaning is engendered. This is essential to psychological well-being. Lifton continues by elaborating that when individuals lose their sense of immortality, daily functioning is impaired, the sense of vitality declines, and anxieties develop regarding disintegration, separation, and death. Most of the nine suicide bombers meet the criteria Lifton identifies as critical for a sense of psychological well-being that necessitates a symbolic immortality. This sense is achieved through the transformative religious experience because it is lacking in other dimensions. Most of these bombers were between nineteen and twenty-five years of age, with limited schooling and social experience. Only one had a work history of any great length. It is evident that the social and psychological conditions of their lives in Gaza and the sense of insecurity and frustration of accomplishment built up to weaken survival coping mechanisms. For these young men, it produced frustration that evolved into rage, attaining unbearable levels. They searched for meaning and found it in sacrifice.

The incidence of suicide among adolescents in Western society is higher than among other age groups. From studies of failed adolescent suicides and the surviving partners in paired suicide attempts, there are indications of some of the same psychodynamics evidenced in these cases. Data from Northern Ireland morbidity and mortality statistics indicate that suicides rose significantly from the beginning of the "troubles" (Fields, 1989) and seemed to level off after the Mitchell Good Friday agreements. Additional evidence can be seen in the incidence of so-called accidental deaths and the "accidental" victimization of additional numbers of suicides. These are suicides attributed to accidental deaths. As described by Lifton (1967), their experiences disrupt several primary symbols, such as "the illusion of personal invulnerability" (p. 481), "faith in the larger human matrix" (p. 481), and the "sense of general continuity of human existence" (p. 488). As a defense mechanism against the pain and threat of war, the "survivor," Lifton writes, "undergoes a radical but temporary diminution in his senses of actuality in order to avoid losing his sense completely and permanently; he undergoes a reversible form of symbolic death in order to avoid permanent physical or psychic death" (p. 500), a phenomenon described by him as "psychic closing off" (p. 500). These young Palestinians chose one form of symbolic immortality: spiritual victory over death, such as belief in the afterlife—life in death rather than death in life, as many survivors would choose (Hazani, 1993). Recurrent depression was reported to have preceded the attack in the majority of individuals studied.

Though no psychiatric examination was conducted before the suicide acts, this postmortem examination of the bombers revealed intense psychic suffering. The reasons given for the attack included general unhappiness, a feeling of inadequacy and depression, low expectation of the future as result of occupation, response to the death or expulsion of other "freedom martyrs," or hatred of Israeli Jews. These problems are multiplied by the earlier-mentioned factors that create the notorious cycle of violence. Depression is anger turned inward and thus individuals can convert the depression and helplessness to suicidal action, giving a sense of control. The subjects of this study evidence feelings of loss of control, which can produce cognitive, behavioral, motivational, and emotional deficits (Seligman, 1975) and can render them incapable of coping with the aversive situation. These individuals maintain less-positive beliefs about survival, and having weaker survival and coping beliefs makes them more prone to see suicide as an acceptable solution.

CONCLUSION

This pilot study demonstrates that some characteristics of the individual and his traumatic experiences are associated with suicide bombing. A number of etiological models (Miller, 1988) have been proposed to account for the political suicide phenomenon. Some psychological studies focus on the characteristics and personality profiles of bombers, while others are sociological, political, religious, and socioeconomic models. The sociological model looks at social forces (for example, marginalization, unemployment, and poverty) and the way these interact to motivate political suicide. The psychiatric model focuses on the psychopathology of the political suicide, while the religious model works from the premise that political suicide may be triggered by the religious belief system.

The results of the study demonstrate that none of these one-factor conceptual frameworks has proven powerful enough on its own to adequately explain Palestinian suicide bombers. These results have favored a multilevel ecological/dynamic model. The sociopolitical matrix interacting with gender identity and personal and interpersonal loss, with religious sentiment fed by symbolic gratification, and the death of optimism as result of the political situation all must be considered as operational factors in the phenomenon of the Palestinian suicide bomber. Understanding the phenomenon from transactional/ecological models removes the enigma imposed by the search for a unique trait or experience shared by all suicidal individuals.

The politics of memory requires transgenerational martyrs, heroes, and villains. Vicarious identification by individuals whose social and political experience limits their development makes righteously indignant true believers.

The fact that these suicide bombings commenced and accelerated during the period of the Oslo Peace Accords is often overlooked. They may be viewed as a symptom of chronic social malaise. Prolonged violence and especially intergenerational violence require much more than a period of political quiescence to disappear. There are significant differences in age, social status, and even gender among the suicide bombers in the 2000–2002 Palestinian uprising. Several possible explanations derive from this study of the nine suicide bombers associated with the period between the first and second *intifada*. Studies of PTSD subjects in many traumatized groups have demonstrated that traumatization is cumulative, and reactions to traumatic stress are often submerged even from the individual traumatized. Rather than having a "vaccination" function, untreated survivors carry hidden, potentially explosive wounds (Fields, 1980a, 1980b, 1986, 1989). Besides the accumulated traumatization, humiliation, and loss of hope that preceded the peace process, the process exacerbated economic and other differences and further fractionated the polity. The breakdown of negotiations and Sharon's visit to the Temple Mount, with the disproportionate force massed against the protesters, symbolized for the most impoverished and marginalized the utter futility of political experience. This realization accompanied, if not preceded, the breakdown of the negotiations.

Suicide committed at a time of civil unrest may often be attributed to hostile acts against the person or "accidents," especially in societies with stringent strictures against taking one's own life. With prolonged violence and occupation, more people become more desperate and also more susceptible to carry out suicidal acts. With few exceptions (one notable is Wafa Idris, the first but not the last woman to enact a suicide bombing), the political bombers have been affiliated with religious groups. The newest phenomenon, as with Idris, has been the succession of female suicide bombers associated with Al Aksa brigades, a secularist militia affiliated with the mainstream Fatah political faction. Currently, the Al Aksa Martyrs Brigade has taken the action to the interstice between the secular and the religious.

There have been several instances of middle-aged men apparently acting on their own who have committed suicide bombings or attacks. Consistent with studies of members of paramilitary groups not particularly noted for suicide missions, there is the profile of righteous indignation or zealotry, with roots far back in history. This is also manifested in secular paramilitary members such as the Irish Republican Army hunger strikers who starve to death, and the Turkish Kurd revolutionaries who likewise embark on hunger strike to death (Juergensmeyer, 2000). These are perhaps more passive-aggressive modes than the Palestinian. The Righteously Indignant truncated in the second stage of legal socialization will, like kamikaze pilots (Japanese suicide bombers in World War II), view death—their own or others'—as a mechanism of retributive justice. Political terror, after all, is as ancient as any other kind of warfare. Violence against Palestinian or Israeli civilians, whether enacted by the regular army forces of a sovereign state or by the "irregulars or paramilitaries," is bound, as Caleb Carr notes in *The Lessons of Terror* (2002), to self-annihilate and make the cause of the perpetrators self-destruct.

REFERENCES

Abu-Lughod, I. (1990). Introduction on achieving independence. In J. R. Nassar & R. Heacock (Eds.), *Intifada: Palestine at the crossroads*. New York: Praeger.

Arnold, M. (1962). *Story sequence analysis: A new method of measuring motivation and predicting achievement*. New York: Columbia University Press.

Carr, C. (2002). *The lessons of terror*. New York: Random House.

Charlesworth, W., Elbedour, S., and Hein, F. (1997). The phenomenon of political suicide: The case of the Palestinian political suicide during the first Intifada. Unpublished report.

Collins, F. (1991). Palestinian economy in chaos after the Gulf War. *The Washington Report on the Middle East Affairs*, pp. 23, 54.

Coopersmith, S. (1981). *The self-esteem inventory (SEI)*. Palo Alto, CA: Consulting Psychologists Press.

Curtis, G. C. (1963). Violence breeds violence—perhaps? *American Journal of Psychiatry, 120*, 386–387.

Darby, J. (1976). Social mobility in Northern Ireland. *Transaction/Society Magazine*. New Brunswick, NJ: Rutgers University Press.

Elbedour, S. (1992). *The psychology of children of war*. University of Minnesota, unpublished doctoral dissertation.

Elbedour, S. (1998). Youth in crisis: The well-being of Middle-Eastern youth and adolescents during war and peace. *Journal of Youth & Adolescence, 45*, 57–65.

Elbedour, S., Baker, A., & Belmaker, R. H. (1999). Psychological responses in family members after Hebron massacre. *Anxiety & Depression 19*, 61–62.

Elbedour, S., Baker, A., & Charlesworth, W. R. (1997). The impact of political violence on moral reasoning in children. *Child Abuse & Neglect, 21*, 1053–1066.

Elbedour, S., Bastien, D., & Center, B. (1997). Identity formation in the shadow of conflict: Projective drawings by Palestinian and Israeli Arab children from the West Bank and Gaza. *Journal of Peace Research, 34*, 217–231.

Farson, S. K., & Landis, J. M. (1990). The sociology of an uprising: The roots of the Intifada. In J. R. Nassar & R. Heacock (Eds.), *Intifada: Palestine at the crossroads*. New York: Praeger.

Fields, R. M. (1976). *Society under siege*. Philadelphia: Temple University Press.

Fields, R. M. (1978). *Hostages and torture victims: Studies on the effects of trauma induced stress*. Proceedings, Second International Conference on Psychological Stress and Adjustment in Time of War and Peace. Tel Aviv University, Israel.

Fields, R. M. (1980a). *Northern Ireland: Society under siege*. New Brunswick, NJ: Transaction/Society Press.

Fields, R. M. (1980b). Victims of terrorism: The effects of prolonged stress. *Evaluation and Change, Special Issue*. Minneapolis Medical Research Foundation.

Fields, R. M. (1982a). Terrorized into terrorist. In F. Ochberg & D. Soskis (Eds.), *Victims of terrorism*. Denver: Westview Press.

Fields, R. M. (1982b). Victims of terror. In D. Rappaport & Y. Alexander (Eds.), *Moral implications of terrorism*. New York: Crane, Russek & Co.

Fields, R. M. (1986). *Psychological profile of a terrorist*. Paper presented at American Psychological Association Convention Invited Symposium, Washington, D.C.

Fields, R. M. (1989). Terrorized into terrorist: Pete the para strikes again. In A. O'Day & Y. Alexander (Eds.), *Ireland's terrorist trauma: Interdisciplinary perspectives.* New York: Harvester Wheatsheaf Press.

Fields, R. M. (1990a). Predicted formula for a terror vocation. In J. E. Lundberg, V. Otto, & B. Rybeck (Eds.), *Wartime medical services.* Stockholm, Sweden: FOA.

Fields, R. M. (1990b). Children of the intifada. *Migration World, 17,* 519–542.

Gabriel, A. (1992). Grief and rage: Collective emotions in the politics of peace and the politics of gender in Israel. *Culture, Medicine and Psychiatry, 16,* 311–335.

Hazani, M. (1993). Sacrificial immorality: Toward a theory of suicidal terrorism and related phenomena. *The Psychoanalytic Study of Society, 18,* 415–442.

Huyck, E. E., & Fields, R. M. (1981). Impact of resettlement on refugee children. *International Migration Review, 15,* 246–251.

Juergensmeyer, M. (2000). *Terror in the mind of god: The global rise of religious violence.* Berkeley, CA: University of California Press.

Knutson, J. M. (1973). *Handbook of political psychology.* San Francisco: Jossey-Bass.

Lerner, M. (1989). Psychological dimension of the Israeli-Palestinian conflict. *Tikkun, 4,* 41–49.

Lifton, R. J. (1967). *Death in life: Survivors of Hiroshima.* New York: Random House.

Lundeberg, M., Fox, P., Brown, A. C., & Elbedour, S. (2000). Cultural influences on confidence: Country & gender. *Journal of Educational Psychology, 92,* 152–159.

Mahjoub, A., Leyens, J., Yzerbt, V., & DiGiacomo J. (1989). War stress and coping modes: Representations of self-identity and time perspective among Palestinian children. *International Journal of Mental Health, 18,* 44–62.

Merari, A. (1994). Terrorism. *Encyclopedia of Human Behavior, 43,* 399–409.

Miller, R. (1988). The literature of terrorism. *Terrorism, 11,* 63–87.

Nixon, A. (1990). *The status of Palestinians children during the uprising in the occupied territories, Parts 1 and 2.* East Jerusalem: Radda Barnen.

Piaget, J. (1932). *The moral judgment of the child.* New York: Harcourt, Brace and World.

Piaget, J. (1954). *The construction of reality in the child.* New York: Basic Books.

Punamaki, R. L. (1996). Can ideological commitment protect children's psychosocial well-being in situations of political violence? *Child Development, 67,* 55–69.

Robins, R. S., & Post, J. (1997). *Political paranoia: The psychopolitics of Hatred.* New Haven, CT: Yale University Press

Roy, S. (1989). Changing political attitudes among Gaza refugees. *Journal of Palestine Studies, 19,* 72–92.

Seligman, M. E. P. (1975). *Helplessness: On depression, development, and death.* San Francisco: Freeman.

Spielberger, C. (1985). *State-trait personality indices.* Psychology Assessment Services (Ed.), Tampa, FL: University of South Florida.

Sprinzak, E. (1991). *The ascendance of Israel's radical right.* New York: Oxford University Press.

Tapp, J. L., & Kohlberg, L. (1971). Developing senses of law and legal justice. *Journal of Social Issues, 27,* 2.

Thabet, A. A., & Vostanis, P. R. (1999). Post-traumatic stress reactions in children of war. *Journal of Child Psychology and Psychiatry, 40,* 385–391.

Yahya, A. (1991). The role of the refugee camps. In J. R. Nassar & R. Heacock (Eds.), *Intifada: Palestine at the crossroads* (pp. 91–106). New York: Praeger.

SUPPLEMENTARY BIBLIOGRAPHY

Achenbach, T. M., Howell, C. T., Quay, H. C., & Conners, C. K. (1991). National survey of problems and competencies among four- to sixteen-year-olds: Parents' reports for normative and clinical samples. *Monographs for Social Research in Child Development, 56,* 1–131.

Fields, R. M. (1983). *Society on the run.* Hammondsworth, England: Penguin Ltd.

McDowall, D. (1989). A profile of the population of the West-bank and Gaza strip. *Journal of Refugee Studies, 2,* 20–25.

Rouhana, N. (1989). Children and the intifada. *Journal of Palestinian Studies, 18,* 110–121.

10

Us & Them: Reducing the Risk of Terrorism

Stephen D. Fabick

"We must live together as brothers, or perish together as fools."

Martin Luther King

As the world gets smaller—with CNN, the Internet, and transportation advances —different cultural groups have more contact with each other. With this comes the opportunity for greater understanding, but also greater conflict. Our enhanced technology requires an enhanced psychology. Our world no longer has the luxury of easy answers such as blind tribal loyalty, ingroup aggrandizement, and outgroup dismissal and disdain.

In a more interdependent world, collaboration trumps competition in the long run, even for the powerful. Wise leaders of powerful groups realize the transitory nature of such a power imbalance. And in a world in which terrorism[1] is the seductive equalizer, the powerful have no other choice ultimately. The asymmetrical warfare of terrorism requires a reassessment of the ways to deal with such threats. Transformative thinking is needed in a world where survival depends more on cooperation than on competition.

Such thinking starts on a personal level with the appreciation that the disenfranchised poor are no less important than others. And it continues with the realization that countries with the highest disparity in wealth have the greatest incidence of stress, violence, and crime (Albee, 2000). Such transformative vision then extends to the powerful fully understanding the sense of threat that others can feel is posed by their greater power, and the privileged having sensitivity to the envy fostered by their bounty and appreciation of the resentment kindled by their higher status. Teddy Roosevelt recognized that those wielding a big stick must speak softly.

It has been argued that people in the majority may be no more prejudiced than people in the minority. But the disenfranchised cannot be oppressive or racist, since such structural violence rests not just on prejudice but also on power. So, because the powerful have more impact socially, economically, militarily, and psychologically, so too do they have greater responsibility to exercise intergroup care and judgment.

Americans don't have to look elsewhere to see the effects of oppression. The original purpose of slavery in America was to maintain an economic advantage for the labor-intensive industries of the South. Unlike slaves in some societies in which prisoners of war were enslaved, American slaves were dehumanized. The residue of this evil is apparent. Though black men constitute less than 6 percent of the general U.S. population, they account for 48 percent of the state prison population (Haney & Zimbardo, 1998). And gross economic disparity continues unabated between blacks and whites in America. Though the majority of whites today are not personally responsible for this problem—that is, they are not racist—they benefit from their "white privilege" and thus are primarily responsible for fixing the problem (McIntosh, 1989). And because of their greater power, whites are more able to effect such change. This burden of American power, a form of modern-day *noblesse oblige*, extends to international relations.

As Benjamin Barber points out in *Jihad vs. McWorld* (1996), many Muslims fear the encroachment of Western culture, i.e., a cultural genocide. Westerners don't need to apologize for everything about themselves, but need to be sensitive to the fears of Muslims. And the West may learn something from its adversaries that can't be learned from its allies. The history of the loss of advantage by a dominant group suggests that for every loss there is a gain. As men in the West have lost some competitive edge at the office, they have gained in their enhanced role in parenting. What can the West learn?

Westerners' greatest "ism" is not racism or nationalism, but materialism. Conversations center on consumption. Western men tend to discuss the acquisition of wealth, e.g., their investments and jobs, and Western women their consumption, e.g., shopping, restaurants, and vacations. The poor in the West shoot each other for jewelry and expensive athletic shoes. Perhaps what the West stands to gain the most from an attunement and responsiveness to the Muslim world is a personal and spiritual renewal. A sense of such an awakening was manifest in New York after the World Trade Center attack. Martin Luther King, Jr., saw the connection between materialism and racism (Wallis, 1994, p. 136):

> We must rapidly . . . shift from a "thing"-oriented society to a "person"-oriented society. When machines and computers, profit motives and property rights are considered more important than people, the giant triplets of racism, materialism and militarism are incapable of being conquered.

RELEVANCE

Are psychological theory, research, and practice relevant in the "War Against Terrorism"? We have seen that multinational military intervention has a place, as does the "dirty business" of intelligence gathering. Certainly, diplomacy plays an essential role in countering the risk of terrorism. But what about psychology? Some track II diplomacy (working with midlevel leaders from large groups in protracted conflicts) relies directly upon psychological research and skills (Rouhana & Kelman, 1994; Lederach, 1995). Reich (1998, p. 279) concludes that psychological research has an important role in the understanding of terrorism:

> Most important for psychological researchers is the need to remember that terrorism is a complicated, diverse, and multidetermined phenomenon that resists simple definition, undermines all efforts at objectivity, forces upon all researchers moral riddles of confounding complexity, and is as challenging to our intellectual efforts to understand it as it is to our collective efforts to control it. It is an example and product of human interaction gone awry and is worth studying and understanding it in the human terms that befit it: as conflict, struggle, passion, drama, myth, history, reality, and, not least, psychology.

However, in applying social science to the understanding of terrorism, we must be cautious, since terrorism is essentially a political phenomenon. We cannot easily extrapolate what is known about violent people in general to terrorists. Kellen (cited in Reich, 1998, p. 49) states,

> Most violent people are not terrorists. What characterizes terrorists is the political, or pseudopolitical, component of their motivations, which ordinary violent people lack. Terrorists . . . have the comparatively rare personality combination of the intellectual (albeit usually not brilliant ones) and the physically violent person in the extreme.

Furthermore, psychologists should not pathologize terrorists' personalities. Hoffman (1998, p. 158) stated, "Contrary to both popular belief and media depiction, most terrorism is neither crazed nor capricious." Terrorists don't voluntarily seek out psychological assessment or treatment. Even when social scientists have access to them after they have been captured, examination of the development of their radicalization is, by definition, post hoc. It is therefore processed through the filter of selective memory and self-justification, as well as intentional omission and deliberate distortion due to judicial contingencies and promotion of the particular political agenda of the terrorist. But they do seek media attention and converts. So terrorists' thinking has been examined in their writings and pronouncements. Overall, researchers (Jager, Schmidtchen, & Sullwold, 1981) who have studied terrorist personalities have concluded that there is no terrorist personality per se. That is, the type of person drawn to and radicalized into a terrorist subculture is unique to the particular political and social context. A terrorist is further socialized and radicalized once within the terrorist group. Moreover, the more insular the group from mainstream society, the greater the likelihood of its members' developing idiosyncratic thinking over time.

Researchers have identified some personality patterns, however. For example, left-wing terrorists are typically more educated, more middle class, and less indiscriminately violent than right-wing terrorists. Religious terrorists tend to be more violent than secular terrorists given the formers' tendency to see the targeted group as infidels. "Holy terrorists" justify more extreme forms of violence by seeing it as retribution for the nonbelievers' immorality, i.e., a "divine duty" (Hoffman, 1995).

Paraphrasing several authors, Reich (1998, p. 27) shows that terrorists have been described as action-oriented, aggressive, stimulus-hungry, and excitement-seeking. Particularly striking is their reliance upon the defenses of externalization and splitting. They exhibit a suspension of rational and empathic thinking in a compartmentalized way about their cause and about the humanity of target outgroup individuals. And though there is some support for psychological motivations such as abusive and neglectful relationships with parents playing some role in vengeance toward authority figures (Jager, Schmidtchen, & Sullwold, 1981), there are no control group studies. And, as previously mentioned, each situation needs to be examined given the multiplicity of variables across societies in which terrorism has manifested. Overall, cultural and political factors may weigh more heavily in the development of a terrorist than individual personality.

Given the commonly reported tendency of terrorists to externalize blame to the target group, to split good and bad into "us" and "them" respectively, to justify their actions, and to dehumanize "them," it makes sense to draw upon the body of research that has addressed such intergroup tendencies, i.e., studies of prejudice and intergroup conflict. Since terrorism is one of the most extreme manifestations of prejudice and conflict that minority group members can perpetrate, it is reasonable to apply such research in our efforts to delineate new paradigms for the research. It also stands to reason that applied programs in intergroup and conflict reduction are relevant in the nascent psychosocial field of terrorism risk reduction.

There is a wealth of research and applied programs in the related areas of conflict resolution (Deutsch & Coleman, 2000) and prejudice reduction (Oskamp, 2000). Much work in social psychology has been done on why individuals identify with a certain group—their reference group—and counteridentify with another (Tajfel & Turner, 1979; Turner, 1985). Such work is relevant in understanding issues of terrorist development and recruitment as well as the support that such individuals receive socially, economically, and politically within their communities.

Research has clarified the conditions under which intergroup prejudice (Oskamp, 2000) and conflict (Fisher & Keashly, 1991) escalate, and aspects of this should apply to the intensification of terrorist threat. Even some work on the identification of types of individuals who are prone to bifurcation of good in their own racial or ethnic group and bad in targeted outgroups (Duckitt, 1992) may help our understanding of people drawn to terrorist action. Such identification might be useful in terms of discriminative profiling for security purposes. Most importantly, the work done in the areas of prejudice reduction and conflict resolution should help inform program development in terrorism risk reduction. As Crenshaw (cited in Hoffman, 1998, p. 247) wrote, "It is difficult to understand terrorism without psychological theory, because explaining terrorism must begin with analyzing the intentions of the terrorist actor and the emotional reactions of audiences."

FOCUS

This chapter will review the role of social identity (Tajfel, 1981), intergroup contact (Allport, 1954), competition (Sherif, Harvey, White, Hood, Sherif, & Campbell, 1988), individual psychodynamics (Volkan, 1988), power (Sidanius & Pratto, 1999), and social cognition (Bandura, 1998), in prejudice and conflict, and by extension terrorism. Then a program developed to moderate group prejudice and conflict—Us & Them: Moderating Group Conflict—will be described in detail.

Theory

Social identity theories assume that group members have a basic need for a positive social identity and that conflict between groups arises from the inevitable comparisons between them. Group identity consists of a variety of dimensions, such as religion, geography, and class. Minorities have trouble achieving favorable social comparisons—and therefore positive feelings about themselves—because of their typically inferior social and economic status.

Tajfel (1981) identifies three ways in which minority group members handle such a problem. If the social system is seen as legitimate and stable, and there are no clear ways to alter the system, such as in a feudal, slavery, or caste system, they acquiesce. In such societies, minority group members usually have internalized the majority group's justification for their lower status to some degree. This lowered self-regard helps maintain the status quo. If the status quo is perceived as illegitimate or unstable by the minority group, the system will be threatened. It is at this stage that states may turn to oppression and terror to preserve their faltering hold on power.

Social, political, and economic changes lead to minority group members' challenging the assumptions of their society about their inferior status. Education, industrialization, urbanization, democratization, capitalism, and mass communication foster comparisons based upon individual merit, not group membership. Such changes sow the seeds of group conflict as the aspirations of the disenfranchised rise. If the majority–minority status is seen as unstable—i.e., the intergroup walls are more permeable—most minority group members will try to assimilate into the majority.

Taylor and McKirnan (1984) suggest that the majority tends to accept highly qualified members of the minority because such assimilation contributes to the stability of the society. Other minority members may be pacified with the expectation that they will move up too if they try hard enough. However, if the system is perceived as not only unstable but also illegitimate, minority group members will move to change their inferior status. Some highly qualified members of the minority are not accepted by the majority or choose not to try. Additionally, some less well-qualified minority members believe that assimilation will not be possible. Then the highly qualified, non-assimilated minority group members begin to raise the consciousness of their group. Self-hate is replaced by pride. They may redefine their group's identity—for example, "Black is beautiful." The minority leaders ascribe responsibility for their lower social status to discrimination and oppression by the majority, not to minority inadequacy. Such consciousness-raising is followed by collective action. The minority begins to struggle against what it now sees as social injustice. The emergence of a charismatic leader is common. Such charismatic leaders may be regressive, like bin Laden, while others are transformative, like Gandhi.

Regardless, the initial response of the majority group is to portray the divisions between their groups as illegitimate or obsolete. But if such attempts fail, the conflict continues, and possibly escalates. If it escalates, the majority may resort to violence and suppression, or it may decide to negotiate to create a mutually acceptable situation. An implication of this research is that to reduce the risk of terrorism, powerful democracies need to be seen not only as militarily and politically strong, but also as legitimate.

One of the most researched theories of intergroup conflict and prejudice is the "contact hypothesis" (Allport, 1954). That research shows that a lessening of intergroup conflict and prejudice occurs under the following conditions: equal status between the groups in the situation; common goals; personal contact (the opportunity to get to know outgroup members as individuals); and support for such contact by each group's authority figures. Such conditions optimize the opportunity for interdependence and development of empathy. The contact hypothesis, and its more recent additions, has been supported by many studies (Pettigrew, 1998).

Intergroup contact under the wrong conditions deleteriously affects relationships. The size of the minority in comparison to the majority, the density of the minority population in a certain area, and the opportunities for superficial (and potentially, competitive) contact between the groups are variables that increase conflict. These factors can increase the sense of threat experienced by the majority. Forbes (1997), a political scientist, emphasized the negative influence of contact between groups when their larger communities are not supportive of such contact, are in conflict, and are disproportionate in size. So he simply extended the scope of the contact hypothesis research to larger constituencies.

A variant of the contact hypothesis is the "realistic group conflict theory" of Sherif (1966). This postulates that intergroup hostility arises from real or perceived competition caused by conflicting goals. The conflict is fueled by the zero-sum nature of the competition. That is, the desired resources are finite, or at least viewed as such; so members of each group believe that gains achieved by members of the outgroup will result in fewer resources for themselves.

Also, Sherif and Sherif (1953) noted that one's *reference group* and one's *membership group* may be different. For example, an individual may belong to a minority group but aspire to and identify with the majority group. Such individuals are typically seen by their membership group as social climbers, disloyal, and mistrusted.

Vamik Volkan (1988) has been the most important psychologist in the formulation of the psychoanalytic approach to intergroup conflict. He described the following stages of the development of self and other images from infancy. First, infants begin to differentiate themselves from the outside world and other people. Simultaneously, they begin forming rudimentary images of others and themselves. They cannot connect both pleasure and pain with the same person (for example, their mothers sometimes feeding them and other times not responding). So they form images of others that are either all good or all bad. Normally, infants begin to meld these opposing images of others and themselves in the second year. However, some images remain unintegrated or primitive, i.e., all bad or good. Later, some of those unintegrated images of self and caretakers are idealized as all good, or devalued as all bad. Then children project those idealized or disparaged images onto certain people. This is done to preserve a sense of internal goodness, safety, and power in the self, one's family, and one's group.

Volkan uses the term *suitable targets of externalization* (STEs) to describe people and objects that are the reservoirs of such images. STEs are culturally determined and include symbols, cuisine, attire, religious icons, and also individuals and groups of people. People experienced as friends, allies, and heroes are positive STEs; enemies are negative STEs.

Volkan and Itzkowitz (1994) describe each member of a group as having an individual identity that is like a garment protecting the individual from threats. But each person in an ethnic, religious, or national group also has a group identity that is like a large tent. Group members aren't preoccupied with the group identification unless they experience it as no longer protecting them. At such times, shoring up the "tent" takes precedence over individual identity needs.

The group identity tent is woven with shared rituals, symbols, leaders, and myths. *Chosen glories,* mythologized and idealized collective achievements and victories, are important in defining "us" versus "them." Even more powerful are *chosen traumas,* which are mythologized losses, injustices, and humiliations suffered by the group. Finally, *borders,* both physical and psychological, clarify the distinction between ingroup and others (Volkan, 1992).

Minorities are common STEs for the psychic discards of the dominant group. So minority group members may be discriminated against because of a mixture of real attributes, but also projected negative qualities of the majority. Unfortunately, more vulnerable minority group members may absorb such characteristics, leading to lowered self-regard.

Another psychoanalytic perspective is offered by Perlman (2002), who spoke of terrorism as a pathogenic response to suffering that is not redressed, a perversion of the search for justice that has been thwarted, and a securing of the need for equality and freedom at any cost. The infliction of humiliation, powerlessness, and terror onto the powerful is experienced as expiation and victory by terrorists. By making the powerful helpless, equality is achieved. But a preferable solution is to achieve equality the other way, by empowering the helpless. "The intifada seemed to turn Palestinians from victims to masters of their fate" (Andoni, 1997). For many, especially men, the feeling of impotence is often intolerable. They would rather be bad. Perlman cited the study of suicide bombers by Ann Marie Oliver and Paul Steinberg of the Center for Middle Eastern Studies at Harvard. They describe such suicide missions as a preemptive strike. Rather than let the enemy kill them, they kill themselves to deprive the enemy and attain control over the inevitable. Volkan has described suicide bombers as "preferring to die physically rather than psychologically."

Bertrand Russell (1938) wrote, "The fundamental concept in social science is power, in the same sense in which energy is the fundamental concept in physics." The asymmetry of power between groups can foster subjugation and oppression. But reprisals by the repressed are not uncommon, terrorism among them. A prolonged sense of powerlessness can have dire consequences (Sashkin, 1984) and result in irrationality and violence (Kanter, 1977).

Social dominance theory (Sidanius & Pratto, 1999) focuses on how group-based hierarchies in society determine disproportionate access to power, wealth, and status, whereas subordinate groups suffer greater disenfranchisement, poverty, discrimination, and imprisonment. Social hierarchies are structured by age and gender generally. Depending on the society, other dimensions for such stratification include: race, ethnicity, caste, clan, religion, class, nation, and many others factors important in a given society.

Coleman (2000) clarifies that power does not have to be a negative factor in group relations. He sees problems stemming from misconceptions about power, such as the concept that there is only a fixed amount of power between groups, that power only flows in one direction (usually from the more powerful to the less), and that power means "power over" not "power with."

However, as demonstrated in the classic Stanford Prison study (Haney, Banks, & Zimbardo, 1973), power can easily corrupt. As religion has been labeled the opiate of the masses, so, too, could power be seen as the "opiate of the elite." Kipnis (1976) described how those having power acquire a "taste for power," an inflated esteem and a devaluing of the less powerful. Fiske (1993) and Mindell (1995) described the insensitivity to the less powerful that is fostered by the possession of power.

Social learning theorist Albert Bandura and others have addressed the perceptual and cognitive distortions that foster violence, including terrorism. He wrote (Bandura, 1998, p. 163),

> From a psychological standpoint, third-party violence directed at innocent people is a much more horrific undertaking than political violence in which particular political figures are targeted. . . . to slaughter in cold blood innocent women and children in buses, in department stores, and in airports requires more powerful psychological machinations of moral disengagement.

Conscious justification of violence allows a person to commit acts normally outside his or her moral code. A psychologically healthy soldier may take pride in his ability to kill the enemy if he believes that he is fighting a just war. The terrorist may think that more people will suffer, especially his people, if he doesn't sacrifice the lives of innocents from the oppressive group. The unconscious mechanism of ingroup–outgroup bias (also known as the ultimate attribution error) facilitates such justifications. It refers to the tendency to imbue our own group members with greater value than the outgroup.

Another means of what Bandura calls the moral disengagement of the terrorist relies on euphemistic labeling. Terrorists describe themselves as "freedom fighters" and refer to "hostages" as "spies," while America sanitizes killing with terms like "collateral damage," "neutralizing," and "surgical strikes." This is another example of ingroup–outgroup labeling bias—our "dissemination of information" is the outgroup's "spreading propaganda," and our "disinformation" is their "lies."

Another example of this "us" versus "them" bias is the finding that people rate aggressive actions of the other as more violent than they rate the action when a member of their own group is the instigator (Duncan, 1976). Similarly, ingroup–outgroup bias leads to an overemphasis on personality as the explanation for ingroup members' virtuous behavior and an overemphasis on context as the explanation for reprehensible behavior by someone in the ingroup. The opposite attribution emphases are true in judging behavior of someone in the outgroup (Taylor & Jaggi, 1974). So terrorists can minimize their slayings as the only defensive weapon at their disposal against an oppressive, intractable regime. Counterterrorists can judge their retaliation as restrained compared with the carnage of the terrorists.

Another way one will relax self-sanction is through the displacement of responsibility. Milgram (Helm & Morelli, 1979) found that 65 percent of students would shock someone until they passed out or died under "optimal" experimental conditions. A key ingredient facilitating that abandonment of normal moral restraint was the assumption of responsibility by the authoritative laboratory professor. Likewise, acts such as suicidal bombings and hostage taking normally proscribed by Islam receive endorsement through circuitous justifications by Shi'ite clerics (Kramer, 1998). Bandura (1998) points out that the most reliable terrorists are those who are bound by a sense of duty to their superiors while relinquishing personal responsibility for the suffering they inflict.

Dehumanization is another psychic tool in the suspension of self-monitoring. It's easier to kill a "Jap" or a "gook" than a person. "It requires conducive social conditions rather than monstrous people to produce heinous deeds" (Bandura, 1998, p. 182). Empathizing with the other is the opposite of dehumanization. If one of the terrorists piloting the hijacked planes on September 11 empathized with his potential victims and their loved ones, he could not have completed his mission. Likewise, terrorism is less likely to be an attractive option to a disenfranchised or oppressed people who feel the humanizing effect of support from the larger world.

The attribution of blame is "another expedient that can serve self-exonerative purposes; one's own violent conduct can then be viewed as compelled by forcible provocation" (Bandura, 1998, p.184). The cycle of violence escalates as terrorists and governments each focus on the latest assault of the other without appreciating the provocative nature of their own violence.

The previously mentioned Milgram studies on obedience underscore the process of what Bandura terms "gradual moral disengagement." Terrorists get socialized into more and more extreme attitudes and modes of violence over time. Sprinzak (1998) writes about the radicalization of the Weathermen. Their opposition to particular social policies grew into increasing estrangement from the society and violent confrontations with police, and eventually they turned to terrorism in an effort to destroy the system.

One group's defense is often experienced by members of the enemy group as an assault. Mistrust and defensiveness lead to caution and control, which can evoke a defensive and hostile reaction, which is then viewed as proof of the initial view. Unchecked, such self-fulfilling prophecies (Merton, 1952) tend to spiral into greater levels of hostility and violence.

THE "US & THEM: MODERATING GROUP CONFLICT" PROGRAM

Need: Within each of us, to some degree, lies the need to split good and bad, that is, to externalize unacceptable aspects of ourselves onto others. Likewise, within each group, there is some tendency to attribute disowned aspects of the group to other groups. Historically, this tendency has been adaptive; yet as our world shrinks due to technological advances, a new approach is required. As nuclear risk remains and terrorist threats grow, we need to adapt. The change in our technology demands a change in our psychology.

Description: The Us & Them program is designed to highlight the dynamics common to prejudice and conflict along many dimensions—for example, race, class, culture, nationality, religion, and ethnicity. Furthermore, education about these common dynamics in the workshop relies on a balance of teaching basic concepts, experiential learning through structured activities, and post-workshop dialogue and action.

"Us & Them" refers to the polarization of two or more groups. Such divisiveness is fueled by an exaggerated sense of one's own group as special and good. Accordingly, other groups are devalued and feared.

The universal tendency to identify with our group and counter-identify with other groups has to do with issues of identity, comfort, and survival. Group boundaries exist to give cohesiveness to groups and to exclude disavowed parts of group members. They tend to provide order and prevent fusion within a large, chaotic world. Group identity tends to confer some sense of belonging, goodness, and worth.

"Us & Them" thinking is magnified at times of an intergroup conflict of interests, such as intensified economic competition, religious conflict, or territorial dispute. And though we realize that prejudice and conflict have important historical, economic, and political causes, we focus on how such tensions are fueled psycho-logically—and how we can moderate them.

Participant Characteristics

Representation. The groups involved in the program should be representative of the major groups involved in the conflict in the region. Efforts need to be made to involve all such ethnic, religious, racial, or national groups. Uninvolved groups may be motivated to derail progress among the involved groups, especially if they feel uninvited in the first place.

Age. Although on several occasions the program has been modified for children (with a shorter duration, simplification of concepts and language, etc.), participants should be adolescents or adults. A children's program may be developed in the future.

Openness. Openness is another important participant characteristic. The majori-ty of participants in past programs were already predisposed to peaceful conflict reduction. However, optimal program impact occurs with participants in the midrange of prejudice toward "them" in the particular conflict. The program is not likely to succeed with the most prejudiced members of the community. And obvi-ously, terrorists and their active supporters cannot be reached by such programs.

Influence. Ideally, we try to involve community leaders. The involvement of such people has the greatest post-program impact on communities.

Conflict intensity. We usually envision the program being implemented before violent conflict. However, we appreciate the cyclical nature of conflict, as well as the need for interventions during intractable conflicts. So there is a role for the pro-gram after cessation of hostilities, since it may help prevent another round of active conflict. However, the more intense the conflict, the less likely it is that disputants will be willing and free to become involved. Doing so could run the risk of their larger constituencies' seeing them as weak or disloyal, and mistrusting or ostraciz-ing them. Therefore, the best time for the program is when intergroup tension is at a moderate level. In terms of Fisher and Keashly's (1991) model of conflict escala-tion—discussion, polarization, segregation, and destruction—the program could be implemented in all but the fourth phase, though the endorsement of communi-ty leaders is essential in the segregation phase.

US & THEM PROGRAM FORMAT

Phase One: The Us & Them: Moderating Group Conflict workshop is the first phase of the three-phase program. The workshop is designed to be experiential, so brief talks by the presenter(s) are followed by more lengthy participant exercises. Each didactic segment covers an aspect of Us & Them dynamics: "What do we mean by Us & Them?"; "Why does Us & Them thinking occur?"; "How does Us & Them thinking develop in children?"; "When does Us & Them thinking escalate?"; "Who is prone to exaggerated Us & Them thinking?"; "The problem with extreme

Us & Them thinking"; and "Resolving extreme Us & Them thinking." Masters for overhead transparencies are provided for each segment of the sample talk.

The experiential activities are the core of the workshop. The exercises are sequenced to facilitate learning objectives in the following order: 1) self-awareness; 2) other-awareness; and 3) a bridge between the diverse groups participating in each workshop. Exercises are categorized by their learning objectives, i.e., self-awareness, other-awareness, creation of a bridge between groups, and in some cases, a combination of two of those objectives.

Phase Two: The second phase of the program occurs after the workshop. It entails formation of dialogue groups (based upon the Study Circles format). Groups have the following characteristics:

- They are composed of eight to twelve people who meet regularly over a period of weeks or months to continue to engage in dialogue. The composition of the group is balanced along the dimension of interest, e.g., race, ethnicity, religion, and so forth.

- A dialogue is facilitated by a mutually respected person from each of the participant groups. The facilitators do not act as experts, but serve the group by keeping the discussion focused, helping the group to consider a variety of views, and asking difficult questions.

- The format of the dialogue can be based on the most relevant discussion guide from the Study Circles Institute.

- The group progresses from a session on personal experience (how does the issue affect me?) to sessions providing a broader perspective (what are others saying about the issue?) to a session on action (what can we do about the issue here?).

Phase Three: The next phase of the program, Joint Community Action, flows from the second. It involves a collaborative project developed and implemented by workshop participants from the diverse groups. Community action can be either a response to group conflicts or a coordinated effort to strengthen intergroup understanding before problems erupt. Projects could involve efforts to reduce neighborhood violence, joint social gatherings, collaborative political action, and so forth. Sample projects are described and relevant resources are provided in the Participant Booklet to facilitate the process.

Presenter's Manual and Participant Booklet: The Presenter's Manual includes relevant research and materials for workshop presentations, such as a sample talk, originals for overhead projector transparencies, many participant exercises, sample agendas for various lengths of workshops, ideas for opening and closing presentations, audiovisual resources, a bibliography, and a typeset brochure with space for the presenter's name and contact information.

The manual also includes the original copy of the Participant Booklet, which features basic workshop material, guidelines for forming dialogue groups after the workshop, ideas for joint community projects, and lists of resources, such as organizations, publications, and videos.

Group Process Considerations

Attention is paid to the dynamics necessary to optimize prejudice and conflict reduction as identified by the previously mentioned conflict hypothesis research. Dynamics include:

- Fostering the equality of participating group members by counter-balancing pre-workshop contact with group representatives; thoughtful seating arrangements in the workshop; balancing the number of participants from involved groups; striving for approximately equal status of participants; and using presenters who are not from participating groups. Presenters demonstrate respect for all participants, as well as for healthy diversity.

- Facilitating participants' common goals, e.g., the superordinate goal of the reduction of intergroup misunderstanding and tension; encouraging participants to engage in a collaborative process to achieve such outcome goals, e.g., introspection of their own attitudes, education about the other group members' experiences to enhance empathy with them, and exercises and follow-up activities designed to create greater connection with participants from the other group(s). Group interdependence is highlighted and valued.

- Establishing a forum for participants to get to know "them" as individuals through the exploration of common interests, experiences, and aspirations (recategorization and cross-categorization; socialization opportunities; and structured dialogue and exercises designed to increase participants' empathic understanding of "them").

- Gaining the endorsement of the participating groups' community leaders. In some communities, it is not advisable to implement the program until tensions decline. If resources permit, holding the program outside the region may provide the psychological space and security conducive to open participation.

Purpose

To help participants understand and moderate their intergroup prejudice and conflict.

Objectives

Knowledge

- Greater awareness of the origins of one's own images of "them," and a reduction in distorted perceptions of "them."
- Increased knowledge of the outgroup participants' history, beliefs, values, culture, perceptions of "us," experience of the conflict, and aspirations.

- Appreciation of the mutual influence between the groups (and the more powerful group's exertion of greater influence).
- Greater sensitivity in dominant group members of the benefits of privilege they have taken for granted and sensitivity to feelings of the disadvantaged group's members.
- Increased knowledge of why and how leaders and the media influence intergroup attitudes and conflict.
- Understanding the power of primary identification, but also the possibility of cross categorization with members of "them" on other dimensions.
- Increased awareness of collaborative processes and possibilities between participating groups.

Skills

- Greater introspection ability in order to more non-defensively and fully see one's own distorted images, stereotypes, and prejudging of "them."
- The ability to talk directly, openly, and constructively to "them" about one's views and feelings about "us," the conflict, and "them."
- The ability to accurately and empathically listen to "them" talk about their views and feelings toward their group, the conflict, and "us."
- The skill to speak up effectively when someone from either group expresses a demeaning or inaccurate representation of either group.
- Enhanced coalition-building skills with the participating groups.

Attitudes

- Realization that group pride does not rely on downward comparisons to other groups.
- Humanizing "them," manifested by greater empathy and respect for "them."
- Increased appreciation of intergroup diversity.
- Increased appreciation of intergroup interdependence.
- Movement toward forgiving "them."
- Ability to envision a more constructive common future.
- Understanding that peace requires conscious, courageous, ongoing action.

Actions

- Intentional and collaborative interaction with "them" during the program.
- Commitment to continue such cross-group interaction after the program.
- Willingness to encourage greater understanding of "them" within one's group.

Sponsoring Organization

Psychologists for Social Responsibility (PsySR) is a U.S.-based, nonprofit, international network of psychologists who draw upon the research, knowledge, and practice of psychology to promote durable peace at community, national, and international levels. With members in forty-seven states of the United States and thirty-nine other countries, PsySR is building a cross-cultural network to facilitate communication about the complex and multidisciplinary problems of fostering cultures of peace.

The Us & Them: Moderating Group Conflict program, originally titled Us & Them: The Challenge of Diversity, was developed by members of the Michigan chapter of PsySR. The program was adopted by the national organization in 1994. Over the past decade, Us & Them programs have been conducted for a wide variety of groups. Programs have focused on problems ranging from international ethnic conflict to racial tension in Detroit.

REFERENCES

Albee, G. W. (2000). Commentary on prevention and counseling psychology. *Counseling Psychologist, 28*, 845–853.

Allport, G. (1954). *The nature of prejudice.* Cambridge, MA: Addison-Wesley.

Andoni, L. (1997, Summer). Searching for answers to Gaza's suicide bombings. *Journal of Palestinian Studies, 36.*

Bandura, A. (1998). Mechanism of moral disengagement. In W. Reich (Ed.), *Origins of Terrorism: Psychologies, Ideologies, Theologies, States of Mind.* Washington, DC: Woodrow Wilson Center Press, 161–192.

Barber, B. (1996). *Jihad vs. McWorld: How globalism and tribalism are re-shaping the world.* New York: Ballantine Books.

Coleman, P. (2000). Power and conflict. In M. Deutsch & P. Coleman (Eds.), *The handbook of conflict resolution: Theory and practice* (pp. 108–130). San Francisco: Jossey-Bass, Inc.

Deutsch, M., & Coleman, P. (Eds.) (2000). *The handbook of conflict resolution: Theory and practice.* San Francisco: Jossey-Bass, Inc.

Duckitt, J. (1992). *The social psychology of prejudice.* New York: Praeger.

Duncan, B. (1976). Differential social perception and the attribution of intergroup violence: Testing the limits of stereotyping of blacks. *Journal of Personality and Social Psychology, 34,* 590–598.

Fisher, R., & Keashly, L. (1991). A contingency approach to third party intervention. In R. Fisher (Ed.) *The social psychology of intergroup and international conflict resolution.* New York: Springer-Verlag.

Fiske, S. (1993). Controlling other people: the impact of power on stereotyping. *American Psychologist, 48,* 621–628.

Forbes, H. (1997). *Ethnic conflict: Commerce, culture, and the contact hypothesis.* New Haven, CT: Yale University Press.

Haney, C., Banks, W., & Zimbardo, P. (1973). Interpersonal dynamics in a simulated prison. *International Journal of Criminology and Penology, 1,* 69–97.

Haney, C., & Zimbardo, P. (1998). The past and future of U.S. prison policy. *American Psychologist, 53,* 709–727.

Helm, C., & Morelli, M. (1979). Stanley Milgram and the obedience experiment: Authority, legitimacy, and human action. *Political Theory, 7,* 321–346.

Hoffman, B. (1995). Holy terror: The implications of terrorism motivated by a religious imperative. *Studies in Conflict and Terrorism, 18,* 4.

Hoffman, B. (1998). *Inside terrorism.* New York: Columbia University Press.

Jager, H., Schmidtchen, G., & Sullwold, L. (Eds.) (1981). *Analysen zum terrorismus 2: Lebenslaufanalysen.* Darmstadt, Germany: Deutscher Verlag.

Kanter, R. (1977). *Men and women of the corporation.* New York: Basic Books.

Kipnis, D. (1976). *The powerholders.* Chicago: University of Chicago Press.

Kramer, M. (1998). The moral logic of the Hizballah. In W. Reich (Ed.), *Origins of terrorism: Psychologies, ideologies, theologies, states of mind* (pp. 131–160). Washington, DC: Woodrow Wilson Center Press.

Lederach, J. (1995). *Preparing for peace: Conflict transformation across cultures.* Syracuse, NY: Syracuse University Press.

McIntosh, P. (1989, July–August). White privilege: Unpacking the invisible knapsack. *Journal of Peace and Freedom,* 10.

Merton, R. (1952). *Social theory and social structure.* New York: Free Press.

Mindell, A. (1995). *Sitting in the fire: Large group transformation using conflict and diversity.* Portland, OR: Lao Tse Press.

Oskamp, S. (Ed.) (2000). *Reducing prejudice and discrimination.* Mahwah, NJ: Lawrence Erlbaum Associates, Inc.

Perlman, D. (2002, January 27). Presentation at American University's Center for Global Peace and the International Peace and Conflict Resolution Program, Washington, DC.

Pettigrew, T. (1998). Intergroup contact theory. *Annual Review of Psychology, 49,* 65–85.

Reich, W. (Ed.) (1998). *Origins of terrorism: Psychologies, ideologies, theologies, states of mind.* Washington, DC: Woodrow Wilson Center Press.

Rouhana, N., & Kelman, H. (1994). Promoting joint thinking in international conflicts: An Israeli-Palestinian continuing workshop. *Journal of Social Issues, 50,* 157–178.

Russell, B. (1938). *Power: A new social analysis.* New York: Norton.

Sashkin, M. (1984). Participative management is an ethical imperative. *Organizational Dynamics, 12,* 4–22.

Sherif, M. (1966). *In common predicament: Social psychology of intergroup conflict and cooperation.* Boston, MA: Houghton Mifflin.

Sherif, M., & Sherif, C. (1953). *Groups in harmony and tension: An integration of studies of intergroup relations.* New York: Harper & Brothers Publishers.

Sherif, M., Harvey, O., White, B., Hood, W., Sherif, C., & Campbell, D. (1988). *The robbers' cave experiment: Intergroup conflict and cooperation.* Middletown, CT: Wesleyan University Press.

Sidanius, J., & Pratto, F. (1999). *Social dominance: An intergroup theory of hierarchy and oppression.* New York: Cambridge University Press.

Sprinzak, T. (1998). The psychopolitical formation of extreme left terrorism in a democracy: The case of the weathermen. In W. Reich (Ed.) *Origins of terrorism: Psychologies, ideologies, theologies, states of mind* (pp. 65–85). Washington, DC: Woodrow Wilson Center Press.

Tajfel, H. (1981). *Human groups and social categories: Studies in social psychology.* Cambridge, England: Cambridge University Press.

Tajfel, H., & Turner, J. (1979). An integrative theory of intergroup conflict. In W. G. Austin & S. Worchel (Eds.), *The social psychology of intergroup relations* (pp. 33–48). Monterey, CA: Brooks/Cole.

Taylor, D., & Jaggi, V. (1974). Ethnocentrism and causal attribution in South Indian context. *Journal of Cross-Cultural Psychology, 5,* 162–171.

Taylor, D., & McKirnan, D. (1984). Theoretical contributions: A five stage model of intergroup relations. *British Journal of Social Psychology, 23,* 291–300.

Turner, J. (1985). Social categorization and the self-concept: A social cognitive theory of group behavior. In E. J. Lawler (Ed.), *Advances in group processes* (Vol. 2, pp. 77–122). Greenwich, CT: JAI Press.

Volkan, V. (1988). *The need to have enemies and allies: From clinical practice to international relationships.* Northvale, NJ: Jason Aronson.

Volkan, V. (1992). Ethnonationalistic rituals: An introduction. *Mind and Human Interaction, 4,* 3–19.

Volkan, V., & Itzkowitz, N. (1994). *Turks and Greeks: Neighbors in conflict.* Huntington, England: Eothen Press.

Wallis, J. (1994). *The soul of politics.* New York: New Press.

NOTE

1. The term "terrorism" is used in this chapter to refer to violence usually committed by non-state entities, in contrast to "terror," which is used by those in power to maintain it.

Afterword

Harvey Langholtz
Series Editor
Psychological Dimensions to War and Peace

In the four edited volumes of the *Psychology of Terrorism,* Dr. Chris Stout and forty-three contributing authors have explored terrorism from the perspectives of psychological theory, therapy, history, sociology, political science, international relations, religion, anthropology, and other disciplines. These authors have brought differing viewpoints and they offer different views. In some cases the reader might even wonder if these authors have been addressing different subjects and different realities.

But this is the fundamental anomaly in the study of terrorism. On the one hand, it is easy to oversimplify and explain terrorism. On the other hand, recent events show us how difficult it is truly to understand terrorism, much less to know how to deal with it both reasonably and effectively. There is no universally agreed-upon definition of terrorism. Views on terrorism are often politically driven and it seems to be easier to cloud the discussion than to agree on an understanding. The issue urgently demands immediate solutions but these solutions appear to be a long way off.

As we look back over the ten years that preceded September 11, 2001, it seems we all missed the signals—the bombing of the Khobar Towers in Saudi Arabia, the U.S. embassies in Kenya and Tanzania, the USS *Cole,* and the federal building in Oklahoma City; the gas attack on the Tokyo subway; and of course the 1993 attack on the World Trade Center itself. Did our world actually change on that one day or were we only coming to realize as we watched the events in helpless disbelief that our understanding of the world had been wrong?

In the long view of history, September 11 will be remembered as a day when we were forced in fear and pain to reexamine some of our fundamental assumptions. And in this long view scholars will look to see what the serious and well-considered reactions were in the months following the event as psychologists and others took the time to reflect on the events of the day. That is what the contributing authors to these four volumes have sought to do in the immediate aftermath of the event: To consider terrorism, the causes of terrorism, people's reactions to terrorist acts, interventions to prevent or contain terrorism, and the possible role psychologists can play in understanding, explaining, and limiting terrorism and its effects.

Index

About the Editor and Advisory Board

CHRIS E. STOUT is a clinical psychologist who holds a joint government and academic appointment in the Northwestern University Medical School, and serves as the first Chief of Psychological Services of the state of Illinois. He served as an NGO Special Representative to the United Nations, was appointed by the U.S. Department of Commerce as a Baldrige Examiner, and served as an advisor to the White House for both political parties. He was appointed to the World Economic Forum's Global Leaders of Tomorrow. He has published or presented more than three hundred papers and twenty-two books. His works have been translated into five languages. He has lectured across the nation and in sixteen countries and has visited more than fifty nations. He has been on missions around the world and has reached the top of three of the world's Seven Summits. He was Distinguished Alumni of the Year from Purdue University and Distinguished Psychologist of the Year, in addition to receiving more than thirty other postdoctoral awards. He is past President of the Illinois Psychological Association and is a member of the National Academy of Practice. He has been widely interviewed by the media, including CNBC, CNN, Oprah, *Time*, the *Chicago Tribune*, and the *Wall Street Journal*, and was noted as "one of the most frequently cited psychologists in the scientific literature" by Hartwick College. A distinct honor was his award as one of ten Volunteers of the Year in Illinois, and both the Senate and House have recognized his work by proclamation of "Dr. Chris E. Stout Week."

DANA ROYCE BAERGER is a practicing clinical and forensic psychologist in Chicago. She specializes in issues related to children, families, mental health, and the legal system. She is on the clinical faculty of the Department of Psychiatry and Behavioral Sciences at Northwestern University Medical School, and is also a staff member of the Children and Family Justice Center at Northwestern University Law School. In her private practice she provides psychotherapy services to individuals, couples, and groups; consults with attorneys regarding clinical and forensic practice standards; and consults with mental health professionals regarding ethical and risk management issues.

TERRENCE J. KOLLER is a practicing clinical psychologist in Chicago. He also serves as Executive Director and Legislative Liaison of the Illinois Psychological Association. He is Clinical Assistant Professor of Psychology in the Department of Psychiatry at the University of Illinois Medical School in Chicago. His areas of expertise include attachment and loss, parent-child interaction, and ethical and legal issues relating to the practice of psychology. He was the 1990 recipient of the Illinois Psychological Association's Distinguished Psychologist Award, and received an honorary doctor of humane letters degree from the Chicago School of Professional Psychology in 1995.

STEVEN P. KOURIS is associate chairman of the Department of Psychiatry at the University of Illinois College of Medicine in Rockford and medical director of the Jack Mabley Developmental Center in Dixon, Illinois. A medical graduate of Des Moines University, he interned at the Mayo Clinic and served clinical residencies at the University of Michigan and Detroit Medical Centers. He also completed an epidemiology research fellowship at the Minnesota Department of Health, and earned degrees in environmental health from the University of Minnesota and in preventive medicine from the University of Wisconsin. An accomplished clinician, teacher, and researcher, he is certified in multiple areas of psychiatry and medicine, and specializes in pediatric and developmental neuropsychiatry.

RONALD F. LEVANT is Dean and professor of psychology at the Center for Psychological Studies at Nova Southeastern University. He chairs the American Psychological Association (APA) Committee on Psychology's Response to Terrorism, and is a Fellow of APA Divisions 1, 12, 17, 27, 29, 31, 39, 42, 43, and 51. He has served on the faculties of Boston University, Harvard Medical School, and Rutgers University. He has authored or edited thirteen books and more than one hundred refereed journal articles and book chapters. He has served as Editor of the *Journal of Family Psychology*, is an Associate Editor of *Professional Psychology: Research and Practice*, and is an advisory editor or consulting editor to the following journals: *American Journal of Family Therapy, Journal of Marriage and Family Therapy, Men and Masculinities, Psychology of Men and Masculinity, Journal of African American Men, Journal of Trauma Practice, In Session: Psychotherapy in Practice*, and *Clinical Psychology: Science and Practice*.

MALINI PATEL is clinical associate professor of psychiatry and behavioral sciences at Finch University of Health Sciences/Chicago Medical School, and Acting Medical Director at a state psychiatric facility. She is board certified with added qualifications in addiction psychiatry. She is actively involved in resident and medical student training programs and has received awards for her teaching and contributions to psychiatric education. She also practices in a community mental health clinic where she sees patients in the Dual Diagnosis and Assertive Community Treatment Programs. She has published and presented on topics related to court-ordered treatment, administrative psychiatry, and substance abuse.

About the Contributors

SHARIF ABDULLAH is an adjunct faculty member at Marylhurst University and Portland State University. An author, proponent, and catalyst for inclusive social, cultural, and spiritual transformation, his work as a humanistic globalist has taken him to more than two dozen countries and to every continent. He received a B.A. in psychology from Clark University and a J.D. from Boston University. He has appeared on several international globalization forums. His writings include *The Power of One: Authentic Leadership in Turbulent Times.* He is founder and president of Commonway Institute in Portland, Oregon.

RUBÉN ARDILA is Professor of Psychology at the National University of Colombia (Bogota, Colombia). He has published twenty-three books and more than one hundred and fifty scientific papers in different languages, mainly Spanish and English. He founded the *Latin American Journal of Psychology* and has been the editor of this journal for several years. His main areas of research are the experimental analysis of behavior, social issues, peace psychology, and international psychology. He has been a visiting professor in the United States, Germany, Spain, Argentina, and Puerto Rico. He is a member of the executive committee of the International Union of Psychological Science.

BENJAMIN BEIT-HALLAHMI received his Ph.D. in clinical psychology from Michigan State University in 1970. Since then he has held clinical, research, and teaching positions in the United States, Europe, and Israel. He is the author, coauthor, editor, or coeditor of seventeen books and monographs on the psychology of religion, social identity, and personality development. In addition, he has a special interest in questions of ethics and ideology in psychological research and practice. In 1993, he was the recipient of the William James Award for his contributions to the psychology of religion.

FRED BEMAK is currently a Professor and the Program Coordinator for the Counseling and Development Program at the Graduate School of Education at George Mason University. He has done extensive work in the area of refugee and immigrant psychosocial adjustment and mental health. He has given seminars and lectures and conducted research throughout the United States and in more than thirty countries in the areas of cross-cultural psychology and the psychosocial adjustment of refugees and immigrants. He is a former Fulbright Scholar, a Kellogg International Fellow, and a recipient of the International Exchange of Experts and Research Fellowship through the World Rehabilitation Fund. He has been working nationally and internationally in the area of refugee adjustment and acculturation for the past twenty years as a researcher, clinician, and clinical consultant and has numerous publications in the area. He has recently written a book in collaboration with Rita Chi-Ying Chung and Paul Pedersen, *Counseling Refugees: A Psychosocial Approach to Innovative Multicultural Interventions*, published by Greenwood Publishing.

BRENDA ANN BOSCH is Clinical and Research Coordinator, Senior Clinical Psychologist, and Lecturer in the Department of Medically Applied Psychology, Nelson R. Mandela School of Medicine, University of Natal, Durban, South Africa. She is a member of several scientific organizations and professional societies. She is a consultant in clinical neuropsychology/disability, dissociative disorders in forensic psychology, traumatic stress, and peer supervision. Her current research and publication thrusts include the relationship between stress and neuropsychological deficits, stress and psycho-oncology, the intensive care unit, and mortuaries/law enforcement.

HENRY BREED has worked more than a decade in the United Nations, having been a Humanitarian Affairs Officer, Assistant to the Under-Secretary-General for Peacekeeping, and Assistant to the Special Representative of the Secretary-General to the former Yugoslavia and to the North Atlantic Treaty Organization. He is currently Political Affairs Officer in the Office of the Iraq Programmed. In past posts, he has been called upon to go to Mozambique, Rwanda, and the former Yugoslavia. In his current post, he has been closely involved in a broad range of international activities within Iraq. He has worked as a consulting editor for UNESCO on issues including education, development, and cultural preservation, and he has been actively involved in a range of environmental activities related to the Earth Summit. Born in Norway and raised in New York, he received undergraduate degrees in music and fine arts from Indiana University in Bloomington. He also holds a master's degree in public administration from Harvard University, a diplôme in international history and politics from the Graduate Institute of International Studies in Geneva, and a master's in international affairs from Columbia University. A member of the Council on Foreign Relations and of the International Institute of Strategic Studies, he was awarded the Beale Fellowship at Harvard and was admitted to the academic fraternity Pi Kappa Lambda at Indiana University. He is also a Fulbright Scholar, a "boursier de la Confédération Suisse," and a Regents Scholar. He lives in New York.

GIOVANNI CARACCI is a Clinical Associate Professor of Psychiatry at the Mount Sinai School of Medicine and Director of Residency Training and Medical Student Education at the Mount Sinai School of Medicine (Cabrini) Program. He is the Chair of the World Psychiatric Association on Urban Mental Health and a member of the Commission on Global Psychiatry of the American Psychiatric Association. He represents the World Psychiatric Association at the United Nations in New York, where he is Chair of the Non Governmental Organizations Executive Committee on Mental Health and Treasurer of the NGO Executive Committee of HABITAT (Center for Human Settlement). His main fields of expertise are international mental health, education, and cultural issues in mental health.

RITA CHI-YING CHUNG received her Ph.D. in psychology at Victoria University in Wellington, New Zealand. She is currently an Associate Professor in the Counseling and Development Program in the Graduate School of Education at George Mason University. She was awarded a Medical Research Council (MRC) Fellowship for postdoctoral work in the United States. Following the MRC fellowship, she remained as a Project Director for the National Research Center on Asian American Mental Health at the University of California, Los Angeles. In addition, she has been a visiting professor at the Federal University of Rio Grande do Sul in Brazil, Johns Hopkins University, and George Washington University, and a consultant for the World Bank. She has conducted research and written extensively on Asian immigrants and refugee mental health and has worked in the Pacific Rim, Asia, Europe, and Latin America. She has recently written a book in collaboration with Fred Bemak and Paul Pedersen, *Counseling Refugees: A Psychosocial Approach to Innovative Multicultural Interventions*, published by Greenwood Publishing.

JOHN M. DAVIS is Professor of Psychology at Southwest Texas State University. He completed advanced work at two German universities and received his Ph.D. in experimental/social psychology from the University of Oklahoma. He has lived and worked as a psychologist in Germany, China, England, and the United States. He has researched and published in the areas of interpersonal relations, refugee stress/adaptation, health psychology, and international psychology. Recent publications include a book chapter (1999) on health psychology in international perspective and an invited article (2000) on international psychology in the prestigious *Encyclopedia of Psychology* (APA/Oxford University Press). His current research interests include international terrorism from the perspectives of social and international psychology, and the influences of ethnic self-identity and attitude similarity on interpersonal and intergroup attraction.

ARTHUR A. DOLE is Professor Emeritus at the University of Pennsylvania Graduate School of Education, and former Chair of the Psychology in Education Division. He is a member of the Board of Directors of AFF, a nonprofit organization that encourages education and research about abusive groups, and a consulting editor of the *Cultic Studies Journal.* His research has focused on the harmfulness of cultic groups.

BORIS DROZDEK is a psychiatrist working at the GGZ Den Bosch/Outpatient and Daytreatment Centre for Refugees, the Netherlands. He is researching, publishing, and teaching in the field of psychotrauma and forced migration.

JONATHAN T. DRUMMOND is a doctoral student in social psychology at Princeton University. Prior to beginning doctoral work, he taught at the United States Air Force (USAF) Academy in the Department of Behavioral Sciences and Leadership as a major in the USAF. His research interests include psychological construction and attributions of legitimacy about political and judicial institutions in the United States and South Asia, retaliatory violence, white separatism, and divergent Aryan identity narratives (present and historical) in Indian Hindutva, Sinhalese Buddhism, and Euro-American Wotanism.

SOLVIG EKBLAD, a clinical psychologist, is Adjunct Associate Professor in Transcultural Psychology at the Karolinska Institutet, Department of Neurotec, Section of Psychiatry, Stockholm, Sweden. She is also Head of the Unit for Immigrant Environment and Health at the National Institute of Psychosocial Factors and Health, Solna, Sweden. She is in charge of the research group "Transcultural Psychology" and supervises Ph.D. and master's level students. At present, she has research grants from the National Swedish Integration Office, the European Refugee Fund, and the Stockholm County Council. She is collaborating with several foreign and local research teams. She is Co-Chair for the International Committee of Refugees and Other Migrants (ICROM), World Federation for Mental Health. She has written many articles and book chapters and has presented papers at international and national conferences in the field of migration and mental health.

SALMAN ELBEDOUR received his Ph.D. in school psychology from the University of Minnesota. After working at Ben-Gurion University, Israel, for six years, and at Bir Zeit University in the Palestinian Authority, he joined the School of Education at Howard University. He is currently an Associate Professor and the Coordinator of the School Psychology Program. His research and clinical interests are focused on psychopathology, maltreatment, child abuse, and neglect. He has published in the areas of cross-cultural and developmental studies of young children and adolescents placed at risk, specifically children exposed to political unrest, family conflict, and school violence. He has published extensively on the impact of the Israeli-Arab conflict on the development and socialization of children in the region. His Ph.D. thesis, "Psychology of Children of War," investigated the traumatic risk, resilience, and social and moral development of Palestinian children of the uprising, or *intifada.*

J. HAROLD ELLENS is a retired Professor of Philosophy, Theology, and Psychology, as well as the author, coauthor, and/or editor of 68 books and 148 professional journal articles. He spent his professional life on the issues involved in the interface of psychology and theology, served for fifteen years as Executive Director of the Christian Association for Psychological Studies, and as Founding Editor and Editor-in-Chief of the *Journal of Psychology and Christianity*. He holds a Ph.D. from Wayne State University in the psychology of human communication, a Ph.D. from the University of Michigan in Biblical and Near Eastern Studies, and master's degrees from Calvin Theological Seminary, Princeton Theological Seminary, and the University of Michigan. His publications include *God's Grace and Human Health* and *Psychotheology: Key Issues*, as well as chapters in *Moral Obligation and the Military, Baker Encyclopedia of Psychology, Abingdon Dictionary of Pastoral Care*, and *Humanistic Psychology*. He is currently a research scholar at the University of Michigan, Department of Near Eastern Studies. He is also a retired Presbyterian theologian and minister, and a retired U.S. Army Colonel.

TERI L. ELLIOTT is a clinical psychologist in New York City, specializing in children and adolescents. She is an Assistant Professor at the Disaster Mental Health Institute (DMHI), where she focuses on children and violence, bullying interventions, disaster response and preparedness, and psychological responses to weapons of mass destruction. She teaches and consults nationally and internationally on topics including children and trauma, crisis intervention, psychological support, and refugee mental health.

STEPHEN D. FABICK is a consulting and clinical psychologist in Birmingham, Michigan. He is past President of Psychologists for Social Responsibility (PsySR), past Chair of the PsySR Enemy Images program, and current Chair of its Conflict Resolution Action Committee. He is also Chair of the Conflict Resolution Working Group of the Society for the Study of Peace, Conflict and Violence (Division 48 of the American Psychological Association). His interest has been in conflict transformation and prejudice reduction. He authored *US & THEM: The Challenge of Diversity*, a Workshop Presenter's Manual. The program was included in President Clinton's Initiative on Race Relations and selected by the Center for Living Democracy as a model program in their book *Bridging the Racial Divide*. The program focuses on transforming group prejudice and conflict.

DON J. FEENEY, JR., is a clinical psychologist and Executive Director of Consulting Psychological Services in Chicago. In practice for more than twenty-five years, he has authored books including *Entrancing Relationships* (Praeger, 1999) and *Motifs: The Transformative Creation of Self* (Praeger, 2001).

RONA M. FIELDS is a clinical psychologist and Senior Associate at Associates in Community Health and Development and Associates in Community Psychology, in Washington, D.C. She has been an Assistant Professor at California State University, a Professor at the California School of Professional Psychology, and an Adjunct Professor at George Mason University and the American School of Professional Psychology. Her research includes studies of terrorism, violence and prejudice, peace-keeping operations and hostage negotiations, and treating victims of torture.

TIMOTHY GALLIMORE is a certified mediator, facilitator, and third-party neutral in conflict resolution. He researches and writes on trauma healing and reconciliation and on violence prevention. He earned a Ph.D. in mass communication from Indiana University in 1992. He was a consultant to the United Nations Development Program for Women and on the USAID Rwanda Rule of Law project to institute a community restorative justice system for trying genocide suspects.

TED G. GOERTZEL is Professor of Sociology at Rutgers University in Camden, New Jersey. His books include *Turncoats and True Believers, Linus Pauling: A Life in Science and Medicine,* and *Fernando Henrique Cardoso: Reinventing Democracy in Brazil.* His articles include "The Ethics of Terrorism and Revolution" and "Myths of Murder and Multiple Regression," and can be found on his Web site at http://goertzel.org/ted.

EDITH HENDERSON GROTBERG, a developmental psychologist, works for the Civitan International Research Center at the University of Alabama, Birmingham, and with the Institute for Mental Health Initiatives, George Washington University, Washington, D.C. Through the International Resilience Research Project (IRRP), she found many answers to the role of resilience in understanding and enhancing human health and behavior. Her articles have been published in *Ambulatory Child Health* and *The Community of Caring,* and some of her books on resilience have been translated into other languages.

RAYMOND H. HAMDEN is a clinical psychologist and Director of Psychology Services at the Comprehensive Medical Center in Dubai, United Arab Emirates. Born in the United States, he was a 1986 Visiting Fellow at the University of Maryland, College Park, Center for International Development and Conflict Management. His research and consultations focused on the psychology of the terrorist and hostage situations. He earned a Ph.D. at Heed University, Department of Psychology, and continued postgraduate study in psychoanalysis at the Philadelphia School of Modern Psychoanalysis. In 1990, he moved to the United Arab Emirates and established his own practice. He holds adjunct faculty positions at institutions including the University of Indianapolis, and has taught at the American Universities in Dubai and Sharjah. He holds Diplomate and Fellow status at the American College of Forensic Examiners and the American Academy of Sexologists. He is licensed by the Dubai Department of Health and Medical Services, as well as by the Board of Psychology Examiners in Washington, D.C. He is also a member of the International Society for Political Psychology and the International Council of Psychologists. He is an ACFE Diplomate, American Board of Psychological Specialties.

FADEL ABU HEIN is a community and clinical psychologist on the faculty of Al Aksa University in Gaza. He was for many years the senior psychologist at the Gaza Community Health Center, where he developed the research program and also instituted a broad outreach service for a traumatized population that had no other mental health resource. He has more recently established his own clinical practice in Gaza in conjunction with his teaching responsibilities at Al Aksa University.

CRAIG HIGSON-SMITH is a research psychologist employed in the Child, Youth and Family unit of the Human Sciences Research Council of South Africa. He is a specialist researcher in the fields of violence and traumatic stress. Previously, he cofounded and managed the KwaZulu-Natal Programme for Survivors of Violence, a nongovernment organization dedicated to supporting communities ravaged by civil conflict in Southern Africa. More recently, he cofounded the South African Institute for Traumatic Stress.

J. E. (HANS) HOVENS is a clinical psychologist and psychiatrist. He has published extensively on the subject of post-traumatic stress disorder. Currently, he is a lecturer on psychiatry at the Delta Psychiatric Teaching Hospital in Poortugaal, the Netherlands.

NIRA KFIR is a clinical psychologist who received her Ph.D. in social psychiatry at the Université de Paris, Sorbonne, Center for Social Psychiatry. She is the Director of Maagalim-Institute of Psychotherapy and Counseling in Tel Aviv. In 1973, she developed a Crisis Intervention program adopted by the Israeli Ministry of Defense, and it is still in use for group work with bereaved families. She developed the psychotherapeutic diagnostic system of Personality Impasse/Priority Therapy.

OLUFEMI A. LAWAL is a Ph.D. candidate at the University of Lagos, Akoka-Yaba, Lagos, Nigeria. He has been a teacher and coordinator at St. Finbarr's College in Lagos, and is now an instructor at Quantum Educational Services, Ilupeju, Ibadan, Oyo.

JOHN E. LeCAPITAINE is Professor and former Chair of the Department of Counseling and School Psychology, University of Wisconsin, River Falls. He has a doctorate in counseling psychology (Boston University), a doctorate in metaphysics, a master of science in school psychology, and a bachelor of science in mathematics. He is a Diplomate Forensic Psychologist and a member of the International Council of Psychologists, the American Psychological Association, the American College of Forensic Examiners, the Institute of Noetic Sciences, the National Association of School Psychologists, and *Who's Who in the World*. He has written a number of articles, receiving the Special Merit award from *Education* for *Schools as Developmental Clinics: Overcoming the Shadow's Three Faces*.

JOHN E. MACK is a Pulitzer Prize–winning author and Professor of Psychiatry at Harvard Medical School who has explored how cultural worldviews may obscure solutions to social, ecological, and spiritual crises. He is the founder of the Center for Psychology and Social Change. He also founded the Department of Psychiatry at the Cambridge Hospital in 1969. In 1983 he testified before Congress on the psychological impact of the nuclear arms race on children. He is the author or coauthor of ten books, including *A Prince of Our Disorder*, a Pulitzer Prize–winning biography of T. E. Lawrence, and, most recently, *Passport to the Cosmos*.

SHERRI McCARTHY is an Associate Professor of Educational Psychology at Northern Arizona University's Yuma campus. She has published research in international journals on a variety of topics, including developing critical thinking skills, anger management training, substance abuse counseling, and the role of psychology in improving society. She has also written books in the areas of special education and grief and bereavement issues. She is active in the International Council of Psychologists' Psychology and Law interest group. She is also active in the American Psychological Association, serving as the Division 2 Teaching of Psychology liaison to the Council on International Relations in Psychology and as the leader of the P3 Global Psychology Project.

CLARK McCAULEY is a Professor of Psychology at Bryn Mawr College and serves as a faculty member and Co-Director of the Solomon Asch Center for Study of Ethnopolitical Conflict at the University of Pennsylvania. He received his Ph.D. in social psychology from the University of Pennsylvania in 1970. His research interests include stereotypes and the psychology of group identification, group dynamics and intergroup conflict, and the psychological foundations of ethnic conflict and genocide. His recent work includes a new measure of intergroup contact, "the exposure index."

STEVE S. OLWEEAN is a psychotherapist with a degree in clinical psychology from Western Michigan University. He is President of the Association for Humanistic Psychology (AHP), and Founding Director of Common Bond Institute. Since 1990, he has served as AHP International Liaison and Coordinator of International Programs. His principal treatment area is trauma and abuse recovery and reframing negative belief systems. His primary international focus is conflict transformation, forgiveness, reconciliation, and humanitarian recovery efforts. He cofounded and each year coordinates the Annual International Conference on Conflict Resolution held in St. Petersburg, Russia. He also developed an integrated Catastrophic Trauma Recovery (CTR) treatment model for treating large populations experiencing trauma due to war, violence, and catastrophe.

DIANE PERLMAN is a clinical psychologist in Pennsylvania, with a special interest in political psychology. She is Co-Chair of the American Psychological Association Committee on Global Violence and Security within Division 48, the Society for the Study of Peace, Conflict, and Violence. She is also a research associate with the Citizens Panel on Ultimate Weapons at the Center on Violence and Human

Survival. She is Vice President of the Philadelphia Project for Global Security, and Liaison to the psychology community for the Global Nonviolent Peace Force. She is also Founding Member of and a research associate for the Transcending Trauma Project, studying adaptation of Holocaust survivors and their children. She is a Fellow of the Solomon Asch Center for Study of Ethnopolitical Conflict at the University of Pennsylvania and was a speaker for two decades for Physicians for Social Responsibility.

MARC PILISUK is a clinical and social psychologist. He is Professor Emeritus of the University of California and a Professor at the Saybrook Graduate School and Research Center in San Francisco. He is a past President of APA Division 48, the Society for the Study of Peace, Conflict, and Violence; a member of the steering committee of Psychologists for Social Responsibility; and one of the founders of the first teach-in.

JERRY S. PIVEN is a Professor of Psychology at New School University and New York University, where his courses focus on the psychology of religion, death, and sexuality. He is a member of the National Psychological Association for Psychoanalysis and author of *Death and Delusion: A Freudian Analysis of Mortal Terror.* He is editor of the series Psychological Undercurrents of History and is presently working on a psychoanalytic exploration of the madness and perversion of Yukio Mishima.

WILLIAM H. REID is a Clinical and Adjunct Professor of Psychiatry at the University of Texas Health Science Center, Texas A&M College of Medicine, and Texas Tech University Medical Center. He is past President of the American Academy of Psychiatry and the Law. He is a fellow of the Royal College of Physicians, American College of Psychiatrists, and American Psychiatric Association. He is also past Chair of the National Council of State Medical Directors, and a U.S. Observer for the Board of Presidents of the Socialist Countries' Psychiatric Associations, Sofia, Bulgaria. He was U.S. Representative, Ver Heyden de Lancey Conference on Psychiatry, Law, and Public Policy at Trinity College, Cambridge University, as well as visiting lecturer, Hunan Medical College, Changsha, Hunan.

LOURENS SCHLEBUSCH is Professor and Head of the Department of Medically Applied Psychology, Nelson R. Mandela School of Medicine, University of Natal, Durban, South Africa. He is a suicidologist, stress management and medico-legal/disability consultant, Chief Clinical Psychologist for the Hospital Services of the KwaZulu-Natal Provincial Administration, and Chief Consultant in Behavioural Medicine at various hospitals in Durban, South Africa. He is a member of many scientific editorial boards, organizations, and societies, and is a reviewer of scientific publications both nationally and internationally. He has many professional listings, honors, and awards. He has made many significant research contributions to his field and has published widely. He is currently researching various aspects of traumatic stress and suicide prevention.

KLAUS SCHWAB is Founder and President of the World Economic Forum, an organization committed to improving the state of the world, and based in Geneva, Switzerland. He has worked in several high-level roles with the United Nations and is now a Professor at the University of Geneva. He studied at the Swiss Federal Institute of Technology, the University of Fribourg, and the John F. Kennedy School at Harvard University.

KATHY SEXTON-RADEK is Professor of Psychology at Elmhurst College and Director of Psychological Services, Hinsdale Hospital/Suburban Pulmonary and Sleep Associates. She has designed conflict resolution and stress management curriculums for elementary and secondary school children and has implemented these programs with inner-city students at risk for violence and substance abuse. She has also constructed and taught anti-violence workshops for teachers. She is the author of more than thirty peer-reviewed articles in the areas of behavioral medicine, applied cognitive behavior theory in school settings, and psychology pedagogy. She is an elected member of her local school board, and a member of the American Psychological Association, Sigma Xi, and the Sleep Research Society.

ERVIN STAUB is Professor of Psychology at the University of Massachusetts at Amherst. He has published many articles and book chapters and several books about the influences that lead to caring, helping, and altruism, and their development in children. His upcoming book is *A Brighter Future: Raising Caring and Nonviolent Children.* He has also done extensive research into and writing about the roots and prevention of genocide and other group violence, including his book *The Roots of Evil: The Origins of Genocide and Other Group Violence.* Since 1999, he has been conducting, with collaborators, a project in Rwanda on healing, reconciliation, and other avenues to the prevention of renewed violence. His awards include the Otto Klineberg International and Intercultural Relations Prize of the Society for the Psychological Study of Social Issues. He has been President of the Society for the Study of Peace, Conflict, and Violence (Division 48 of the American Psychological Association) and of the International Society for Political Psychology.

MICHAEL J. STEVENS is a Professor of Psychology at Illinois State University in Normal. He is a Fellow of the American Psychological Association, serving as Chair of the Committee for International Liaisons of the Division of International Psychology. He is also a member of the Advisory Board of the Middle East Psychological Network. He is an honorary professor at the Lucian Blaga University of Sibiu, Romania, where he completed Fulbright and IREX grants. In 2000, he received the Recognition Award from the American Psychological Association for his work in international psychology.

TREVOR STOKES is Professor of Child and Family Studies, Professor of Psychology, Professor of Psychological and Social Foundations of Education, and Professor of Special Education at the University of South Florida, Tampa. He received his bachelor's degree with first-class honors in psychology at the University of Western

Australia, a Ph.D. in developmental and child psychology from the University of Kansas, and Ph.D. Clinical Psychology Augmentation at West Virginia University. His research, teaching, and clinical activities involve the behavior analysis and developmental assessment of aggression within families, with a focus on techniques for interception of violent repertoires by children.

TIMOTHY H. WARNEKA treats adolescents and children in a community mental health center near Cleveland, Ohio. He specializes in working with sexually aggressive and/or aggressive juveniles. He has studied the martial art of aikido for more than twelve years and incorporates aikido principles into his psychotherapeutic work. He is President of Cleveland Therapists, Ltd. (www.clevelandtherapists. com), a referral site for mental health professionals. He is President of Psyche & Soma Consulting, Ltd., an organization that offers training and consultation on a variety of mental health subjects.

MICHAEL WESSELLS is Professor of Psychology at Randolph-Macon College and Senior Technical Advisor for the Christian Children's Fund. He has served as President of the Division of Peace Psychology of the American Psychological Association and of Psychologists for Social Responsibility. His research examines psychology of terrorism, psychosocial assistance in emergencies, post-conflict reconstruction, and reintegration of former child soldiers. In countries such as Angola, Sierra Leone, East Timor, Kosovo, and Afghanistan, he helps to develop community-based, culturally grounded programs that assist children, families, and communities affected by armed conflict.

ANGELA WONG is a University of California student in sociology and social welfare. She is a research assistant and an intern providing assistance at homeless shelters.